European Labor Aristocracies

WITHDRAWN

Marc Linder was educated in the United States and West Germany. He received a Ph. D. in politics from Princeton University and a J. D. from Harvard Law School. He has taught economics and political science in the United States, West Germany, Denmark, and Mexico. Author of several books in the areas of political economy and jurisprudence, he is currently an attorney in the migrant farmworker division of Texas Rural Legal Aid in the Rio Grande Valley.

Marc Linder

European Labor Aristocracies

Trade Unionism, the Hierarchy of Skill, and the
Stratification of the Manual Working Class before
the First World War

Campus Verlag · Frankfurt

CIP-Kurztitelaufnahme der Deutschen Bibliothek

Linder, Marc:
European labor aristocracies : trade unionism,
the hierarchy of skill, and the stratification of the
manual working class before the first World War /
Marc Linder. – Frankfurt/Main ; New York :
Campus Verlag, 1985.
   ISBN 3-593-33457-7

Table of Contents

List of Tables

And even today the book, as the current scientific mode
of production teaches, is an obsolete mediation between
two different card filing systems. For everything that
is essential is found in the card file of the researcher
who wrote it, and the scholar who studies in it
assimilates it to his own card index.

Walter Benjamin, Einbahnstrasse

Preface

You know that in our industry it is entirely different from
the cotton industry, and the steel industry in this respect.
Our employers are not capitalists in the sense that these
large organizations are. We meet our employers every day,
call them Tom, Dick and Harry; we meet them from time to
time when we have a little trouble. They understand our
troubles and we understand theirs. You know we have a
lot of members in our trades union movement in the building
industry who get up and preach about capitalism and all
that kind of thing, and who would have us at one another's
throats with our employers, who say we have nothing in
common with them. Gentlemen, we have everything in common
with them. ... (1)

This study originated in 1970 in connection with an investigation
into the background and motivation of demonstrations conducted
in May of that year on Wall Street by members of building
trades unions in ostensible solidarity with President Nixon and
the American invasion of Cambodia. (2) Further research indicated that a political-economic conjunctural logic did, ultimately,
lie behind this seemingly un-class conscious behavior. In order
to determine whether the peculiarities of construction work had
generated such tactics in the past, a full-scale history of the
American construction industry and building trades unions was
written; in order to test the resulting working hypotheses in
a different socio-political context, briefer histories were assembled for numerous European countries.

At this point an "epistemological rupture" occurred: with
construction workers relegated to the role of one exemplar of
a species, the problem orientation shifted to the basic theoretical issues underlying the alleged separatist political ideologies
and actions of the better-situated strata of the working class
throughout the capitalist era. Since the prevailing theoretical
constructs proved, however, almost wholly devoid of mediated
empirical studies, (3) detailed historical illustrations became
necessary both to judge the reality-content of existing theories
and to help formulate more adequate explanations.

A companion volume devoted to the United States is in
preparation.

Acknowledgments

Public thanks are due the staffs of the following libraries for having made their resources accessible: McGill University; Aarhus University, Arbejderbevaegelsensbibliotek, Danmarks Statistik, Det Kongelige Bibliotek, Roskilde University; Frankfurt University, Free University of Berlin, Württembergische Landesbibliothek; British Library, British Library of Political and Economic Science, Edinburgh University, National Library of Scotland; Colegio de Mexico; Chalmers Tekniska Högskola; Balch Institute, University of Baltimore, Boston College, Brandeis University, Brookings Institution, Bryn Mawr College, University of California at Berkeley, University of California at Los Angeles, University of California at Santa Barbara, Catholic University, University of Chicago, City College of New York, City University of New York, Clark University, Columbia University, Cornell University, Duke University, Eleutherian Mills, Federal Reserve Bank of New York, Federal Reserve Bank of Philadelphia, Fordham University, Gettysburg College, Harvard University, Haverford College, Hoover Institution, Hunter College, University of Illinois, Indiana University, Institute for Advanced Study, Jewish Labor Committee, Johns Hopkins University, University of Kansas, Library Company, Library of Congress, Lincoln University, Massachusetts Institute of Technology, Middlebury College, University of New Hampshire, University of New Mexico, New York Public Library, New York State School of Industrial Relations, Northwestern University, University of Oregon, University of Pennsylvania, Pennsylvania State University, Princeton University, Rice University, Rutgers University (New Brunswick), University of Southern California, Stanford University, Swarthmore College, Tamiment Institute, Temple University, University of Texas at Austin, United States Department of Labor, Vassar College, University of Virginia, University of Washington, Wesleyan University, Williams College, University of Wisconsin, Wisconsin State Historical Society, Yale University.

Chapter 1
Introduction

Unskilled labor must become skilled before it can gain rights. (1)

Although capitalist societies of the nineteenth and twentieth centuries have been decisively molded by conflicts between labor and capital, cleavages within the working class have constituted a crucial element specifying the structure of national political systems. In recent years, for example, much attention has been devoted to the issue of fissures between: blue-collar and white-collar workers; the working class and the marginalized stratum of semi-permanently unemployed and welfare recipients variously characterized as the lumpenproletariat, working poor, non-working poor and underclass; public sector and private sector employees; and the old and the new working class. (2) In connection with racial, ethnic, generational, sexual and organizational divisions, working class politics have been conspicuously preoccupied with intra-class controversies in the United States. (3)

For the past one hundred and fifty years the notion of an aristocracy of labor has enjoyed widespread currency: not only in left-wing political circles, but also among journalists (4) and scholars (5) it has served as a fungible element in attempts to explain or denounce the fractionation of the working class. The overarching principle of division within a politically relevant stratification of that class has been perceived as being rooted in the formation of a stratum whose superior conditions have led it to articulate and pursue social, economic and political goals without reference to the interests of other, atomized, strata which, despite the latter's numerical preponderance, it has been able to outflank organizationally. This long conceptual tradition notwithstanding, the notion of an aristocracy of labor has not been accorded theoretical treatment adequate to the level of generalization that its use has often implied. (6)

In particular, analysis of the relations of proletarian strata to one another has not been furthered by arguments--whether tautological, definitional or conceptual in accordance with their

14

degree of sophisticatedness--that insist that capital, as the essential social relationship in capitalist societies, cannot be overridden by any differentiations within wage-labor in forming the basis of new class boundaries. (7) Although this value-theoretical foundation of class antagonism (8) serves a heuristic purpose in relation to authors who posit that the chief issue is the analysis "of the strictly speaking fluid nature of the worker's whole fate" (9) or who base their stratificatory classifications on "an analytic act of violence", (10) "this most general concept of class antagonism" (11) is manifestly inadequate to the task of analyzing the class structure of a particular country at a particular point in history. If the terminological barriers raised by the question of class-imputation are eliminated by focusing attention on the factors that tend to influence the conditions of working class homogeneity, then the aforementioned value-theoretical objections become untenable. For if adherents of this position concede that the various material forms of labor (such as skilled and unskilled labor), as those in which the relationship between capital and labor appears to the agents of production, differentially shape the latter's consciousness, then it is inconsistent to contend that the stratification of the working class derived from these material forms of labor must inevitably be "completely arbitrary." (12)

The fact that the concepts used to analyze differentiation within the working class are located on a different level of abstraction from those characteristic of the relationship between capital and labor does not disqualify them as adequate scientific reflections of social reality. The denial of their validity rests upon the moral imperative that "scholarly discussion must" concentrate on those aspects of the relationship between capital and labor which "compel all wage workers" to overcome their spontaneous mutual competition. (13)

Historical research concerning the formation of national labor aristocracies must observe two methodological considerations. First, intra-national uneven development is an on-going process that continuously generates intraworking class restratification. Moreover, uneven development itself develops unevenly (14) so that one period may create the basis for an increasingly homogeneous working class whereas the next generates predominantly heterogeneous elements. By undermining the economic foundations of one version of the notion of an end of class history, such constant restratification casts doubt on the thesis of permanent embourgeoisement. (15) Second, it is crucial to scrutinize the specific political-historical nature of the "superior" working class strata; for just as the mathematical existence of a lowest one-fifth of the income

15

recipients of a society does not suffice as a qualitative indicator of poverty, (16) so too the highest-paid one-fifth or one-tenth of wage earners does not automatically constitute an aristocracy of labor. (17) Wage differentials, for example, similar to those prevailing in nineteenth-century Britain have been documented for earlier centuries. (18) Yet the class structure of societies prior to the rise of industrial capitalism makes it inappropriate to impute to artisans in pre-capitalist societies the political functions associated with classical labor aristocrats. (19)

The structure and distribution of skills within the manual working class is accorded overriding significance as a stratificatory principle in the historical-empirical chapters which follow. (20) Industrial capitalism itself created skilled labor and the latter's conceptual counterpart, unskilled labor, in a fourfold sense: 1. qua complicated and simple labor, respectively, they are represented and become commensurable in the commodity values produced by the aggregate labor of society; in this relation complicated labor and simple labor are qualitatively undifferentiated expressions of abstract labor; quantitatively, however, complicated labor exists as intensified or multiplied simple labor; 2. qua qualified and unqualified labor, respectively, they are forms of concrete labor, qualitatively different as technological agents in the production of useful objects; (21) 3. for the capitalist employers of skilled labor it is essential that the quantitative relationship between the value created by skilled labor and the reproductive cost of skilled labor power be no less favorable than that obtaining between unskilled labor and unskilled labor power; non-fulfillment of this condition would, ceteris paribus, manifest itself as a below-average rate of profit among capitals that are heavily reliant upon skilled labor and would result in diminished demand for and hence a (temporary) superabundance of the latter; and 4. for the owners and sellers of skilled and unskilled labor (power) differential working and living conditions derive from the introduction into the sphere of dependent labor of an attenuated version of the "principles of stratification" that regulate the unequal and hierarchical distribution of "more essential" social positions and functions on the one hand and the accompanying "rewards," "rights" and "perquisites" on the other in society at large. (22)

It is in particular this last aspect that forms the focus of interest below. The crucial task of analysis consists not so much in confirming the existence of this hierarchy of privilege within the manual working class as in setting it in relation to the overall structure of social class as it evolved during one historical period. To what degree, in other words, did the common experiences of manual working class life in the spheres of production and reproduction neutralize the divisive effects of intra-class stratification? Or, seen from a different perspective, to what degree did the privileged stratum of the working class use the economic, social and political "power and prestige" attaching to its "scarce skills" (23) to undermine the mechanisms that gave rise to the inequalities peculiar to capitalist societies in general? (24)

Parts I and II, dealing with Britain and Europe respectively, are of unequal length and subject to qualitatively different kinds of treatment. This disparity reflects the divergent historical paths taken by the aristocracy of labor in the two zones. The Continental patterns serve as virtual negative case histories illustrating the national specificity of class relations. Within each Part, too, the emphases are far from uniform. Thus chapters 2 and 3, devoted to the pre-Chartist and Chartist periods respectively, undertake to reconstruct the early history of the labor aristocracy in Britain on the basis of contemporary qualitative accounts; although no attempt is made to gauge the social structure statistically, the chapters demonstrate that the peculiarities of the prevailing political structure imparted a distinct character to the putative labor aristocracy. Chapter 4 traces the idea-historical origins of Marx's and Engels' conception of the aristocracy of labor back to the attack that the leftwing Chartist, Ernest Jones, mounted on craft unionism in the 1840s and 1850s.
   Marx's and Engels' scattered references to the notion of a labor aristocracy are systematically elaborated in chapter 5 with a view to inspecting their immanent theoretical logic and historical accuracy. In this context a diverse body of empirical indicators relating to the socio-economic structure of mid-Victorian Britain is set forth. An alternative theoretical approach to the study of national labor aristocracies, which is adumbrated in chapter 6, is then developed in the remaining chapters. Chapter 7, which concludes Part I, focuses on the impact of intra-working class differentiation on the evolution of a British labor aristocracy during the quarter-century preceding the First World War.
   In Part II attention is shifted to Continental Europe. Chapters 8 and 9 examine the two major industrial capitalist nations, Germany and France respectively. Sketches of labor aristocracies in several of the less advanced nations of Europe (such as Austria-Hungary, Denmark, Italy and Russia) are contained in chapter 10. Finally, chapter 11 synthesizes the new insights emerging from this study.

Part I
The Labor Aristocracy in Britain

Capital and Labour seem
By our Maker joined;
Are they not like giant twins
In the world of mind?
Up the hill of progress bright
March we on in tether.
Making difficulties light.
Pulling all together.
So shall we in concord joined
Shew to wondering mankind
Capital and Labour
Are our oars to pull the boat,
Are our wings to soar aloft,
In our high endeavour? (1)

Chapter 2
Early Socialism and Trade Unionism
(1820s and 1830s)

The decade beginning with the mid-1820s witnessed a new stage
in the development of the consciousness and of the organizations
of the British working class. The rise of political reform, co-
operative, socialist and general--indeed revolutionary--trade
union movements reflected and reinforced this transformation. (1) The internal struggles accompanying the political
and economic constitution of the proletariat as an effective
class force represented the first nationally significant instances
of the politicization of the socio-economic stratification of manual
workers.

One of the most condemnatory indictments of the labor aristocracy and at the same time perhaps the earliest precise semantic
reference stems from the Ricardian utopian socialist, William
Thompson. (2) In his book, Labour Rewarded, written in 1826
and published the following year, Thompson founded his ac-
cusation on a topos that has remained a mainstay of anti-labor
aristocratic criticism until the present day--namely, that of
exclusionary trade societies, which drew their power from a
system of unnecessarily rigid and extended apprenticeship. (3)
Thompson saw little correlation between wage levels and
skill (4) because he regarded differences in skill as comparatively minor and subsidiary to other factors.

> Whether one class of laborers is better paid than another,
> as weavers than agriculturists or hatters, is a mere matter
> of chance and change, depending on the fluctuations of the
> market, and on corporation or other exclusions of force,
> legal or not legal, restraining the freedom of competition. (5)

Although the effective skill-content separating various "classes"
may have been largely fictitious, the institutions protecting
and inflating such differentials

> give a factitious elevation to the remuneration of particular
> classes of laborers; while the great mass of the industrious
> remain at that competitive point of remuneration which
> enables the laborers to live out their average round of

years, and to leave behind them a new race to continue the routine of unattractive, unrequited, toil. Those classes of trades or subdivisions of classes which are the best remunerated ... are the mere aristocracy of trades, possessing no superior utility, skill or good disposition, with no more pretensions to superior merit than any other aristocracies, but frequently partaking of the vices of all aristocracies, full of unsocial antipathies to those less remunerated than themselves. ... (6)

The quasi-hereditary procedures for transmitting its privileges to the next generation constituted one of the most invidious aristocratic attributes of this class of labor inasmuch as

unequal remuneration renders it the interest of those possessed of skill in any department of industry to conceal from all others the mode of acquiring the peculiar manner of operating, which, improved by habit, becomes skill. Those who are skilled having families ... will teach their children alone. ... (7)

As long as the labor aristocracy rested on secure technological foundations, the gulf between it and the rest of the working class was unlikely to become politically or socially explosive. But as education spread, trades' mysteries lost their status, legal compulsory apprenticeship was abolished (8) and machinery displaced skilled labor, common laborers and their children were enabled to acquire the skills required by industry. (9) Once industrialization had reached this stage, trade unions had to decide whether they would

resort to force, law-supported as to apprenticeships, or illegal as to intimidation ... to put down the competition of the great majority of the Industrious, and thus erect a bloody--for force will lead to blood, and without blood no aristocracy can be supported--aristocracy of Industry. (10)

The scenario that Thompson evoked for the case that the aristocracy of labor preferred resistance, while appearing historically unrealistic in the light of the experience of the past century and a half, seems peculiarly suited to the mind of an Irish landlord who chose to analyze this stratum of workers analogously to that of the British nobility. Thompson predicted that,

The unskilled laborers would every where form a league with the capitalists; and being the majority in point of physical strength, and having, moreover, justice and the legally armed bands of the country on their side, they would by the underbidding of their labor defeat every where all the efforts of Trades-Unions. ... (11)

Thompson's analysis proved valid, however, in the sense that over time labor aristocratic positions in various trades were eroded. Even during this period some labor aristocrats underwent a rapid and dramatic process of absolute economic immiseration. (12) But these were relatively autonomous economic processes as the agents of which capitalist employers functioned; there do not appear to have occurred any successful (or unsuccessful) revolts by "'plantation slaves'" against "'palace slaves,'" (13) let alone ones in which the bourgeoisie and the armed forces supported the former. The fact that the ruin of certain sectors of the labor aristocracy did not mean the disappearance of this stratum as a whole--which was periodically replenished by the creation of new categories of skilled workers--constituted an even more cogent refutation of Thompson's claims.

The weakness of Thompson's approach was rooted in his misconception of the course of capitalist industrialization, on the one hand, and of the political behavior of working class strata, on the other. It is implausible--in regard to the first issue--that labor aristocrats, merely by means of the institutional methods outlined by Thompson, but against the grain of capital accumulation and in spite of underbidding on the labor market by the unskilled and of determined resistance on the part of employers, could have maintained a technologically obsolete position in the long run. (14) And in point of fact, the end of the eighteenth and the beginning of the nineteenth century appear to have been characterized by more accretions to than deductions from the skilled trades. (15) In those instances, in which trade unions of the skilled engaged in isolated sectional struggles for the preservation of technologically superfluous occupational roles, they were generally defeated. (16) Bourgeois and socialist attacks on trade unions overlapped precisely in such cases of "aristocratic tyranny", which collided with the rights of property on the one hand and working class solidarity on the other.

Thompson's analysis of potential class collaboration was based on a conception of the labor aristocracy as a combative and essentially retrogressively disruptive force within capitalist society. As such, it incurred the hostility of the bourgeoisie and of the other strata of the proletariat. Thus alliances between any two of these three groupings would, in accordance with the logic of Thompson's argument, have been tactical ones with the "enemy's enemy" rather than ones founded on positive common interests. Given his timebound misconception of the unilinearity of capitalist industrialization and his exclusive concentration on a certain type of waning labor aristocracy, Thompson could establish no basis for collaboration between such a working class stratum and the industrial bourgeoisie. It is, nevertheless, worth reflecting on the factors that precluded such cooperation.

During the 1820s and 1830s trade unions were not treated by the bourgeoisie as possible instruments for the introduction of notions of class conciliation into the minds of the proletariat; instead, they were fought and smashed, their members jailed, transported and executed. (17) Although labor aristocrats may have been regarded as distinct from other working class strata, they were not yet welcomed as respectable labor businessmen, committed to private property and the free market. Preferable perhaps to certain violence-prone groups that were undergoing rapid de-skilling and deteriorating conditions, they were none the less perceived as attempting to exercise a more systematic and insidious control by interfering with day-to-day operations of private profit-making production facilities. Trade unions still constituted an alien force.

The rather solid front which the working class maintained during the struggle for universal male suffrage left little room for a policy designed to divide that class by conferring the right to vote on a part of it. Once it had secured Parliamentary reform for its own benefit, the bourgeoisie no longer found it necessary to compensate any of its erstwhile working class political allies. (18)

Although the middle classes do not appear to have attempted to play various strata of the working class off against one another during this period, some anti-working class authors and socialists believed that labor aristocrats were being recruited for special purposes. One of the most notable of these contemporary sources was the anonymous pamphlet entitled, On Combinations of Trades. Using as his point of departure the claim that "the interests of low and high-priced labour ... are far more conflicting than those which divide the classes living in the enjoyment of various degrees of comfort," (19) the author asserted that "the single benefit of upholding a class of highly-paid artizans ... outweighs all" "serious evils resulting from trades' unions. ..."

> In every civilized society ... the importance of this class of men has been recognised. Whilst compulsory labour existed, they interposed between the patricians and the slaves, but in free countries they are called upon to discharge higher duties. In forming the connecting link between wealth and poverty, they serve to stimulate the latter, and indeed

their existence furnishes almost the only motive to exertion to the English working classes. (20)

In embryonic form the aspects alluded to by the anonymous author represented a component of the attributes of the classical labor aristocracy; yet this particular type of labor aristocracy was peculiar to a period in which the working class and its sales organs, the trade unions, had not yet been firmly institutionalized as responsible economic agents. At this point the labor aristocracy still symbolized an ideological intermediate station on the road out of wage labor into economic "independence," whereas in subsequent years the social advancement of this stratum qua stratum of and in the working class became a subjective motivating factor. (21) The function ascribed to the labor aristocracy during the pre-Chartist period was not so much one of having divided the loyalties of the working class as having created an escape mechanism. In the event, the author of On Combinations of Trades was disappointed by the efficacy of the mechanism which he praised; for although he deemed it more rational for the skilled to seek alliances with the classes above them--with whom they did not compete--, they persisted in attempting to join forces with the very strata beneath them that were capable of underbidding them when trades were open. (22)

Socialist organs also recognized the possibility that skilled workers might ally themselves with the bourgeoisie. A particularly striking example occurred in the building trades in which, however, the situation was complicated by a struggle between large and small capitals. The Pioneer, the trade unionist organ of the Builders' Union, warned editorially that "many of the skillful and more intelligent workmen have forsaken their order, and persevered in gaining a footing among the middle classes." (23) The socialist Poor Man's Guardian devoted several articles to refuting the notion that building operatives were better advised to work for small masters than for the then burgeoning class of larger general contractors. It endeavored to destroy the myths surrounding the relations between small masters and workmen (24) by claiming that small masters all wanted to become large capitalists; since their small capitals placed them in an inferior competitive position, they wanted to "excite a hatred of the large capitalists" in order to monopolize the labor force. The existence of such a conspiracy seemed demonstrated to the journal by a remark of a master plumber to the effect that he hoped that the operatives would rather work at four shillings a day for the small masters than at six shillings for the "gormandisers." (25) A week earlier the journal had observed that one of the advantages of being

25

employed by large contractors was that there were fewer of them. (26)

Behind the facade of malicious rejoicing at the prospective demise of petty-bourgeois elements (27) lurked an apparent fear that relatively well-situated artisans might seek limited political reforms together with their employers. (28) To the extent that early English labor aristocratic artisans gave evidence of harboring class collaborationist tendencies, these have been traced back to the fact that the comparatively slow tempo of the industrial revolution in England allowed craftsmen and their small employers to resist the entry of large-scale industry more successfully. (29)

Further support for this position was provided by a contemporary account of the socially stabilizing influence of the political unions as a consequence of their members' having been "drawn from the class of respectable tradesmen, and of the mechanics and artizans in populous cities"; for

> surely, no one will have the hardihood to assert that such men can have the remotest interest in hurrying their country into the vortex of revolution. Has the trader any motive for bringing on a state of things which all deprive him of his all ...? Has the mechanic who earns his 25s. 30s. or 35s. a week, any interest in inflaming the passions of angry and ignorant men, who will burn the manufactory to which he carries his labour; or ruin the manufacturer from whom he received his wages? Yet these are the men who have united together, in the hope of carrying such measures as will enable them to participate more largely in the rich resources which the skill of their hands has raised. ... (30)

Contemporaries began to comment upon still another aspect of the labor aristocracy during this period--the relations of the skilled to (their) laborers in the same trades. Alexander Somerville recounted that, "The masons were intolerable tyrants to their labourers." After having witnessed a mason strike a laborer gratuitously--ironically enough after a group of masons had been declaiming against tyranny and aristocracy--Somerville, who objected to the physical and moral abuse inflicted on the laborers, was told that "the privileges of masons were not to be questioned by labourers." (31) There is also some evidence that, in spite of the absence of systems of co-exploitation of laborers by skilled trade unionists in the building trades, the latter were able to enforce their high wages in part because contractors managed to maintain their profits by lowering the wages of the unskilled. (32)

26

Although employers tended to regard themselves as the chief victims of the "tyranny" of trade unionism, (33) others preferred to emphasize the detrimental effects on working class groups. Archibald Alison, sheriff of Lanarkshire during the events surrounding the conspiracy trial of the Glasgow cotton spinners in 1837-1838, provided a particularly vivid account of a trade union-enforced dual labor market. According to his testimony before a Parliamentary committee, membership in every trade was restricted to close relatives so that others were driven into trades in which no combinations or prohibitions were possible; there they were employed as day laborers, masons' laborers, porters and hand-loom weavers. "The tendency in practice clearly is to establish a monopoly of skilled against the efforts of unskilled industry, and to fence in the monopoly of skilled labour by a power of intimidation to which the working classes find it impossible to make any resistance." (34) After having affirmed that trade unionism represented "a complete system of castes," Alison became involved in the following exchange with M.P. O'Connell:

Thus making a species of aristocratic class amongst the labouring population?--Exactly; I have long been convinced that the system is just a system of the aristocracy of skilled labour against the general mass of unskilled labour ...; for the real sufferers are not the masters so much as the other workmen who are excluded. (35)

Contemporaries also commented on labor aristocratic relations in such traditional trades as carriage making (36) and printing. (37)

Other contemporaries doubted whether labor aristocrats could in fact preserve their privileged positions by means of strikes. Thus a commission studying the "State of Protection of Manufacturing Industry" in connection with the establishment of a constabulary questioned "the soundness of an opinion that has been expressed that strikes are of service in sustaining skilled labourers, or an 'aristocracy' of skilled labourers." It was the commissioners' view that those workers had the most to gain from strikes who were able to block, by virtue of their industrial position, a greater number of workers, some of whom might have been more skilled than the strikers. (38) The commission believed that such strikes would ultimately lead to the introduction of laborsaving machinery. (39)

The foregoing survey has avoided the issue of developing quantitative criteria for demarcating a labor aristocracy. Yet the economic distance between labor aristocrats and the rest of the working class must have been larger and growing more rapidly during a period which even "revisionist" social and economic historians acknowledge to have been one of increasing immiseration for significant sectors of the proletariat than during the second half of the nineteenth century. (40) Considerable social distance also obtained between labor aristocrats and other proletarian strata; artisans often viewed the unskilled sectors of the manual working class with contempt. (41) In these respects working class solidarity was still subordinate to intra-class divisions. The very fact, for example, that Luddite croppers in direct conflict with machinery, on the one hand, (42) and London artisans producing luxury commodities by means of centuries-old techniques, on the other, belonged to such disparate spheres of societal life meant that long-term political and economic cooperation between them was by no means self-explanatory. The emergence rather than the absence of such a coalition impressed contemporaries. This cleavage within the working class was created by the uneven quantitative and qualitative development of capital accumulation in various branches and regions; the transition from pre-industrial forms of labor to industrial capitalist forms left a unique imprint on each trade and occupation. In the context of this fundamental restructuring of British society, policies implemented by the ruling classes made a decidedly subsidiary contribution to further differentiation within the working class. (43)

While living under--and neither forgetting nor allowing others to forget the--quite different conditions from those of their "classmates," (44) labor aristocrats do not appear to have opposed the latter's interests insofar as they were directed toward the reconstruction of society. Despite frequently conflicting claims at the points of production, employment and income distribution--claims which labor aristocrats did not scruple at asserting regardless of the possible consequences for the unskilled--, the labor aristocracy often assumed a role of leadership in the formation of radical and socialist movements. (45) Autonomy rather than opposition characterized its relationship to the working class at large.

Such were the possibilities in a period when craftsmen could still dream of production cooperatives and when artisans who desired to become independent, self-employed masters could still be integrated into the same movement with factory operatives who sought to share in common the newly emergent mass means of social production. (46) As long as both movements were guided by anti-capitalist attitudes, the former could be shielded from the socio-economic antagonisms that were beginning to fissure the working class. (47)

Chapter 3
Chartism

The fact that the existence of Chartism as a coherent national movement compelled every stratum and grouping within the working class to wake a definite stand in words and/or actions on the issues raised by the Charter, facilitates an evaluation of the labor aristocracy during the period from the mid-1830s through the 1840s. For their part, adherents of the Charter publicly applauded or condemned the labor aristocracy for what they perceived as friendly or hostile acts toward their movement.

The London Working Men's Association, founded in 1836 by and for members of the working class (1) whom J.S. Mill regarded as the "most respectable and well-conducted men" among that class, (2) formed the organizational spark of the Chartist movement. While the Working Men's Association itself has been referred to as a "labor aristocracy" providing political leadership, (3) the 3,000 workers in attendance at the meeting in London in February of 1837 at which the Charter was publicly formulated have been characterized as "the elite of the London working class." (4)

The peculiar role of the London artisans may be traced back to the fact that London in the 1830s was "probably the only English city in which there was a considerable body of highly skilled artisans, for there alone was there a large wealthy and leisured class whose wants could find employment for skilled handicraft." (5) Ernest Jones, the left-wing Chartist leader, denounced this class of artisans for having been withdrawn from productive labor and thus demoralized. In this way there arose "an aristocracy of labour out of the higher paid trades" who looked "down on the less fortunate--class is thus established within class, each having its separate interests, jealousies and objects; and an oligarchy is empowered to divide and rule." (6) To be sure, Jones did not concern himself with the variegated nature of the London artisanate, which included "masses of slop tailors, poverty-stricken chambermaster shoemakers and miserable fancy cabinet-makers," who were neither craftsmen, nor independent nor educated.

In addition there was a sort of customary hierarchy among the trades, those with higher status usually receiving higher earnings. These trades at the top formed a kind of "aristocracy." Such were compositors, engineers, calico printers, shipwrights, coachmakers, bookbinders, coopers, and many upholsterers. These were aloof from labour movements because of social snobbery, higher earnings and more secure protection from their trade societies. The real basis of artisan radicalism lay among trades lower down in the hierarchy, especially shoemakers, tailors, plasterers, carpenters and stonemasons, all of which were on the same status level. ... (7)

These skilled artisans took great pains to strengthen their trade unions which enabled them to maintain their socio-economic status. But it was precisely the developed consciousness of their successes in these areas that made them "resentful of their exclusion from full political rights." (8) Yet the basis of labor aristocratic achievements required a defense of the general political-economic framework that made trade unionism viable. Hence trades that remained aloof from inter-trade union cooperation--such as printing, engineering, shipbuilding, bookbinding and cooperage--contributed few members to the Chartist movement; rather, they tended to restrict their support for Chartism to times during which all organized labor faced a political threat in the form of legislation. (9)

Both in London and in other parts of Britain obvious differences in interests existed between the labor aristocracy and other working class strata giving their allegiance to the Charter. The labor aristocracy, which played a considerable part in the movement until 1842, supported it on the basis of "steady political conviction" rather than as a result of recurrent economic pressure. The tradition within which the aristocracy of labor unfolded its political activity plainly set it apart from other groups.

The labour aristocrats had assets which enabled them to develop a mature political awareness well in adavance of the mass of the working force. They had time to read and study. Through their trade unions they had long acquired the habit of association, and their position on the social ladder facilitated a traffic in ideas between themselves and the radical lower class of tradesmen, attorneys, dissenting ministers and small masters. (10)

Although little proof has been adduced in support of the assertion that the respectable artisan in the political unions of the 1830s leaned more toward the side of the bourgeoisie than to

that of "his class comrades from the factories," (11) it seems
plausible that labor aristocrats were at least in part motivated
by considerations other than those that were imposed upon the
burgeoning class of industrial (especially textile) workers.
Those who, on the other hand, worked at home on hand looms
in direct competition with machine industry, received wages
less than one-eigth of those of workers in large-scale industry
who treated the former as "pariahs." In desperate need of
state intervention, these domestic workers entered the Chartist
movement in large numbers. (12)

Given this constellation of intra-working class forces, the
years of the most intense Chartist activity (1837-1842) were
characterized by a mutually ambivalent relationship between
labor aristocratic trade unions and the Chartists. Although
there were unambiguous examples of rapprochement created by
friendly gestures by trade unions (13) reciprocated by enthusiastic recognition on the part of Chartist leaders, (14) dis-
sension was easily provoked. Thus at the Chartist convention
in Birmingham in 1839, which took up the issue of a general
strike, a delegate was able to claim that unanimity could be
found only among the worst-paid workers; charging that the
working class, like the bourgeoisie and the nobility, had its
own aristocracy, he argued that those earning thirty shillings
per week were unconcerned with those earning fifteen shillings
who, in turn, remained indifferent to the problems of those
earning but five or six shillings weekly. (15) The fact that
this was not an isolated voice expressing the view that only
the most oppressed and resolute would participate in a general
strike, (16) makes it plausible that Chartist activists had had
prior experience with the political consequences of differential
working and living conditions within the working class.

Yet the severe depression of 1836-1842 (17) and the decline
in living standards, which also affected the better-paid artisans, (18) meant that purely trade unionistic attempts to
maintain standards by influencing supply and demand on the
labor market had proved ineffective. (19) Nevertheless, "the
manifest absurdity of persuading starving men to remain on
strike until the whole political machinery of the country had
been altered, must have quickly become apparent to the
shrewder Trade Unionists." (20) Chartism failed, consequently,
to "capture" the trade union movement, thus falling short of
the achievement at the height of the Owenite agitation in
1833-1834. (21)

It has also been argued that, with the improvement in
economic conditions in the 1840s, Chartism lost its momentum
and began to decline. (22) Yet such an explanation, as applied

to labor aristocrats, contradicts the aforementioned thesis according to which labor aristocratic attachment to Chartism was based on a theoretical-political understanding which was relatively unaffected by economic fluctuations. Alternatively, Helévy has contended that once Chartist agitation had been directed against the workhouse and the trade unions had received assurances that they no longer needed to fear persecution by the state, the unions withdrew from the movement, turning it into "an insurrection of the canaille." (23)

It is true that during the upswing of 1842-1845 (24) and especially after the successful obstruction in 1844 of a Parliamentary bill designed to expand the powers of justices of the peace in adjudicating disputes between masters and servants (25) some trades began to turn away from Chartism. The claim that, "The Trades Unions of London, embodying the élite of the operatives, always stood aloof from the agitation," (26) may have retained some validity with regard to the highest echelons of the labor aristocracy, but scarcely applied to the broader category of organized artisans. The occupational composition of the nominees to the General Council of the National Chartist Association in 1841 (27) and that of the registered members of the Chartist National Land Company in 1847 (28) illustrate the significant participation of skilled tradesmen in the Chartist movement of the 1840s. Moreover, numerous strikes, in the building trades for example, in the early and mid-1840s, (29) underline the stage of integration of the two movements.

With the revival of Chartism during the depressed years of 1846-1848, the skilled trades undertook to close ranks with other sectors of the working class. The National Association of United Trades, which was formed in 1845, proved to be the chief vehicle of this cooperation. Although the Webbs stressed the moderate nature of the policies pursued by this organization, (30) the mere fact that several trade unions had urged their members to join (31) impressed the Chartist leadership.

> For the first time in the history of the working classes, the aristocratic and the poorer sections of the array of industry, have cordially held out the hand of mutual help and friendship to each other. The starved, oppressed and suffering handloom weavers, and the still more miserable slave of competition, the frame-work knitter, had sat down side by side with the joiner, the mechanic, and the engraver. (32)

Other instances may be adduced of aristocratic trade unions' having narrowed the traditional gulf between themselves and the lower orders. In connection with the conviction of nine members of the Journeymen Steam-Engine and Machine Makers and Millwrights' Friendly Society in 1846, growing out of action by the union against systematic overtime and the piece master system, William Newton, an officer of the union, commented on the effects of the aid offered his union by other trades: "They (the members) had been called the aristocracy of the trades, and thought too proud to join with carpenters, plasterers, stockingers, and weavers, but he disclaimed the imputation. (Loud cheers.)" (33) Newton conceded that engineers had previously been insufficiently acquainted with the idea of association since they had been able to defend themselves; but they would have to begin helping their poorer brethren. (34) Newton's speech reveals that certain of the more secure labor aristocratic organizations remained aloof not only from the "residuum," but from the purely trade movements of skilled building tradesmen as well. (35)

The later 1840s also witnessed denunciations of labor aristocrats for their continued sectionalism. Writing in a periodical edited by Feargus O'Connor and Ernest Jones, one author accused the trade unions of "narrow-minded conceit": "The distinguishing feature of the present movement is the struggle of the democracy against the aristocracy of its own class." (36) William Peel, the general secretary of the National Association of United Trades, complained in 1852 that in the years 1845-1847 his organization had not been joined by

what are usually designated the "skilled trades," who were presumed to possess superior intelligence and superior resources. But, alack! there exists, unfortunately, an aristocracy of labour as well as of title and rank, and equally tenacious of dignity; and those higher class of British workmen declined fellowship in the same movement with their less favoured brethren. (37)

Peel's retrospective condemnation of the aristocracy of labor was colored by and ultimately merged with the strictures Ernest Jones was meting out during these years. (38)

The behavior of labor aristocrats during the Chartist finale--the demonstration in London on April 10, 1848 at which time the third petition, containing almost six million signatures, was submitted to Parliament--generated considerable animosity among those who continued to uphold Chartist traditions. Writing three years after the fact, Ernest Jones contended that if three million of seven million male adults were enfranchised, the majority would be composed of special constables of April 10, 1848--namely, middle class professions, clerks, shopkeepers, foremen and aristocrats of labor. (39) Although there is no reason to assume that Jones was deliberately falsifying history, the available evidence does not corroborate his claim. The reports in The Times on the days preceding and following April 10, 1848 made no reference to recruitment of special constables among the ranks of artisans. Statements made before the House of Commons on March 13, 1848 by Gladstone, Labouchere and Grey concerning the swearing in of the special constables singled out the coalwhippers of London--a group of poorly paid, underemployed, unskilled laborers who unloaded coal from ships. (40) In point of fact, skilled workmen appear to have been heavily underrepresented among the 170,000 volunteers who were enrolled to safeguard public order on April 10, 1848. Their absence from the ranks of the demonstrators, (41) however, symbolized the class-straddling role which they performed during the Chartist period as a whole and constituted the closest approximation to "classical" labor aristocratic behavior exhibited by organized artisans during these years. (42)

The maturation of British capitalism during the 1830s and 1840s subordinated ever larger numbers of workers to manifestly capitalist relations of production. This common experience of wage labor generated, in spite of countertendencies toward intra-working class stratification, a politically more unified proletariat which found a partial and temporary expression in Chartism. At the same time, the mobilization of theretofore unorganized laborers crytallized out an antagonism to the better-situated stratum of skilled trade unionists that had largely remained latent in the pre-Chartist period. The fact that both sectors could cooperate to the end of realizing the democratic demands of the Charter helped mask the partial conflict of interests between them. This clash referred, on the one hand, to the means to which desperation drove each sector, and, on the other, to the differing degrees to which each could rely on trade unionistic practices. As long as anticapitalist and socialist principles did not guide the labor movement, (43) the latter continued to be considerably influenced by the relatively autonomous effects of differential branch capital accumulation on the division of labor and on the conditions of various strata. (44)

Since the major aspects of labor aristocratic behavior and attitudes uncovered for this period derived from the sphere of intra-working class relations, they point to the fact that the phenomenon under review was not one of the aspirations of one sector of the working class to leap over class barriers,

but rather that of the resistance of a stratum formerly associated with petty bourgeois elements (45) to falling victim to
the degradation that was engulfing many unskilled manual
laborers. The embitterment accompanying the attempts by this
stratum to preserve socio-economic distance between itself and
the lower strata was revealed most distinctly in the struggle
against unlimited apprenticeship and the use of "cheap
men." (46) In this confrontation, however, the skilled were
arrayed not with but against employers since the latter benefited from the substitution of lower for higher "priced" workers. (47)

If this situation brought skilled trade unionists into a zero-
sum confrontation with their unskilled and unorganized replacements, it also precipitated a conflict with employers, who were
perceived as the subjective agents of deteriorating conditions.
The numerous strikes conducted over these issues bore witness
to the intensity of the antagonism. Under these circumstances,
capitalists were more likely to seek to exploit the division of
interests between unskilled and skilled workers by allying
themselves with the former than with the latter, as the opponents of the labor aristocracy would have had it. (48) The
alliances which the upper stratum of artisans entered into with
the radical petty bourgeoisie for political reasons not only did
not flow from economic cooperation--they were blocked by opposition to trade unions and strikes by parts of the employing
class. (49)

The 1830s and 1840s represented, then, a period in which
labor aristocrats reacted in a complex fashion to the forces they
experienced. The Chartist movement itself documented the cooperation that democratic traditions, hard times and common
resistance to governmental oppression forged among various
strata of the working class. The influx of laborers from agricultural to industrial pursuits in an urban environment and the
concomitant broadening and deepening of the experience of
cpaitalist industrial wage labor contributed to this closing of
ranks. (50) Nevertheless, past and present patterns as well
as future perspectives of well-being remained disparate enough
to cause a relative socio-political autonomization of the labor
aristocracy vis a vis worse-situated manual laborers. (51) This
autonomy was, however, even more sharply accentuated over
against the employing class as economic agents and political
participants.

Still unrecognized as fully legitimate negotiators on behalf
of the aggregate class or even of sectorizalized segments of
sellers of the commodity labor power, skilled trade unionists,
far from being treated as the favored "palace slaves" of the

bourgeoisie, were still engaged in a struggle that transcended what Gladstone, two decades later, characterized as "a natural mode of what we may call self-defence in the friendly strife which must always go on between the capitalist and the labourer." (52)

Chapter 4
The Transition from the Age of the Chartists to the Age of Capital: The Radical Left-Wing Naturalization of the Notion of an Aristocracy of Labor (1)

As a means of examining the transition from the preclassical labor aristocracy of the first half of the nineteenth century to the formation of the classical labor aristocracy during the second half of that century, it is useful to scrutinize the views of a left-wing leader of the period, Ernest Jones. As a key figure in the Chartist movement of the 1840s and a chief organizer of moribund Chartism of the 1850s, he was a significant contemporary participant-observer during this transition. Moreover, as one of Marx and Engels' closest British political friends, he contributed to their knowledge of labor politics while his own theoretical approach was shaped by theirs. Although Jones did not coin the term "labor aristocracy," (2) his repeated explication of it helped gain it a place among left-wing, especially Marxist, shibboleths. In fact, no author prior to Lenin recurred so frequently to this notion as Jones.

For Jones the essence of the labor aristocracy lay not so much in superior living and working conditions as in the existence of trade unions per se; it was not the latter's exclusionary absuses that formed the crux of the matter, but rather their normal, ideal-type, functions. And although Jones's failure to arouse the poor probably intensified his bitterness toward the labor aristocracy, (3) his fulminations against trade unionists were basically motivated by his conviction that their short-sightedness was bound to injure them materially in the near future and had already weakened the democratic and socialist movements by having destroyed working class unity.

Trade unionism had, according to Jones, been founded--and continued to be based--on the fallacy that workers were able, by means of combination, to maintain a fixed standard of wages. Such an approach did not, however, touch on the causes of declining wages, which could be summarized under the rubric: The supply of labor must run ahead of the demand for it. This course of events could, in Jones's view, be avoided if the number of masters wanting men increased or if the number of men wanting masters decreased. Trade unions, however, exerted no influence on these two factors. By pointing to a series of counteracting factors, Jones implicitly sought to meet the possible objection that an increase in the demand for labor could absorb the unemployed. (4) This theoretical possibility was thwarted by the increasing mechanization of industry and agriculture and the ensuing refinement of the division of labor; these processes resulted not only in a relative diminution in the number of workers per unit of capital, but also brought about deskilling, which eliminated premiums on training and weakened traditional craft power. Jones also adduced such factors as the increasing employment of women and children and the intensification of labor (which enabled capitalists to avoid hiring additional workers by obtaining more work from the existing stock) as elements fostering the growth of un-employment. With regard to the issue of diminishing the number of men wanting masters, Jones believed that capitalists could defeat cooperative efforts by causing the supply of labor to increase more rapidly than cooperatives could absorb it. (5)

Jones was manifestly describing the causes and effects of what was to gain fame in Capital as the reserve army of the unemployed. (6) Yet Marx, who was a reader of and contributor to Notes to the People, which was edited by Jones, did not subscribe to the latter's conception of trade unionism as Sisyphean labor. (7) Marx, who took a long view of the deve-lopment of anti-capitalist consciousness, (8) recognized that as long as capitalism prevailed, unions were necessary both as defensive organs of the marketers of labor power (9) and as promoters and galvanizers of class consciousness. (10)

Jones's judgment on trade unions resulted in part from an exaggerated notion of how quickly the logic of capital accumu-lation would seize the previously unrevolutionized crafts and subject the better-situated workers to the processes of dequalification and immiseration that other artisans had experienced. (11) Jones underestimated the tenacity with which artisans could cling to privileged positions in various branches; similarly, he viewed the process of homogenization of the work-ing class (and even of the petty bourgeoisie) too optimisti-cally. Moreover, his unilinearly cataclysmic conception of capitalism allowed no room for the periodic creation of new laboring elites. Rather, he believed that

> the aristocracy of labour is being fast driven down into
> the ranks of the wage-slave--the small retail shopkeeper
> and the small farmer are fast disappearing beneath the
> dull level of hired labour--while the class below this again
> is widening with fearful celerity. (12)

Predicting a levelling down of the wage hierarchy, Jones urged that it was in the "vital interest" of the labor aristocracy "to prevent reductions in the wages of the ranks beneath" it. (13) As a result of his underestimation of the conservative technological forces at work in some branches (14) or of the non-unilinear nature of technological change as well as of the adaptive policies of unions in others, (15) Jones failed to perceive the long-term necessity of trade unions under capitalism.

It was in particular the Amalgamated Society of Engineers, the foremost national union of mid-nineteenth century Britain, that inspired Jones with contempt for the labor aristocracy. This union, which had amalgamated in 1851, became involved in a strike-lockout in 1852 following the rejection by employers of demands for the abolition of systematic overtime and of the piece-master system as well as that for the exclusion of un-skilled workers from self-acting machines. (16) Although the Webbs suggested that the London Executive of the union had refused to support this latter demand, (17) it was the policy of the Engineers to pay, from the subscription provided by other unions and the public, seven shillings a week to skilled non-members and only three shillings a week to laborers. William Newton, a member of the Executive, justified this structure on the basis of the higher standard of living to which the skilled had become accustomed. (18) But a scholar with full access to the union's archives observed two decades later that the skilled non-members were granted more because, as the more dangerous competitors, they had to be treated more generously lest they ally themselves with the employers. (19) Jones was outraged: "That's brotherhood, is it? That's opposing class-legislation, is it?" (20) The system of benefits apparently led to a certain degree of disaffection within the ranks of the unskilled. (21)

Although the Amalgamated Society of Engineers was forced to send its members back to work on the employers' terms, it was not, as Jones fancied, destroyed. Jones's view was, nevertheless, vindicated in the sense that the character of the union was crucially modified by this experience, which consolidated the narrow, exclusionary, craft-protective approach of the early nineteenth century. (22) This process of change was exemplified by the decision of the Engineers to expunge its rules seeking to abolish overtime and piece-work. (23) The conciliatory and pacific attitude, which was to become the characteristic of this model New Model union, was illustrated by the following resolution which the Executive Council adopted unanimously.

That in the opinion of this meeting, the resistance of Labour against Capital is not calculated to enhance the condition of the labourers. We therefore advise that all our future operations should be directed to promoting the system of self-employment in associative workshops as the best means of effectually regulating the conditions of labour. (24)

Generalizing from the pattern set by the Amalgamated Society of Engineers, the Webbs argued that "the contemporary trade movements either did not observe or failed to realise the tendency of this attempt to retain or reconstruct an aristocracy of skilled workmen." (25) But the claim that a conscious attempt was made to (re-)establish an aristocracy of labor does not follow from the developments under review. For if the term was meant in the sense of a stratum, enjoying superior conditions, such an aristocracy had existed continuously throughout the nineteenth century and thus did not require reconstruction. If, on the other hand, the Webbs had in mind a relation of dominance within the working class, it would still have to be shown how the labor aristocracy intended to exert its leadership over other working class strata. In view of the consensus of scholarly opinion to the effect that the Engineers stood aloof from general political movements, (26) there is no reason to assume that labor aristocrats aspired to the status of collective representative of the working class vis a vis other classes and the state. (27) Nor would it have been accurate to include among the characteristics of the emerging labor aristocracy the displacement of unskilled workers from the forefront of economic struggles; for the Engineers recieved considerable moral and financial support from this sector of the working class. (28)

The only substantial support for the Webbs' view lies in the sphere of capital-labor relations; for here the Engineers' conciliatory policy could be interpreted as an attempt to come to terms with capital at the expense of the rest of the working class. Although seemingly plausible, such an interpretation encounters important counter-evidence. Resistance by employers to conciliation constitutes the weightiest counter-argument. To begin with, many employers regarded the dispute of 1852 "as a challenge to capitalism, particularly the freedom of employers as property owners to do what they liked with 'their' workshops." (29) Moreover, many large engineering firms refused to recognize the Amalgamated Society of Engineers for many years. (30)

This is not to say that numerous employers did not, in the ensuing years, pursue a paternalistic course toward workers, whose organization they resisted; such paternalism may also have intentionally nurtured divisions within the work force. But classical labor aristocratic relations between capital and labor, although they may have made their first appearance in the early 1860s, could, primarily for two reasons, not have flourished until the later 1860s or 1870s. (31) First, the cumulative prosperity rendering such a constellation of forces possible and desirable to the subjective agents concerned, did not evolve until this later period; and second, state-mediated recognition of the role of trade unions did not assert itself until that time.

Since Jones looked upon aristocratic aspirations as fruitless, thwarted as they were constantly by the forces of production, he was unconcerned with such a hypothetical reconstruction. (32) Jones seems at times to have believed that the labor aristocracy had already swung over to the side of the working class at large. Thus in 1851 he was persuaded that the skilled artisan and common handicraftsman with superior wages "belong assuredly to the working classes--and, though, certainly forming the aristocracy of labour, are as widely distinct from the veritable middle class, as they are from the pauper." (33) In contrast with this plausible analysis of working class stratification, from which Jones was able to conclude that, "The privileged classes can no longer reckon on the support of the majority" of the labor aristocracy, (34) the following year he contended that the bill, proposed by Lord John Russell, to reduce the qualification of borough voters from an annual rent of ten pounds sterling to five would, by doubling the power and influence of the labor aristocracy, mean that "the veritable working order will be the loser by the measure" since the labor aristocracy "would side, as it ever has sided, with the oppressor. ..." (35) Jones pointed out that even under the new bill household suffrage would still exclude "the navvie, bricklayer, mason, costermonger, mechanic and artizan, who may not have constant permanent employment, and thus shift from town to town as the tide of work ebbs from spot to spot." (36)

Jones's final and perhaps most damning charge against aristocratic (and, in fact, all) trade unions was one that had been uttered before (37) and that continued to be echoed by left-wing critics.

Why! the Trades' Union has been the greatest upholder (unintentionally) of the present system. It has made working-men uphold it and defend it, by teaching them to believe that their wages could be kept up without a political change. It has been one of the most anti-democratic institutions of the modern time,--it has taught them to look at the capitalist as a thing of nature; at wage slavery as a thing of right. ... (38)

Resuming the theme in a similar vein, Jones denied that unions functioned as a palliative, but claimed that even if they did so function, they would be harmful because "they make the evil just bearable--whereas, if it were not bearable, it would be blown sky high at once." For Jones, the advocates of trade unionism were "the POLITICAL OPIUM-EATERS" of the day. (39)

This type of impatience with the chief defensive organ of the working class has traditionally been associated with periods of revolutionary turmoil when the opportunity has been perceived of removing the conditions that render trade unions necessary. Yet the 1850s were not such a period, especially when compared to the preceding decades. Jones's views on trade unionism must, then, be seen as the outgrowth of a lack of understanding of contemporary political trends by Jones and/or as a remnant of an earlier movement that tended to see capitalism as a temporary aberration that could be overcome quickly rather than as a necessary stage of social development. (40)

In light of this clearly non-Marxist and even anti-Marxist conception of trade unions, (41) it is surprising that Engels judged Jones's propagandistic abilities so enthusiastically. (42) One explanation lies in their common desire to mobilize the working class to transcend trade strikes. Thus Marx predicted in 1853 that a continuing depression would transform a series of strikes for higher wages into a defensive struggle against wage reductions that would encompass the political level; the trade unions created during the strike would then be of inestimable value. (43) He cited approvingly Jones's Chartist agitation, which stressed that the success of the labor movement and an enduring improvement in working and living conditions ultimately depended on gaining control of legislation. (44) Marx valued this political approach especially in England, where the struggle for universal suffrage would, in Marx's view, become a socialist achievement to a much greater degree than in Europe since the majority status of the proletariat would provide it with political power. (45)

Marx and Engels' support for Jones may also have derived from the former's overoptimistic estimation of anti-capitalist trends in the British working class. Marx's articles in the New-York Daily Tribune were replete with references to the "war" that was raging in England's factory districts. Marx was of the opinion that these strikes had "revolutionized" the industrial proletariat; once food prices has risen and wages declined, "the political consequences" would manifest themselves. (46) Marx maintained that for the first time the lower strata of the unskilled had initiated the strikes, whereas in the past the skilled factory workers such as engineers and cotton spinners had been in the forefront of industrial conflicts, which then took hold of the lower strata and, finally, of the artisans. (47)

Although several "fierce" conflicts broke out during the mid-1850s, they were "years of steadily expanding trade" and "a blank" for labor historians. (48) According to the Webbs, "with the exception of the building trades, Trade Unionism assumed ... a peaceful attitude." (49) In particular, the Operative Stone Masons engaged in several strikes for higher wages and shorter hours. (50) A correspondent to Jones's People's Paper praised the masons as the staunchest of any workers for trade purposes, but was "sorry to say politics, to the majority of them, are a dead letter. They have got the mistaken notion, so peculiar to high-paid trades, that they can keep wages up by the means of strikes." (51) Since this notion did not, as far as many masons and other artisans were concerned, prove to be so "mistaken" as this correspondent and Jones imagined, it is comprehensible why labor historians and practitioners in the tradition of the Webbs assessed such movements and unions on a completely different plane from the political one on which Marx operated.

Yet the issues involved are not clear-cut. Although there is evidence to the effect that artisans at the end of the 1840s and during the 1850s developed a disinclination to become personally involved in political activity, (52) the material assembled by Henry Mayhew in the years 1849 to 1851 revealed an entirely different picture of the political participation of working class strata in London.

In passing from the skilled operative of the west-end to the unskilled workman of the eastern quarter of London, the moral and intellectual change is so great, that it seems as if we were in a new land, and among another race. The artisans are almost to a man red-hot politicians. They are sufficiently educated and thoughtful to have a sense of their importance in the State. It is true that they may entertain exaggerated notions of their natural rank and position in the social scale, but at least they have read, and reflected, and argued upon the subject. ... They begin to view their class, not as a mere isolated body of workmen,

but as an integral portion of the nation, contributing their quota to the general welfare. ...
The unskilled labourers are a different class of people. As yet they are as unpolitical as footmen, and instead of entertaining violent democratic opinions, they appear to have no opinions whatever; or, if they do possess any, they rather lead towards the maintenance of "things as they are," than towards the ascendancy of the working people. (53)

Conditions in London were, however, owing to the absence of a factory proletariat and to the large number of outworkers, casualized unskilled laborers and lumpenproletarians, not representative of Britain at large. (54) Moreover, the type of political attitudes noted by Mayhew performed a peculiarly integrative function instead of expressing an oppositional spirit among the labor aristocracy. The foregoing considerations merely confirm that no stratum of the working class manifested consistently organized resistance to capitalism as a social formation during the 1850s.

Marx himself was constrained to concede this latter point in connection with Jones's abandonment of several parts of the Charter in an attempt to forge an alliance with the radical bourgeoisie. (55) Marx tried to explain Jones's behavior by referring to the unfavorable political "tone" prevailing at that time in the English working class. (56) This incident also motivated Marx and Engels to introduce into the discussion of the labor aristocracy a topos that became prominent in the subsequent Marxist tradition. "Jones has decidedly sold himself (but at the lowest possible price) to the Bright coterie." (57) To be sure, the denunciation of venality was still only metaphorical; this restriction was removed by the 1870s, but even in the 1850s Engels was prepared to expand the indictment. He conjectured privately that Jones's comprimising was bound up with the circumstance

that the English proletariat is in fact becoming more and more bourgeois, so that this most bourgeois of all nations seems finally to want to reach the point at which it will possess a bourgeois aristocracy and a bourgeois proletariat in addition to the bourgeoisie. For a nation that exploits the whole world, this is to be sure in some measure justified. Only a couple of really bad years can help, and since the discoveries of gold they are not easy to bring about. By the way, I must say that it isn't clear to me at all how the mass of overproduced (commodities), which the crisis gave rise to, has been absorbed. (58)

Engels alluded to four themes that came to occupy a crucial position in the controversy surrounding the labor aristocracy: 1. the English proletariat as a whole had achieved a privileged status vis a vis that of other nations; 2. this status derived from England's internationally dominant industrial role, which apparently permitted the English proletariat to participate in the gains accruing from the world market; 3. the political and social consciousness of the proletariat could be jolted only by an economic depression; and 4. (implicitly) if such a depression did not materialize, the tendency toward working class embourgeoisement would be strengthened.

The first two points appear to have been Engels' original contributions: he was the first to have postulated the existence of a "special form of the labor aristocracy" comprising an entire national working class, (59) and to have pointed to England's world market position as its source. Although the third point, which Marx also stressed, implies the fourth, Engels appears to have been the first to have coupled misery and revolution so tightly; (60) in so doing, he rendered a version of Marxist theory vulnerable to the criticism that fairly steadily rising real wages could undermine the revolutionary potential of the working class over long periods of time. (61) Moreover, given the fact that real wages stagnated during the 1850s while capitalist incomes grew quickly, (62) Engels' own reasoning should have led to the conclusion that the labor movement should have assumed more radical forms of expression during the 1850s.

The tentativeness of these new hypotheses was shown by the fact that Engels made no attempt to seek differentiations within the working class. If this omission derived from the empirical circumstance that the gap between labor aristocrats and other proletarian strata was not widening and/or that domestic intra-working class stratification was receding in importance vis a vis the increasing differentiation between the British working class and other national working classes, then the set of hypotheses would have to be rejected as having no explanatory value with regard to the directions taken by the labor movement in the period from 1848 to 1858. (63)

In summary, then, neither Jones nor Marx and Engels presented theoretical or empirical arguments that convincingly demonstrated the ascendancy of the aristocracy of labor to working class hegemony; they did not even marshal evidence supporting the claim that a significant gap was emerging between the labor aristocracy and the remainder of the working class. (64) Engels' major innovation--the domestic social stratificational consequences of Britain's world market dominance--proved adequate to postulating a nationally favored working class, but did not yet specify mechanisms that could explain differential intra-working class effects.

In the end, therefore, the theoretical legacy of these socialist discussions of the labor aristocracy became an ambiguous one. On the one hand, it consolidated an earlier, pre-"scientific socialist," tradition, which had focused on the debilitating effects a labor aristocracy could and did have on the political progress of the working class. On the other hand, however, Jones and his mentors failed to develop an appropriate framework for analyzing the socio-economic and hence political perspectives of a privileged stratum. They were for this reason unable to formulate a strategy for unifying the working class in Britain as long as they proceeded from the false assumption that the labor aristocracy was bound to disappear in the course of the next cyclical waves of capital accumulation.

Following his break with Marx and Engels, Jones began to accept the former's views on trade unions. In connection with the strike-lockout in the London building trades in 1859 Jones defended the wage and hours demands of the skilled artisans. While taking a cynical, circulation sphere-approach of characterizing these demands as being, like other dealings in property, "a fair common business-like transcaction," he rejected the masters' suggestion that building workers, as highly paid tradesmen, should compare their lot with that of woolcombers.

> No! Compare it with your own, you rich employers, grown wealthy out of the labour of your men! Because the woolcomber starves, it is no reason why the carpenter should be worse off, but it is a reason why the woolcomber should fare better. The test, whether a working man receives wages enough, is not the minimum paid to labour of any kind but the true test is the profits of the employer. (65)

Jones thus effected a shift from his overwhelming reliance on moral categories of intra-working class solidarity to class-unifying economic ones of wages and profits. No longer was the skilled worker being agitated to accept his decline to the level of the worst-paid; on the contrary, he was being urged to establish the principle of relative as well as real wage bargaining. (66) In this sense Jones anticipated Marx's own insight according to which high wages alone were no indicator of socio-economic improvement since wage labor expressed a whole range of human degradation, brutalization and ignorance. (67) This convergence of views was perhaps one reason that Engels, three days after Jones's death, told Marx that Jones had been "among the politicians the only educated Englishman who au fond" had sided with them completely. (68)

Chapter 5
Marx and Engels and the Labor Aristocracy of Mid-Victorian Britain

The present chapter serves the dual purpose of systematizing and evaluating Marx's and Engels' views of the labor aristocracy by confronting them with a comprehensive empirical analysis of the contemporary British labor aristocracy. The former task derives its justification above all from Marx and Engels' influence on subsequent generations of Marxist political leaders who relied heavily on this source for strategical inspiration. To the extent that revolutionary politics were informed by these discussions, their analysis transcends the history of ideas. Subsidiarily, Marx and Engels must be regarded as authentic contemporary sources as a result of their firsthand knowledge of British working class leaders from Chartism to New Unionism.

A. The Structure and Distribution of Skills within the Manual Working Class

The very fact that Marx's and Engels' scattered and often passing remarks on the labor aristocracy have first to be systematized, provides prima facie evidence that they did not constitute a coherent theoretical structure for analyzing this phenomenon let alone uncover "the laws of the formation of the working class." (1) Marx and Engels originally became interested in the notion of a labor aristocracy in connection with its widespread usage in Chartist circles. (2) At first, Marx and Engels wrote within this tradition; that is to say, the issue which they saw confronting revolutionaries in the United Kingdom did not relate to the absence of a socialist movement --the strength of which they in fact overestimated--but, rather, to its slow progress. In contrast with the Chartists, however, Engels in particular shifted his attention from a privileged stratum to a privileged nation of proletarians. (3) Thus as early as 1851 Engels, referring to a movement to found schools and libraries for the working class, informed Marx that the freetraders of Manchester were using "the prosperity or semi-prosperity in order to buy the proletariat." (4) Despite Engels' undifferentiated mention of "the proletariat," it is manifest that in practice schools and libraries could be of use only to the actively literate who also had some leisure time at their disposal--in other words, to an elite. (5)

This emphasis on the privileged status of the British proletariat as a whole, although arriving at a contrary result, was based on an argument similar to one deployed in the Communist Manifesto written at the outset of the cyclical depression in 1847-1848.

> The interests, the life-situations within the proletariat tend more and more toward equality inasmuch as machinery more and more obliterates the differences of work and depresses wages almost everywhere down to an equally low level. (6)

Here Marx and Engels insisted upon the levelling influence of capitalist industrialization on the skill and hence income hierarchy within the working class. (7)

Once the cyclically determined conditions of the working class improved, however, the increasingly uniform and unifying effects of a national capitalism contributed to a diminished resistance to capitalist exploitation. Writing in the midst of a strong upswing in 1850, Marx and Engels argued:

> There can be no question of a real revolution in this general prosperity in which the forces of production of bourgeois society are developing as luxuriantly as is altogether possible within bourgeois relations. ... A new revolution is only possible in the wake of a new crisis. The former is, however, just as certain as the latter. (8)

Marx and Engels saw no reason to alter their view of the long-term dynamic levelling influence of capitalist industrialization; indeed, whole chapters of Capital are devoted to an investigation of the transformation of working and living conditions wrought by the ascendancy of the machine qua capital. The origin of the stratification of skills within the manual working class could be found, according to Marx, in the preceding period of (capitalist) Manufaktur. (9) Here a new division of labor evolved within the artisanal producing unit. (10) Various operations, formerly performed by a single craftsman, now became life-long activities of individual workers. At first, these work-processes were assigned by matching the various requisite degrees of strength, dexterity and mental attention with the natural attributes of the available labor force. Once the manufactory system had created its own basis, it began to develop "workers who by nature are fit only for a one-sided special function." (11)

At this point a two-fold stratification process unfolded consisting of a continuum of and a sharp division between groups of skilled and unskilled workers.

> Since the various functions of the aggregate worker are simpler or more complex, lower or higher, its organs, the individual workers, require very different degrees of training and therefore possess different values. Manufaktur thus develops a hierarchy of workers to which a scale of wages corresponds. (12)

But the new stage of social production did not limit its impact to the creation of gradations of skill; it also seized upon the simplest operations present in even the most skilled work-processes and designated laborers to perform them.

> Now they too are released from their fluid connection with the more substantive aspects of the activity and become ossified as exclusive functions. Manufaktur thus produces in every craft which it embraces a class of so-called unskilled workers which the craft shop strictly excluded. ... The simple separation of workers into skilled and unskilled emerges alongside the hierarchical graduation. (13)

This two-fold process of de-skilling also involved a general downward pressure on wages by reducing the training required by the skilled and eliminating that accorded the unskilled. Marx did not, however, venture a qualitative, let alone a quantitative, evaluation of the consequences of the redistribution of skills on the redistribution of incomes within the working class. In other words, he did not state whether the transformation of the skill structure--from one in which, presumably, a relatively large number of relatively highly skilled workers predominated to one in which the skill level was shifted downwards along the entire continuum so that the new lower end became more prominent--issued in a more or less equal skill distribution.

This already ambiguous perspective was further complicated by two modifying counter-movements. The first, which Marx termed an "exception" to the general trend toward diminished training time and cost, derived from the circumstance that the decomposition of the labor process in certain instances generated new synthetic functions, little known or unknown in craft production, which necessitated lengthier apprenticeships. (14)

And it was precisely the jealous and tenacious protection of apprenticeship rights and other customs by adult male workers which Marx singled out as having been chiefly responsible for the fact that during the entire period of Manufaktur the number of unskilled remained "very limited by the predominant influence" of the skilled. (15)

The victorious advance of large-scale, mechanized industry in competition with various lower stages of production entailed, according to Marx, an acceleration of the de-skilling trends already adumbrated. The new division of labor became one of the distribution of workers under the subordination of specialized machines; at this stage Marx saw the emergence of the second counter-movement: the formation of a crucial distinction between those really employed at machine tools and their helpers (mainly children). Apart from these two "major classes" he enumerated a "numerically insignificant" sector, occupied with the control and repair of machinery, including engineers, machine-builders and joiners: "It is a higher, in part scientifically trained, in part artisanal working class, outside the circle of factory workers and only attached to them." (16)

With the exception of this latter grouping, which Marx evidently considered marginal, manual laborers were therefore experiencing deteriorating and increasingly homogeneous conditions. The tendency of Manufaktur to turn the worker into a crippled abnormality, to deprive him of his knowledge, skill and autonomy, combining them with concentrated force in the form of antagonistic capital, (17) underwent an intensification: exploitation by capitalistically employed machinery brought in its wake an increasingly common experience of a tyrannical factory regime, an assault on bodily organs and functions and and intensified and lengthened working day devoted to a progressively less substantive activity. (18)

The relatively inconspicuous role played by skilled labor in modern industrial capitalism reappeared in Marx's discussion of the reduction of complicated to simple labor in connection with possible objections to his theory of value. While observing that the character of average unskilled labor varied from country to country and cultural epoch to epoch, Marx insisted that, "Simple labor forms by far the greatest mass of all labor of bourgeois society. ..." (19) To this claim he appended the contention that an examination of "any set of statistics" would corroborate the preponderance of unskilled labor. (20) Unfortunately, Marx neither adduced such data nor explicated their long-term trends. In point of fact, given the quality of census data in the United Kingdom during Marx's lifetime, such an analysis would have proved a major and complex scholarly undertaking.

Marx returned to this issue in Capital in which work he was inclined to illustrate skilled labor by reference to jewelers who numbered but several thousand in 1861, the last census year for which material was available to Marx while writing the first volume of Capital. (21) Marx's choice of an occupation so clearly rooted in a former stage of production techniques and so obviously marginal to contemporary capitalist production raises the suspicion that Marx was presenting a distorted image.

A possible explanation of Marx's procedure emerges from a footnote which Marx attached to the aforementioned reference. (22) In his scepticism of the claims of exceptional talent and training required of skilled labor (23) Marx echoed the sentiments expressed by Adam Smith nearly a century before. (24) Marx underscored the importance of factors lying outside the sphere of economic and technological necessities.

> The difference between ... "skilled" and "unskilled labour" rests in part on mere illusions, or at least differences which have long since ceased to be real and only linger on in traditional convention; in part on the more helpless situation of certain strata of the working class which permits them less than others to obtain the value of their labor power by sheer obstinacy. In this context accidental circumstances play such a great part that the same kinds of labor change place. Where, e.g., the physical substance of the working class is weakened and relatively exhausted, as in all countries of developed capitalist production, brutal kinds of labor, which demand much muscle-power, are in general converted into higher kinds of labor vis a vis much finer kinds of labor which descend to the rank of simple labor, as, e.g., the labor of a bricklayer ... in England occupies a much higher rank than that of a damask weaver. (25)

Since this passage is crucial to an understanding of Marx and Engels' subsequent views of the labor aristocracy, it is imperative to analyze it in some detail. It was evidently Marx's conviction that the elimination of the need for arcane knowledge and elaborate manual skills, which had been effected in the wake of the supersession of handicraft technology by a machine-based division of labor, had progressed so far that virtually or tendentially all modern manual labor could be performed by most individuals with a minimum of training. (This is not to argue that Marx deemed the rigorous specialization associated with the capitalist division of labor necessary or desirable in a socialist society.)

Marx specified two major sets of causes underlying the
continued social recognition--i.e., in the form of higher
wages--of technologically obsolete skills. (26) One derived
from the power of certain trade unions to enforce the maintenance of lengthy apprenticeships and limited access to the
trade, thereby preserving an artificially high wage rate
relative to other trades. (27) The other referred to the ability
of some organized workers to mitigate the tyrannical oppression
of their immediate employers.

Given Marx and Engels' thesis according to which only the
fear of trade unions could impel capitalists to pay workers the
value of their labor power, the latter of the two foregoing
cases is logically unexceptionable. The former, however, appears more problematic. Empirically, relatively few trade unions
--encompassing relatively even fewer workers--in the latter
part of the nineteenth century were able to enforce apprenticeship regulations stringent enough to restrict entry into a
trade. The Webbs singled out the Boilermakers, the Sheffield
Cutlers and the Stonemasons as the only larger unions effectively maintaining such rules, whereby only the Boilermakers
were completely successful. Of the approximately 1,500,000
trade unionists recorded in 1895, the Webbs estimated that
900,000 were protected by no apprenticeship rules; 500,000
belonged to unions professing adherence to apprenticeship
rules yet in fact permitting free entry (these included the
metal, building and printing trades); only 90,000 were covered
by apprenticeship rules which were actively enforced, whereby
only 15,000 belonged to unions effectively restraining entry. (28)

Even if Marx had been correct in asserting that socially
relevant numbers of trade unionists were able to enforce payment of wages, over the long-term, in excess of the current
reproducible value of their labor power, then he would not only
have contradicted his own application of the law of value to
wage determination, but would still have had to explain how
the subjective volition of a factor of production could overcome
the dual workings of capital accumulation in destroying the basis
of craft privilege and creating a reserve army of the unemployed
to act as a wage-depressant. (29) Under these circumstances it
appears more plausible to propose the working hypothesis that
Marx and Engels erred in exaggerating the extent to which
capitalism had, already in their time, undermined the genuinely
craft occupations; similarly, they tended to underestimate the
extent to which new skilled occupations were being created. (30)

To be sure, in the context of the many vague definitions
of skilled labor which abounded at that time and later, Marx's
scepticism was scarcely unfounded. Thus Palgrave's Dictionary

of Political Economy reported that skilled labor ordinarily implied "general intelligence, foresight, energy, and honesty," qualities which depended "largely on inherited race character, and on early environment and training." (31) In a further definitional move, the Dictionary posited that skilled labor could be distinguished from the unskilled variety by the fact that its transfer to another area involved a greater "industrial loss" than was the case among the unskilled. (32) This criterion is either tautological--because it equates the loss of high wages with "industrial loss"--or, in some instances, empirically untenable.

Yet it is clear that some criteria must be adduced. Three which focus on essential distinctions between grades of labor are: 1. "a thorough and comprehensive knowledge of processes involved in the work"; 2. "the exercise of considerable independent judgment"; and 3. "a high degree of manual dexterity." (33) Occupations demanding such skills are clearly ones that cannot be mastered within a short period of time; both theoretical knowledge (of natural laws) and experience are necessary. The fact that "independent judgment" plays an important part implies that the work flow is not repetitive since new and unexpected though perhaps predictible problems may arise.

Although the skilled-unskilled spectrum constitutes a continuum without fixed borders, it is possible to specify certain occupations requiring these qualities and others characterized by their absence. (34) Thus a group of carpenters who can build a house on their own are as skilled according to these criteria as the laborers who fetch the lumber are unskilled. This distinction does not imply, however, that these laborers, by virtue of years of observation and practice, could not become carpenters without a formal apprenticeship. Nor, on the other hand, does it imply that all carpenters are skilled, (35) for a further division of labor and the introduction of machinery may alter the skill requirements so that none of the three aforementioned criteria is fulfilled. (36) A serious investigation of the role of the skilled in nineteenth century British industry would, therefore, presuppose a concrete study of the changing technological requirements of labor in each major branch. But neither Marx nor any subsequent economist has conducted such a study. (37)

To return to the factors bringing about an "accidental" division between skilled and unskilled trades: the specific examples adduced by Marx seem ill-suited to prove his point. The premium supposedly paid for physical strength in countries characterized by physical debilitation and exhaustion of the proletariat should be detectable in the wages of such workers as hod carriers or bricklayers' helpers who performed literally backbreaking labor. Yet the large and relatively constant wage differentials between these two groups and building trades journeymen during the nineteenth century suggest that skill was not a negligible factor. (38)

The only empirical evidence Marx offered in support of his claim that skilled labor occupied an insignificant position within the aggregate British national labor supply stemmed from Samuel Laing's National Distress, published in 1844. Here Marx found data indicating that of a total English and Welsh population of eighteen million, the existence of eleven million rested on unskilled labor; the fact that Laing reckoned better paid factory workers and bricklayers among the working middle class amused Marx. (39)

Although Marx's choice of a man as a witness who in Marx's time had become a respected figure in government suited his scholarly and propagandistic tactics of allowing the bourgeoisie to indict itself, it was not appropriate to documenting his historically more sweeping assertions. To begin with, Laing's book appeared in the same year as the results of the occupational census for 1841. (40) As a result, Laing apparently had no access to the latest data, for he cited data from 1831; (41) the data cited by Marx referred, according to Laing, to the "present," but no date or source was mentioned. (42) At the time, in other words, Marx published Capital (43) these data were three to four decades old; from 1830 to 1870 enormous changes had marked the British economy which it was incumbent upon Marx to show as having further diminished the positional value of skilled labor. Yet Marx, who devoured virtually every statistical work published by the British government, made but sparing published use of the decennial censuses.

Laing's value as a source on living conditions in mid-century Britain was further vitiated by the fact that his perceptions were strongly shaped by the severe immiseration which textile operatives--who represented 28.3 per cent of all manufacturing workers in 1841 (44)--had undergone during the first half of the nineteenth century. Thus Laing noted that the hand-loom weavers, who together with their families numbered 800,000, were counted among the lowest level of employed persons although at the outset of the century they had "stood at the head of British operatives in amount of earnings, intelligence, education, and general respectability." (45) Laing projected the experience of the hand-loom weavers into the future of all unskilled adult manufacturing labor, making "exception of a

comparatively small number of skilled labourers and artizans." (46) Of 2,500,000 persons deriving their subsistence
directly from manufacturing, one-third were "plunged in
extreme misery, and hovering on the verge of actual starvation"; another third, however, were earning "high wages,
amply sufficient to support them in respectability and comfort." (47) But even this "upper class of highly-paid workmen
connected with machinery" came to know distress in the years
following the crisis of 1837. (48)

Laing persisted, however, in giving prominence to the
distinction between common laborers "and all the superior
descriptions of workmen, such as carpenters, shoemakers, &c.,
who exercise what is strictly speaking a handicraft, in contradistinction to common brute labour, and to labour which is
mechanical or a mere link in the operations of a great
machine." (49) Although Laing incurred Marx's scorn for having included manual workers in the middle class, he exhibited
ambivalence in this matter. On the one hand he specified that
only "a few of the best paid and most respectable operatives"
belonged to the middle class; indeed, he modified this straitifi-
cation even further by conceding that, "The lower members of
this class, such as the bricklayers, masons, &c., hardly come
within the denomination of the middle class." (50) On the
other hand, he insisted that the skilled artisans did occupy
"an intermediate position between the common labouring class
and that of retail dealers, &c." (51) Laing introduced yet
another stratum, observing that common handicraftsmen,
exercising a craft that demanded some period of apprenticeship
and earning wages decidedly superior to those of common labor,
were in fact closer to the laboring classes in education, feelings
and habits of life, although they could theoretically attain the
same standard of civilization as small shopkeepers. (52)

The upshot of this review of Laing's essay is the insight
that, despite the assault which capitalist industrialization had
mounted against the working and living conditions of millions
of British workers, differentials between/among manual working
class strata apparently widened. Although Laing may be interpreted as having implied that the base of the proletarian
stratification pyramid had become broader over time, he also
appears to have witnessed an increasing distance between top
and bottom.

But Laing could not report on the burgeoining of new
methods of production calling for a large increment to the stock
of skilled workers. Although the latter may, in terms of
versatility, have lagged behind their predecessors, they
nevertheless differed sufficiently from "average" unskilled

laborers to have rendered it profitable for their employers to pay them above-average wages regardless of the abolition of apprenticeship and entry restrictions. (53)

Attempts by nineteenth century British economists to resolve these issues were unsatisfactory, in part because they relied on generalizations dictated by political-ideological needs of the late-Victorian English bourgeoisie confronting growing socialist agitation rather than on empirical studies. (54) One of the most prominent "optimists" in the field was Robert Giffen (55) whose opinions were often elevated to standing dogma. (56) Giffen's only support for the claim that the aristocracy of labor had, by the 1880s, become a greater proportion of the working classes than fifty years earlier, and that a "substitution of artisan classes for rude labourers" had taken place, consisted in the argument that, "It would have been a miracle if with all the increase of machinery and development of artistic skill which had been going on, any other change had taken place." (57) Although machinery may have exerted the influence alluded to by Giffen--as, for example, when the operator of a complicated excavating machine replaces manual shovelers (58)--, there is no a priori reason to assume that this was in fact the case. It would be equally justifiable to make the apodictic statement that the thrust of mechanization was, as had been the case in textiles, to replace skilled men with unskilled men, women and children. (59) For in point of fact, males above the age of twenty as a share of all those employed in manufacturing declined from 60.5 per cent in 1841 to 49.8 per cent in 1881; the corresponding figures for textiles and dyeing were 43.6 per cent and 28.1 per cent respectively. (60)

Apart from direct evidence supplied by concrete studies of individual trades (see below), there is still another indicator supporting the view that a shift in the skill structure took place in favor of the more highly skilled. (This argument does not provide sufficient proof that a labor aristocracy was formed, but merely that the number of unskilled diminished whereas the number of those with at least a modicum of skill rose.) The source of this evidence is George Wood's generally accepted observation that approximately three-eighths of the increase in real wages between 1850 and 1900 stemmed from a shift in employment from the lower to the higher paying branches. (61)

Marx's analysis of capitalist development did not lead to this result; on the contrary, Marx saw capitalist mechanization and division of labor as steadily operating to create ever simpler labor tasks so that the skill structure was being and would continue to be compressed downwards. (62) In terms of income, Marx would also have expected a negative shift effect

--diametrically opposed to that discovered by Wood--to make itself felt in the long run; in other words, apart from wage movements in individual branches or occupations, the average wage level would, in Marx's view, be depressed by shifts from higher to lower paid categories. (63)

If Wood's analysis is acknowledged as correct, then one of two possible moves is available from Marx's position. Either Marx's conception of wages' following, in the long-term, a course parallel to that of the value of labor power (including training costs) is propounded--in which case it would have to be conceded that the shift to higher wage categories reflected a shift to higher skill categories; or, a divergence between wage and value of labor power (in particular the skill component), resulting in a long-term excess of the price over the value of labor power, must be assumed.

As strange as it may appear, (64) Marx and Engels did opt for some variant very close to the latter possibility. By having rejected the general notion that skill would continue to play a significant part in the capitalist division of labor; and by having further denied that wage differentials were based on corresponding real skill differentials; and, finally, by having become convinced that (the allegedly widespread) long-term apprenticeships did not rest on technological necessities, Marx implied and Engels expressly argued that for almost a half-century of unprecedented capitalist growth the trade unions organizing such skilled workers had been able to impose their will on employers and the state. (65)

Marx's published work does not indicate that Marx was aware of and/or troubled by this theoretical inconsistency. This lack of concern rested on at least two considerations: 1. Marx (and Engels) adhered to the view that the social and technological forces of capital accumulation would soon sweep these remnants away (66); and 2. Marx expressed scepticism about the size of differentials within the working class. It was not differences in material well-being as such that Marx perceived as possible sources of proletarian disunity, but rather the effects of exclusionary trade unions on political consciousness and action. (67)

Engels, on the other hand, doubtless in part because he led an active political life during the socialist renaissance of the 1880s and 1890s, felt compelled to resolve the aforementioned theoretical inconsistency. In Britain's world market and colonial hegemony he found the economic basis of the profits which enabled capitalists to pay to skilled workers wages in excess of the value of labor power. Engels was considerably less precise, however, with regard to the motivations of capitalists in dispensing this largess; but he hinted that a probable goal was political co-optation, which at times was extended to the entire British working class. (68)

B. Working Class Income

One of Marx's earliest and most detailed empirical discussions of aggregate working class income is found in his inaugural "Address of the Working Men's International Association." (69) In it Marx underscored the disparity between the unprecedented industrial progress recorded in Britain between 1848 and 1864 on the one hand and the unalleviated poverty of the masses on the other. (70) He conceded that a minority of workers in Britain (and Europe) had obtained an increase in real wages although for most workers rising money wages had been neutralized by rising prices. (71)

Both this short outline and Marx's much more detailed account in Capital (72) have been criticized on the grounds that Marx did not adduce conclusive empirical evidence of the direction in which aggregate or average working class income changed during this period. (73) This objection is justified in the sense that Marx did not present any aggregate real wage indicators; the wealth of unsynthesized data cited by him referred mainly to the "badly paid" part of the working class which he claimed--without documentation--formed, together with agricultural laborers, the majority of that class. (74) Several factors may be responsible for this logically incomplete approach. First, a significant segment of contemporary public and scholarly opinion upheld the notion that the working class had shared little if any in the expansion of British production. (75) Second, Marx had devoted earlier sections of Capital to historical illustrations of deteriorating conditions within the process of production which he deemed an essential component of immiseration. (76)

Moreover, the theoretical objections to Marx's claim of unabated poverty have been inadequate to the task. The basic argument runs as follows: during the period in question the two basic sources of an interior, exogenous reserve army of the unemployed--agricultural migration and competitive destruction of handicrafts--were becoming exhausted; at the same time, commodity exports were increasing rapidly enough to overcompensate for capital's own endogenous superannuation of workers. Consequently, the reserve army of the unemployed did not operate to depress wages. (77)

With regard to the first factor, the release of agricultural workers actually peaked during the period under review. Whereas the number of male agricultural laborers and indoor farm servants above the age of twenty had risen in England and Wales from 762,594 in 1841 to 812,447 in 1851 (an increase of 6.5 per cent), between the latter date and 1871 it declined to 655,718 (a decrease of 19.3 per cent). (78)

As far as handicrafts are concerned, although the only relevant data from this period do not allow of a direct comparison, (79) a random examination of them corroborates the theoretical expectation that the average number of employees per industrial establishment was on the rise. In this context the plausibility of the assumption that the shift of labor from the pre-capitalist and petty-capitalist sectors to the capitalist sector of industrial production ceased during this period is diminished. (80)

Testing the claim that the growth of exports to the non-capitalized world created more employment than was lost through the mechanism of an increasing organic composition of capital is extremely complicated. Nevertheless, an attempt may be made to approximate some orders of magnitude. From 1851 to 1871 employment in manufacturing in Great Britain rose by about twenty-two per cent. (81) During the same period, exports of manufactured goods from the United Kingdom rose by about 122 per cent. (82) Although total exports to Northern, Western and Central Europe, the United States and Canada grew more quickly than those to the rest of the world, (83) the data as a whole enhance the plausibility of this particular claim.

There are, additionally, three indicators of labor market conditions which do not confirm the view according to which the reserve army of the unemployed was not being replenished. First, unemployment among skilled trade unionists--the only available data--averaged about five per cent from 1851 to 1871, reaching a high of 11.9 per cent in 1858 and peaking again during the crisis and depression of 1867-1869. (84) Figures for individual unions such as the Iron Founders and London Compositors neared one-fifth in some years. (85) The level of unemployment was, moreover, as high as at any time in the latter half of the nineteenth century. (86)

Second, the number of paupers in receipt of relief (exclusive of vagrants) in England and Wales rose from 860,893 in 1851 to 1,081,926 in 1871. (87) This increase of 25.7 per cent was only marginally lower than the growth of total population. (88)

The third indicator of a general redundancy on the labor market was the explosive growth in emigration after 1847. (89)

In order to avoid confusing British with Irish emigration, United States immigration data can be used as an illustration. From the inception of the collection of such data in 1820 until 1847, the number of British immigrants never exceeded 24,000; then from 1848 through 1851 the average annual level doubled to more than 48,000; from 1852 to 1861 the annual average declined to about 39,000; and finally from 1862 to 1871 it jumped sharply to more than 67,000. (90) Although it is patent that emigration of this magnitude must have relieved some of the downward pressure on the wage level deriving from the unemployed, even the new amalgamated trade unions began to despair of the efficacy of emigration funds as an expedient to reduce surplus labor. (91)

It must, finally, be noted that even at this time British capital export represented a significant channeling of investment away from potential employment opportunities in the United Kingdom. In this sense it weakened the bargaining position of British workers by braking capital accumulation and hence the demand for labor. (92) Although the relative weight of capital export in the British economy was to grow later in the pre-World War I period, even in the third quarter of the nineteenth century the commitment was sizable. Thus, whereas in 1855 the gross trading profits of companies had been sixteen times larger than net property income from abroad, by 1875 they were less than seven times greater. (93) It has been estimated that "Britain's foreign wealth had swelled by 1875 to Ł 1,200,000,000." (94) The possible connections with stagnating real wages were manifest enough for contemporary middle-class radicals to express concern about the trend away from domestic and toward foreign investment. (95)

But perhaps the most telling reason for seriously considering Marx's summarization of working class living standards during the 1850s and 1860s lies in the fact that more recent scholarly studies have not only confirmed Marx's views, but have also revealed that Marx judged the improvement in the condition of the better paid workers too favorably. According to this body of literature, real wages (with unemployment taken into account) did not reach and consolidate a new plateau until after the crisis and depression of 1866-1868. (96) Moreover, the data indicate that the wages of skilled workers rose no more rapidly than those of the mass of workers. Thus an index of the real wages of London artisans reveals that the values recorded in 1850-1852 were not permanently exceeded until the years following 1869. (97) Other detailed wage studies have revealed similar trends. (98)

The evidence pertaining to the functional distribution of income also supports Marx's position. Three independent surveys of the wage share all show a decline. According to a contemporary statistician, Leone Levi, this share of total income declined from 43.5 per cent in 1866-1867 to 41.4 per cent in 1882-1883. (99) A decade later, Arthur Bowley estimated that from 1860 to 1891 average manual labor wages had risen forty per cent compared with an increase of forty-seven per cent in total national income on the average. (100) Finally, a modern study indicates that income from employment as a share of total domestic income declined from 52.1 per cent in 1855 to a low of 46.2 per cent in 1871, and did not surpass the initial value until 1883; if net property income from abroad is added to obtain gross national product, then the share of employment income in 1900 (50.9 per cent) was lower than in 1855 (51.0 per cent). (101)

In Capital, the first edition of which was published three years after Marx had written the "Address" for the First International, Marx returned to the theme of the better and worse paid sectors of the working class. Although Marx cited the limits of his book as the reason for focusing on the badly paid workers, (102) his two-fold conviction that they formed the majority and that "the misery of the working masses" would continue unabated under capitalism (103) doubtless reinforced the design of the expository architecture. In this context, his sparse and unsystematic comments on the best paid workers did not serve to contrast the two groups, but rather to underscore the insecurity, poverty, deprivation and misery shared by both. (104)

In a short passage devoted to miners, Marx noted that they purchased their wages--which made them one of the highest paid categories of British workers--at the expense of very poor working and housing conditions. (105) Then in a separate section (106) Marx very briefly discussed the effects of the crisis of 1866-1867 on "the best paid part of the working class, its aristocracy," namely iron shipbuilders in London. (107) The heart of the passage consisted of a very lengthy quotation from a newspaper documenting how hundreds of men, who had previously belonged to the best paid skilled workers of Britain, had been compelled to seek shelter in workhouses because their reserves had been exhausted. (108)

It is significant that Marx chose to dwell on these two factors in his brief references to the best paid. For he was manifestly convinced that: 1. capitalist mechanization would both undermine the technological basis of higher craft incomes

and lead to a deterioration of working conditions; (109) and
2. during periods of crisis and depression the aggregate working class, subject to tendentially homogeneous conditions,
would coalesce politically.

Marx and Engels retained their conviction that revolutionary
movements ebbed and flowed in intimate connection with the
upswings and downswings of the industrial cycle. (110) In
later years, however, they refined this causal nexus. Engels
in particular sought to demonstrate that a generation of the
English working class, enjoying historically unique privileges
based on the world market supremacy of British capital, would
be succeeded by a proletariat reduced to standards of living
common to other European national working classes. The correlation between economic misery/immiseration and revolution
came to be more stratum-specific. Thus Engels warned Eduard
Bernstein that the misery of hand-weavers, engaged in a
fruitless struggle with capitalist industry, could make them
susceptible to socialist views but that those in a hopeless
situation would reach out for any available means of res-
cue. (111) Trade unionists, too, would have to experience
hard(er) times before anything could be "done with them." (112)

Numerous indicators show that both of the leveling/unifying
factors imputed to Marx's conception of capitalist progress
were operating during the period in question. An illustration
from a branch with which Marx had some acquaintance may
suffice here. From August 1859 to February 1860 a large and
intense building trades strike-lockout took place around the
issues of a nine-hour day and union recognition. (113) Marx,
reporting on the beginning of the strike for a German emigré
newspaper, spoke of the "brutal obstinacy of the masters" who
had arrogated to themselves the same authority vis a vis their
"'hands'" as American plantation owners vis a vis their slaves.
Acknowledging that such attitudes and treatment generated
"that concentrated, conscious class hatred ... which is the
most certain guarantee of a societal overturn," Marx praised
the sacrifices suffered by other workers throughout Britain
who were providing financial support to those on strike or
locked out. (114) In spite of strike and lockout benefits, (115)
men who had been earning five and one-half shillings per
day (116) soon exhausted their funds. (117) In summarizing the
"state of open war" which had raged between labor and capital,
the Registrar-General stated:

> This distress produced ultimately a sensible effect on the
> mortality of the men and their wives. As long as there was
> bread, the poor children, however, apparently had it; until

weakened, cold, ill-clad, they at last died in unusual numbers as the severe weather came on towards the close of the year. (118)

Although de-skilling brought about by technological change remained marginal in the building trades compared with the transformations other industries were undergoing and/or had already underwent, it was none the less advancing. Painting in particular, subjected to increasing "jobbing" between the 1830s and the 1860s, was flooded by unskilled painters and became casualized. (119) As a result, painters were known as the unhealthiest occupational group during these years. (120) In carpentry and joinery, labor-saving tools and a further division of labor served to undermine the position of the tradesmen. (121) Largely as a result of the piecework connected with subcontracting and sweating, wrote one of the deans of orthodox political economy, "A carpenter in London, and in some other places, is not supposed to last in his utmost vigour above eight years." (122)

C. Marx's and Engels' Progressive Disillusionment with British Trade Unions

Despite his relativization of the socio-economic disparities between the majority of poorly paid workers and minority of better paid ones in Britain, (123) Marx remained sceptical of the trade unions of the skilled in their contemporary form. An understanding of Marx's position is, however, complicated by the fact that his criticisms were sometimes directed against trade union leaders, at other times against the membership and at still other times against the entire working class. Thus in 1864 he made the failure of the continental European revolutions of 1848 responsible for the ensuing "castration" of the British working class. Large scale emigration, induced by the discovery of gold in California and Australia, deprived the labor movement of irreplaceable members. Finally, other former leaders, "bribed" by the "bait" of greater employment and temporarily higher wages, swam with the current. On the other hand, the apathy of the masses reached historically unprecedented levels so that the working class became reconciled to its political nothingness. (124)

Marx's position becomes even more ambiguous in light of the growing class polarization of wealth and poverty which he described for this period. (125) By allowing such exogenous factors as the discovery of precious metals, the failure of other national labor movements and corruption to counteract the theoretically predictable outcome of an extended period of capital accumulation, Marx, to be sure, punctured the rigorously economist categorical framework often attributed to him; (126) at the same time, however, he did not succeed in plausibly uncovering systemic causes of the course pursued by the labor movement and the British working class as a whole.

During the 1860s Marx appears to have sustained the hope that the trade unions of the skilled would expand the scope of their operations to include the organization of the worst paid workers, participation in and leadership of general social and political movements and mobilization of the masses for the overthrow of "wage slavery." (127) In connection with the recruitment of trade union support for the International at the end of the 1860s, Marx was convinced that he had made some progress in converting several trade union leaders to a perspective closer to his own. (128) He was particularly impressed by Robert Applegarth, the secretary of the Amalgamated Society of Carpenters and Joiners. (129) Engels, who in general was even more sceptical of English trade union leaders than Marx, became so enthusiastic as a result of an attempt by a member of the House of Lords to elicit Applegarth's support for the preservation of landed property in exchange for legislation favorable to trade unionism, that he ridiculed M.P.'s who fancied that they had the whole labor movement "in their pocket" because a few leaders had flirted with them. (130)

Soon, however, Marx's attitude toward existing trade unions became increasingly critical. (131) By the early 1870s (132) Marx stated at a session of the London Conference of the International that he had altered his views on trade unions which he now considered

> an aristocratic minority. The poor workers could not belong to them: the great mass of the workers, who were driven daily by economic development out of the villages and into the cities, will long remain outside the trade unions, and the poorest of the poor would never belong to them. (133)

Marx then proceeded to disparage the achievements of trade unions which, in his view, were powerless without the International. (134) Although these remarks must be read in connection with a proposal to attain administrative decentralization by means of an international federation of trade unions, (135) the sharp tone revealed that Marx had been deeply disappointed by the failure of the trade unions to adopt an aggregate anti-

capitalist approach. It also underscored the baselessness of
Bakunin's charge that Marx and Engels viewed the "wretched
proletariat" "with the deepest contempt" and founded their
revolutionary strategy on the privileged stratum of bourgeois-
ified workers. (136) A year later, at the Haag Congress of the
International, Marx made his opinion of the "so-called leaders
of the English workers" even more explicit, claiming that they
"were more or less bought by the bourgeoisie and the government." (137)

Toward the end of the 1870s Marx's condemnation of the
British trade unions became even more comprehensive. Speaking of the years following 1848 as "the period of corruption"
which had mired the working class deeper and deeper in
demoralization until it had become "the tail" of Liberal Party
capitalists, Marx charged that the leadership had definitively
passed into the hands of venal trade union leaders and professional agitators who devoted themselves more to supporting
Liberal foreign policy than to coming to the aid of starving
strikers. (138)

Numerous factors may account for the transformation that
occured in Marx and Engels' assessment of British trade
unions. Certainly not the least important was their disillusion-
ment upon discovering that the Reform Bill of 1867 and other
election and voting reforms, to which they had attributed
great potential significance, (139) had not galvanized the
working class into building its own party or pursuing a course
independent of that set by the bourgeoisie. (140)

Marx's reactions did not prove to be unique; much less
radical socialists shared them. Thus the Webbs, writing in the
1890s, set forth an indictment which corroborated many of the
charges made by Marx. (141) They observed, for example,
that the legislative recognition achieved by trade union leaders
had been gained at the price of abandoning the class approach
of compulsory maintenance of the standard of living in favor
of the bourgeois principle of freedom of contract for the individual worker. (142) They also confirmed that adherence by
the officially acknowledged leaders of the trade union world to
bourgeois economic views had led to a growing disaffection
among the rank and file from that leadership. (143) The class
collaboration that followed in the wake of legislative recognition,
made so much of by Marx, also occupied a prominent place in
the Webbs' narrative. (144) Finally, the Webbs agreed fully
with Marx's assessment of the political labor movement as the
tail of the Liberals. (145)

Engels, too, shared these views. In the most explicit and
ambitious analysis of the labor aristocracy ever published by

him or Marx, Engels not only set forth what was to become
a standard Marxist explanation in terms of England's world
market hegemony, but also sketched the political strategy
employed by the bourgeoisie in cultivating working class passivity. According to Engels, Chartism's extinction, taken
together with the renewed economic upswing after 1848,
enabled the industrial bourgeoisie, flushed with victory in the
wake of the abolition of the corn laws, to attach the English
working class to its own Liberal Party. Moreover, strong common sense instructed the capitalist class in the impossibility
of establishing complete social and political dominance without
the support of the proletariat. (146)

Engels' evaluation of the allegedly conciliatory class politics
pursued by English industrialists was influenced by Marx's
conception of the peculiar class structure prevailing in England.

> In no other country have the intermediate stations between
> the millionaire commanding whole industrial armies and the
> wages-slave living only from hand to mouth so gradually
> been swept away from the soil. There exist here no longer,
> as in continental countries, large classes of peasants and
> artisans almost equally dependent on their own property
> and their own labour. (147)

Modern scholars have also stressed the fact that at least
through the third quarter of the nineteenth century, England
differed from continental European countries in lacking a
significant number of relatively prosperous petty bourgeois,
farmers, civil servants and office workers. (148)

In lieu of more precise cross-national data for nineteenth
century Europe, the following selected comparative data may
serve to indicate relative orders of magnitude for Britain,
Germany and France. Between the census years of 1841 and
1891 the number of farmers and graziers in England and Wales
fluctuated between 225,000 and 250,000. (149) In France,
3,266,705 farms were enumerated in 1866 and 1,967,590 in
1896. (150)

Seen in terms of relative population size, these figures
reveal that in the mid-1860s, when the French population was
one and three-quarters times as great as that of England and
Wales, French farmers were more than thirteen times as numerous as their English and Welsh counterparts; by the mid-1890s,
when the French population was only one and one-quarter
times as large, French farmers were still almost nine times as
numerous. (151)

Careful estimates for Germany show that between 1855 and 1895 the number of independent farmers, woodsmen and fishermen rose from 2,130,000 to 2,564,000. (152) Thus with a population only seventy to eighty per cent larger than that of England and Wales, Germany accounted for eight to eleven times as many farmers. (153)

Although the relative number of civil servants, professionals and white collar employees appears to have been roughly equal in Britain, Germany and France in the latter half of the nineteenth century, (154) the number of employers and self-employed in manufacturing, handicrafts and trade appears to have been at least twice as great in the two continental countries as in Britain. (155)

In spite of this empirical verification of the relative insignificance of buffer classes between the bourgeoisie and proletariat in Britain, the generally plausible interpretation built by Engels on this basis reveals itself, when applied to concrete measures and policies, as undifferentiated, in particular with regard to historical timing. For a quarter-century passed after 1848 before significant sections of industrial capital could be said to have accepted labor organizations and the principle of collective bargaining. Not only does Engels seem to imply that the years immediately following 1848 were marked by a new phase of capital-labor relations, but his language also suggests that the change derived from a voluntaristic strategy, consciously and unilaterally formulated by industrial capitalists as a social and political class. (156)

This historical image unequivocally contradicts Marx's analysis of the struggles surrounding the passage of the Ten Hours Act of 1847 and subsequent acts. Marx stressed that the capitalists at first fought passage of the bill, then sought to undermine its effective enforcement and, finally, had recourse to judicial maneuvers. Marx, moreover, left no doubt that enactment was due mainly to working class struggles to assert its "political economy" vis a vis that of the middle class and subsidiarily to Conservative support in revenge for the elimination of the corn laws. (157) More striking still is the fact that Engels' account in the 1880s contradicted not only the notes which he made in 1868 of the relevant passages from Capital, (158) but also his own articles on the Ten Hours Act written in 1850. (159)

Similarly, it was decades before manufacturers "cajoled and protected" trade unions as beneficial institutions (160) if indeed they can be said ever to have done this on a societally relevant scale in the nineteenth century. Numerous viciously conducted strikes and lockouts in the 1850s and 1860s scarcely contributed

to an environment of conciliation. G.D.H. Cole is therefore
almost certainly justified in stating that prior to the 1870s
"most employers were ... far more intent on smashing Trade
Unions than on negotiating with them." (161) It was not until
the success of the leading trade unionists before the Royal
Commission on Trade Unions from 1867 to 1869 in allaying the
fears of some segments of the ruling classes concerning the
goals of the unions, (162) and especially not until these classes perceived that an enfranchised working class would not
engage in disruptive political activity, that trade unions received legislative sanction. (163)

To recapitulate, then, Engels appears to have interpreted
events of the 1850s and 1860s too deterministically in terms
of the capital-labor constellation of the 1870s and 1880s. That
the trade unions of the skilled and their employers had come
to terms with each other within the existing socio-economic
framework he took to have been the result of long-term class
planning reaching back four decades. In so doing, Engels
deprived the various struggles for enhanced democratic
rights and better working and living conditions of their appropriate positional value within the history of mid-Victorian
class conflict; instead, they were derogated to a secondary
role of empirical contingencies causally ornamental to the
decisions and policies of capitalists and their venal allies in
the leadership of the labor movement. The social, political and
cultural complexity inherent in the ascendancy of a social
stratum and its interactions with the ruling classes was
abandoned in favor of apodictic generalization. Ironically, for
example, it was precisely the debate surrounding the Reform
Bill of 1867 that for the first time underscored the conscious
class tactic of granting privileges to a part of the working
class as a means of influencing it (see below section G), yet
Engels failed to comment on this stratum-specific course of
action. It remains to be determined whether Engels' economic
explanation was equally mechanistic.
    Marx's and Engels' views on the British labor aristocracy
have been faulted on other grounds. As the Chartist traditions
became progressively dissipated in the 1860s and 1870s, (164)
Marx and Engels reformulated the issue of the political context
of the labor aristocracy: the failure of an existing revolutionary
movement was transformed into the total absence of anti-capitalist organizations within the working class. A modern critic
has construed this sequence to mean that Marx and Engels
tried to explain the rise of a non-socialist trade union movement
by having recourse to the thesis of the labor aristocracy

because "(t)he obvious interpretation--that a certain share of
the new wealth created by the development of industry under
capitalism went to the mass of the workers--had to be rejected." (165)

This line of reasoning displays a number of weaknesses.
First, Marx and Engels neither devised the thesis of a labor
aristocracy nor applied it first to this particular turn of socio-
political events; others and they themselves had employed it
in partial explanation of a different phenomenon. Second, far
from rejecting--let alone having to reject--"the obvious interpretation," Marx and Engels did, as was noted above, take
account of rising wages and their consequences for revolutionary action. The third and most decisive weakness relates to
the implication that Marx and Engels believed that the
existence of the labor aristocracy explained why no revolution
had taken place in Britain. (166)

This question clearly encompasses a much broader spectrum
of social forces than those focusing on the causes leading to
the rise and consolidation of an exclusionary trade union
movement pursuing peculiarly narrow social and political goals.
The key role of a labor aristocracy in such a trade union
movement suggests itself much more readily than in the context
of the failure of a revolutionary political movement to emerge.
For even superficial considerations would place crucial emphasis
on the conditions and consciousness of the mass of workers
--and not of the labor aristocracy--in any evaluation of the
reasons underlying the absence of a revolutionary party. And
in point of fact, Engels did plump for this kind of analysis
although it proved at times to be at loggerheads with other
arguments used by Marx and Engels.

The relationship between trade unions and revolutionary
parties/movements is an extremely complicated one which Marx
and Engels never analyzed in detail for Britain. In fact, apart
from historical illustrations in the first volume of Capital,
which do not deal with this issue directly, neither Marx nor
Engels wrote any serious, scholarly study of politics and
economics with special reference to the labor movement of
Victorian England.

D. The World Market

Engels' original contribution to the debate surrounding the
labor aristocracy consisted in his insistence upon Britain's

world industrial hegemony and colonial dominance as the material basis of bourgeois support of a favored stratum or, as Engels often expressed it, of the entire English working class. (167) Engels, as already noted, had broached this subject in a letter to Marx as early as 1858. In the 1880s Engels' private correspondence was replete with variations on this theme. To Marx he motivated his decision to suspend his cooperation with the weekly, <u>The Labour Standard</u>, by referring to the lack of public influence generated by his articles. The basic cause of this failure Engels saw in the fact that, "The British working man just doesn't want to go any further, he must be shaken up by events, by the loss of the industrial monopoly." (168) A year later Engels returned to the subject, once again implicating the entire working class. In response to a query from Karl Kautsky concerning the attitude of the English workers towards Britain's colonial policy, Engels wrote that in this matter and all other political matters they thought as the bourgeoisie did, presumably because they were "also feasting smartly upon England's world market and colonial monopoly." (169)

The next year Engels explained to the leader of the German Social Democrats, August Bebel, that "a really general labor movement" would not arise until the workers felt that England's world market monopoly had been broken; for as long as they remained the tail of the bourgeoisie in the economic exploitation of this monopoly, they would remain the tail of the Liberals. (170) Engels underscored the significance of foreign trade profits for domestic class struggle by using the negative example of Germany. In view of the strategy of German exporters--namely, to demand protective import tariffs in order to compensate for the losses incurred in dumping abroad--, it became necessary for German industrialists to replace the surplus value not realized on the world market by depressing wages. This inversion of the English model would, according to Engels, lead to an exacerbation of class conflict in Germany. (171)

That Engels was convinced of the historically unique conditions underlying the comparatively tranquil period of English labor relations was revealed by his prediction that no single country--not even the United States--would ever be in a position to assume the monopolistic role enjoyed by England between 1840 and 1870; competition among Germany, the United States and the United Kingdom would, moreover, lead to chronic overproduction on world markets and an inevitable deterioration of working class conditions. (172) Engels continued to hold such views into the 1890s. (173) Engels thus conceived of the labor aristocracy--particularly that of a whole national working class, but in lesser measure that of a stratum too-- as absolutely restricted in time and place. The peculiar historical conditions giving rise to it would be replaced by those generating intensified class struggle throughout the world.

It is important in this connection to separate analytically from this specific set of world market factors another class of factors that, in Engels' mind, set Britain apart from other countries of the second half of the nineteenth century. Although chronologically and causally related to the aforementioned set, this class exerted its own influence. This class of factors was rooted in the circumstance that British capitalists, as the representatives of the period's premier industrial capitalist nation, were subject to "a law of modern political economy" that insured the gradual abandonment of practices of fraud so characteristic of the precapitalist sphere of circulation. With the growth of the market, bilking consumers and other businessmen became counterproductive compared with other uses of time. As industry expanded, analogous changes in the forms of direct exploitation of wage laborers also asserted themselves: industrial magnates "had better things to do" than to devote themselves to devising and executing new methods of "gypping" their workers. Consequently, numerous reforms such as the abolition of the truck system were carried out. (174) Moreover, as the scale of industrial plants grew, capitalists and managers realized that "unnecessary quarrels" with workers and their representatives should be avoided since the loss of production and profit associated with them exceeded their potential benefits. As long as such "concessions" remained the prerogative of large capital, they also served the purpose of squeezing out smaller business that could not yet afford such enlightened attitudes. (175)

Since Britain was the first capitalist society to have eliminated such abuses, at least in the leading branches, the British working class was relieved of such chicanery at a time when continental workers were feeling the brunt of it. To be sure, Engels also interpreted this differential development to mean that the British working class would also be the first to recognize the source of its misery in the capitalist system itself rather than in its abuses. (176)

In spite of this extended pre-history of private observations on the effects of England's world market domination on the proletariat, it was not until 1885 that Engels published his views--that is to say, at a time when this monopoly was already "irretrievably broken." (177) Here, for the first time, Engels introduced a stratum-specific modification, noting that whereas the working class as a whole participated in the resulting advantages "to a certain degree," the latter were distributed "very unequally": "the privileged minority pocketed the greatest part," but even the masses received temporary benefits. (178) For this reason socialism had expired with Owenism and for the same reason it would be renewed with the collapse of the world market monopoly. (179) Since Engels believed that this collapse had already taken place, it must be assumed that he considered a time-lag necessary until the English proletariat became conscious of its altered situation.

This assumption is corroborated by a remarkable letter written by Engels to Bebel several months after having composed the article cited earlier. As one of the by-products of the international overproduction crisis anticipated by him, Engels hoped that the old trade unions would be swept away.

> These have retained the character of gilds, which has clung to them from the very beginning, and it is becoming more unbearable every day. You people believe perhaps that any worker in the branch can join up with the mechanics, carpenters, masons, etc. without further ado? Not at all. Whoever wants to join has to have been attached as an apprentice for a series of years (mostly 7) to a worker who belongs to the union. This was supposed to limit the number of workers, but was completely useless--except that it harvested the teacher money for which he in fact did nothing. This lasted until 1848. Since then, however, the colossal upswing in industry has produced a class of workers just as numerous or even more numerous than the "skilled" workers of the Trades Unions, who do as much work or even more but can never become members. These people have been bred as it were by the gild rules of the Trades Unions. But do you think that the Unions would ever consider doing away with all this old rot? Not in the least. ... (T)hese fools want to reform society according to their own views, but do not want to reform themselves in accord with society's development. They stick to their traditional superstition which only hurts them instead of getting rid of this stuff, thus doubling their numbers and power and in fact becoming what they less and less remain, namely unions of all workers of the trade against the capitalists. I believe that will clear up for you much of the behavior of these privileged workers. (180)

The context in which Engels made these remarks suggests that he was implying that England's world market domination had acted as a shield behind which unions of the skilled had been able to enforce apprenticeship and entry regulations in which employers could acquiesce. Such a thesis is problematic for two reasons. First, as already noted, Marx and Engels appear to have held an exaggerated notion of the extent to which restrictive entry practices were successfully enforced by trade unions toward the end of the nineteenth century. (181) Second, the correspondence between the leading export branches and those allegedly or actually characterized by restrictive apprenticeship systems was marginal. The textile industry, which from 1860 to 1890 accounted for about two-thirds, and until 1913 for more than one-half, of all United Kingdom exports of manufactured goods, (182) lacked a skilled labor aristocracy based on lengthy apprenticeship. (183) Other industries with larger numbers of labor aristocrats, such as printing and building, were hardly involved in exporting at all. The working conditions in another major export trade, namely coal mining, precluded the emergence of an aristocracy of labor. (184)

In point of fact, only three major industries employed large numbers of labor aristocrats and simultaneously relied heavily on the world market--iron and steel, machinery and shipbuilding. The British iron and steel industry, which exported approximately two-fifths of its output in the latter half of the century, (185) accounted for 46.0 per cent of world pig iron and 35.9 per cent of world steel production between 1875 and 1879; not until the 1890s was it supplanted by Germany and the United States as the leading producer, and it was only in the first decade of the twentieth century that Germany attained the first rank as exporter. (186) In machine tools, Britain maintained its supremacy in almost all fields during the nineteenth century. (187) Finally, Britain accounted for three-fifths of world shipbuilding tonnage well into the twentieth century. (188)

Of the unions in these three industries it was generally true that they restricted membership to the skilled although only the United Society of Boilermakers and Iron Shipbuilders preserved full apprenticeship rights. (189) Vitally strengthened by this enforcement, the Boilermakers proved to be the only one of the unions in these industries which organized virtually all the skilled in its trades. (190) The Amalgamated Society of Engineers, on the other hand, managed to represent only one-third to one-half of the skilled machine-tool workers after 1875. (191) The Amalgamated Association of Iron Workers, an organization almost exclusively of iron puddlers, experienced a drastic decline in membership in the 1870s. (192) The

Engineers rejected the admission of the unskilled until as late as 1912. (193) The Boilermakers went so far as to organize the defeat of platers' helpers in a dispute in 1882, while the holders-up were admitted in the same year under the condition that they not participate in unemployment or superannuation benefits. (194) In the iron and steel industry, even where entry by the unskilled was formally permitted, it was to little avail since the union afforded them no protection against their de facto employers--the (sub-)contractors such as puddlers and rollers who formed the leadership of the union. (195)

These three branches, all belonging to the metal industries, witnessed explosive employment growth in the latter half of the nineteenth century. From 1851 to 1881 the numer of men employed in England and Wales in the manufacture of machinery, ships and iron and steel rose from 176,400 to 408,000. This increase of 131.7 per cent exceeded by a large margin that of: all manufacturing (86.9 per cent); all males in manufacturing (29.8 per cent); the entire occupied population (37.8 per cent); and of the entire population (44.8 per cent). As a result, these occupations represented 18.2 per cent of all males employed in manufacturing in 1881 compared with 10.2 per cent in 1851. (196) Alone from 1851 to 1871, iron and steel manufacture rose from the twenty-fourth to the tenth largest employer, while engine and machine making rose from thirty-seventh to eighteenth place. (197) By 1881, only coal mining and carpentry occupied more male manual workers than iron and steel manufacture. (198)

During this period metal trade unions also expanded their membership apace. The Amalgamated Society of Engineers, which numbered 5,000 at its formation in 1851, counted 46,101 members in 1881; the Iron Founders grew from 4,073 members in 1850 to 11,448 in 1881; similarly, the Boilermakers and Iron Shipbuilders numbered 20,676 in 1881 compared to 1,771 in 1850. (199) Union membership clearly grew at a more rapid rate than employment in these branches, although this fact was largely a function of the extremely low initial values. But even if the 1860s are taken as a starting point, membership in the engineering and shipbuilding unions grew more quickly than employment. (200) An estimate of a fifteen per cent degree of organization for the entire metal, engineering and shipbuilding sector for the year 1888 (201) would also serve as an upper limit for earlier years. (202)

These metal-based industries represented a significant deviation from the type of trade in which the highly skilled and paid artisanate traditionally had worked. Formerly, the bulk of such craftsmen had been employed in small-scale crafts such as printing, silversmithery, carpentry, etc., which had been relatively little affected by capitalist industrialization. (203) This vast new increment to the labor aristocracy tended to be concentrated in large works, confronted by huge masses of machinery. Thus according to the factory returns of 1871, the almost 100,000 English and Welsh establishments covered by the Factory Acts employed, on the average, about twenty-one persons. But in the manufacture of machinery the average was eighty, in iron mills, 141; at blast furnaces, 236; and in iron shipbuilding, 426. (204) The approximately 2,500 establishments in these three branches, representing 2.5 per cent of all those covered, accounted for twenty-nine per cent of the moving steam power reported. (205)

The emergence of these industries as new sources of, and Engels' annoyance with labor aristocrats are ironic when it is recalled that Marx and Engels discounted the possibility of the creation of significant numbers of skilled workers by industrial capitalism. In machine making, for example, although the transition from handmade to machine-made machine during the first four decades of the nineteenth century led to the demise of the all-round millwright and the emergence of a division of labor among turners, fitters, pattern makers, erectors and others, the development of machine-using industries placed greater demands on machines so that greater accuracy and speed were required of the operators. Moreover, the new machine-making machines "still left the major proportion of the engineering work from patternmaking to fitting and erecting, in the hands of the skilled worker with hand tools." (206) From the 1850s to the 1880s, little basic change in engineering technology occurred other than increased specialization of the fitter; investment assumed a labor-using character. (207) Textile machinery manufacture, in particular, "was the outstanding nineteenth century case of a skill-intensive monopoly." (208) It appears that the majority of engineering workers remained skilled until World War I. (209) Not until after the 1890s, at any rate, did capital intensive technological change begin to oust engineers from their position as labor aristocrats. (210)

In these areas, machine making probably stood mid-way between shipbuilding, with its rigid apprenticeship system, (211) and the regulated occupational progression of the steel industry. (212) In shipbuilding, scattered returns from various parts of Britain between 1866 and 1883 revealed an almost invariant fifty-two per cent share of total employment accounted for by the skilled. (213) Similar data for iron and steel production pointed to the skilled as a sizable minority, averaging about two-fifths of the work force. (214)

Engels was, consequently, correct in claiming that the economic upsurge of the second half of the nineteenth century brought in its wake a capital intensification and division of labor which ushered in the era of the unskilled industrial worker who was largely excluded from trade unions. From a moral and political perspective similar criticisms had been made earlier by laissez faire liberals and Christian socialists. (215) Orthodox economists, too, bemoaned the fact that exclusionary unions of the skilled (such as bricklayers) were fast becoming "an oligarchy of manual laborers" aspiring to protect privileges. (216) Aristocrats condemned them for their tyranny. (217) What caused this course of events to appear particularly odious to Engels was his apparent conviction that these new skills, unlike those that in fact necessitated long periods of training, were artificially maintained by union-controlled apprenticeship programs. Although this view exaggerated the unions' strength, (218) it was true that the New Model unions in building, engineering and shipbuilding helped shape a tracking system which insured that boys, upon entering a trade, were virtually "labelled as future skilled craftsmen or as future unskilled labourers, with little or no chance of rising into a higher grade." (219) A few occupations, on the other hand, did demand uncommon skill and strength, which could not be acquired over short periods of time. (220)

Engels was not without predecessors with regard to the claim that the working class could achieve a more advantageous material position as a result of the superiority enjoyed by sectors of the national capital in producing industrial commodities for the world market. Robert Torrens had discussed this possibility as early as the 1830s. (221) And Thornton had mentioned the "qualified monopoly" held by the United Kingdom in coal, iron, cottons, woollens and machinery as having enabled unions in these trades to increase their wages without jeopardizing the advantages accruing to their firms on the world market. (222) In contrast with these economists, however, Engels insisted that the gain, though unequally distributed, accrued to the entire national working class.

It is therefore necessary to dwell on the mechanisms that might have permitted a rise in the level of real wages in accordance with Engels' assertions. To begin with, Engels' position involved certain inconsistencies. If, as Engels maintained, the restrictive practices of trade unions represented an attempt to thwart technical progress, then the leading British industries must have been disadvantaged vis a vis their European and United States competitors. Yet despite contemporary entrepreneurial complaints to that effect, (223) modern research does not attach great significance to these putative blocks in explaining Britain's economic decline prior to World War I. (224) If, on the other hand, the competitive position of British capital was not adversely affected by trade unions, then it is not clear how the latter were harming themselves, as Engels claimed.

A further inconsistency in Engels' conception of world market-supported gains to the working class relates to the chronological course of development. Explanations of British trade union opportunism based on that country's world industrial supremacy are "obviously inadequate" because the set of labor aristocratic attitudes and policies became particularly salient at the time "when English capitalism grew rather niggardly." (225) Table 1 documents the decline of the United Kingdom as the worlds's leading industrial producer.

Table 1. Shares of World Industrial Production, 1820-1920 (in per cent) (226)

	U.K.	U.S.	Germany		U.K.	U.S.	Germany
1820	50	10	--	1880	28	28	13
1840	45	11	12	1890	22	31	14
1850	39	15	15	1900	18	31	16
1860	36	17	16	1910	14	35	16
1870	32	23	13	1920	14	47	9

Thus until approximately 1870, the industrial output of the United Kingdom was a great as that of the United States and Germany combined; by the first half of the 1880s, however, the United States surpassed the United Kingdom, and by the second half of the first decade of the twentieth century Germany achieved the same result. (227)

Although Britain's share of world industrial markets held up much longer than its share of output, it too experienced a decline, albeit one differentiated according to product. Other estimates than those underlying Table 2 indicate a similar trend. (229) Although Britain's competitiveness on the world market continued at a high level, it had peaked about 1870, before Germany and the United States emerged as industrial powers. (230) Thus in the thirty-two years between 1840 and 1872, manufactured exports of the United Kingdom increased 352.9 per cent compared to a rise of only 51.4 per cent in the following thirty-two years. (231) That Britain's

world industrial trade monopoly was being broken is illustrated
by the high but declining shares in the three sectors under
discussion.

**Table 2. Shares of World Exports of Manufactured Commodities,
1880–1913 (in per cent)** (228)

	U.K.	U.S.	Germany	France
1880	41.4	2.8	19.3	22.2
1890	40.7	4.6	20.1	17.1
1900	32.5	11.2	22.2	15.8
1913	29.9	12.6	26.5	12.9

**Table 3. Britain's Share of World Exports in selected Metal
Industries, 1880–1913 (in per cent)** (232)

	1880	1890	1899	1913
Iron and steel	60.5	56.1	49.3	35.6
Metal manufacture	42.2	42.8	30.6	25.6
Ships and railway material	80.8	74.9	56.5	48.2

In fact, Britain's export position in these sectors deteriorated
even more than these figures reveal because exports tended
to be concentrated in older product lines (such as locomotives,
ships and textile machinery) rather than in "the most recently
developed products" (such as motor vehicles, machine tools
and electrical machinery). As a result, "Britain by the late
nineteenth century could not compete effectively with American
and German domestic production" of iron and steel goods. (233)
But even if British industrial supremacy were granted, it
would still have to be shown how British workers benefited
therefrom. To begin with workers directly employed in one
of the leading export branches: it is feasible to arrive at a
rough estimate of the extent to which they were able to "feast
smartly"on this world monopoly. In 1871, the United Kingdom
exported machinery valued at Ł 4,257,000. (234) Factory
returns from the same year showed that 166,981 persons were
employed in the United Kingdom in the manufacture of
machinery. (235) If seventy per cent of the workers are
assumed to have been skilled, and fifteen per cent of the
exported value is reckoned as gross profit, (236) then somewhat

less than £ 5.5 would have been available per worker for distribution. If it were further assumed that one-fourth of this sum had been "converted into 'crumbs,'" (237) this portion would not have amounted to the average weekly wage of an engineer in Manchester in 1871. (238) Even if a much smaller group of workers were taken as the recipients of these benefits, such as the membership of the Amalgamated Society of Engineers, which was 38,000 at this time, (239) the "monopoly premium" accruing to them would still have accounted for only one-fifth to one-sixth or less of the difference between the annual wages of a mechanic and those of the average worker in the United Kingdom. (240) In order to control for skill as a variable, unskilled laborers in favored world market branches may be compared with those employed in other branches. In point of fact, the wages of laborers in the iron and steel industry were no higher than those of the average town laborer and only little higher than those of agricultural laborers. (241) Along these lines, then, it is not possible to prove that world market-induced "premia" skewed the distribution of income within the favored branches any more than between them and other branches. (242)

Even apart from the complicated theoretical issue of whether one nation can exploit another by means of foreign trade alone, (243) it is difficult to reconcile such exploitation with the fact that British exports were largely destined not for "the inhabitants of Africa, Asia and the Americas," (244) but for the other capitalist countries of the world. In 1880, for example, thirty-eight per cent of British iron and steel exports went to the United States (245) at a time when wages there were higher than in Britain. (246) But even with regard to colonial countries such as India, a question arises concerning the mechanism by which imports of steel or of machinery would have led to the exploitation of Indian workers and the participation therein by English workers producing those exports. (247) Rising productivity and hence profits appear to offer a much more plausible interpretation of branch-specific higher wages. (248)

Two approaches have been formulated to marshal support for the claim that British workers as a whole benefited from Britain's colonial-imperial position. (249) The first refers to cheap food imports which began to reach Britain in the 1870s (250) from colonial areas. Strong corroboration of this view is provided by the fact that Britain alone of the major capitalist nations experienced a decline in the cost of living during the last third of the nineteenth century; partly as a result of this circumstance, real wages also grew most quickly in that country. (251) Despite the perspicacious objection that such gains were scattered and fortuitous, (252) this approach appears plausible yet lacks any stratum-specific validity.

The second approach emphasizes the huge stock of foreign investment accumulated by "Britain". This fund increased approximately ten-fold in the six decades preceding the First World War, (253) while net property income from abroad rose fifteen-fold from Ŀ 13 million in 1855 to Ŀ 200 million in 1913. (254) As a share of net national product, such income tripled from 2.2 per cent in 1855 to 6.6 per cent in 1885, while it more than tripled as a share of domestic non-employment incomes, rising from 4.3 per cent to 14.1 per cent. (255)

Although these were large sums in the aggregate, per capita distribution would, again, have been marginal. In 1867, for example, R. Baxter included about 841,000 adult males in his class of "higher skilled labour and manufactures." (256) In the same year, net property income from abroad totaled Ŀ 28,000,000. (257) If the assumption is once again made that one-quarter of this amount would have been available for redistribution to a labor aristocracy, little more than eight pounds sterling would have accrued to each labor aristocrat in England and Wales. This sum would have represented approximately one-eighth of such a worker's annual income (258) and even less of total family income. If Engels' notion of the corruption of the entire working class is employed as the basis of calculation, then the per capita sum would have amounted to one or two pounds sterling per annum, or perhaps two per cent of the income of a manual working class family. (259)

Regardless of the quantitative dimensions of this "bribery account," (260) a question still remains concerning the socio-economic mechanism facilitating the redistribution of colonial-imperial incomes from the primary recipients to the final consumers. A relatively straightforward procedure--and one analogous to that mentioned in the case of foreign trade profits--would have required domestic industrial companies to re-channel some of the profits appropriated in the putative super-exploitation of colonial and other workers to their English employees in order to secure their good will. In point of fact, however, British industrial firms were only marginally involved in direct overseas investment during the nineteenth century. (261)

A notable exception to this tendency was the large-scale involvement by British railway construction contractors in Europe, Asia, North and South America and Australia. (262) A patron-labor aristocrat relation, however, emerged only very faintly in this context. (263) In the first instance, railway

construction laborers (navigators or navvies) were, for the
most part, not highly skilled. (264) They received wages on
a par with those of other industrial laborers, (265) although
in little industrialized areas their wages may have exceeded
those of country and agricultural laborers "in consequence
of the lawless body of men employed, the urgency of the
work ... and the men being perfectly aware of the necessity
that there was for this work being completed by a given
time. ..." (266) The reputation for "fairness" acquired by
such contracting magnates as Thomas Brassey rested not on
their recognition of and negotiations with trade unions, (267)
but rather on their intervention in the subcontracting system
in order to eliminate abuses. (268) Finally, considerable doubt
attaches to the aristocratic stature of a group of workers
referred to as "the refuse of the Community." (269)

The possible redistributive effects of the receipt of foreign
investment income depended on the socio-economic composition
of the primary recipients. The major investors in British
foreign capital issues (270) were: 1. the increasing number
of late-Victorian middle class professionals; 2. the wealthy;
3. the commercial classes of large trade centers; 4. rentiers;
and 5. banks and life insurance companies. (271) Aside from
directly eleemosynary objects--which would not have benefited
labor aristocrats--such income recipients would have spread
their largess basically by virtue of their purchasing power
to employ "those who produce personal services (e.g. to
gardeners and domestic servants) and ... those who make
luxury goods" such as artists and dressmakers. (272) In
point of fact, the period from 1851 to 1881 witnessed a very
large increase in the number of domestic servants--63.9 per
cent compared to an increase of 30.6 per cent in manufacturing
employment and of 44.9 per cent in population in England and
Wales. Artists experienced similar growth, while outdoor
servants (included among the aforementioned domestic servants)
increased almost five-fold. (273)

Such occupations have not traditionally belonged to those
associated with manual labor aristocrats; they were largely
filled by women and remained virtually unorganized. Moreover,
such a vast siphoning of investment funds either abroad or to
unproductive employment in Britain must have diminished the
demand for productive labor and hence improved the bargaining
position of employers. (274) In this context, the suggestion
that workers "will probably be worse off than before" becomes
plausible. (275)

Although aggregate gains to the working class may have
been slight, the significant shift of British capital interests

(and hence, indirectly, of employment interests) from the
domestic to the world market might have had positive political
ramifications for the bourgeoisie if it had been accompanied
by working class support for Britain's "international posture".
Engels alluded to such support when he spoke of working
class adherence to bourgeois foreign policy. Yet the urgency
of such advocacy did not manifest itself until the colonial
issue emerged more sharply from the 1890s onwards. (276)
But in more subtle ways the perception of joint interests made
itself felt even earlier. In the 1860s, for example, the leaders
of the Engineers and of the Ironfounders declined to seek
membership in the First International because, it has been
reasoned, their unions could bargain successfully with employers as a result of Britain's world market position; and since
one of the main points of attraction of the International to
unions consisted in its aid in dissuading foreign strike-breakers
from coming to or remaining in Britain, the leaders of these
particular unions saw no practical need for cooperation. (277)

On balance, then, the alleged positive correlation between
world market dominance and aggregate working class or labor
aristocratic reconciliation with the ruling class has found only
a modicum of support. Foreign trade profits could have been
shared to some extent with the direct producers of the relevant
branches, but they would have accounted for but a small part
of skilled-unskilled wage differentials, which contemporaneously
obtained in other capitalist countries without access to world
market monopoly profits. Theoretical arguments, moreover,
render recourse to this mechanism of economic lass cooperation
suspect. The cheap food thesis retained the greatest plausibility, but it was devoid of a stratum-specific dimension. This
argument would, nevertheless, be difficult to reconcile with
Engels' implicit use of it because the cost of living did not
begin to decline until the 1870s, that is, after the "enormous
upswing" of the 1850s and 1860s and during the "chronic state
of stagnation" in the 1870s and 1880s. (278) Finally, gains
resulting from the redistribution of foreign investment incomes
were found to have been not only moderate in size (as a
consequence of a luxury consumption-triggered multiplier
effect), but acquired by non-surplus value producing salaried
strata.

E. Economic and Social Differentiation within the Working Class

In order to arrive at a better understanding of Engels' position, it is necessary to review the picture he drew of the consequences of Britain's unique economic dominance for working class incomes. The following major points can be distilled from his presentation: 1. even during the "unheard of expansion" between 1848 and 1868, the mass of workers experienced only a temporary improvement of their situation, which was constantly being counteracted by the effects of the reserve army of the unemployed; 2. although Engels offered an ambiguous account of the 1870s and 1880s, he seems to have implied that economic stagnation had brought in its wake a general deterioration of working class living standards; (279) and 3. a permanent (i.e., for the period from 1848 to 1868) improvement was the privilege of two groups of workers: a. factory workers whose working conditions were subject to legislative protection enjoyed an enhanced state of health and "moral superiority" owing to their concentration in large numbers; and b. trade unionists in branches employing (almost) exclusively adult males who had theretofore resisted attempts to devalue their labor power or to usurp their jobs altogether by the introduction of women, children and machinery. For certain workers, such as engineers, carpenters and joiners and construction workers, Engels apparently perceived the period of privilege as having extended into the 1880s since he considered that the best proof of the undoubted improvement of their situation was the fact

> that for more than fifteen years not only have their employers been extremely satisfied with them, but they too have been extremely satisfied with their employers. They form an aristocracy in the working class; they have managed to exact a relatively comfortable position, and they accept this as final. They are the model workers of Messrs. Leone Levi and Giffen (and also of the philistine Lujo Brentano), and they are indeed very nice, tractable people for every reasonable capitalist in particular and for the capitalist class in general. (280)

When Engels concluded that, at the time of writing, a privileged minority was still excepted from the misery and insecurity of existence that still haunted the mass of workers, (281) it is unclear whether he included both "protected departments of the working class" among the elite.

In order to clarify Engels' position, it is necessary to dwell shortly on these two departments. The number of English and Welsh workers covered by the Factories Acts in 1871 totaled about two million of whom about one million were males above the age of eighteen; another 400,000 Scots (of whom about 200,000 were adult males) and 125,000 Irish (including 50,000 male adults) were also protected. (282) Although the condition of the women and children may have improved, they may be neglected as politically irrelevant for Engels' analysis; the Irish workers will also be omitted from discussion because of the dependant status of Ireland. Of the remaining 1,200,000 adult males one-half were employed in metal manufacture and building, two trades in which males predominated. An additional 130,000 adult males earning above-average wages in branches employing few women or children may be counted among this factory elite. (283) In other words, approximately 730,000 men or three-fifths of the men (or three-tenths of all persons) covered by the Factories Acts in Great Britain in 1871 could be included under the rubric of privileged workers.

For the year 1870 it has been estimated that little more than 140,000 workers were trade unionists in the United Kingdom. Almost all the trades represented by them were mentioned in the preceding paragraph (coal miners being the major exception); the vast majority of them were employed in metal manufacture and building. (284) It may, therefore, be supposed that the significant overlapping that existed between these two "departments" became more extensive in the 1870s and 1880s. (285)

With this clarification, it is possible to proceed to a point not discussed by Engels in this context. Although obscured by the aforementioned overlap, the distinction between the older stratum of the skilled (such as printers, coachbuilders, jewelers and carpenters) and the newer stratum (employed especially in metal manufacture) must be emphasized because of the differential material foundation and ideological perspectives of the two strata. The former group was concentrated in industries as yet little affected by capitalist mechanization and de-skilling; these craftsmen retained varying degrees of autonomy vis a vis their small employers and often considerable access to self-employment and even employer status. (286) Journeymen, having long enjoyed relatively high social status, (287) strove to defend their position against future down-grading. The new skilled workers, on the other hand, "did not possess any societally recognized status, but were intruders" in the existing "hierarchy." (288) Not only did this new stratum have "to prove its active loyalty vis a vis the system if its life ideals were to be bound up with that system," (289) the technological demands of the new machine-based industries as well as the latter's owners and managers actively solicited its identification with the social system. (290)

In the light of this differential movement of technology and ideology, it would be misleading to suggest that the Engineers were developing trade unionism in the same environment as the Carpenters or Stonemasons for example. At the same time, however, the two strata evolved neither in isolation from each other nor as ideal types. Thus, although the general tenor of trade unionism during these years may have been one oriented towards reconciliation with capital, other currents never disappeared. As the secretary of the Amalgamated Society of Engineers, William Allan, testified before the Royal Commission in Trade Unions in 1867, (291) the interests of employer and employed were not identical. "I scarcely see how that can be, while we are in a state of society which recognizes the principle of buying in the cheapest and selling in the dearest market. ... And you can never reconcile those two things." (292)

Engels' theses can now be analyzed point by point.
1. The discussion of the period from 1848 to 1868 has already shown that (Marx and) Engels' assessment of working class incomes has been verified by modern research. For this, as for the subsequent period, a question remains concerning the mechanisms by which capitalist society secured the allegiance of a class whose incomes were not only not rising, but actually declining in the aggregate compared to those of the ruling classes.
2. The issue of real wages for the period through the middle of the 1880s is not so straightforward. It has been firmly established that the general index of money wages rose through 1874 at which point it began to decline; the fall continued through 1879 with the previous peak not surpassed until 1890. (293) At the same time the cost of living declined sharply enough to offset the fall in money wages until the mid-1870s; at this point real wages fell several percentage points. Not until 1883 was the previously recorded peak level of real wages exceeded. (294) But even if average time lost on account of unemployment is considered, real wages did continue to climb, albeit at a considerably slower rate. (See Table 4.)

Such aggregate data do not suffice to test Engels' claims since they may conceal the stratum-differentiated aspects that constitute the core of Engels' position. (296) It is necessary, therefore, to employ a series of indicators in order to approach this issue. One significant indicator of the spread or abatement of extreme poverty is the extent of pauperism. (297)

Table 4. Rates of Increase in Average Real Wages in the United Kingdom, 1865–1884 (adjusted for unemployment) (295)

1865–69 to 1870–74	1870–74 to 1875–79	1875–79 to 1880–84
13.0 per cent	4.1 per cent	3.1 per cent

Table 5. Number of Paupers (exclusive of vagrants) in Receipt of Relief in England and Wales on January 1, 1870–1890 (298)

1870	1,079,391	1880	837,940
1871	1,081,926	1881	803,126
1872	977,664	1882	797,614
1873	887,345	1883	799,296
1874	829,281	1884	774,310
1875	815,587	1885	784,155
1876	749,593	1886	807,633
1877	728,350	1887	817,289
1878	742,703	1888	825,509
1879	800,426	1889	810,132
		1890	787,545

From the peak value in 1871 to the lowest value recorded in 1877, the number of paupers on relief declined by more than 350,000, i.e., by almost one-third; the period through the 1880s witnessed a small rise, but the average of approximately 800,000 for the years 1878 to 1890 represented an historical low since records had been kept beginning in the 1840s. Given an increase in population of 27.8 per cent between 1870 and and 1890 in England and Wales, (299) a sharp drop in the rate of pauperism ensued. (300)

Another sign of the failure of late-Victorian capitalism to undermine the foundations of generations of urban misery and degradation was the discovery by Charles Booth and his co-workers in the mid-1880s that almost 1,300,000 Londoners, equivalent to 37.4 per cent of the working classes or 30.7 per cent of the total population, had to be classified as "poor" or "very poor." (301) Findings such as these have led one cautious modern investigator to conclude that, although "gains clearly predominated over losses," after the 1860s

> it was still possible, and indeed likely, that the absolute number of those whose lot deteriorated was equal to or greater than it had been in the early decades of the century, for the overall growth in numbers permitted this sector of the population to diminish relatively, yet to increase absolutely. Moreover with the growth in the absolute size of the areas of dilapidation and dereliction, in the East End of London and in the provincial cities, the degree of degeneration possible within them might well have increased. (302)

Still a further approach to the measurement of the course of wages among the mass of workers consists in comparing the latter's nominal wages with the price index and with the general wage index. Money wages began to decline in general from their peak at the turn of the industrial cycle from prosperity to depression in 1873-1874; they continued to decline during the period under review until after the depression year of 1886. (303) A composite, weighted average index showed a decline of about five per cent. Most industries clustered about this point. Whereas the printing and cotton industries disclosed a small rise during these years, coal miners and iron puddlers, subject to a sliding scale which geared wages to the prices of the commodities they produced, experienced disastrous declines of one-third or more. Yet with a simultaneous decline of more than one-fifth in the retail price index, almost all industries registered real wage gains. (304)

In summary, then, it has not proved possible to derive an unambiguous synthetic judgment of the change in wages of the mass of workers during the 1870s and the first half of the 1880s. For although official pauperism declined, concentrated urban poverty apparently did not diminish; and although a fall in the cost of living more than compensated for the fall in money wages, unskilled labor both in the branches covered by Bowley's and Wood's wage surveys and in those outside these studies may have fared worse than their statistically recorded co-workers. On the whole, however, whatever aggregate gains were won do not appear to have been large and stemmed largely from cheaper overseas food. Thus, even if Engels' position is partially confirmed with regard to this point, the bourgeoisification of a class experiencing stagnation or immiseration remains to be explained.

3. Engels' most interesting remarks were reserved for the strata he characterized as labor aristocrats. Since the 1850s and 1860s have already been discussed, the following analysis is limited to the 1870s and 1880s.

In the first instance, Engels appears to have exaggerated the ability of the unions of the labor aristocrats to defend and improve their conditions. There is, for example, no evidence that construction workers successfully thwarted the introduction of machinery; the Amalgamated Society of Engineers certainly failed in its industry in 1852 and 1897-1898. The fact that relatively few women and boys were employed in the building trades (305) presumably had at least as much to do with the strenuous nature of the physical requirements of the trade as with trade union exclusionism. (306) Finally, "the best proof" of the improvement of the condition of the labor aristocracy does not, contrary to Engels' claim, consist in pointing to the aristocrats' alleged satisfaction with their employers, but rather in an examination of that condition.

Data on the living and working conditions of the best paid trade unionists are, fortunately, relatively plentiful. Tucker's index of the wages of London artisans reveals that money wages declined from 1872 to 1887; but a significant decline in the cost of living led to a rise in real wages of 37.2 per cent. (307) If, however, these data are compared with the general indices constructed by Wood, a surprising result emerges: money wages (which are cited here because Tucker and Wood used different cost of living indices) of the London artisans declined by 1.0 per cent during this fifteen-year period while Wood's general wage index rose 2.1 per cent; with 1870 and 1885 as the reference years, the general index rose twice as much as that of the London artisans--12.0 per cent as opposed to 6.1 per cent. (308)

There is general agreement that in particular the latter half of the 1870s was marked by declining money wages and rising unemployment among trade unionists. (309) The greater degree of organization normally enabled unions to offer greater resistance to wage reductions. (310) Yet Bowley's wage indices show that the level of money wages in the building trades stagnated from 1876 to 1890. (311) Similar patterns were registered in engineering and shipbuilding as well. (312) Data from individual trade unions reveal different patterns. The Amalgamated Society of Carpenters and Joiners recorded a decline in monetary wages beginning in 1874; the Operative Bricklayers in 1876; the Operative Stonemasons in 1877; the unionized building trades as a whole experienced stagnation from 1876 through the 1880s. (313) Wood indicated that the

Amalgamated Society of Engineers did not achieve any general increase in wages for its members from 1866 to 1882, while most other skilled trades recorded declines in the 1870s and 1880s. (314)

In spite of the gains in real wages, setbacks in certain areas did plague the better paid workers during the 1870s and 1880s. In some cases working hours, which were shorter for organized workers, (315) were lengthened again during this period. (316) Moreover, with the transition from daily to hourly wages in the building trades, "a man could be dismissed at a moment's notice when the hour's work was up, and therefore, although they might reckon so many hours a week for the man to earn 39s. 41/2 d., it was a very rare thing for carpenters to earn full money." (317)

The relative development of conditions between labor aristocrats on the one hand and the mass of the workers on the other can, furthermore, be examined in the light of the available information concerning differentials between them. There is, first of all, ample testimony of a qualitative nature from contemporaries. Although it was not unambiguous, the predominant current from the 1860s onwards (318) tended to view the economic and social gap between labor aristocrats and the "residue" either as a new phenomenon or as significantly wider than in earlier times. Thus one observer of the working class contended that "the disparity between the wages of artisans, mechanics, and labourers" had been "less" when he had been a youth than in the 1860s. (319) About the same time an image was invoked that became common in subsequent years--namely, that the skilled "look on the other or labouring class as one with whose members they cannot associate out of the workshop, while in the workshop the labourers are treated as servants." (320)

By the 1880s contemporaries were convinced of the existence of a widening gulf between the skilled and the unskilled. (321) The growing rates of unemployment among the organized toward the end of the 1870s and the beginning of the 1880s (322) were accompanied by a surge of demarcation disputes among un- ions. (323) The renewed increase in official pauperism probably indicated an even sharper deterioration in the employment situation of the unskilled. (324) Whether they denounced or extolled labor aristocrats, political observers were obviously more impressed by the latter's socio-economic status than they had been in recent decades. (325) In particular the Industrial Remuneration Conference, held in 1885, heard several particip- ants stress the widening gulf between "the aristocracy of labour" and "the residuum", the former having "gained very

considerably" and the latter but "a little" during the previous
generation. (326) Edith Simcox went so far as to assert that

> there is more difference between the skilled artisan of to-
> day--an educated trade unionist, politician, and, probably,
> social reformer,--and the residuum of the industrial popula-
> tion, than there was a century ago between the steadiest
> mechanic and the most loutish labourer. (327)

But no empirical data were adduced to support this far-reach-
ing claim of intra-working class polarization. (328)

A more direct procedure for analyzing wage differentials
between the skilled and the unskilled consists in comparing
the available data for each group. This task is complicated
by the unsystematic nature of data collection in the nineteenth century. As a result, no comprehensive comparisons
exist.

At the outset it is worth noting that the aggregate differential is composed of two analytically separable components:
1. differentials between the skilled and the unskilled within
branches; and 2. differentials between relatively high-paying
and relatively low-paying branches. The aggregate differential
is, furthermore, determined by shifts in the ratio of skilled
to unskilled workers and of those employed in high-paying
to those employed in low-paying branches. Most studies of
wage differentials in the nineteenth century have focused
solely on differentials within branches.

In the 1880s contemporaries were divided on the issue of
whether labor aristocrats represented a larger or smaller
proportion of the manual working class than in previous
times. (329) And in retrospect it is difficult to reconstruct
their share. Nevertheless, several indicators are useful. The
fact, for example, that the wage pyramid was flattened by the
mass shift of workers from the lower to the higher-paying
industries meant that in order for a widening of wage differentials to have expanded the aggregate differential, it would
have had to have offset this considerable shift effect. Since,
moreover, the data underlying the formation of the wage pyramid
refer to occupations as well as to industries, a widening of
intra-branch differentials would require further explanation.

Hobsbawm has offered such an explanation by having recourse to "peculiarities in the British labour market"--to wit,
the large supply of female and child labor which "depressed
the standards of many non-aristocrats." (330) Two major
objections may be raised to this argument. First, on the
theoretical level it is based on the mistaken--and for a Marxist,
like Hobsbawm, self-contradictory--notion that "(t)he main

reason" for wage differentials between the skilled and the unskilled "under capitalism is that the industrial reserve army of unemployed and underemployed, which determines the general movements of wages, affects different categories of workers differently." (331) Although fluctuations in the price of labor power are determined by supply and demand factors synthesized in the changing size of the reserve army, the level of wages is determined by the reproduction value of labor power which includes a component for skill (i.e., training costs). During the last six decades of the nineteenth century--a period long enough to provide some notion of the value of labor power in contradistinction to that of fluctuations in its price--the wage level of the skilled was higher than that of the unskilled not because many replacements were always available for the latter but not for the former; rather, many replacements were always available because little skill was required. Although Hobsbawm is justified in stressing the significance of precapitalist labor market factors such as custom in wage determination, his exclusive reliance on supply and demand disregards the transformation of occupational skills brought about by differential capital accumulation.

Second, the reference to the oversupply of female and child labor could have been relevant only if its variations had coincided with those of the wage differential. In point of fact, however, the proportion of women and children among those employed in manufacturing actually declined slightly from 1851 to 1881. (332)

It is, therefore, not surprising that a comparison of the average weekly wage of a London artisan with that of a town laborer reveals a narrowing of the differential during the nineteenth century. (333) Other general studies of wage differentials for the period beginning with the 1870s do not indicate any notable widening of differentials. (334)

The following observations can be made with regard to individual industries: in the building trades, following a small widening in the 1850s and 1860s, the gap between the skilled and the unskilled narrowed in the 1870s and 1880s; (335) in shipbuilding, differentials moved in different directions in different localities; (336) the gap between the wages of fitters and laborers in Manchester engineering firms declined during the 1870s; (337) in the cotton industry, the differential between spinners and weavers rose somewhat; (338) in other industries, particularly in those with few labor aristocrats, differentials appear to have risen. (339)

No body of data, then, has been adduced that supports the claims advanced by contemporaries concerning the widening gap between labor aristocrats and the remainder of the working class. This discrepancy may be explained by two factors. First, often contemporaries meant "the residuum" when referring to other segments of the working class; this lowest stratum--not to be confused with the bulk of the nonskilled--may in fact have been undergoing absolute and relative immiseration as witnessed by the increasing number of paupers in the late 1870s and early 1880s. Second, the less skilled may have been subject to considerably more unemployment than the skilled; this would have resulted in lower annual earnings and worse conditions in general than could have been captured by the foregoing daily or weekly wage data.

Some additional data are worth citing in order to supplement the analysis of Engels' assessment of the "comparatively comfortable situation" that labor aristocrats were alleged to have gained for themselves. Although contemporaries were agreed that labor aristocrats were better situated than other workers, opinion was divided with regard to the degree of their prosperousness. Again, the participants at the Industrial Remuneration Conference shed considerable light on the matter. Edith Simcox, for example, insisted on a comparison between the skilled artisan and the yeoman of yesteryear.

> Unstinted food, clothes of the same pattern as the middle class, when house-rent permits, a tidy parlour, with stiff, cheap furniture, which, if not itself luxurious or beautiful, is a symptom of the luxury of self-respect, and an earnest or better taste to come, a newspaper, a club, an occasional holiday, perhaps a musical instrument. ... We may even go so far as to admit that the prosperous operative is better off in comparison with the unprosperous middle-class man than ever before. (340)

And although Alfred R. Wallace disagreed inasmuch as he denied that the incomes of the skilled allowed of "much leisure for intellectual culture and the refinements of existence," (341) both touched on the indispensable prerequisite of the "moderate comfort" enjoyed by the "highest skilled" (342)--steady employment. Simcox formulated it indirectly when she noted that trade union benefits were "a poor substitute for wages" and a temporary one at best; (343) Wallace went further in reminding his listeners that periods of depression thrust the unskilled as well as the skilled into pauperism and starvation. (344)

A number of social statistical surveys conducted in the mid-1880s served to stress the potential fragility of labor aristocratic prosperity (345) at a time when estimates placed the magnitude of this upper stratum at between one and two million. (346) A report on the wages of manual laborers in 1886 revealed sharp differences in the distribution of earnings among industries. Table 6 synthesizes the aggregate data.

Table 6. Distribution of Wages in the United Kingdom, October 1886 (in per cent) (347)

	Men	Women	Lads/Boys	Girls
Half timers	--	--	11.9	27.2
under 10s.	0.1	26.0	49.7	62.5
10s. to 15s.	2.4	50.0	32.5	8.9
15s. to 20s.	21.5	18.5	5.8	1.4
20s. to 25s.	33.6	5.4	0.1	--
25s. to 30s.	24.2	0.1	--	--
30s. to 35s.	11.6	--	--	--
35s. to 40s.	4.2	--	--	--
above 40s.	2.4	--	--	--
Total	100.0	100.0	100.0	100.0

Average

    weekly wage   24s. 9d.   12s. 11d.   9s. 2d.   6s. 5d.

Apart from the enormous differences between the men and the other groups--most adult men earned above 20s. per week whereas the vast majority of women and children received less than 15s.--, among the men eighteen per cent earned more than one-quarter more than the average of slightly less than 25s. for all men. In the following industries, however, more than one-half of the adult male employees received more than 30s. weekly (the figures in parentheses indicate the percentage of men earning such wages): printing and engraving in newspaper printing works (77.2); tin plate works (63.5); cooperage works (56.3); wood shipbuilding (55.5); building trades (51.6); brass work and metal wares (50.1). (348) Iron and steel shipbuilding, pig iron (blast furnaces) and engineering fell into an intermediary grouping with percentages of 46.4, 20.9 and 24.7 respectively. (349)

Among the chief industries in which an above-average share (i.e., above 24.0 per cent) of the adult male workers earned less than eighty per cent of the aggregate male average (i.e., below 20s) were: china clay works (88.6); linen manufacture (57.6); jute (57.3); silk (53.6); distilleries (53.6); roads, pavements and sewers (48.7). (350) Significantly, the higher paying metal industries also contained large groups of such low paid workers: shipbuilding (18.9); engineering (29.5); and pig iron (blast furnaces) (33.5). (351)

The foregoing data provide a misleading account of the income situation of manual workers inasmuch as they do not take into consideration the losses resulting from unemployment and other absences from work (caused, for example, by sickness and accidents). The building trades may be taken as an example of the effects of time lost on wages. According to the survey of October 1886, 10.9 per cent of building tradesmen earned less than 20s. per week. A survey of London, conducted in March 1887, revealed that twenty-seven per cent of the 30,000 men covered were out of work; the corresponding rates of unemployment in the building trades were: carpenters and joiners, twenty-seven per cent; masons and bricklayers, thirty-seven per cent; painters and plumbers, thirty-three per cent. Similarly, whereas fifty-three per cent of the total sample had experienced some unemployment since October 31, 1886, the corresponding figures for the aforementioned building tradesmen were considerably higher--fifty-nine, seventy-nine and seventy-two per cent respectively. (352) As a further illustration of the dire straits into which skilled workers could fall, this survey also revealed that a greater percentage of out-of-work carpenters and joiners were receiving charity assistance than of all persons sampled. (353)

Charles Booth's survey of London in the 1880s and 1890s disclosed a similar pattern. Many highly paid and well organized artisans such as building tradesmen, coopers, shipwrights, bookbinders, engineers and goldsmiths, suffered very large losses from unemployment, ranging from one-sixth of expected annual incomes among building tradesmen to two-thirds among caulkers. (354) In numerous trades, moreover, considerable deductions resulted from a relatively short working life caused by particularly dangerous or unwholesome conditions. Thus in 1867 the secretary of the London Master Builders' Society informed the Royal Commission on Trade Unions that the average working life in the building trades was shorter than that of all classes; he instanced bricklayers, who could expect to work 9.2 years. (355)

A final and, as a synthetic expression of the circumstances of an entire working and earning life, particularly informative indicator of comparative occupational prosperity can be constructed from data on wills and letters of administration in 1858. Of the 102,049 men who died during that year, 15,558 (i.e., 15.2 per cent) left wills valued, on the average, at Ł 3,469. (356) Since the occupational rubrics applied to those leaving wills correspond but imperfectly to the ones used in the Report of the Registrar-General of Births, Deaths, and Marriages (for 1860-1861), only rough estimates can be made, on an occupational basis, of the proportion of those who died and left wills and letters of administration. In comparison with the one man in five who left a will or letter in the total population, one in ten tailors, one in fourteen boot and shoemakers and three in five farmers left such documents; among bakers and carpenters the proportion was equivalent to that of the aggregate average. (357) Much more precise data, however, can be derived concerning the size-distribution of wills according to occupation. Unfortunately, they do not distinguish among employers, employees and the self-employed; consequently, the differences among occupations may in part be a function of the varying sizes of retained profits in accordance with differences in average sizes of establishments. Table 7 shows the percentage of will valued at less than Ł 20 and more than Ł 1.000.

Table 7. Percentage of Wills left by Males in England in 1858 valued at below Ł1,000, by selected Occupation (358)

Occupation	below Ł20	above Ł1,000
All males	5.9	31.5
Clergy	1.8	71.6
Merchant	0.9	71.3
Esquire, gentleman, independent	2.9	62.1
Physician, surgeon	2.1	52.6
Army	6.3	46.9
Draper	2.3	43.6
Builder	3.7	37.6
Navy	1.7	35.3
Grocer	0.8	31.1

Table 7 (continued)

Miller	2.9	29.5
Cotton manufacture	15.6	25.9
Farmer	6.2	22.9
Commercial clerk	4.9	21.1
Hotel keeper	2.6	17.0
Tailor	11.5	16.6
Shipwright	6.1	16.3
Painter, plumber, glazier	4.2	16.0
Butcher	6.6	15.8
Engineer, machine and tool maker	5.9	14.7
Mariner	5.0	14.1
Blacksmith	10.6	13.8
Baker	7.8	12.2
Shopkeeper	2.5	10.8
Gardener	8.2	10.7
Boot and shoemaker	8.9	7.9
Carpenter-undertaker	12.9	4.9
Bricklayer	13.5	4.3
Laborer	20.9	1.3

The list, which is ordered from the highest to the lowest
percentage of wills valued at more than Ł 1,000 and which contains all occupations in which more than one hundred men were
enumerated--engineers and shipwrights, though below this
threshold, were included for comparative purposes--, shows
that such "aristocratic" occupations as carpentry and bricklaying were located much closer to common laboring than to
white collar, business or professional categories. In fact, only
these trades and shoemaking registered more men leaving less
than Ł 20 than more than Ł 1,000. On the other hand, the
table also discloses significant gaps between laborers and other
manual workers with regard to the ability to save and to
bequeath sums ten to twenty times greater than annual income.
This lifetime bottom-line perspective, as it were, underscores
the overall differential in levels of living standards and in life-

chances for the next generation between aristocrats and non-aristocrats, although it does not, unfortunately, reveal how such differentials evolved over time.

F. Engels' Accusation of Class Collaborationist Trade Unionism

If, in connection with charges of tractability and docility, Engels had merely meant that craft unions had not developed into fortresses of anti-capitalist guerrilla warfare, then few contemporaries would have contradicted him. If, however, as has become evident, he was also denouncing trade unions and their members for having abandoned the principles of combative confrontation in favor of a conscious policy of subordination to capital and its agents in exchange for meager privileges, then additional proof would have to be adduced to support Engels' position.

Engels' own presentation is self-contradictory since it fails to explain why employers would have been "satisfied" with workers who were allegedly strong enough to thwart the former's will with regard to the introduction of machinery. Even if such behavior was, from Engels' standpoint, reactionary because it impeded the development of the forces of production, it would scarcely have made unions appear "tractable" to employers. Second, Engels was doubtless exaggerating when he claimed that nine-tenths of all strikes were provoked by capitalists in order to check overproduction. The most obvious counter-evidence is to be found in the building trades in which strikes for shorter working hours and in opposition to wage-cutting by speculative builders constituted two major types. In part because the building trades experienced trade fluctuations almost immediately, construction workers were characterized by an "infectious habit" and "irrepressible impulse" to strike. (359) Significantly, building accounted for 598 or more than one-quarter of all recorded strikes during the 1870s; the carpenters and joiners participated in more strikes during this time than any other occupational group. (360) The strike in favor of the nine-hour day, which was contested by 10,000 workers in London for twelve weeks, illustrated the lack of satisfaction that workers and employers felt for each other. The divisive attitude on the part of the Stonemasons, however, indicated that the unions of the skilled were often not "satisfied" with one another; this lack of solidarity--even among aristocrats--constituted one of the aspects of narrow-mindedness that Engels was attacking. (361)

The strike in support of the nine-hour day conducted by the Amalgamated Society of Engineers in 1871 was a further example of aristocratic militance, especially since it also embraced successful efforts at organizing additional workers. (362) Evidence of the continued confrontation between capital and aristocratic labor was also provided by the Stonemasons' strike in London in 1877-1878, the unsuccessful outcome of which --brought about by the depression, the importation of American and European strike-breakers and harsh anti-union penalties imposed by the judicial system--led to a drastic decline in membership within a few years. (363)

Although the major source of militance during the period prior to thre rise of New Unionism was located outside the aristocratic unions--in mining, textiles and agriculture (364)--, representatives of the employing class were convinced that trade unions were still "maintaining, in a modified form, their belligerent character and aims." (365) Yet neither group of unions mounted a concerted assault on the foundations of capitalism. Non-aristocratic unions such as the Miners accepted the principle of classical economic orthodoxy according to which wages should fluctuate with coal prices. (366) And in spite of the lack of proof that trade unions based their strategy on the assumption that capitalism was eternal, (367) their day-to-day economic struggles--beyond which they did not proceed once male suffrage had been secured for most eligible workers-- did not call into question the social status quo. (368)

Nevertheless, even the most aristocratic unions remained ideologically prepared and economically compelled to struggle against the deterioration of conditions that capitalist development periodically mandated and as the subjective agents of which employers were perceived as remorselessly functioning. (369) Although the goals pursued by trade unions and their aristocratic members may have been narrowly economic and even selfish, such an orientation was not unique to Victorian England or to the most highly skilled workers. The peculiarities of British trade unionism in the nineteenth century resulted in part from the pioneering nature of British capitalism and in part from Britain's classical social structure; the latter reflected rapid proletarianization which the more homogeneous ruling class was able to manage more efficiently than was, for example, the case in Germany where a political role was virtually foisted upon the labor movement. But even in Britain deep-seated social conflicts were incapable of permanent peaceful channeling. In particular, "The contradiction could not be borne forever" that "a man cannot be simultaneously proud and prostrate; but on that contradiction was founded the respectability of the Victorian working classes." (370) The coming decades would force the British working class to make decisions about the reconcilability of its goals in the context of a rapidly changing socio-economic formation.

G. The Second Reform Bill: The Parliamentary Debate on the Political Co-optability of the Labor Aristocracy

The Parliamentary debates leading to the passage of the Reform Bill of 1867 disclosed the keen interest taken by the ruling classes in the division of the working class into what they perceived as two sharply distinguished strata. The fact, however, that such discussions had been conducted as far back as the time of the Reform Bill of 1832 (371) indicated that "the great Victorian shibboleth and criterion, respectiability," (372) had, in very material forms, staked its claim to societal validity long before the advent of post-Chartist tranquility.

The whole point of the complicated Parliamentary wrangling over the appropriate residential rental level as a criterion for enfranchisement consisted in devising a procedure to separate the "lower class of artisan" and mechanic, that is, "the rank and file of the industrial army," from the "upper class artisan." For although the two classes, to some extent, shared the same opinion, the latter had "a position to maintain," and it was "his interest to stand well with the upper classes." (373) During the debates themselves, John Bright, for example, enunciated the principle that "the residuum" had to be excluded from the franchise, whereas "the intelligent and honest working-men" were to be accorded voting rights. (374) While Gladstone was at pains to reduce the rates sufficiently to enfranchise the skilled, (375) Robert Lowe, a bitter opponent of extending the franchise even to "the elite of the working class," elicited laughter from his colleagues by referring to the politics of laborers earning eight shillings per week. (376)

Some elements of the ruling classes, aware that suffrage would have to be broadened to some extent in any event, feared that the poorer strata of the working class would prove to be too erratic in judgment to be susceptible to the proper electioneering cues. Experience with the "upper class workmen" who had been voters prior to the Reform Bill of 1867 (377) indicated to some at least that they were "amenable to influence from their masters." (378) Yet opinion on the issue was divided.

R. Dudley Baxter, the statistician, stated at one point in his testimony that the "lower class" workers would not be amenable to the same influence as the "upper class" artisans, (379) but later testified that the "mill hands" would also vote with the masters "except when it came to a question of labour." (380) Others feared that, precisely because he was "intelligent," the "superior" artisan was "the most easy game for the agitator." (381) Still others--as different as Bright and Lowe--feared that venality would result from the enfranchisement of a dependent class, while others, clearly speculating on this possibility, welcomed the opportunity. (382)

The fact that no M.P. had, at the outset, envisioned the Reform Bill that ultimately emerged from the Parliamentary maneuvering casts considerable doubt on the thesis that the ruling classes had formulated a strategy to co-opt the labor aristocracy. (383) Such a thesis is further weakened by the fact that passage of the bill was hastened by riots and other disturbances brought on by the economic crisis of 1866 as well as by the incorporation of many trade unionist artisans into the Parliamentary struggle as a reaction to a court decision in 1867 declaring unions to be in restraint of trade and hence ineligible for friendly society status. (384) The lowering of the rental limit to five pounds sterling meant, moreover, that a large segment of the male urban working class--and not merely the better paid strata--became enfranchised. (385) The diffusion of suffrage to virtually all sectors of the working class--with the exception of the poorest urban casual laborers and agricultural laborers (386)--underlay Prime Minister Derby's famous "leap in the dark," which was tantamount to the admission that co-optation had not been the guiding strategy of those in power. (387) Although some employers and political leaders may at times have cherished the notion that a tutelage could be exercised over the more literate strata of the proletariat, considerable suspicion--if not outright fear--of the current and potential power of trade unions caused second thoughts. The latter focused not only on the so-called Sheffield outrages, but also on the strength manifested by organized workers in long-term strikes. (388)

By the 1870s, new nuances were becoming perceptible in the relations of employers to the skilled unionists and in those of the latter to the unskilled. Legislative recognition of trade unions, achieved between 1867 and 1875, discouraged strikes that might have exhausted carefully accumulated assets. (389) The increased emphasis placed by unions on the ability of members to earn the standard union rate (390) reflected, from the perspective of the working class as a whole, not so much a polarization of the skill continuum (391) as an attempt to avoid dilution of membership regardless of dilution of skills. In certain trades, however, that were relatively little threatened by mechanization and thus exposed to a comparatively minor competitive threat from the unskilled, unions sometimes supported efforts at organizing the unapprenticed. (392) Nevertheless, the general estrangement of the skilled and the unskilled--especially insofar as they coincided with the organized and the unorganized--had progressed far enough to induce a foreign observer to venture the prognosis that at some future time the unskilled, severed off as a fifth estate, would be compelled to accomplish their goals on their own. (393)

British observers, too, were already speaking of a "gulf" that had become "fixed" between artisans and unskilled laborers. Thomas Wright synthesized this view of sectional antagonism based in part on the differential effects of a "habitually overstocked" labor market. (394)

> The artisan creed with regard to labourers is, that the latter are an inferior class, and that they should be made to know and kept in their places. In the eyes of unionist and non-unionist mechanics, any clever or ambitious labourer who shows a desire to get out of his place, by attempting to pick up or creep into "the trade" to which he is attached as an unskilled assistant, is guilty of deadly sin. ... In the same way artisans' wives hold the wives of labourers to be of a lower social grade, and very often will either not "neighbor" with them at all, or else only in a patronising way. (395)

This attitude on the part of the skilled could have been vitally reinforced by two phenomena: 1. a tendency toward de-skilling that was rendering the formally unapprenticed potential competitors in certain industries undergoing technological change; and 2. a desire on the part of the skilled to place as much distance as possible between themselves and the unskilled at a time when the Liberals and the Conservatives were casting about for politically reliable sections of the working class. Such a constellation would have represented evidence in support of Engels' position since: 1. indicated that a former elite stratum was fighting a rearguard struggle against the effects of technological change on the structure of the labor force; whereas 2. pointed to an attempt at class cooperation between the more farsighted elements of the ruling classes and the upper stratum of the working class. (396)

The plausibility of this line of reasoning is impaired by the circumstance that employers would have had little motivation to form an alliance with skilled workers who stood in the path of the processes of de-skilling that mechanization necessitated. (397) The counter-argument, according to which many Radical employers in large firms traded union recognition for political support, appears insubstantial. (398) Two further counter-arguments are, however, more promising. One locates the acceptance of the unions of the skilled by large employers in the latter's perception that the former contributed to the exhaustion of "those sources of secondary exploitation" that had formerly sustained smaller competitors. (399) This thesis gains plausibility in branches of the newer, large-scale metal industries, (400) but fails to explain why the skilled recorded their greatest successes in the old crafts marked by small firms. (401) The other counter-argument stresses the fact that some farseeing employers recognized "the exposed position of property and of its need to find outside support." (402) Although, once again, eminently plausible, this claim fails to explain the obvious shortsightedness of a policy that, by consciously alienating the majority of workers, would have only exacerbated class antagonisms and prepared an even more destabilizing explosion in the future.

H. Engels on New Unionism

In order to document the argument that what Marx and particularly Engels deemed so opportunistic in the unions of the labor aristocrats was not solely a function of their allegedly privileged position, it is worth examining Engels' own assessment of the New Unions of the unskilled that were formed at the end of the 1880s.

From the outset, Engels wrote with great enthusiasm about the fact that the dockers' strike of 1889 had demonstrated that the most immiserated stratum of unskilled workers, concentrated in the largest slum in the world, was capable of organization. (403) Moreover, he took pains to emphasize that the unions of the unskilled "differed completely from the old organizations of the labor aristocracy and cannot pass on to the same conservative paths" because their members were too poor and their jobs too insecure. (404) Although formally similar to the old trade unions, the new unions were strike and struggle organizations as opposed to friendly societies. Whereas the old unions accepted the wage system as a "definitive fact" once and for all, the unions of the unskilled were formed at a time when the faith in the eternal nature of the wage system had already been broken. The leaders were either conscious or emotive socialists, while the membership was "free of the inherited, 'respectable' bourgeois prejudices that confuse the minds of the better-situated 'old' unionists." (405) Given the claim that the unskilled looked with scorn upon those who preached the identity of interests between labor and capital, and given, further, Engels' optimism concerning the future of socialism in Britain, it was no surprise that Engels also predicted the coming defeat of the aristocratic unions. (406)

Yet from the very beginning Engels seems to have been conscious of the dangers inherent in the organizational efforts by and on behalf of the unskilled. Thus, although he perceived and indeed welcomed the aid provided the dockers by merchants and the "great mass of the bourgeoisie" who hated the "dock monopolists" for their exploitative policies toward customers as well as toward workers, (407) he was later constrained to admit that the dockers had been "spoiled by the subsidy of the philistines and don't want to spoil things with the bourgeois public." (408) In addition to fearing that leaders such as John Burns and even Tom Mann might have fallen victim to various baits of respectability set by the bourgeoisie, (409) Engels became alarmed that the Dockers had not only refused to cooperate with the Gas Workers, but had also begun to close their membership lists and even to protest against the immigration of "foreign paupers" such as Russian Jews. (410) The gradual debilitation of the Gas Workers and of the Dockers led Engels in 1891 to complain that the old unions were once again in control. (411)

This was not the place to explain why "(t)he 'new unionism' of 1889 thus became uncomfortably like the 'old unionism' it had once fought." (412) The point was, simply, to illustrate that low wages, concentrated poverty, casual labor and the absence of monopolizable skills were not, contrary to Engels' recurrent enthusiastic outbursts, guarantors of a politically connected, let alone socialistically oriented trade unionism.

I. Conclusions

This chapter has shown that Marx's and Engels' analysis of the labor aristocracy contained significant gaps; further reflection will reveal that their analyses were in fact self-contradictory. For Marx, the overriding developmental process in the context of the formation of the working class was the increasing homogeneity of working and living conditions attendant upon capitalist industrialization. The increasing organic composition of capital, accompanied by a deepened division of labor and a diffusion of de-skilling, produced and would continue to produce technological and socio-economic conditions that swept away the barriers between and among working class strata that had been erected, particularly during the period of Manufaktur.

Such a sequence of events left little room for the rise and expansion of a skill-based labor aristocracy. Consequently, Marx tended to see the origins of the labor aristocracy in various remnants of pre-capitalist custom and convention as well as in a series of non-essential, accidental features of British capitalism in the nineteenth century.

Engels introduced the notion that Britain's world market and colonial monopoly lay at the base of its labor aristocracy. Paradoxically, then, the labor aristocracy was being fostered, from this perspective, by the same set of forces that, according to Marx, were leading to its demise--namely, the fact that capitalist industrialization had made its breakthrough in Britain. Although Engels did periodically add a stratum-specific component to his analysis in the form of an unequal distribution of foreign profits within the working class, he reversed the meaning Marx had given to the homogenization of the working class: now the British working class as a whole was perceived as having been elevated to the status of a privileged national proletariat vis a vis other proletariats.

This position was, however, interpreted as merely temporary; with the collapse of Britain's unique world economic domination, its favored proletariat would be depressed to the level of other national working classes. Increasing competition and overproduction would eliminate the possibility of the rise of a labor aristocracy in other nations. Engels conceived of this stratum as a historically unique and nationally specific phenomenon. (413)

The logical hiatus in Marx's and Engels' argumentation emerged between the fundamental economic theory, which predicted the submergence of intra-proletarian disparities, and the manifest existence of a numerically significant and socio-politically powerful sector of skilled trade union members. This gap was bridged by means of recourse to a set of unmediated conjectures concerning the voluntaristic aspirations both of these artisans to underpin their position and of their immediate employers (and of the latter's political representatives) to weaken the proletariat by appealing to the venality of its more prosperous members and leaders.

Chapter 6
Some Preliminary Results: An Alternative Theoretical Perspective

The deficiencies and insufficiencies of Marx's and Engels' conception of the labor aristocracy manifested themselves even more acutely in the two decades between Engels' death and World War I. In the dominant form that Lenin gave to it, the new view of the labor aristocracy was relieved of its internal theoretical tensions (i.e., inconsistencies) at the expense of a definite superficialization. The ambigious legacy that Marx and Engels had left in the form of the aforementioned hiatus between economic prediction and voluntaristic reality was eliminated by discarding all economic theory on the level of the influence of national capital accumulation on the structure of the working class. (1) Consequently, imperialist profits on the one hand and an even more extreme version of voluntarism and corruption on the other hand became the sole relevant variables. (2)

This approach, by virtue of its redefinition of Engels' concept of monopoly to include "(e)very cartel, trust, syndicate," (3) claimed to account not only for the preservation of the source of foreign superprofits and hence of the labor aristocracy in Britain, but also for the possibility of the rise of a labor aristocracy in Germany, France and the United States (4) as well as in such peripheral nations as Denmark. (5) Yet complete reliance on "imperialist superprofits" as the economic basis of the labor aristocracy divorced from any attempt to make the mechanism underlying the redistribution of "crumbs" plausible (6) offered a weak foundation for a theory of political action. This was so much more the case in light of the quasi-psychological and quasi-moral notions that were grafted on to this economic basis. (7)

This superficialization of Marx's and in particular of Engels' conception of the labor aristocracy within the Leninist tradition exerted an increasingly deleterious influence on politics and theorizing precisely because the scattered views of Marx and Engels were elevated to the status of a theory that actually guided Party tactics. Indeed, this theory soon gained a near-monopoly status so that the working class was perceived in dichotomous terms--a small corrupt upper stratum versus the masses made incorruptible by poverty. (8) The fact, moreover, that the mechanisms that were alleged to generate and to perpetuate the labor aristocracy were never set forth let alone empirically tested (9) stemmed from and in turn consolidated a hypothesis-turned-dogma.

In contradistinction to the positions adumbrated above, that emerging here de-emphasizes the whole set of variables relating to corruption--that is, strategies formulated by ruling classes or individual employers in order to influence certain strata of the working class; similarly, policies explicitly orienting trade unions toward alliances with employers or with the capitalist class are not regarded as crucially important. Although such conscious class collaborationist tendencies surely existed and even flourished, they are by themselves too general--by virtue of being common to all class societies--to be of heuristic value in understanding the course of class conflict in Europe and the United States during the nineteenth and twentieth centuries. (10) Exclusive emphasis on the subjective motivations of class agents obscures the underlying societal development that rendered such collaboration possible and, at times, successful.

Attention will also be shifted away from foreign-generated profits as a source, if not of corruption, then at least of differentials among working class strata. The theoretical and empirical arguments already marshaled against the use of this variable retain their validity for the period after 1890 as well. The emergence, moreover, of national labor aristocracies in countries that did not appropriate a significant colume of "imperialist superprofits" (11) or in ones that in no straight-forward way could be designated as exploiters of less develop countries (12) is taken as prima facie evidence that this source did not represent a necessary condition of the rise of a favored proletarian stratum.

Instead, the approach developed here focuses on those processes that brought into being decisively heterogeneous interests among various working class strata; by "decisive" is meant a heterogeneity strong enough to cause these strata to pursue their goals separately--indeed, at times even antagonistically--rather than jointly. The formation of a labor aristocracy represented one partial, subordinate aspect of this general phenomenon of the absence of working class commonality. Concentration on this stratum is, therefore, a heuristic device for making the entire issue of the lack of material, political and organizational proletarian homogeneity accessible to analysis.

Given the outstanding part played by the labor aristocracy within the trade union movement, however, this laboring sector has acquired a theoretical interest out of proportion to its numbers.

At issue, then, are those societal forces that were powerful enough to overcome other forces that, according to Marx's working hypothesis, "should" have created the foundation upon which anti-capitalist working class unity was to be molded. Even if Marx's reasoning were rejected, that is, if it were, for example, assumed that some variant of social-democratic integration of the working class into capitalist society were the "normal form" of proletarian political participation, (13) the factors underlying this positive or "negative integration" (14) would still have to be elucidated. In this sense, Marx's theorizing would remain the discursive point of departure.

Since the major force of Marx's theory of working class homogenization turns on an analysis of the forms of capital accumulation and their influence on the conditions, states of consciousness and actions of the working class, criticisms of various theories of the labor aristocracy for being based on the technological criterion of skill are unwarranted. (15) To argue that relations of production--and not technological change--are decisive for class relations is, in this context, tantamount to emptying the argument of substance, especially if by the term "relations of production" is meant the global setting of capitalist exploitation. If the rigidity of this invariant global interpretation is removed, however, then it becomes clear that more than mere nuances distinguish the relations of production and of class that obtain, for example, in a steel plant, owned by a publicly held corporation that operates ten other plants employing 100,000 workers, and those in a carpentry firm owned by a working carpenter who employs three carpenters earning three-fifths of the "capitalist's" combined "earned and unearned income." (16) As the relationship between relations of production and technological change revealed by this illustration indicates, the categories of "skilled" and "unskilled," which are often perceived as underlying the privileged and non-privileged strata respectively, are in effect abbreviations or code names for much more comprehensive sets of societal relations.

In its cruder variants, the theory of the labor aristocracy seeks to set the limit, as it were, above which attempts to relieve exploitation at the source are no longer triggered. Yet this approach is clearly insufficient because better-situated workers have often participated in revolutionary movements whereas low paid workers have often joined counter-revolutionary movements en masse. (17) Consequently, more specific conditions remain to be enumerated with regard to the transformation of potential class conflict into actual anti-capitalist action. A relatively high standard of living and the relatively secure perspective of the maintenance of that standard associated with trade unionism of the skilled have, in other words, been empirically necessary but not sufficient conditions for the rise of a labor aristocracy. They have not been sufficient for the obvious reason that, unless the forms of capital accumulation assumed by any particular branch have been such as to render the retention of entrenched skills reconcilable with competitive branch profitability, firms have been forced to revolutionize the skill structure and, where necessary, to combat the unions resisting the transformation.

But just as the enjoyment of relatively good working and living conditions has not guaranteed that any body of workers perceived itself as able to fend for itself independently of other working class strata, so the existence of such self-imagined labor aristocrats has not per se implied that individual capitalists solicited or even welcomed this elite despite the fact that the very fractionating of the working class symbolized by the labor aristocracy may, in certain countries and during certain periods, have been in the long-term interest of the capitalist class. (18) Indeed, often employers may have seen little advantage at all in acquiescing in the "greedy" demands of one group of workers in exchange for the latter's exclusion of unskilled workers from their organizations. Such compliance by employers depended in individual instances on such factors as the share of the skilled in total firm-level employment and the likelihood, cet. par., of the self-organization of the remainder of the work force--i.e., on how splintered this sector was by occupational, racial, ethnic, generational, sexual, linguistic, religious and other traits.

But isolated instances of some type of labor aristocratic relationship between an upper stratum of workers and their direct employers would not have sufficed to invest this sector of the working class with any decisive influence on the class structure as a whole; and only if the constellation of class forces had been restructured to ease the strains of class conflict--from the standpoint of the ruling classes--in the course of facilitating the maintenance of existing property relations, would the phenomenon of a labor aristocracy have merited the attention that generations of contemporary supporters and detractors have devoted to it.

A labor aristocracy could have exerted societally relevant effects of the magnitude indicated primarily on two different levels--within the trade union movement as a whole and within the national political system. To the extent that unions of the skilled obtained hegemonic control over the labor movement in many capitalist countries during the nineteenth century, considerable scope was created for mobilizing and channeling resources on behalf of the unorganized. But, once again, a decision on the part of labor aristocrats and/or their leaders not to make such an organizational effort a major priority need not have been solicited, encouraged or even suggested by the bourgeoisie. As long as economic conditions were expansive enough to provide for rising labor aristocratic standards without leading to a deterioration of standards among the remainder of the working class that would have compelled the latter to organize itself at all costs, the unions of the skilled would have experienced little socio-economic incentive to seek a widening of their ranks.

Incorporation of the national political system into an international comparative analysis of labor aristocracies underscores the importance of national-historical peculiarities in comprehending class alignments. For explicit political attempts on the part of ruling classes to favor and to solicit support, in turn, from a stratum of the working class presupposed, at a minimum, an elaborated structure of formal, and a modicum of substantive, democracy for the non-ruling classes. This criterion made Britain and the United States, for example, potential centers for the creation of a labor aristocracy; Germany, with its constitutionally prescribed exclusion of the non-propertied classes from the authoritative institutions of political power, (19) offered a significantly less favorable framework within which nationally uniform privileges could be bestowed on a segment of the working class; in France, the century-long tradition of violent revolution--combined with a relatively well entrenched petty bourgeois agricultural sector--created a socio-political environment that made class collaboration appear less desirable and plausible to the relevant classes than was the case, for example, in Britain, the United States or the Scandinavian countries.

The remaining chapters represent an attempt to sketch the essential national characteristics promoting and/or undermining the rise of a labor aristocracy in the major European capitalist societies prior to World War I.

Chapter 7
The British Labor Aristocracy from the Depression of the 1880s to the First World War

> ... I was told that men at the front, daily confronted with death and needing shells to protect and defend themselves, wrote home to their fellow trade unionists entreating them not to surrender any of the privileges of their craft, although strict adhesion to these privileges was impeding the supply of the munitions they so sadly needed. (1)

During the quarter-century preceding the First World War Britain underwent significant economic, social and political changes which affected the working and living conditions of the labor aristocracy and its relations to other strata and classes. The cumulative consequences of these developments, together with the upheaval brought on by the war, transformed the basis, structure and role of the labor aristocracy in British society.

A. The Trend Reversal of Basic Economic Variables

During the period under review a number of economic trends which had become manifest in the latter part of the 1870s and in the 1880s were accelerated, whereas others, which could be traced further back into the nineteenth century, were reversed. A further turning point at the outset of the new century introduced an element of irregularity into the internal structure of the period as a whole. (2)

Industrial production: Although the severe depression of the 1870s (3) suspended the series of relatively high growth rates of industrial production extending back to the end of the eighteenth century, (4) instead of creating the preconditions of renewed economic growth--as had been the function of previous cyclical depressions--it ushered in a period of comparatively minimal growth which lasted until World War I. (5) During the twenty-five years preceding the war, growth rates amounted to one-half to two-thirds of those recorded between

1811 and 1877. (6) The annual growth rates of gross national product exhibited roughly analogous patterns. (7)

Profitability: Calculations of the profitability of British capital during the prewar period disclose a sharp decline during the depressions of the 1870s and 1880s, followed by an upsurge during the latter part of the 1890s; the opening years of the twentieth century then witnessed another steady decline. (8)

The following patterns emerge from an examination of the components of profitability. (9) The capital-output ratio declined throughout the entire second half of the nineteenth century; after an abrupt reversal at the turn of the century, followed by a period of stabilization, the capital-output ratio attained the level that had been recorded at the close of the 1880s. (10) Whereas capital-intensity (i.e., capital per worker in constant pounds of 1913) stagnated between 1879 and 1899, it rose by 18.4 per cent from 1899 to 1909. (11) Productivity, or output per worker, also exhibited a markedly lower rate of growth during the decades following the 1880s. (12) The share of wages in total income also fell somewhat during the 1890s and the early twentieth century. (13)

International trade and income: Although here, too, a break in the series of growth rates may be observed, the decline must be viewed in the context of Britain's earlier absolute dominance and of the very high rates of growth attained prior to the depression of the 1870s. This pattern applied to commodity exports (14) but particularly to net property income from abroad which, from the turn of the century to World War I, rose as a share of net national product. (15)

Real wages: Nearly unanimously both contemporaries (16) and more recent scholarship (17) agree that the fifteen years preceding the war witnessed an unambiguous reversal of the trend toward rising real wages which had extended far back into the nineteenth century. (18) Thus Tucker's index of the real wages of artisans in London, which rose by 79.2 per cent between 1866 and 1897, declined by 10.3 per cent from the latter year to 1914, receding to the level of 1890. (19) Kuczynski's index of net real wages of all workers (which takes unemployment and--beginning in 1912--social security contributions into consideration) reveals a similar pattern, peaking in 1901 and falling to a twenty-year low in 1909, 15.1 per cent below the peak value. (20) (See Table 8.)

Of the components of net real wages, the level of unemployment did not rise during the period in question, (22) whereas the cost of living, the decline in which had contributed powerfully to rising real wages during the last third of the nineteenth century, increased sharply from 1896 to World War I, (23) thus

113

Table 8. Net Real Wages in the United Kingdom, 1833-1914 (21)
(1900=100)

Economic Cycle	Index	Economic cycle	Index
1833-1842	51	1880-1886	80
1843-1849	53	1887-1895	91
1849-1858	57	1895-1903	99
1859-1868	63	1904-1908	95
1869-1879	74	1909-1914	93

exerting considerable downward pressure on real wages. If, as has been argued, (24) the lack of working class militancy in late-Victorian England was in part attributable to the quasi-automatic increases in real wages generated by a continuous cheapening of consumer goods, (25) then the upsurge of labor radicalism in the years preceding the war may have been fomented by the reversal of the trend in costs and real wages. To the extent, however, that the working class perceived its supply of such goods as dependent upon free trade, it may have been motivated merely to rally to the Liberal party in its opposition to the Conservative tariff reform campaign. (26)

In summary, then, a group of interconnected economic variables such as production, productivity and profitability indicates that the twenty-five, and in particular the fifteen, years preceding the war witnessed a significant curtailment of the expansiveness of British capital. Extending over several business cycles, this development signaled the incipient eclipse of British by German and especially American capital. (27) Although the share of British output that was exported rose, (28) the competitiveness of British industry deteriorated on a broad front. (29) The restrictions imposed on British capitalism as a whole by this less favorable constellation of international economic relations were only partially alleviated by the enormous growth of capital exports, especially during the decade before the war. (30) Since banking capital and sectors of the petty bourgeoisie--rather than industrial capital--constituted the principal agents of foreign investment, (31) savings and/or capital invested abroad represented a deduction from potential domestic accumulation--quite apart from the potential losses stemming from the reinvestment of the enormous profits on this investment abroad or from their repatriation for purposes of consumption by the investing strata. (32)

Thus at a time of rising living costs, that is, when increases in money wages were necessary to insure a stationary or enhanced standard of living, capitalists and politicians of the major bourgeois parties "really felt that the system could not afford to make" "the moderate concessions which would still have quelled the unrest." (33) For given the intensity of foreign competition, increased wages would--cet.par.--have led not only to reduced profit margins and the loss of further markets but also to "a flight of capital to lands where labour could be exploited with less hindrance." (34)

These epoch-making shifts within the hierarchy and interdependence of national capitals (35) lowered the upper limits of the bargaining position available to a labor movement that not only scrupulously observed the rights of private industrial property but also conceded the necessity of an internationally competitive profit on that capital. (36) Once economic constraints rendered the "progress" enjoyed by the cooperating elements of capital and labor less than "bright," (37) continued acquiescence in declining standards of living was as likely to guarantee the stagnation of trade unionism as rebellion against that deterioration was likely to radicalize the unions. Consequently, the prewar years of the twentieth century seemed almost destined to become a turning point for the British working class and its political organizations.

B. Differentiation within the Working Class

1. Changes in Class and Occupational Structure

With the advent of a question in the census of 1891 inquiring whether the respondent was an "employer," "employed" or "working on own account," the reliability of empirical statements concerning the British class structure improved significantly. (38) Table 9 illustrates this tripartite division at the three censuses of 1891, 1901 and 1911 for a broadly defined industrial sector.

During these two decades the number of employees rose by 30.2 per cent whereas the number of employers and self-employed declined by 11.8 per cent and 2.7 per cent respectively. The proletarianization of the industrially occupied thus took place basically by means of an increase in employees and a decrease in employers whereas the self-employed were able to maintain their numbers.

The development of the industrially occupied female population showed a greater shift toward employees as a result of considerable losses among employers and the self-employed.

Table 9. Class Structure of Males, aged ten Years and upwards, occupied in Industry (39) in England and Wales, 1891, 1901 and 1911 (40)

	1891 No.	%	1901 No.	%	1911 No.	%
Employers	265,543	4.7	206,723	3.2	234,212	3.3
Employed	5,159,005	91.4	6,090,194	93.0	6,719,457	93.7
Working on own account	222,881	3.9	250,645	3.8	216,873	3.0
Total	5,647,429	100.0	6,547,562	100.0	7,170,542	100.0

Table 10. Class Structure of Females, aged ten Years and upwards, occupied in Industry (39) in England and Wales, 1891 and 1911 (40)

	1891 No.	%	1911 No.	%
Employers	37,590	2.5	24,765	1.4
Employed	1,266,279	84.8	1,574,193	90.2
Workers on own account	189,123	12.7	146,500	8.4
Total	1,492,992	100.0	1,745,458	100.0

Between 1891 and 1911 the number of female industrial employees grew by 24.3 per cent, whereas the number of employers and self-employed declined by 34.1 per cent and 22.5 per cent respectively. (41)

Employees of both sexes as a share of the industrially occupied rose from 90.0 per cent in 1891 to 93.0 per cent in 1911; during the same period the share of employers declined from 4.2 per cent to 2.9 per cent whereas the self-employed fell from 5.8 per cent to 4.1 per cent. The aggregate number of industrial employees rose from 6,425,284 to 8,293,650. This increase of 29.1 per cent was somewhat greater than that of the entire occupied population (27.7 per cent) (42) as well as that of the entire population of England and Wales (24.4 per cent). (43) This general trend toward formal proletarianization of the work force did not apply to the agricultural sector, in which a significant decline in the number of wage laborers accounted for the aggregate loss of those occupied in agriculture, whereas the number of farmers and working family members rose somewhat. (44)

The increasing size of industrial establishments provided a further indication of the trend toward large-scale capitalist employment. Although no data were collected before the war pertaining directly to this characteristic, (45) the ratio of employees to employers (i.e., excluding the self-employed) may function as a guide to the direction and magnitude of the concentration of employment.

Table 11. Ratio of Employed to Employers among Males and Females, aged ten Years and upwards, in Industry (39) in England and Wales, 1891 and 1911 (40)

1891		1911	
Employed	6,425,284	Employed	8,293,650
Employers	303,133	Employers	258,977
Ratio	21.2 : 1	Ratio	32.0 : 1

With the increase in the number of employees twice as great as the decrease in the number of employers (29.1 per cent and -14.6 per cent respectively), the ratio of employees to employers rose by more than fifty per cent.

The proletarianization of manual workers was accompanied by strong growth among professional, (state) administrative, clerical and commercial employees. (46) The relative numerical influence of this sector is revealed in Table 12, which presents a heterogeneous stratification system of the entire occupied population.

Whereas the professional/clerical and service sector occupations increased their total share by 6.1 per cent, domestic (largely indoor female) servants and those occupied in agriculture (largely male laborers) witnessed the largest declines. The industrial proletariat continued to constitute slightly more than one-half of the occupied population (58.6 and 58.7 per cent of occupied males in 1891 and 1911 respectively), whereas the heterogeneous category comprising the industrial bourgeoisie, petty bourgeoisie and proletarianized out-workers proved to be the only one that declined relatively and absolutely. Among males these losses assumed only marginal proportions, varying significantly from trade to trade with some trades recording considerable gains. Thus, for example, the number of employing and self-employed plumbers and painters grew considerably; the number of self-employed bricklayers rose moderately while

Table 12. Distribution of the occupied Population, aged ten Years and upwards, among non-overlapping Classes, Sectors and Occupational Groupings in England and Wales, 1891 and 1911 (47) (in per cent)

	1891	1911	Change
Industrial proletariat	50.4	50.9	0.5
Service sector (48)	10.1	13.3	3.2
Professional/clerical occupations	9.4	12.3	2.9
Domestic servants	14.2	11.6	-2.6
Agricultural sector	10.3	8.1	-2.2
Industrial employers/self-employed	5.6	3.8	-1.8
Total	100.0	100.0	0.0

employing bricklayers declined in number. (49) The number of self-employed carpenters and joiners stagnated while their employing counterparts suffered large losses; in masonry losses were high in all classes. (50) Compared to the somewhat favorable situation in the building trades, (51) that prevailing among such artisans as tailors, shoemakers, goldsmiths, blacksmiths and watchmakers was precarious. (52)

As the comparatively constant share of employees in many branches shows, however, the growth of the industrial proletariat in relation to industrial employers and the self-employed was largely attributable to the above-average growth among those occupied in industries with relatively few employers or self-employed. Whereas the total male industrial population grew by 27.0 per cent between 1891 and 1911, the corresponding percentages in the aforementioned industries amounted to: metals and machinery (52.1); mining (60.1); railways (72.5); chemicals (78.7); and gas, water, etc. (114.1). (53)

In spite of the relatively late expansion of a so-called middle class, (54) the industrial proletariat retained its status as the numerically dominant socio-economic contingent. Growth among clerical employees was especially marked in national and local government as well as in commerce. The fact, however, that the highest growth rates were registered among female employees (55) suggests that part of this intermediate stratum represented a non-manual counterpart of the industrial proletariat. (56) Strong economic grounds for viewing the inclusion of such employees in "the middle class" (57) with scepticism are provided by the wage parity that existed on the eve of World War I between female clerks and female skilled and semi-skilled manual workers as well as between male clerks and skilled male manual workers. (58)

Although such considerations do not constitute a refutation of arguments that emphasize the economic, social and cultural differences between the "new lower middle class" and the upper stratum of the manual working class, (59) they do cast some doubt on the claim that England lagged far behind Continental European countries with regard to the formation of a social stratum situated between skilled manual workers and the bourgeoisie. (60) For if the new or lower middle class was composed of white-collar, technical, supervisory and service employees in contradistinction to the "old" middle class, which was largely made up of independent artisan producers, farmers, shopkeepers and professionals, (61) then England had long led its Continental counterparts because of its early elimination of many small property owners. (62) Table 13 documents the relative weight of two basic elements of the largely non-employing middle class in England and Wales and in Germany.

Table 13. Persons in government and professional Occupations as a Share of all occupied Persons in England-Wales and Germany, selected Census Years (63)

England-Wales		Germany	
1881	4.6	1882	3.2
1891	5.1	1895	3.8
1901	5.6	1907	4.4
1911	6.2		

Not only had the commercial sector expanded much earlier in England than in Germany, but domestic servants, whose socio-economic and cultural conditions of employment separated them sharply from profit-producing wage workers, bulked twice as large in the English labor force as they did in Germany. (64) The fact, however, that significant numbers of lower middle class employees such as postal workers, teachers and salespersons organized themselves in comparatively militant trade unions, (65) suggests that the gap in living and working conditions between them and manual workers was not politically insuperable.

Apart from the fundamental societal bifurcations of capital versus labor (66) and manual versus mental labor, a whole series of socio-economic characteristics contributed to shaping the contours of intra-working class differentiation.

a. Age

With the progressive elimination of child labor, the work force became more homogeneous by becoming increasingly composed of adults.

Table 14. Children, ten to fifteen Years old, in the Labor Force in England and Wales, 1891 and 1911 (67)

| | Boys | | Girls | |
	1891	1911	1891	1911
Total number	419,209	314,534	262,194	182,476
Percentage of all boys/girls this age	26.0	18.1	15.3	10.4
Percentage of entire male/female labor force	4.8	2.7	6.7	3.8

The number of employed boys declined by 25.0 per cent; among girls the dcline reached 30.4 per cent. (68) Thus by 1911 approximately ninety-seven per cent of all occupied persons were over fifteen years old. The disappearance of children from the labor market enhanced the possibilities of cooperation and solidarity within the working class by withdrawing from employers a particularly docile mass of exploitable labor and by preventing parents from using their children to supplement family earnings marginally (69) at the expense of the competitive position of the entire proletariat.

b. Sex

During this period, as during the entire century extending from 1851 to 1951, (70) women represented a relatively small and unchanging share of the total occupied population. From 1891 to 1911 this proportion declined slightly--from 30.9 per cent to 29.7 per cent; within the industrial proletariat the corresponding figures were 19.7 per cent and 19.0 per cent. (71) Similarly, the participation rate of females in the labor force moved within narrow limits, declining from 34.4 per cent in 1891 to 32.5 per cent in 1911. During the same period the participation rate of males rose marginally, from 83.1 per cent to 83.9 per cent. (72)

In a number of other respects the demographic composition and labor force distribution of female workers militated against lifelong attachment to wage work in an employment context conducive to integration into the male-dominated organizations of the working class. Thus in 1901 only 152,000 women were trade union members, constituting 7.5 per cent of all trade unionists; although female membership more than doubled (to 335,000) by 1911, its share of 10.7 per cent (73) represented only one-half of its share of the industrial proletariat. The cotton industry, which accounted for the majority of female trade unionists and a considerable proportion of female industrial wage workers, proved the major exception to the tendency of women to join unions less frequently than men. (74)

Briefly, the female labor force consisted overwhelmingly of a successively replenished supply of younger cohorts of unmarried women. Thus in 1911, 77.4 per cent of all occupied women were unmarried, 14.1 per cent married and 8.5 per cent widowed; the corresponding labor force participation rates of these three groups amounted to 54.5 per cent, 10.3 per cent and 30.1 per cent. (75) In 1901 the patterns were very similar: 52.3 per cent of unmarried women and 13.2 per cent of married/widowed women were "engaged in occupations." (76) In that year, unmarried women aged fifteen to thirty-five accounted for 19.8 per cent of all women over ten years of age; yet they also accounted for 62.7 per cent of all occupied women; similarly, they accounted for 60.2 per cent of all unmarried women but 80.4 per cent of all occupied unmarried women. (77) On the basis of a labor force participation rate of 69.7 per cent--more than twice as high as that of all women--these women constituted a majority of the female work force. In light of the fact that most women eventually married (78) and that only one in ten married women worked, (79) relatively few women were compelled to develop a social consciousness appropriate to those for whom lifelong labor outside the home, in cooperation with others similarly situated, had become an unalterable necessity. (80)

The location of women workers within the social division of labor also exerted an adverse influence on their opportunities to become active in working class organizations, which were increasingly linked to the advance of capitalist forms of economic enterprise. Female employment was, however, in the process of being shifted away from these most unfavorable locations. Although the share of women employed in domestic positions declined, this sector continued to account for the largest segment of employed women, declining from 43.5 per cent in 1891 to 35.9 per cent in 1911. (81) The number of women employed at home--particularly as out-workers of the clothing and textile industries--, which had approached 300,000 in 1901, also declined. (82) This kind of work, "largely undertaken by the quite destitute, who undercut one another," rendered home-workers "helpless and unorganised," unable to "protect themselves." (83)

Within the industrial proletariat women remained heavily concentrated in the textile and clothing industries despite the fact that progressive mechanization throughout manufacturing industries led to their utilization in place of men who had formerly been employed at technologically less advanced means of production. (84) Thus from 1891 to 1911 the proportion of the female industrial proletariat employed in these two industries declined from 78.4 per cent to 73.2 per cent. Significantly, the textile industry, in particular cotton manufacture, with a long tradition of highly concentrated female employment, (85) was staffed by an above-average share of older married women, whose attachment to the labor force contributed to the afore-mentioned above-average degree of trade union organization. (86) Apart from these industries, women outnumbered men in few major occupations, bookbinding and paper box manufacture being two examples. (87) Women in several other occupations increased their numbers relative to men although they remained a distinct minority. (88)

c. Urbanization

The cohesiveness of the British working class was enhanced during these years by virtue of its being drawn closer together spatially in the course of urbanization. Although the progressive concentration of the population in urban areas had characterized British industrialization throughout the nineteenth century, (89) the pattern of urban growth underwent two important modifications after the census of 1881. First, London ceased to grow more rapidly than England and Wales as a whole; after having increased its share of the total population from one-tenth to one-seventh from 1801 to 1881, London experienced a decline to one-eighth by 1911. (90) Whereas London --the industrial structure of which deviated from that of the country at large inasmuch as it was dominated by small masters, skilled labor, relatively small amounts of capital investment and the production of consumer goods (91)--began to grow more slowly, the industrial cities of the Midlands and of the North of England witnessed growth sufficient to enable the cities with populations in excess of 100,000 to overtake London. Such urban areas increased their share of the total population from slightly more than one-seventh in 1881 to more than one-fifth by 1911. (92) During this thirty-year period the number of such cities rose from nineteen to thirty-four—a gain of fifteen compared to an increase of fourteen during the half-century preceding 1881. (93)

Second, the growth recorded by cities of more than 250,000 inhabitants proved more striking still. Prior to 1841 no city other than London had attained this size; from that year until 1881 each census registered one additional city of such size; between 1891 and 1911 the number of these cities doubled from five to ten. Of these ten cities, eight were located within a square measuring 150 kilometers on each side, bordered by Leeds in the north, Hull in the east, Birmingham in the south and Liverpool in the west. (94) Their share of the total population rose from one-thirteenth in 1891 to one-eight in 1911. (95)

By 1911 more than one-third of the population of England and Wales inhabited cities of more than 100,000 persons. In this respect Britain's population remained considerably more concentrated than that of any other country, with Germany and France attaining a level two-thirds and one-third respectively of that of British urban concentration. (96) The fact that English trade unionists overwhelmingly lived and worked in these same areas underscored the urban orientation of the industrial working class. (97)

d. Supervisory Personnel

The emergence and growth of a numerically significant group of shop-floor supervisory personnel (foremen), recruited largely from the ranks of the skilled industrial proletariat, (98) would, upon preliminary inspection, seem to have created greater differentiation within the manual working class by having introduced into the latter an element functionally allied with and acting as agents of the industrial bourgeoisie. (99) And in fact the material privileges accruing to the occupants of such positions did intensify the competition for them in contemporary Germany, thereby detracting from working class solidarity; (100) in the United States, moreover, the association of the rise of native-born or Northwest European English-speaking workers into supervisory positions with the entry of Southern and Eastern European immigrants into subordinate unskilled industrial positions introduced a consciously manipulated element of ethnic divisiveness. (101) The peculiarities of British industrial development, however, and in particular of the organizational forms of capitalist enterprise, modified the effects of the rise of the industrial foreman on the structure of the working class.

123

Empirically it is not possible to specify a trend in the growth of this stratum since the prewar British censuses did not contain any questions on this subject. The only nationally representative data were generated by an inquiry into earnings conducted by the Board of Trade in 1906. (102) Extrapolations based on the "proportion of foremen to operatives" (103) indicate that by 1911 the number of industrial foremen (104) had reached approximately 175,000. (105) The fact that foremen increased more rapidly than all other manual working class groups during the succeeding half-century (106) may indicate that the same pattern obtained during the period under review. (107)

The bulk of industrial foremen were employed in textiles, coalmining, construction, metal-making and metalworking. (108) But it is in the metal industries that the organizational transformations affecting the need for foremen can best be studied. (109) Earlier in the nineteenth century, numerous industries in Britain had been characterized by a system of subcontracting in which considerable areas of managerial authority over labor and production had been delegated to workers whose mode of payment had encouraged them to maintain wages at the lowest possible level since a fixed sum had been set aside for all workers. Such a system of "co-exploitation"

> enabled small-scale enterprise to expand operations without raising unmanageably-great masses of circulating capital, it provided "incentives" to all groups of workers worth humouring, and it enabled industry to meet sharp fluctuations in demand without having to carry a permanent burden of overhead expenditure. (110)

At a certain point in the course of the overall development of economic, technological and organizational factors, the lack of direct capitalist-managerial control of the work force and the process of production began to restrict the production and accumulation of profit. (111) From the standpoint of differential branch technology,

> This challenge of coordination and control that led to the development of modern factory management initially appeared in those industries where high velocity of throughput required careful control to assure steady use of a plant's equipment and working force and where, at the same time, such effective coordination could not be assured by the careful designing of plants and works. In the mechanical industries, where continuous process machinery and plants permitted mass production, and in the refining and distilling

industries ... improved plant design and machinery were in most cases enough to synchronize the processes of production and to assure intensive use of equipment and personnel. But in the metal-making and metal-working factories, organization and management of men became more critical than plant design. (112)

Although this analysis refers to the rise of scientific management in the United States, it applies with some time-lag to prewar British industry. (113) Of prime interest in the present context is the fact that the first re-organizational schemes that represented a threat to so-called inside contractors attempted to blunt expected resistance by offering subcontractors and foremen disproportionally large shares of "the savings resulting from increased productivity." (114) It was not, however, until the advent of the more thoroughgoing plant management reforms associated with Frederick W. Taylor that the previously exalted position of the contractor/foreman was fundamentally undermined. Taylor accomplished this by "introducing two broad and sweeping changes in the art of management. ..." (115) On the one hand, foremen (as well as workers)

> should be entirely relieved of the work of planning, and of all work which is more or less clerical in nature. All possible brain work should be removed from the shop and centered in the planning or laying-out department, leaving for the foremen and gang bosses work strictly executive in its nature. (116)

On the other hand, the increased scale of production rendered the foreman incompetent to attend to all the functions that devolved upon him; consequently, the ensuing division of labor within foremanship created a demand for more, though less qualified and experienced, foremen. (117) Charles Booth observed this status as early as the late 1880s among the foremen in London, whom he assigned to the highest class of wage earners, characterizing them as "the non-commissioned officers of the industrial army":

> They have nothing to do with the planning or direction ... of business operations; their work is confined to superintendence. They supply no initiative, and having no responsibility of this kind they do not share in profits. ... (118)

Thus in the case of Britain, the supplanting of inside contractors by company foremen initially led to a more homogeneous manual working class by removing from it a section that had been of it but that had also actively participated in its exploitation. But whereas the subcontractor not only shared the working conditions of his subordinates but also stood in an antagonistic market relationship to the owners of capital, the foreman had become the latter's salaried agent. In this regard he stood in sharp contrast not only to the mass of the unskilled--whose proliferation coincided with his rise (119)--but even to the highest-paid skilled workers with whom Booth classified him: "... the foreman of ordinary labour generally sees things from the employer's point of view, while the skilled artisan sees them from the point of view of the employed." (120) It was not until a later period that the routinization of foremanship moved such employees "closer to workers." (121) During the period under review, however, the income, living conditions, security and social milieu of the foreman clearly set him apart from his erstwhile classmates. (122)

Paradoxically, then, the transformation of the semi-autonomous inside contractor into a formally dependent employee (123) rendered the British proletariat more compact by segregating out from it an element whose material interests were fundamentally at variance with those of the class as a whole.

e. Trade Union Membership

The growth of trade union membership, especially in industries and occupations previously little organized, exerted a powerful unifying influence on the British working class. For the United Kingdom as a whole, membership rose by 162.4 per cent--from 1,576,000 to 4,135,000--between 1892 and 1913. (124) Female membership quadrupled, accounting for one-ninth of total membership by 1913. (125) In 1891 approximately one-fifth to one-fourth of the male industrial proletariat was organized; by 1911 the degree of organization had risen to the range of three-tenths to one-third; by the outbreak of the war perhaps two of every five male manual industrial wage workers were trade unionists. (126) Though considerably lower, the degree of organization of the female industrial proletariat doubled from 1891 to 1911, rising from one-fourteenth to one-seventh; by 1914 almost one in five industrial working class women was a trade unionist. (127)

In some branches, such as mining, shipbuilding and cotton manufacture, the degree of organization exceeded the overall average; in others--metals, building and clothing for example-- a below-average share of workers was organized. (128) And although the skilled male workers of the building trades, engineering, coalmining, shipbuilding, metallurgy and cotton ccntinued to dominate numerically, notable advances were recorded by transport and general (unskilled) workers. (129) Outside the industrial working class, unionization spread to the "black-coated" proletariat, becoming well entrenched among postal employees, teachers and national government employees in general. (130)

f. Ethnic Composition

Relative ethnic and racial homogeneity had long characterized England: by 1911, 96.5 per cent of the population of England and Wales was returned as having been born there. (131) Whereas the share of those born in Scotland remained almost unchanged between 1861 and 1911, that of those born in Ireland declined steadily from 3.0 per cent to 1.0 per cent; in absolute terms the decrease amounted to more than 225,000 from a peak of slightly more than 600,000. (132) Toward the end of the nineteenth century England experienced an influx of population from outside the British Empire, in particular from Europe. Between 1881 and 1911 the number of foreigners born abroad and living in England increased by 141.4 per cent--from 117,999 to 284,830. (133) Although the share of such aliens doubled during these three decades, it remained less than one per cent. (134) Moreover, the bulk of these European immigrants lived in London, thus limiting their influence on the country as a whole. Ethnically, Russian Jews predominated, while occupationally aliens were concentrated in tailoring. (135) On balance, then, the movements of immigrants provided few impulses toward change in the class structure. (136)

g. Pauperism

The long-term reduction in the number of paupers during the latter part of the nineteenth century contributed to a coalescence of the working class, softening the distinction between the working and the non-working poor. This global conclusion, drawn from data in the aggregate, is subject to certain modifications of detail. In the first instance, both the mean annual number of paupers and the percentage of the total population receiving relief rose during the first decade of the twentieth century. (137) The total, for example, of more than 900,000 paupers recorded in 1909 and 1910 had not been reached for almost forty years. (138)

Although only two people in one hundred were receiving relief under the Poor Law on the eve of the war, (139) compared

to five or six people in one hundred fifty or sixty years
earlier, (140) such comparisons reveal nothing of the concentration and distribution of official poverty. Thus although
average daily pauperism in 1906-1907 amounted to slightly under
800,000 (141) or approximately one person in forty-seven in
England and Wales, the total number receiving relief at one
point or another during this time was more than twice as
great. (142) In other words, in addition to the two per cent
of the population that was permanently pauperized, a somewhat
greater proportion was compelled to have recourse to relief at
times of extraordinary distress. Such intermittent pauperism
was in large part brought on by the unemployment associated
with cyclical depressions and declining trades. (143) The differential effects of such unemployment on the protected and
unprotected sections of the working class will be taken up
later; here it suffices to point to the socio-economic proximity
of a large pool of potential paupers to the hard core of permanent paupers. (144)

In another important respect, however, the working and the
non-working poor were becoming increasingly segregated from
each other: the share of able-bodied adults among total paupers
was declining whereas that of the insane and idiots on the one
hand and of aged and infirm adults on the other was rising. (145) Moreover, by 1906 paupers between the ages of
sixteen and sixty represented only one per cent of all persons
in this age group whereas paupers above the age of sixty accounted for almost sixteen per cent of those over sixty years
old. (146)

The results of this survey of the pauperized section of the
population during the late-Victorian and Edwardian periods
are not unambiguous. It seems plausible that the long-term
decline in the number of permanent paupers helped consolidate
the working class as an active and productive force; the incorporation of a large periphery of casually and/or periodically
poor into the relief system probably exerted a counteracting
influence. The upshot of these developments may not have
altered the relations between the working and non-working
poor at all but rather have insulated and isolated the remaining, relatively protected, sections of the working class from
these more vulnerable ones. Furthermore, the fact that the
latter were thrown back on the resources of the state in the
form of Poor Law relief, old age pensions, etc., while the
former continued to rely on their traditional institutions of
self-help (trade unions and friendly societies), drove a wedge
between them politically.

128

2. The Skill Structure

> Labourer is a good word in itself, but it has to be discarded
> because it has acquired a special and limited sense, in which
> it is contrasted with artisan; while the latter word evidently
> excludes the unskilled labourer. ... (147)
> ... The curious store of illiterate scientific knowledge
> possessed by the puddler ... who has acquired his know-
> ledge by his own unaided application of the Baconian method
> of inductive research. He has observed, experimented,
> generalised, and deductively applied the principles thus
> induced, and all without ever having heard of any other
> Bacon than which is salted, and without being able to ex-
> pound his knowledge in any other form than practical
> lumps of malleable iron. (148)

Despite the central role that has been ascribed to skill as a
force for structuring the manual working class, (149) this
criterion is much less accessible to quantification than those
discussed above. In the absence of any aggregate data (150)
it is necessary to form an impression concerning the trend of
skill distribution by means of an examination of technological
changes in prominent branches and occupations. Shifts in skill
distribution based on such changes together with disaggregated
employment trends should provide a reliable account of the
overall development.

Two definitional caveats are in order at this stage. First,
from the fact that the census of 1911 recorded 295,343 male
general laborers compared to 594,128 returned in 1891, (151)
it does not follow that a relative or absolute diminution in the
number of unskilled occurred; rather, the decline "simply
denotes ... improvement in the returns and does not imply
any change in the numbers. ..." (152) Second, the custom of
referring to all those carrying on a skilled trade as skilled (153)
is a statistical pitfall; for although it is valid and useful when
comparing, for example, carpenters and carpenters' laborers,
it proves to be misleading when applied to occupations caught
up in technological upheaval. It should also be borne in mind
that, at least during the "first generation," such de-skilled
occupations were often filled by the formerly fully-skilled and
did not represent the kind of semi-skilled positions that contemporary observers were wont to single out as offering an
important sphere of upward mobility for the unskilled. (154)

Table 15 serves as a first approximation to a quantitative
estimate of the trend in the number of skilled manual workers.
In it are shown employment data relating to the most significant
skilled occupations; that is, the great majority of the skilled

were located in these trades which, in turn, employed proportionally more skilled than other trades or industries. These data in themselves, however, do not indicate the actual number or percentage of skilled at the outset or close of the period.

Table 15. Male Employees in the major skilled Occupations (155) in England and Wales, 1891 and 1911 (156)

	1891	1911
Building Trades		
Bricklayer	117,673	93,312
Carpenter/joiner	182,409	176,978
Mason	72,206	43,764
Painter/decorator	99,199	150,174
Paperhanger/whitewasher/plasterer	23,733	25,985
Plumber	35,544	52,139
Slater/tiler	5,253	6,946
Metal/Engineering Trades		
Blacksmith/striker	113,030	105,759
Boilermaker	34,742	47,878
Cutler	15,418	12,504
Erector/fitter/turner	83,370	151,298
Iron/steel manufacture (157)	190,067	214,715
Machinist (158)	69,485	160,170
Millwright	5,280	5,138
Railway engine driver/stoker/cleaner	40,008	69,683
Shipwright (159)	63,796	84,249
Toolmaker	10,592	23,827
Wheelwright	19,589	17,325

Table 15 (continued)

Traditional Trades	1891	1911
Brush/broommaker	7,643	8,438
Cabinetmaker/upholsterer (160)	57,591 (161)	68,553
Coach/carriagemaker (162)	32,638	57,472
Cooper	14,522	12,539
Currier	18,241	14,176
Glassmaker (163)	21,975	27,187
Goldsmith/silversmith/jeweler	14,960	16,733
Hatter (164)	13,958	12,091
Lithographer	7,486	11,692
Pianomaker (165)	9,039	12,717
Printer	73,288	107,052
Saddler	17,058	14,415
Tailor	83,117 (166)	92,344
Watchmaker	12,189	8,544
Woodcarver/gilder	8,233	7,844

An analysis of the data presented in Table 15 is facilitated by the overview shown in Table 16.

Table 16. Male Employees in the major skilled Occupations in England and Wales, 1891 and 1911: Summary (167)

Trade	Number	%	Number	%	Change in %
Building	536,017	34.1	549,298	28.7	2.5
Metal/engineering	645,377	41.0	892,546	46.6	38.3
Traditional	391,938	24.9	471,797	24.7	20.4
Total	1,573,332	100.0	1,913,641	100.0	21.6

The number of men employed in skilled trades rose substantially --by 340,000 or more than one-fifth. But as a share of the male industrial proletariat (168) this stratum declined slightly--from

30.5 per cent in 1891 to 28.5 per cent in 1911. The shifts among the three great categories of skilled trades are instructive. The metal and engineering trades, which were basically products of nineteenth-cenutry industrialization, grew much more rapidly than the building and traditional skilled trades, both of which originated in pre-capitalist and pre-industrial conditions. Although the stagnation in the building trades is manifest, the moderate growth in the traditional trades is largely definitional: if the cutlers, millwrights and wheelwrights, who were traditional artisans who happened to work in metal, are shifted to the traditional trades, and the coachmakers to the metal trades, (169) then the growth rate in the traditional trades drops to 12.4 per cent whereas that in the metal and engineering trades rises to 43.5 per cent. According to such a classification, almost every other tradesman was employed in the metal or engineering trades in 1911 compared to two of every five in 1891. (170)

The slight decline in the skilled as a share of the industrial proletariat, alluded to above, is inconclusive because the proportion of skilled in the so-called skilled trades has not yet been ascertained. The following observations will help fill this gap. Although the introduction of a separate rubric for laborers in numerous branches at the census of 1901 and 1911 is reflected in their exclusion from the figures for 1911 in Table 15 and Table 16, (171) their inclusion in the employment figures for 1891 necessarily inflates the latter. It is, unfortunately, impossible to quantifiy the overstatement of the skilled since many of the laborers were not classified under their trades but as "general laborers," a category which became progressively depleted in 1901 and 1911 as separate rubrics were inserted.

Building trades: Scattered data collected over several decades indicate that, even apart from the issue of the extent of the reduction of skill levels within skilled occupations, the latter were progressively supplanted by unskilled labor. Whereas a wage survey of eight cities conducted in 1877 had revealed that one-quarter of building workers were laborers, (172) by the 1920s it was estimated that one-half of the labor force in building was unskilled. (173) Within the skilled occupations, "steel frames and concrete and machine-made joinery were disturbing the old technical framework," (174) a development that had found expression in a decline in apprenticeship on the one hand and increased recruitment from the ranks of the "attached" (175) laborers on the other. (176) Moreover, the trade which registered the largest advance, painting, was commonly acknowledged to have been staffed by large numbers of little accomplished "brush-hands" (177) so that one specialist characterized the painters as a whole as semi-skilled. (178)

On balance, then, building experienced such a pervasive pattern of de-skilling that the statistically recorded stagnation in the number of skilled ought to be regarded as masking a significant real decline.

Traditional Trades: The task of discovering the contribution of these trades to the overall industrial skill pattern is simplified by the fact that only one-third (179) of them registered a significant increase in numbers (the numbers in parentheses represent the increase to the nearest thousand): cabinetmaking (11); glassmaking (5); lithography (4); pianomaking (4); printing (34); and tailoring (9). Since printing accounted for half of this aggregate increase, it will be reviewed first.

With the diffusion of the linotype machine from the 1880s onward, the apprenticeship system came increasingly to be circumvented as a training process so that large numbers of boys and females gained access to the trade. (180) Thus from 1891 to 1911 the number of female printing employees rose more than fivefold--from 4,133 to 21,834; if in 1891 one female printer was returned for every eighteen males, by 1911 this ratio had been reduced to one to five. The association between de-skilling and the influx of women is underscored by two further facts: 1. whereas more than half of all female printers in 1911 were under twenty years old, fewer than one-quarter of the males belonged to this age-group; and 2. almost all the females were concentrated in the group, "others in printing," whereas the more highly skilled compositors remained an almost exclusively male domain. (181) In the related trade of lithography, the relative growth of female employees was greater still, the ratio of men to women having fallen from twenty-four to one in 1891 to five to one in 1911. (182)

Just as the growth in employment in printing was largely a product of the increased demand for newspapers and books spawned by the extension of public education to the working class, (183) so too expansion of the clothing industry was due to increased demand by the working and middle classes for factory-made, mass-produced clothing attendant upon the introduction of the sewing machine and the subdivision of labor. (184) In tailoring, too, the more rapid growth of female labor may be taken as an index of the reduction in the required level of skill. Thus the share of women among employed tailors rose from forty-eight per cent in 1891 to fifty-five per cent in 1911. (185) And although a large core of highly skilled English journeymen continued as a vital force in the bespoke trade, it was subject to erosion not only at the hands of less skilled females but also of the chiefly Jewish sweated shops. (186)

A somewhat different situation evolved in cabinetmaking, which changes in census classifications render difficult to capture statistically. (187) Although the trade remained virtually all male, in the absence of systematic apprenticeship "excessive specialization of skill" manifested itself "not in the making of parts, but in the making of or working on one, or a very few, out of a large variety of articles, to any of which an all-round man would be able with equal ease to turn his hand." (188)

The glass trades, which were not revolutionized by new technologies until after World War I, (189) not only remained highly skilled but were able, through the agency of the unions of the Flint Glass Makers and Glass Bottle Makers, to maintain rather rigorous apprenticeship rules. The Webbs attributed this extraordinary power to restrict entry to the fact that "the work is carried on, not by individual craftsmen, but by associated groups of highly skilled wage-earners. ...." (190) By its very nature, however, such a "policy" was ill-designed to contribute to the growth of the skilled sector since "limiting the numbers has been so effectively carried out that capitalists who, when trade is brisk and profits large, might desire to set up new works in competition with the old establishments, are actually stopped by the difficulty of obtaining an adequate supply of skilled workmen." (191) In point of fact, the increase in employment recorded by the entire glass industry lagged behind that of the male industrial proletariat as a whole.

Finally, the small absolute gain among the pianomakers did not exert any notable influence on the aggregate balance between the skilled and the unskilled.

In light of the improbability that the "skilled" trades experiencing absolute declines in numbers witnessed a rise in the share of the skilled within them--let alone one large enough to compensate for a fall in total employment--, it appears likely that the number of skilled employees in the traditional skilled trades declined during this period. If this claim seems to contradict the relatively high rates of apprenticeship registered by the census in 1911, (192) it must be borne in mind that the distinction between apprentices and boys used for their "immediate commercial utility" was in the process of being obliterated. (193) Apprenticeship was, in other words, no longer an unambiguous index of skill. But even in those trades in which apprentices were not disguised boy laborers, the former were, owing to their increasingly specialized training, "supported above the abyss of unskilled labour by the fragile bridge of a single aptitude. A new invention, a reorganisation of the industry, a change in the demand for commodities, may render their peculiar skill useless and precipitate them into the gulf." (194)

Metal and Engineering Trades: Within these trades, growth rates vary widely even when the traditional trades among them are excluded. Table 17 recombines the remaining eight trades under four industrial rubrics.

Table 17. Male Employees in the major skilled Occupations of the Metal and Engineering Trades in England and Wales, 1891 and 1911: according to Industry (195)

Industry	Occupation	1891	1911	Change (in %)
Engineering	Erector, etc.			
	Machinist			
	Toolmaker	163,447	335,295	105.1
Shipbuilding	Boilermaker			
	Shipwright	98,538	132,127	34.1
Railways	Coachmaker			
	Engine driver	72,646	127,155	75.0
Iron/steel		190,067	214,715	13.0
Total		524,698	809,292	54.2

The dominant contribution made by the engineering trades is conspicuous: by more than doubling, the machinists and allied tradesmen accounted for three-fifths of the growth in the relevant metal and engineering trades and one-half of the entire increase in all skilled occupations.

Although the two trades grouped under "railways" exhibited a very high rate of growth, the skilled component is difficult to isolate. Among the coachmakers, the more highly skilled artisans engaged in the production of luxury coaches declined, whereas the more heavily mechanized construction of railway carriages employed increasing numbers of workers. (196) Since the unskilled railway engine stokers and cleaners were returned together with the engine drivers, the differential movements of skilled and unskilled workers cannot be determined. Yet the relative ease with which the drivers themselves could be replaced casts some doubt on their classification as skilled employees at all. (197)

Although employment growth in shipbuilding was only moderate, the processes of mechanization and subdivision of labor, which decimated the ranks of the skilled in many other trades, did little to undermine the latter's position in this industry. The extraordinary maintenance of a stringent apprenticeship system (198) and the steady growth of the Boiler Makers and Iron and Steel Shipbuilding Society toward the status of exclusive and comprehensive organization of the skilled (199) may indicate that the skill level of the skilled remained intact. (200) On the other hand, the increasingly bitter conflicts between the skilled and the unskilled of this industry, precipitated by the former's exclusion of and contempt for the latter, (201) may point to fears harbored by the skilled that technological development was bringing about a situation in which their tasks could be performed by those with less or little formal training. (202) It therefore seems pluasible to conclude that some (indeterminate) growth in the number of skilled shipbuilders occurred between 1891 and 1911.

Total growth in employment in the manufacture of iron and steel was quite limited. The labor-saving consequences of capital-intensive innovations, particularly in steel production, did not manifest themselves as a result of the compensating effects of enlarged output. (203) Technological change did, however, alter the skill structure of the work force much more rapidly in foundries and smelteries. (204) The iron and steel industry offers a case not of the further polarization of skills but rather of the homogenization of the work force by means of the compression of the skill structure at both ends toward a middle ground of the semi-skilled. (205) Given the small increase in aggregate employment in this industry, it seems reasonable to assume that the number of skilled declined. (206)

Finally, the enormous increase in the number of fitters, turners, erectors and allied tradesmen must be examined. The period extending from 1890 to World War I witnessed a minor revolution in the engineering workshop in the form of the introduction of the capstan, turret lathe, milling machine, grinder, vertical borer and radial drill. (207) Many of these capital-using technologies not only reduced the demand for skilled labor in general by substituting semi-skilled and unskilled labor for it, (208) but also narrowed the skill requirements of numerous skilled positions. (209) During the prewar years, however, this process had not yet undermined the position of the skilled craftsman. (210) The increasing stress, for example, placed on the tolerances, complexity and intricacy of engineering products meant that skilled fitters and erectors continued to be in great demand. (211) Empirical confirmation of the high skill-content involved in machine-making was provided by the measures taken during the war to replace the skilled manpower lost to military recruitment. Although it had long been the vogue in British business circles to lay the blame for industrial retardation and lagging competitiveness on the restrictive practices of trade unions, (212) when the opportunity finally presented itself to effect "dilution" of skilled labor, it did not suffice

> to say to labour, "Abandon your practices." Means had to be found by which persons admitted to the work could perform it. A skilled man carrying out a job of work in the engineering trade carried out a fairly considerable number of processes. Each process might be in itself comparatively simple, but the interrelation and correlation of them all involved a high degree of skill. It was useless for the skilled man to agree that an unskilled man should take his job--because he could not. What was necessary was that it should be divided into its component parts, and that foolproof machines should be introduced, each capable of turning out a particular part and such as could be attended by semi-skilled or unskilled machine minders. (213)

Despite the significant advances registered by the semi-skilled and unskilled, the doubling of engineering employment permitted considerable increments within the ranks of the skilled. (214) Although this increase in the number of skilled engineers may have sufficed to offset decreases elsewhere in the metal and engineering trades, they were not great enough to yield an aggregate absolute increase for all the skilled trades. Indeed, the foregoing discussion points in the direction of a not insignificant decline in the absolute number of skilled employees. Given the enlargement of the industrial proletariat during this period, the relative decline of the skilled must have been greater still.

The relative diminution in the number of skilled did not automatically generate an equivalent increase in the share of the unskilled; for it was precisely during this period that semi-skilled workers began appearing in large numbers, (215) that is, industrial workers whose machine-based skills were acquired through on-the-job experience rather than through formal training and apprenticeship. They first appeared in cotton weaving, which was in turn the first great industry not characterized by craft dominance or subcontracting; in other words, sharply differentiated, caste-like divisions between the skilled and the unskilled were absent in this industry. (216) Although not machine-based in the manner of the textile industry, the railways and the coal mines, both spheres of rapidly growing employment, also represented industries in which the traditional rigid demarcations between skilled and unskilled were absent. (217)

What was new about the semi-skilled who became prominent from the 1890s onward was that they worked in industries that had been marked by the strict and virtually permanent separation of the skilled from the unskilled upon entry. During these years "semi-skilled" came to imply a position that called for skills only in parts of a trade in contradistinction to the all-round training required in skilled positions. (218) This evolution of a skill continuum through the creation of a broad sector of semi-skilled workers originated in the engineering trades and gradually spread to those branches which consumed engineering products. (219) The expansion of the semi-skilled at the expense of the extremes of the skill continuum was not only commented upon by contemporaries, (220) but was subsequently incorporated as a historical phase into a typology of industrial skill stratification. (221) Although this schema has been advanced as evidence in refutation of Marx's theses concerning the tendency toward a more uniform distribution of skills throughout the working class, (222) the developments that it reflected initiated a growing homogeneity of the skill structure. (223) Another component of this criticism has, to be sure, been directed at Marx's expectation that the new distribution of skills would be situated at a low and lower level as capital accumulated. One method of judging these conflicting claims consists in determining whether the movement from skilled to semi-skilled positions exceeded that from unskilled to semi-skilled ones. (224)

The preceding discussion has already disclosed that, in the aggregate, the number of skilled industrial workers declined. The fact that the semi-skilled became an object of social observation during this period is prima facie evidence that their numbers rose--a conclusion that is strongly supported by the growth of industries employing them on a large scale, such as mining, cotton and railways. The expanded application of machinery and ever deepening subdivision of labor within branches formerly staffed largely by artisans provided another source of growth of the semi-skilled even where total employment was falling off. (225)

The situation among the unskilled is not quite so transparent. The absolute decline in the number of working children and the below-average increase in the number of female industrial employees indicates that two important components of unskilled labor were losing ground. (226) The continued excessing of significant proportions of the agricultural laboring populations, on the other hand, provided a substantial source of unskilled industrial labor. The decline in the share of male agricultural laborers below the age of thirty-five from 41.5 per cent of all male agricultural laborers in 1891 to 35.1 per cent in 1911 meant that approximately 70,000 prime-age males became available to replenish the ranks of the unskilled in industrial pursuits. (227) Strong growth characterized employment in five major unskilled occupations outside manufacturing: the number of messengers, dock laborers, carmen, coalheavers and gas workers rose from 423,498 in 1891 to 661,622 in 1911-- a gain of 56.2 per cent. (228) Given the rise of industries such as chemicals, which were based largely on unskilled labor, (229) the spread of the sweating system, which was likewise a large- scale employer of unskilled labor, (230) and the general advance of mechanization and the division of labor, it appears that the unskilled sector must have enlarged its share of the labor market. (231)

To recapitulate: 1. the skilled declined absolutely and relatively; 2. the semi-skilled grew most rapidly in absolute and relative terms; and 3. the unskilled probably increased absolutely and almost certainly came to account for a larger share of the working class. (232) Given the dearth of empirical studies relating to inter-generational occupational mobility and recruitment prior to World War I, (233) it is difficult to make substantive statements without running the risk of falling victim to ecological fallacies. In the context of an overall growth in the industrial proletariat, inter-generational occupa- tional shifts probably played a greater part than did the mobil- ity experienced by given individuals. Specifically, it seems unlikely that large numbers of workers either left the ranks of the skilled (except to retire) or joined them from "below". (234) As access to apprenticeship shrank, skilled workers were con- fronted with the necessity of placing their children in less skilled (in most instances probably semi-skilled) jobs. (235) Thus inter-generational recruitment to semi-skilled occupations represented downward as well as upward mobility.

Although these trends appear to point to a more uniform distribution of occupational skills, the underlying homogeniza- tion of the industrial proletariat need not, at least in the short- term, have manifested itself in a heightened subjective unity of purpose. (236) For with the rise of the semi-skilled and the increasing penetrability of what was formerly a wall nearly impervious to incursions from the less skilled, the growing competition between the skilled and the semi-skilled in the economic sphere may have rendered cooperation in political con- flicts with employers and the state apparatus tenuous. (237) Ironically, then, the sharper cleavage or quasi-bifurcation that had once characterized the English working class may have permitted the skilled to view political solidarity with the unskilled as an act fraught with few personal risks or disadvantages since direct economic competition was virtually absent. But once this largely moral motivation gave way to a more complex political-economic calculus, once common interests became intertwined with areas of potential or actual conflicting interests and, finally, once a tutelary and/or patronizing relationship was transformed into once of segmented rivalries, then the progressive compression of the occupational skill hierarchy may, by having brought the extremes into closer contact, have released new tensions. Not until the working class gained sufficient experience with the consequences of this socio-economic propinquity to create organizational means of coping with them, would the enlarged objective basis of commonalities be perceived as such. That there was nothing inherently automatic about this coincidence of being and the consciousness thereof, was amply demonstrated by the period under review, which in many respects was one of convulsive transition. (238)

3. Income and Working and Living Conditions

Two central issues are raised in this section: 1. Did the gap between those sectors of the working class enjoying a higher material standard of living and better working conditions and those located on significantly lower levels of economic well-being widen, narrow or remain stable? and 2. Is it necessary to relativize the traditional image of the former group? That is to say, were systematic elements of socio-economic insecurity and subordination, characteristic of wage-labor in general, prevalent or dominant enough to set this group apart from the strata/classes "above" it?

A resolution of these questions forms a necessary though scarcely sufficient prerequisite to a resolution of the issue of whether such material differentiation represented a factor fissuring the working class. Although sectional political attitudes and actions were not motivated solely by such narrowly economic relations as wages and hours, the former are incomprehensible without a thorough cataloging of the latter. (239)

a. Income

Although data on wage rates, usually in the sense of minima established by agreements, are abundantly available for many industries and occupations, little information was collected on a uniform national basis relating to wages actually received.

The two returns that provide the most detailed information
--those of 1886 and 1906--were compiled for one specific week;
the annual wage figures constructed on the assumption that
such wages were earned every week for a year (240) are fictitious since they abstract from unemployment and other causes
of lost wages. (241) Nevertheless, the depth and comprehen-
siveness of the two inquiries permit considerable insight into
the structure of working class incomes. (242)

The report of 1886 covered somewhat more than 350,000
adult male manual workers (243) compared to the more than
1,900,000 covered by the report of 1906. (244) Since compliance
by employers was voluntary, "the returns were not proportional
to the numbers employed in the industries as wholes"; (245)
agricultural workers were excluded from both reports, (246)
building tradesmen were omitted in 1886 (247) and miners were
excluded in 1906. Apart from discrepancies in industrial classification between the two surveys, the latter also differed inasmuch as the first survey was restricted to wages earned in full
or normal workweeks, whereas the second survey collected data
on such workweeks as well as on those containing overtime and
short-time. (248) In direct comparisons of the two surveys,
only data on full-time workers in 1906 will be used.

Table 18 focuses on the extremes of the wage hierarchy in
1886 and 1906. (249)

**Table 18. Distribution of weekly Earnings among full-time adult
Males in the United Kingdom, 1886 and 1906 (250)**

	1886		1906	
	Number	%	Number	%
Total	355,838	100.0	1,296,606	100.0
Under 20 shillings	85,342	24.0	177,719	13.7
40 shillings +	8,712	2.4	174,055	13.4

The lowest and highest wage groups, together, accounted for
somewhat more than one-quarter of all men in both years. Yet,
whereas those earning under twenty shillings were ten times
as numerous as those earning forty shillings or more in 1886,
by 1906 the two groups were of approximately equal size. This
relative shift from the lower to the higher wage groups, (251)
which was not merely a monetary phenomenon, (252) is analyzed
in greater detail in Table 19.

As Bowley, the contemporary economic statistician, observed:

Thus there was a shifting all up the scale, but the highest
tenth gained most, 33 per cent., and successive sections

141

Table 19. Structure of weekly Earnings among full-time adult Males in the United Kingdom, 1886 and 1906 (253)

	1886 s. d.		% of median	1906 s. d.		% of median	Change in earnings, 1886-1906 in %
Lowest decile	16	7	68.6	19	6	66.5	18
Lower quartile	20	0	82.8	23	4	79.5	16
Median	24	2	100.0	29	4	100.0	21
Upper quartile	29	5	121.7	37	2	126.7	26
Highest decile	34	7	143.1	46	0	156.8	33
Mode	22	8		23	10		
Average	24	11		30	6		22

below less, till the lower quartile advanced only 16 per cent. The general shape of the distribution, however, hardly changed; in both years the lower quartile is about four-fifths and the upper quartile about five-fourths of the median, and the lowest decile is about two-thirds and the highest decile about three-halves of the median. The mode, however, dominated by the wage of the ordinary unskilled labourer, has dropped from near the average to near the lower quartile. (254)

Although no radical changes can be detected, it is nevertheless clear that the higher income groups garnered the lion's share of the total increase in wage income. The downward deviation of the modal income of the unskilled from the median/mean income and the concomitant shift of the semi-skilled into the median income position (255) underline the growing numerical importance of the latter in spite of the continued preponderance of the former. Both the widening of the gap between the wages of the unskilled and the skilled as well as the relative displacement in numbers, (256) may, however, have been exaggerated by the sampling procedures employed in the smaller survey of 1886. (257)

To the extent that the disparity between the wages of men and women reflected that between the wages of the skilled and the unskilled, the twenty years that elapsed between the two surveys did not effect any substantial realignment: across all trades women continued to receive weekly wages only marginally in excess of one-half of men's earnings. (258)

Further evidence in support of the notion of a relatively stable distribution (259) of the working class population at the polar extremes of the income scale is provided by a number of poverty studies conducted in several British localities. (260) The comprehensive social survey of London, directed by Charles Booth in the latter half of the 1880s, disclosed that 38.9 per cent of the working class population were "poor" or "very poor" or belonged to the "lowest class--occasional labourers, loafers and semi-criminals." (261) Similarly, his detail study of East London revealed that 40.7 per cent of the population in families headed by male industrial proletarians could be so classified compared to the 10.2 per cent classified as belonging to families of males of "higher class labour" and of "the best paid of the artisans." (262) A further study by Booth in 1893, restricted to adult males in regular employment--a condition which Booth himself recognized as having distorted the distribution toward the better-paid--indicated that seventeen per cent of the 75,000 Londoners sampled received weekly wages in excess of forty shillings. (263) Moreover, the relationship of the highest and lowest deciles and of the upper and lower quartiles to the median was almost identical with that established by the national wage survey in 1886. (264)

A study of York--a city of fewer than 100,000 inhabitants-- at the turn of the century ascertained that approximately forty-three per cent of wage earners and their families lived in poverty. (265) Both this study and one conducted a decade later in Reading and three other towns (266) underscored the stable share of the most impoverished sector of the working class by situating one-sixth of the latter in "primary" poverty. (267)

A study conducted in urban districts throughout the United Kingdom in 1904 captured an important dimension of the extent to which wage differentials among various strata of the working class expressed themselves in distinct levels of real consumption. Table 20 summarizes the results.

In spite of the fact that families with weekly incomes in excess of forty shillings were larger than all other families, their per capita income was almost twice as great as that of families earning less than twenty-five shillings per week (about eight shillings and four shillings respectively). Although the most prosperous working class families outspent the lowest-income families in every category of food expenditures, they managed to devote ten per cent less of their aggregate incomes to food than the poorest families. In real per capita terms, the gap between the consumption of the two extreme groups

Table 20. Average weekly Cost and Quantity of certain Articles of Food consumed by urban Workmen's Families in the United Kingdom, 1904 (268)

Limits of weekly income	Under 25s.		25s.- 30s.		30s.- 35s.		35s.- 40s.		40s.+	
Average weekly family income	21	$4\frac{1}{2}$	26	$11\frac{3}{4}$	31	11	36	$6\frac{1}{4}$	52	$0\frac{1}{2}$
Average no. of children at home	3.1		3.3		3.2		3.4		4.4	
Cost										
Bread/flour	3	0	3	$3\frac{3}{4}$	3	$3\frac{1}{2}$	3	$4\frac{1}{4}$	4	$3\frac{3}{4}$
Meat	2	8	3	$4\frac{3}{4}$	4	$3\frac{1}{2}$	4	$5\frac{1}{2}$	5	$10\frac{1}{2}$
Bacon	0	$6\frac{3}{4}$	0	9	0	$10\frac{1}{2}$	0	$11\frac{1}{2}$	1	$3\frac{3}{4}$
Eggs	0	$5\frac{3}{4}$	0	$8\frac{1}{2}$	0	11	1	0	1	$4\frac{3}{4}$
Fresh milk	0	8	0	$11\frac{3}{4}$	1	$3\frac{1}{4}$	1	$4\frac{1}{4}$	1	$7\frac{3}{4}$
Cheese	0	$4\frac{3}{4}$	0	$5\frac{1}{2}$	0	6	0	6	0	8
Butter	1	2	1	7	1	$10\frac{1}{4}$	2	0	3	$0\frac{1}{2}$
Potatoes	0	$8\frac{3}{4}$	0	$9\frac{3}{4}$	0	$10\frac{1}{2}$	0	$10\frac{1}{4}$	1	$1\frac{3}{4}$
Vegetables/fruit	0	$4\frac{3}{4}$	0	7	0	10	0	$11\frac{3}{4}$	1	$3\frac{3}{4}$
Tea/coffee/cocoa	0	$11\frac{1}{4}$	1	$2\frac{1}{2}$	1	$4\frac{1}{4}$	1	$5\frac{1}{2}$	1	$10\frac{1}{2}$
Sugar	0	8	0	10	0	$10\frac{3}{4}$	0	$11\frac{1}{4}$	1	3
Other items	2	$8\frac{1}{4}$	3	$2\frac{3}{4}$	3	10	4	$5\frac{1}{4}$	5	10
Total food expenditures	14	$4\frac{3}{4}$	17	$10\frac{1}{4}$	20	$9\frac{1}{4}$	22	$3\frac{1}{2}$	29	8

Table 20 (continued)

	Under 25s.	25s.- 30s.	30s.- 35s.	35s.- 40s.	40s.+
Per cent of family income spent on food	67	66	65	61	57
	Quantities (in lb.) (269)				
Bread/flour	28.44	29.97	29.44	29.99	37.76
Meat	4.44	5.33	6.26	6.43	8.19
Bacon	0.94	1.11	1.19	1.38	1.82
Fresh milk	5.54	7.72	9.85	10.34	12.63
Cheese	0.67	0.70	0.79	0.77	1.02
Butter	1.10	1.50	1.69	1.89	2.78
Potatoes	14.05	15.84	16.11	15.87	19.83
Tea/coffee/cocoa	0.63	0.73	0.77	0.82	1.01
Sugar	3.87	4.62	4.79	5.21	6.70

of working class families ranged from almost one hundred per cent in milk to five per cent in bread and flour.

Despite the considerable differences in consumption between these two extreme groups, the consumption patterns of even the "wealthiest" working class households were characterized by reliance on the familiar staples of bread, potatoes, butter, sugar and tea. (270) Daily per capita meat consumption in families earning more than forty shillings weekly averaged a mere three ounces (compared to two ounces in families with weekly incomes below twenty-five shillings). (271) On the assumption that adults drank no milk, children in the most "affluent" working class families consumed a half-pint daily (compared to three-tenths of a pint for children of the poorest families). (272) These quantitative comparisons serve as a three-fold reminder of: 1. the low levels of consumption of the entire British working class; 2. the relatively favorable position of those workers who received above-average wages; and 3. the large gap that separated the latter stratum of workers from the middle and upper classes in terms of income and consumption. (273)

This last point is underscored by a study of prewar income tax returns and surveys of salaried employees. Table 21 portrays the hierarchy of annual earnings for various "occupational classes" on the eve of the war.

Table 21. Average annual Earnings of Males, by occupational Class, in the United Kingdom, 1913/14 (274)

Occupational class	Ł	As a percentage of the Earnings of the Unskilled
Higher professionals	328	521
Managers	200	317
Lower professionals	155	246
Foremen	113	179
Clerks	99	157
Skilled manual workers	99	157
Semi-skilled manual workers	69	110
Unskilled manual workers	63	100

According to these annual averages, which do not take into account income losses resulting from unemployment, sickness or accidents, skilled men (275) were situated closer to clerks and foremen in terms of income than to semi-skilled and unskilled workers. Although deductions for typical working class income losses would doubtless have segregated the skilled somewhat from foremen and clerks, who were less likely to suffer spells of unemployment, the fact that the less skilled experienced even more unemployment than the skilled (276) may have served to differentiate the manual working class even further. There is, however, reason to believe that such losses prevented artisans with weekly earnings equal to or slightly in excess of those of clerks from maintaining a standard of living equivalent to the latter's. (277)

If attention is focused on losses owing to unemployment, (278) then the stratum of skilled males must be viewed in a more differentiated manner; for unemployment did not affect these workers uniformly: on the contrary, it tended to be concentrated within relatively small minorities. Thus, for example, approximately one-fifth of the membership of the London Society of Compositors drew unemployment benefits each year from 1894 to 1907; from 1904 to 1907, 8.6 per cent of the membership, that is, about two-fifths of the members receiving benefits, drew benefits each year and accounted for more than fifty-six per cent of aggregate unemployment benefits received. (279) Although the percentage of trade unionists experiencing unemployment at some point during a year was five to ten times greater than the annual mean, even in depressed years, fifty to sixty per cent of the membership were able to "escape unemployment altogether." (280)

On the assumption that the higher-paid men within each trade largely coincided with the group subject to relatively little unemployment, (281) tens of thousands of skilled workers received annual wages in excess of the annual salaries of tens of thousands of clerical employees (282) and of a considerable section of foremen. (283) There existed, in other words, a societally significant area of overlap between the upper reaches of the stratum of skilled manual workers (especially insofar as they were trade unionists) on the one hand and the lower and middle groups of clerks and the worst-paid foremen on the other. It is just as patent, however, that the chasm between skilled workers and professional or managerial employees was both greater than that which separated the skilled from the unskilled and unbridgeable. (284)

In the absence of representative national data relative to the incomes of employers and the self-employed, (285) similar comparisons with those of artisans are precluded. It seems reasonable to assume, however, that the picture drawn of East London by Booth bore a tolerable measure of resemblance to "class relations" (286) elsewhere in Britain.

Table 22. Percentage of selected Groups of occupied Males belonging to the highest Income Groups in East London, 1886/87 (287)

Occupation	Higher comfortable	Well-to-do (288)
Laborer	0.1	0.0
Police, soldier, etc.	6.9	0.0
Artisan	10.4	0.0
Shop assistant	11.8	0.0
Railway servant	37.6	0.0
Foreman	98.0	0.0
Home industry (non-employer)	17.1	0.3
Dealer (small shop)	31.6	6.5
Salaried clerk/agent	40.1	21.8

Table 22 (continued)

	Higher comfortable	Well-to-do (288)
Subordinate professional	38.1	23.2
Small manufacturing employer	55.0	29.2
Dealer (large shop--employing assistants)	30.5	67.6
Professional	8.1	91.9
Large manufacturing employer	0.0	100.0

A tenth of the male artisans (289) and three-eights of railway servants were classified as performing highly paid work as were one-ninth of the shop assistants and one of every four-teen or fifteen policemen and soldiers; one-sixth of home-workers but virtually all foremen were so ranked; two-fifths of the clerks fell into the same group but a further fifth was "well-to-do"; one-third of small shopkeepers and more than one-half of small manufacturing employers were very "comfort-able," but another three-tenths and one-sixteenth respectively were "well-to-do."

These figures tend to confirm the national data: some overlap existed between the best-paid skilled tradesmen on the one hand and foremen, lower white collar employees and small employers on the other. (290) As in the case of the foremen, however, relatively few skilled workers received incomes as large as those of their immediate employers.

A comparison of the income tax returns of the 451,000 em-ployees who earned more than Ł 160 in 1911-1912, and were thus subject to income taxation, with various data relating to the more than 16,000,000 employees below this limit offers another perspective from which to situate skilled workers' wages within the hierarchy of "earned" incomes. Among all adult male manual workers sampled in 1906, 14.2 per cent earned forty shillings or more per week; (291) if this share is applied to the average of the size of the male industrial proletariat for 1901 and 1911 (Table 9), approximately 900,000 men of this class may be reckoned as having earned at least two pounds weekly during the middle of the first decade of the twentieth century. (292)

Earnings of two pounds weekly would have resulted in an annual income of Ł 104 if no losses of income had been in-curred. If, however, it is considered that workers generally spent the equivalent of two weeks on unpaid holidays (293) and trade unionists were, on the average, unemployed three per cent of the time in 1911-1912, (294) then almost seven per cent would have to be deducted from the hypothetical annual income. Although trade unionists earning in excess of forty shillings weekly could expect to recover one-quarter of wages lost to unemployment of short duration in the form of benefits, (295) additional losses were to be expected in the form of illness and accidents. Thus in an unexceptional year, an artisan earning two pounds per week might receive gross wages of ninety-five pounds.

In 1911-1912 such an income sufficed to locate a male toward the top of the seventh decile among male employees and in the lower range of the eigth decile of all employees. (296) Approximately one-fifth of "earned" income recipients, numbering somewhat over 2,500,000, ranked above this core of the most highly paid and regularly employed skilled tradesmen numbering fewer than 1,000,000. If this position deteriorated in some measure during the half-century preceding the war, (297) then this decline was in large part caused by the above-average growth in the number of higher-paid clerical, administrative, professional, managerial and supervisory salaried employees rather than by a decline in the number of skilled or a widening of the gap in income between the former and the latter.

The foregoing data underscore the location of a large number of relatively well-paid skilled workers as far removed from unskilled laborers as from teachers, draftsmen and laboratory assistants. (298) It remains to be seen whether this intermediary position obtained in other areas of material well-being. But before this issue is examined, the more detailed data must be analyzed that pertain to the wages of skilled and unskilled workers in various branches.

A number of studies dealing with the evolution of skill differentials in various British industries reveal no pervasive pattern other than relative stability. A study of time rates of certain categories of skilled and unskilled workers in building, shipbuilding, engineering and on the railways from the 1880s to 1913 disclosed insignificant shifts. (299) A comparison of the hourly wage rates of bricklayers and their laborers as well as of masons and their laborers shows that a differential of fifty per cent existed for four decades preceding World War I; the differential between plasterers and their laborers remained stationary until 1910, at which time it rose slightly; only the differential between slaters and their laborers diminished steadily. (300) An attempt to gauge the relative gains of the skilled, unskilled and semi-skilled by examining weekly wages of representatives of these "grades" of labor in building, coal-mining, cotton manufacture, engineering and on the railways proved inconclusive. (301) Other studies have similarly failed to detect new patterns in skill differentials. (302)

The Earnings Enquiry of 1906 provides the greatest detail of any source concerning the distribution of wages in narrowly defined branches and sub-branches. (303) Table 23 reveals how diverse the pattern of concentration of wage earners was at the extremes in various industries.

Table 23. Distribution of weekly Earnings among Men Employees in various Industries in the United Kingdom, 1906 (304) (in per cent)

	Full-time men			All men		
	Under 20s.	40s.-49s.	50s.+	Under 20s.	40s.-49s.	50s.+
Paper/printing	6.8	14.7	10.0	8.9	16.0	10.1
Metal/shipbuilding/engineering	7.6	13.9	9.0	13.0	13.5	8.0
Building/wood-working	5.7	13.4	3.0	12.6	13.6	3.1
Textiles	18.4	9.6	4.4	21.0	8.5	3.8
Clothing	7.2	8.3	4.6	16.6	7.0	4.2
Pottery/brick/glass/chemical	9.1	8.2	3.9	14.4	7.9	3.4
Miscellaneous	9.5	6.9	2.7	13.4	7.4	3.0
Public utility services	12.0	7.6	1.6	17.6	7.0	1.6
Railway service	21.7	5.5	3.1			
Food/drink/tobacco	16.4	5.5	2.0	13.4	7.4	3.0

Table 24 is an abbreviated version of Table 23 as applied to women in their chief industries of employment.

To begin with the immense gap between men's and women's wages: in the textile and clothing industries the majority of women received a wage that only a minuscule proportion of men earned whereas, at the other extreme, virtually no woman earned the forty shillings or more per week that one of eight or nine men received. This skewed distribution itself repre-

Table 24. Distribution of weekly Earnings among full-time Women Employees in the Textile and Clothing Industries in the United Kingdom, 1906 (305) (in per cent)

	Under 15s.	30s.+
Textiles	52.1	0.6
Clothing	66.7	1.6

sented a marked shift from the situation in 1886 when nine of ten women earned less than fifteen shillings weekly and no women received more than thirty. (306) The concentration of earnings at the lowest level was even more pronounced among children. (307) On the average, the weekly wages of women ranged from somewhat more than one-half (e.g., in textiles) to one-third (e.g., in printing) of those of men. (308)

Among men the wage structure varied sharply from industry to industry; whereas almost one-quarter of full-time men in paper and printing earned more than forty shillings, only one-fourteenth of those in food, drink and tobacco reached this level; at the other extreme, more than one in five railway servants earned less than twenty shillings weekly whereas only one in seventeen or eighteen building trades workers and wood-workers was found in that range. (309) Generally speaking, those industries with the highest proportions of men earning more than forty shillings (i.e., paper/printing, metal and building/woodworking) were also characterized by the lowest proportions of men earning less than twenty shillings; and similarly, those industries with the lowest proportions of highly paid men also employed the highest proportions of low-paid men (public utilities, railways and food/drink/tobacco). The major exception to this relatively high negative correlation between shares of best-paid and worst-paid men is found in the textile industry, which employed a slightly above-average share of the former and a considerably above-average share of the latter. (310) This anomaly was a product of the concentration of male textile workers in the cotton industry, which imprinted its peculiar wage structure on the entire textile industry; none of the other textile branches revealed this twofold concentration at the extremes. The bipolarity in cotton manufacture resulted from the large number of foremen and spinners on the one hand and of piecers on the other (see below).

As this latter example illustrates, the underlying causes of the wage hierarchy peculiar to each branch are best studied in conjunction with an examination of the special conditions obtain-

ing in the branches constituting each industry. The fact,
however, that the aforementioned bipolarity was largely absent
on the industry level, if analyzed together with the rough
correspondence between the share of high-paid men and the
level of average industry-wide earnings, means that the inter-
industry wage hierarchy derived in large measure from the
shifting proportions attaching to the extremes surrounding
the seventy to eighty per cent of male employees in each industry who earned between twenty and forty shillings weekly.
In other words, the relative proportions of skilled and unskilled
exerted a dominant influence on inter-industry differentials.
The latter did not assume the form of an across-the-board
premium, as it were, which would have elevated the wages of
the unskilled in the highest-wage industry to the level of the
skilled in the lowest-wage industry. (311) The presence of
some men in metallurgy, shipbuilding and engineering earning
upwards of four pounds per week not only did not preclude
the existence of a stratum earning less than twenty-five
shillings, but, through the mechanism of the subcontracting
system, virtually presupposed it. (312) Other high-wage industries employed low-paid unskilled groups too. (313) Only
agriculture, in which the average weekly wage of little more
than eighteen shillings amounted to only two-thirds of the all-
industry average, appears to have developed a relatively
homogeneous wage structure--concentrated at the low end. (314)

Table 25 presents an overview of the inter-branch wage
hierarchy and the intra-branch distribution of wages for all
the more important branches covered by the Earnings Enquiry
of 1906 in descending order of average weekly earnings.

Those branches with the highest average wages were, in
general, identical with those with the highest shares of men
earning in excess of forty and sixty shillings as well as with
those with the lowest shares of men earning below twenty
shillings per week. Bookbinding, building, gas, harbor construction and tramways were exceptions in the sense that their
rank with reference to average weekly earnings was considerably
higher than their rank with reference to the shares of men in
the highest and lowest wage groups. This means that a very
large proportion of these workers was concentrated in the
middle group earning thirty to forty shillings. With the exception of cotton and hosiery, all branches in which more than
seventeen per cent of full-time men earned forty shillings or
more employed less than ten per cent at below twenty shillings.
Although clearly falling within this group, lace, iron/steel,
pig iron and engineering/boilermaking all revealed large proportions of men earning below twenty shillings.

Table 25. Average weekly Earnings of full-time Men and their Distribution in selected Branches in the United Kingdom, 1906 (315)

Branch	Av. weekly earnings s./d.	60s.+	40s.+	Under 20s.
			(in per cent)	
All full-time men	30/ 6	1.7	13.4	13.7
Tinplate	42/ 0	13.0	55.7	4.8
Lace	39/ 6	13.2	44.1	6.2
Iron/steel	39/ 1	12.3	30.8	6.2
Printing	36/10	7.1	30.0	3.9
Shipbuilding	35/11	5.5	23.6	5.1
Pig iron	34/ 4	3.4	27.9	6.9
Bookbinding	34/ 1	1.3	19.1	2.6
Tailoring (bespoke)	33/ 6	6.4	22.1	5.1
Cabinetmaking	33/ 0	1.6	18.9	4.7
Building trades	33/ 0	1.0	17.8	4.0
Gas supply	32/ 6	1.1	19.3	3.0
Engineering/boilermaking	32/ 5	2.1	19.6	9.1
Porcelain, etc.	32/ 4	2.1	21.8	6.1
Tailoring (ready-made)	31/11	3.2	19.1	6.5
Construction of harbors	31/10	5.7	17.5	1.0
Hosiery	31/ 5	1.8	20.6	11.5
Railway carriage building	30/ 9	1.4	15.6	9.2
Tramway/omnibus service	30/ 6	0.2	8.6	2.0
Shirts, underclothes, etc.	29/10	2.5	16.9	14.1
Cotton	29/ 6	0.5	18.9	16.0
Coach/carriagemaking	29/ 2	0.6	9.9	9.6
Chemical manufacture	29/ 1	0.8	9.7	6.1
Paper manufacture	29/ 0	4.1	15.2	14.2
Leather/tanning, etc.	28/11	1.1	11.5	10.3
Harbor/dock service	28/10	1.2	10.1	5.1

Table 25 (continued)

Branch	Av. weekly earnings s./d.	60s.+	40s.+ (in per cent)	Under 20s.
Boot/shoemaking (ready-made)	28/ 8	0.3	6.7	6.5
Bleaching/printing, etc.	27/ 8	3.4	12.2	16.8
Saw milling, etc.	27/ 4	0.6	9.1	14.3
Woollen/worsted	26/10	1.2	6.4	15.2
Railways (not electric)	26/ 8	0.9	8.7	21.6
Brick/tile/pipe	26/ 7	0.5	5.9	11.7
Carpet	26/ 7	0.4	7.5	19.4
Food/drink/tobacco	26/ 4	0.8	7.6	16.4
Silk	25/ 8	0.4	3.6	19.4
Linen	22/ 4	0.8	5.3	44.4
Jute	21/ 7	0.0	1.5	49.1
Road/sanitary services-- county/rural district councils	17/11	0.0	0.3	66.5

At the other end, most of the branches with low average earnings were also characterized by low proportions of men earning high wages and high proportions earning low wages. Textile bleaching proved to be an exception--like cotton--in that it employed an above-average share of men earning sixty shillings or more and less than twenty shillings. Boot/shoe-making resembled tramway service in that very few men earned extreme wages. (316)

Thus metallurgy, engineering and shipbuilding as well as printing employed an above-average proportion of highly-paid men; among these, printing alone employed an unexpectedly low proportion of low-paid men. The textile branches with relatively high average weekly earnings resembled the metallurgical branches inasmuch as they employed unexpectedly large proportions of low-paid men.

A much more homogeneous wage structure obtained on the level of occupations, indicating that aggregate working class income distribution was largely a function of the distribution of workers among various occupations. Although this relation

154

expresses, on the one hand, the relatively trivial insight that the more narrowly defined a location within the division of labor the more likely it is that "equal pay for equal work" will prevail, (317) it serves, on the other hand, to underscore the critical importance of skill in wage differentiation.

The concentration of workers at the extremes of the wage hierarchy was, consequently, much more pronounced on the level of individual occupations than on the branch or industry level. Thus numerous occupations were recorded in which more than three-fifths of all men earned in excess of forty shillings-- platers, caulkers and riveters in shipbuilding, certain grades of cotton spinners and of lace makers and open-hearth steel piece workers having been some of the best-paid. (318) Numerous laborer occupations were returned in which virtually no employee reached this plateau. (319)

That the rather great dispersion of earnings on the aggregate level was largely a function of the occupational distribution can be seen by direct comparisons. Thus for all full-time men, earnings at the upper quartile were fifty-nine per cent greater than at the lower quartile. (320) In the cotton industry, which has already been shown to have been one of above-average wage dispersion, the corresponding figure was seventy per cent; yet with the exception of one numerically insignificant grade of weavers, none of the individual cotton manufacturing occupations even approached this degree of dispersion. (321)

One outstanding source of increasing inequalities of income distribution within the working class was the process of urbanization insofar as workers were withdrawn from less populous areas in which the relatively underdeveloped stage of the division of labor and specialization found expression in a more homogeneous wage structure. This process of urban-induced differentiation may be illustrated with reference to the building trades. In 1906, 27.4 per cent of full-time (26.3 per cent of all) building tradesmen earned two pounds or more in large towns compared to 10.7 per cent (11.4 per cent) in small towns; at the other extreme, only 1.5 per cent (8.9 per cent) of building workers in large towns earned less than one pound compared to 5.9 per cent (12.2 per cent) in small towns. (322) In other words, in small towns, five-sixths of full-time building tradesmen earned between one and two pounds weekly compared to only seven-tenths in the large towns. (323)

The foregoing data, chiefly actual weekly earnings, represent the single most important facet of differential living conditions; yet they remain seriously deficient insofar as they fail to provide any direct indication of the regularity of such wages. (324) In lieu of any collection of data relating to genuine annual--let alone lifetime--wages it is necessary to allude to several indirect indices of sources of wage "shortfalls."

b. Unemployment

Although income losses resulting from unemployment worked extreme hardship on those whose full-time regular earnings permitted subsistence at or near the poverty level, and although even for wage earners ranged toward the upper end of the wage-rate spectrum a contemporary found it "difficult to see how any rate can be devised to protect even the moderately thrifty against depressions of extraordinary length," (325) no comprehensive national data were gathered during the prewar period. Such ignorance reflected the absence of a comprehensive unemployment insurance system.

By far the longest time-series was a by-product of the unemployment benefits financed by members of certain trade unions. Coverage extended to a third or less of all trade unionists, never exceeding one million during this period; (326) even within the section of the labor force organized in unions, coverage may not have been representative since some stable industries such as railways were exluded altogether whereas others were disproportionally represented. (327) This source may, however, be used to judge the course--though not the volume--of aggregate unemployment and is, moreover, considered an accurate description of the number of wholly unemployed in the reporting unions. It neglected, however, both shortened workweeks--prevalent in mining and cotton--and the regular underemployment of casual laborers on building sites, the docks and elsewhere. (328)

Between 1890 and 1914 the rate of unemployment for all trade unionists included in the returns fluctuated from a low of 2.0 per cent (1899) to a high of 7.8 per cent (1908); in 1909, 13.0 per cent of the members of unions in engineering, metallurgy and shipbuilding were unemployed; in the printing and bookbinding unions the rate of unemployment never exceeded 5.7 per cent (1894). (329)

The Unemployment Insurance Act of 1911 covered approximately 2,250,000 workers in building, construction of works, shipbuilding, mechanical engineering, ironfounding, vehicle construction and sawmilling. (330) For the two-year period from the inception of data collection in September 1912 to the outbreak of World War I in August 1914, the mean monthly rate of unemployment amounted to 3.9 per cent compared to 2.4 per cent among trade unionists. (331) Since the latter consisted largely of skilled workers whereas the former included the unskilled as well, it is plausible to conclude that the unskilled experienced higher rates of unemployment than the skilled. (332) Further support for this view is provided by the fact that by far the largest number of applicants under the Unemployed Workmen Act of 1905 were classified under the rubric, "General or Casual Labor." (333)

In spite of this apparent differential between the skilled and the unskilled, many of the former also suffered great losses as a result of irregular employment. Thus Booth's study of male workers in London in the 1890s estimated that the weekly average earnings of skilled building tradesmen for an entire year amounted to five-sixths of the normal weekly rate; for coopers, shipwrights, caulkers, goldsmiths, bookbinders and brushmakers the annual weekly average formed a still smaller share of the normal weekly rate. (334)

But even had unemployment been equally distributed between the skilled and the unskilled, the fact that the former, insofar as they were members of trade union benefit systems, were more amply protected against the vicissitudes of the labor market would have created a new form of inequality. For whereas the Unemployment Insurance Act provided seven shillings per week, (335) trade unionists received at least this much and often twice as much. (336) Hundreds of thousands of unionists who were not covered by their labor organizations as well as large numbers of better-paid non-unionists could also rely on benefits from their friendly societies, (337) whereas "the residuum" was forced to have recourse either to the exiguous means afforded by charitable agencies or to the intentionally degrading workhouse and/or outdoor relief under the aegis of the Poor Law. (338)

On the whole, then, the effects of unemployment weighed more heavily on the less skilled and lower-paid although the introduction of a compulsory plan of insurance served to diminish the gap in protection for the small minority newly enrolled. Within the stratum of better-paid skilled workers several groupings can be discerned: 1. the best-paid and most steadily employed men in occupations/trades subject to relatively little unemployment (e.g., printers, engineers, railway engine drivers); 2. those subject to more irregular employment but whose trade union (and/or friendly society) benefits provided a measure of relief (e.g., carpenters, iron-founders); 3. those whose unions offered no unemployment insurance benefits but whose wages enabled them to afford membership in friendly societies (e.g., bricklayers, masons); and 4. the remainder, who formed a considerable proportion of those of whom it was said that:

Every depression leaves behind it a trail of those who have sunk from the ranks of the steadily-employed to those of the casual labourer; and often when they fall they do not rise again, but becoming and remaining "casuals," their placers are quickly taken by new men. (339)

c. Other Sources of Wage Losses

Chief among the other causes of reduced or lost income were sickness, accidents, old age and strikes. In certain respects the patterns of differentiation in these areas resembled those of unemployment. Thus, for example, the major trade unions offered a superannuation benefit ranging from five to ten shillings per week in accordance with age and length of membership. (340) The virtually universal, non-contributory old age pension, authorized by Parliament in 1908, granted, at age seventy, a full five shillings weekly to those (still) earning less than twenty-one pounds annually and as little as one shilling per week to those with incomes not in excess of Ł 31 10s. 0d. Those still in receipt of incomes above this sum--i.e., about twelve shillings weekly--received no state pension. (341) With the transfer of large numbers of ex-workers from Poor Law relief rolls to pensions, the gap in income between the ex-skilled and the ex-unskilled narrowed, although those of the former receiving pension benefits from trade unions or friendly societies also received them from the state in most instances. (342) Despite a joint pension payment of ten shillings for married couples, incomes for all strata of the working class remained in the range of one-third to one-half of average peak earnings, thereby insuring greater homogeneity--at or near the poverty level--of the superannuated proletariat.

The national health insurance program, the first part of the National Insurance Act of 1911, was, like the old age pension system, nearly universal though contributory. Sick pay did not, on the average, attain the levels offered by trade unions or friendly societies, (343) but unlike the benefits of these organizations, medical treatment was also included. (344)

The Workmen's Compensation Act of 1897, amended and extended in 1900 and 1905, marked a further step toward greater equality between unionists and non-unionists inasmuch as it compelled employers to pay employees one-half of their wages for time lost as a result of on-the-job accidents as well as of certain industrial diseases such as anthrax and lead, mercury, phosphorous and arsenic poisoning. (345)

Regardless of the differential levels of compensatory income accruing to various strata of the working class, workers in certain industries and occupations suffered a greater incidence of sickness, accidents, disabilities, early retirement and death than others. (346) It remains to be seen whether the better-paid workers bore or were spared the brunt of these afflictions.

Census returns on "'pensioners' and 'retired' according to former occupation' offer a body of crucial--although not un-ambiguous--data synthesizing the cumulative lifetime results of the economic exertions of working class individuals. Table 26 indicates the ratio of pensioners and retired persons to those still occupied in certain age-groups.

Table 26. Pensioners and retired Persons per 100 occupied Males in selected Age-groups in England and Wales, 1901 and 1911 (347)

		All ages	55-	65-	75 and older
Total	1901	2.85	8.24	31.41	101.78
	1911	3.69	9.10	43.73	161.90
In workhouses	1901	0.57	1.67	8.37	24.14
	1911	0.63	2.09	9.21	23.88
In lunatic asylums	1901	0.32	0.69	0.92	1.44
	1911	0.37	0.81	1.11	1.99
Elsewhere	1901	1.96	5.88	22.12	76.20
	1911	2.69	6.20	33.41	136.03

In the aggregate, the share of unoccupied men rose from 1901 to 1911 in all categories and age-groups with the exception of those over seventy-five in workhouses. The most impressive increases, registered in the two oldest age-groups classified as "elsewhere," were largely due to the introduction of old age pensions in 1909. (348) To what extent the increases in retirement at ages fifty-five to seventy as well as the rising incidence of workhouse confinement for men ages fifty-five to seventy-five reflected the inability of older workers to withstand the strains of accelerated and intensified machine-controlled labor processes is difficult to judge. (349) Nevertheless, the growing use of various--and ever more complicated and regressive--payment-by-result wage systems, particularly in metallurgy, engineering and textiles, underscored the desire of employers to reduce labor expenditures per unit of output during this period. (350)

The data in Table 26 are, in abbreviated fashion, occupationally specified in Table 27.

Table 27. Workhouse Residents and other Pensioners and retired Persons not in Lunatic Asylums, by former Occupation, per 100 occupied Males in England and Wales, 1911 (351)

Occupation	Work-house	Else-where	Occupation	Work-house	Else-where
General laborer	4.39	1.99	Gardener	0.56	2.12
Navvy	2.06	0.71	Baker	0.54	2.66
Dock laborer	1.77	0.63	Carman	0.48	0.94
Bricklayers'			Butcher	0.43	3.01
laborer	1.54	0.49	Pavior	0.42	2.03
Agricultural			Erector/fitter/		
laborer	1.39	1.80	turner	0.41	1.79
Boot/shoemaker	1.30	2.25	Cotton		
Masons' laborer	1.24	0.76	manufacture	0.36	1.79
Coachman	1.23	2.98	Printer	0.35	1.57
Bricklayer	1.20	1.83	Plumber	0.31	1.36
Blacksmith	1.04	3.48	Wool manufacture	0.30	2.34
Painter	1.02	1.08	Commercial clerk	0.23	1.07
Cabinetmaker	1.00	1.62	Coalminer	0.22	1.56
Builders' laborer	0.99	0.48	Railway servant	0.17	3.67
Coachmaker	0.98	3.27	Teacher	0.11	5.07
Carpenter	0.94	3.22	Farmer	0.10	8.51
Tailor	0.76	2.04	Police	0.08	22.10
ALL MALES	0.63	2.69	Civil service		
Ironfounder	0.62	1.70	officer/clerk	0.05	15.47
Domestic servant	0.58	2.41	Bank/insurance		
			officer/clerk	0.03	4.38

The preponderance of laborer occupations in the group with an above-average incidence of workhouse confinement is as conspicuous as their absence from the group with below-average rates of confinement. The above-average rates among boot/shoemakers, blacksmiths, cabinetmakers, coachmakers and tailors were associated with the decline of these traditional crafts. (352) The high rates in the traditional building trades --carpenters, bricklayers and painters (353)--reflected the extraordinary problems of unemployment and casualization of employment in this industry. (354) The better-paid workers, such as printers, engineers and coalminers, and the regularly employed railway workers all exhibited low rates of workhouse confinement; the low rates among textile workers may in part have been due to local institutions of collective self-help. (355) The familiar gap in living standards between the best-paid manual workers and the white collar employees was reproduced not only in the latter's very low rates of workhouse residence but even more clearly in their location in the highest ranks among those classified as "elsewhere"--that is, real pensioners.

Although the laborer occupations were by and large located at the extreme low end among pensioners, the overall correlation between workhouse and pension is difficult to explain: many high-paid trades with low rates of workhouse confinement also exhibited low rates of pensioning; on the other hand, several trades with above-average rankings in workhouse confinement also ranked high in the range of the pensioners (e.g., blacksmiths, carpenters and coachmakers). Such discrepancies may have been due to a number of factors. The latter group of trades may have been characterized by an upper stratum of extremely well-paid men, but since the census also included the self-employed and employers under these occupational rubrics, many non-wage earners may have been represented in the group of pensioners.

Apart from technical and demographic explanations of occupational variations, (356) one basic ambiguity inherent in the data must be taken into account: a comparatively small proportion of an occupation may have been pensioned either because conditions were such that workers did not live to be pensioned (either because they died or because wages were too low to permit retirement) (357) or because the work was not so taxing as to preclude further employment of the elderly. But in spite of ambiguities, the familiar pattern reappears: the skilled fared better than the unskilled but worse than the non-manual employees.

The national collection of data relating to accidents was not comprehensive enough to generate detailed occupational comparisons. Nevertheless, the records concerning industrial fatalities show that of the 141,907 persons killed between 1880 and 1914, 27.9 per cent (39,592) were employed in relatively high-wage coalmining. On the railways, death was as regular as employment: five hundred deaths annually were registered during this thirty-five-year period. (358) Occupational diseases and the deaths resulting from them were similarly distributed across the whole range of occupations: lead poisoning, for example, affected the highly paid plumber as well as the less well-paid potter. (359) Although the relatively skilled building trades were said to be not unduly unhealthy or dangerous, (360) the highly skilled printers suffered from chest diseases. (361) Many unskilled workers, particularly those in the more modern manufacturing processes such as those that characterized the chemical industry, were also exposed to a wide variety of industrially related diseases. (362)

Although the data on annual mortality disclose some familiar patterns of occupational stratification, they also underscore the pitfalls inherent in mechanistic conceptions of the relationship between income and mortality. (363) For the huge gap in mortality between urban and rural areas overshadowed that between skilled and unskilled occupations. From 1890 to 1892, for example, the mean annual mortality of occupied males in industrial districts in England and Wales was almost twice that in agricultural districts for those between the ages of fifty-five and sixty-four. (364) At the same time the mean annual mortality of male metalworkers in this age-group was less than forty per cent greater than that of barristers and physicians, whereas that of building tradesmen was less than sixty per cent greater than that of school-teachers. (365) Although certain individual trades exhibited very high death rates, (366) many categories of agricultural and non-agricultural laborers fared better than many skilled groups. (367)

Infantile mortality is subject to little of the ambiguity characteristic of the occupational stratification of adult mortality. Table 28 reveals a strikingly high negative correlation between legitimate infantile mortality on the one hand and class or stratum on the other.

The steady progression of rates from the highest to the lowest income groups--with the familiar exception of the agricultural laborers--is confirmed by a comparison of infantile mortality in families the heads of which were employed as skilled tradesmen and as laborers in the same industrial branch. Infantile mortality among laborers' families ranged from thirteen to sixty per cent higher than among the families of the following skilled groups to which the laborers were occupationally subordinated: masons, fitters, bricklayers, plasterers, builders

Table 28. Legitimate infantile Mortality by Occupation/Class of Parent in England and Wales, 1911 (368)

Occupation/Class	per 1,000
Middle and upper class	76.4
Shopkeepers, etc.	106.4
Skilled	112.7
Semi-skilled	121.5
Unskilled	152.5
Textile workers	148.1
Miners	160.1
Agricultural laborers	96.9
Aggregate working class	132.5

and carpenters. (369) The extraordinarily high rates recorded for families of miners and iron and steel workers (370) suggest either that diseases contracted at workplaces were transmitted to the unborn or very young or that mining communities and mill towns were environmentally unwholesome for all inhabitants regardless of occupation. (371)

The data set forth in this section have not disclosed a uniform pattern of differentiation within the working class: although the familiar hierarchization of structural advantages and disadvantages applies to some indicators (e.g., old age security), the distribution of other "goods" (e.g., health) appears almost random among proletarian strata.

d. Other Indicators

Remarkable variations in the length of the average workweek prevailed throughout this period; although compression of the range of workweeks was fostered by the incorporation of ever greater categories of workers into maximum hours legislation and by the spread of trade unionism, greater homogeneity had to await further extension of both of these factors. (372) The structure of working hours was not oriented toward the skill structure of the working class but rather toward the industrial and branch structure. For this reason both skilled workers and their "attached" laborers tended to work the same number of hours: since their tasks were coordinated with each other, the one group could not, by and large, work without the other. (373)

At one end of the spectrum, a significant sector of the iron and steel industry worked upward of seventy hours per week in a complex shift system; (374) the above-average wages of this industry were thus in part a function of the relatively long workweek. Other branches in which employees worked more than sixty hours per week included tanning, baking, soap and candle making, butchery, sugar refining, hosiery and tram driving. (375) Plumbers, tinplate workers, miners, shipbuilders, engineers, printers and building tradesmen in some localities achieved a workweek of forty-eight or fewer hours. (376) The bulk of the working class, including most textile workers, worked between fifty and sixty hours per week. (377)

Selected indicators of living conditions and "life-chances" in general once again reveal the familiar pattern. A striking illustration is provided by the occupational composition of the male inmates of local and convict prisons: in 1911, fully 27.4 per cent were classified as laborers. If the total numbers employed in these various occupations are compared with the inmate population, the laborers were disproportionally represented in comparison with groups of skilled workers. (378)

Although the findings of Booth's survey of London concerning residential crowding (379) confirm the expectation that the most severe crowding occurred among laborers and the lowest incidence of crowding among white collar employees and professionals, the above-average incidence among skilled workers with relatively high wages--such as building tradesmen, machinists and printers--underscores the seriousness of the impact of irregular wages on living conditions. (380) It also serves to relativize the gap in living standards between those with high hourly wages but subject to much unemployment and those who were steadily employed at average wages.

The degree to which the wives and children of unskilled and skilled workers functioned as "earners" outside the home (381) offers a very different kind of indicator of living conditions. The structures of the two groups proved to be quite similar: in 1911, only the man worked in 43.3 per cent of the skilled households compared to 39.4 per cent of the unskilled; in 31.0 per cent of the skilled families at least one child worked compared to 29.6 per cent of the unskilled; and 4.5 per cent of the wives of skilled men worked compared to 7.3 per cent of those of the unskilled. (382)

If, in accordance with the values of the period, employment of wives outside the home was regarded as a step to be taken only in the last resort, (383) then differential rates of employment of working class wives may be an indicator of the relative earnings of the adult male and of the degree of fulfillment of an idealized social norm. The foregoing data may, however, conceal important occupational and geographical distinctions. (384) In mining and iron and steel mill towns, which were almost exclusively male domains, wives found little access to employment. (385) Evidence indicates that among the wives of skilled workers recourse to employment occurred chiefly as a consequence of unemployment or irregular employment among husbands. (386) In spite of these variations, however, the customary standard of living was maintained in the vast majority of skilled and unskilled households without income derived from extra-housewifely employment.

e. Conclusions

At the outset two questions were posed which it has been the purpose of this section to resolve. One related to the evolution of material differentiation among working class strata; the other concerned the extent to which the material advantages accruing to the upper stratum of the manual working class modified its location within the class structure which was determined by its subordination to capital--a status it shared with other proletarian strata.

The weight of the evidence marshaled above supports the view that the hierarchization of material conditions underwent a small degree of compression. The major factors contributing to this outcome were: 1. the stability of wage differentials; and 2. the introduction of various state insurance benefit systems, which offered the greatest advantages to those who were neither well-paid nor members of trade unions. Although the confrontation of the results of the national wage surveys of 1886 and 1906 pointed in the direction of a further polarization of working class incomes, methodological differences in survey procedures were significant enough to cast doubt on the underlying reliability of the comparison. Finally, the spread of trade unionism to previously unorganized occupations and branches promoted a tendency toward equalization of working conditions. (387)

A resolution of the second issue has proved more complicated. The empirical aspects are easily recapitulated. Although approximately fifteen per cent of the male industrial proletariat earned weekly wages in excess of two pounds, a sizable proportion of these workers had, for a variety of reasons, to be excluded from any substantively and societally meaningful upper stratum of the working class. Chief among these workers were: 1. those who, as a consequence of unemployment or other forms of irregular employment, failed to maintain this wage-level week for week throughout the year (e.g., many building tradesmen); 2. those whose hazardous or unhealthful working conditions would have rendered virtually any level of compensation inadequate as a source of material privilege (e.g., coalminers); and 3. those who "paid" for their high annual incomes by working extremely long hours (e.g., some iron and steel workers). These and other considerations discussed above underscored the improbability that more than one-tenth of the male industrial proletariat could count on earning in excess of one hundred pounds annually. (388)

The great majority of this narrowly defined upper stratum belonged, in terms of Weber's conceptual scheme, to the same "negatively privileged acquisition class" and shared the same "class situation," which generated a similar "typical chance" of providing itself with goods, as the rest of the proletariat. (389) Such common deprivation included low levels of real consumption, extraordinary hardship attendant upon the interruption of regular full-time employment (especially pronounced in old age), exposure to industrial accidents and diseases and a lifelong psychological burden of insecurity rooted in a realistic appraisal of "life-chances." Only a minuscule segment of the working class escaped these typical features of working class life to any significant degree. If, in terms of income and consumption, the upper stratum approximated to patterns established by the lower and middle grades of clerical employees and foremen, it found itself clearly in the mainstream of proletarian life in relation to the peculiar uncertainties, dangers and damages inflicted by industrial capitalism upon its material producers. (390)

Although this stratum was situated, to use Weber's terminology once again, in the same ownership class (391) as the proletariat at large inasmuch as both were "negatively privileged" in relation to the means of production, the form in which the members of the skilled upper stratum participated in the micro-authority structure vis a vis their "attached" unskilled co-workers introduced a significant element of heterogeneity of interests. (392) Inter- and intra-generational class mobility, a crucial component in the consolidation and perception of class, (393) was almost as restricted in the upper stratum of the working class as in the strata below it; but since this "'closure'" (394) also applied to the mobility between these two sectors of the working class, it rendered them relatively rigid and socially segregable. (395)

Sharing characteristic traits with various classes and strata, the upper stratum of the proletariat often appeared equidistant between adjacent social groupings. Its position within the class structure, in particular its relationship to other proletarian strata, warrants closer scrutiny with a view to determining whether it was a class sui generis.

C. The Ambiguous Class Status of the Aristocracy of Labor

> We ... have managed to create a great mass of middling well-to-do people, hovering on the verge of the middle class, prosperous artisans, small tradesmen, and the like; ... in spite of all their innate good qualities the class does little credit to our civilization; for though they live in a kind of swinish comfort as far as food is concerned, they are ill housed, ill educated, crushed by grovelling super-stitions, lacking reasonable pleasures, utterly devoid of any sense of beauty. (396)

Although the upper stratum of the working class acted within the framework imposed on the aggregate working class by the relations between capital and labor, it also entered into a peculiar set of relations with the working class strata below it and petty-bourgeois and bourgeois classes above it. From the interaction of these two constellations of class forces there emerged a stratum-specific class position which will be analyzed in this section. Here attention is focused on the primary economic relations created by differential integration into the division of labor and the process of production as well as on the derivative aggregate socio-economic structure. The follow-ing section will concentrate on trade unions and political parties as organizational reflections of and reactions back on to these underlying relations.

From the vantage point of the observer of the British working class and labor movement during the post-World War I period, it seems almost banal to emphasize the contradictory class forces to which the prewar labor aristocracy was subject. To many contemporaries--skilled and unskilled workers, socialists and anti-socialists alike--, however, the conflicts between the upper and lower strata of the working class appeared so immediate, acute and basic as to have rendered the former a distinct and autonomous class pursuing interests hostile and antagonistic to those of the unskilled. The Webbs, for example, recorded that at the time of the rise of New Unionism, the unskilled laborer regarded the trade societies of the skilled "as aristocratic corporations with which he had as little in common as with the House of Lords." (397) A conservative German observer contended that in the course of the nineteenth century the English working class had ceased to be identical with the English proletariat since the uppermost stratum of the former had in fact fused with the bourgeoisie. Although this author's conceptual framework, which applied such defining coordinates of the bourgeoisie as standard of living and possession of a savings account, a small house, a life insurance policy and "one or several shares in a large factory," (398) was not rigorous, more stringent criteria were brought to bear in the claim that not only could and did workers still become entrepreneurs, but that the transition to the possessing and educated classes was easier for the sons of labor aristocrats than it had been for the latter. (399)

Such statements welcoming the alleged merger of the labor aristocracy with the bourgeoisie echoed, in substance, scattered criticism from the ranks of the working class. The latter emphasized the desire of "the great majority of the best members of the working classes ... to raise themselves out of those classes" (400) and the susceptibility of the more prosperous men remaining within the working class to ideologies and policies supporting private property. (401) Perhaps the most extreme confirmation of the bifurcation of the working class to have been articulated by a representative of the labor aristocracy was elicited from Robert Knight, general secretary of the Boiler Makers and Iron and Steel Shipbuilding Society, during his testimony before the Royal Commission on Labor. After having affirmed that "a cleavage of interests as between the skilled workman and the employer, and ... a corresponding cleavage of interests as between the unskilled and skilled workman" prevailed, (402) and having urged "the labourers to keep their place" within the division of labor and authority, (403) Knight was engaged in the following dialog with Commissioner Gerald Balfour:

Q. Yes, but if you carry that principle very far you would separate the working classes into cast-iron divisions, and it would be impossible for a man to pass over from the class to which he belonged to another class. Do you think that would be desirable?
A. I do not think it would be desirable for a man of one class to go to another class; and, in fact, for the interest of the man, I do not think it would be desirable.
Q. You think it would be desirable to maintain such an arrangement as would keep a working man in the class to which he originally belonged all his life?

A. Do you mean that we should be agreeable for a labourer to come and do a mechanic's work?
Q. Provided he was able to do it?
A. But we have never found that to be so. (404)

A highly placed representative of capital was also constrained to acknowledge the existence of heterogeneous and inimical interests within the working class.

Q. Would you consider it generally to the advantage of the working classes that a man should be able to pass readily into a higher department of labour than that in which he has hitherto exercised his skill?
A. I am bound to say that if you take a closed society, the addition of other members who are not members, so to speak, of the corporation in one sense is not an advantage. I think it is for the advantage of the country generally, but I cannot say that I think it would be to the advantage of a closed corporation. (405)

Left-wing socialists, industrial unionists and syndicalists carried this reasoning a step further by propagating the notion that skilled labor, virtually by its very essence, stood opposed to the mass of labor. Although this particular version gained prominence in the United States, (406) another analysis, claiming applicability to "all the more advanced countries," (407) regarded the labor aristocracy as the most recent manifestation of the universal tendency of every "higher social group" to exploit a "lower group." (408)

Although these contemporaries, preoccupied as they were with certain aspects of the role and behavior of organized labor aristocrats, overlooked the general framework of capital-labor relations which trade unionism was not in a position to transcend, they nevertheless succeeded in drawing attention to the peculiarities of class relations that benefited the labor aristocracy. The foundation upon which these peculiarities rested was located in the process of production; as the skill and authority structure at the level of the individual producing unit underwent significant changes, so did the internal structure of the working class (409) and its relationship to "higher" strata and classes. It has been suggested, for example, that the growth of the stratum of non-manual employees in commercial, clerical and lower professional occupations introduced disequilibrium into existing class relations by upsetting the relatively stable position that the labor aristocracy had occupied between the mass of workers and the urban middle class. (410) Yet, despite the plausibility of the conjecture that the loss of status occasioned by the emergence of this intermediate stratum may have motivated labor aristocrats to seek closer organizational and political ties with the less skilled, (411) it is also plausible that the former, having found themselves declassed, resisted fusion with the less skilled and strove instead to preserve their remaining privileges. (412) In point of fact, labor aristocrats reacted to these contradictory forces in a complex fashion. (413)

Precisely how the domination of the unskilled by the skilled flowed, at the level of the individual production unit, will be explored below. But before this discussion can be incorporated into an aggregate societal analysis, the transmission mechanism, by which such localized and specialized hierarchies became virtually universally acknowledged segments of the national class structure, must be mentioned. How, specifically, did skilled workers in certain industries gain and maintain intra-class supremacy over less skilled workers in other industries with whom they had no direct contact? Apart from the issue of the international economic paramountcy of the industries (such as iron and steel, engineering, shipbuilding and cotton) in which immediate relations of superordination and subordination obtained, the crucial means of the majoritization of the working class by the skilled proved to be the trade unions. For these not only excluded the unskilled for the most part, but also acted as the economic and political representative of the whole class vis a vis the bourgeoisie and its various fractions. The emergence of organizations of the less skilled coincided with the relative increase in their numbers as generated by more advanced stages of capital accumulation and rendered the role of the skilled as unambiguous agent of the whole working class untenable. The synthetic organizational expression of this altered constellation of working class forces will be examined below (see section D). (414)

The unskilled abounded in numerous industries in which the skilled played virtually no part--on the docks and in coal-portering, for example. Such "unattached" laborers (415) must be contrasted with "attached" laborers, who were directly subordinated in terms of skill and authority to largely ap-prenticed craftsmen. Although artisans in general would scarcely have counted any unskilled laborer "as a brother and certainly not as an equal," (416) the central and almost sole zone of physical propinquity between the two strata witnessed the greatest enforced distance. As "a servant unto servants," the unskilled laborer was "the hewer of wood and drawer of water to society in general, and to the mechanic, his immediate Lord and master, in particular."

... (T)here is no place in which class distinctions are more sharply defined, or strongly, if need be, violently maintained than in the workshop. Evil would certainly befall any labourer who acted upon even a tacit assumption that he was the social equal of the artisan. ... (417)

If intermingling with the unskilled outside of carefully guarded limits of custom and authority was shunned, descent into or relegation to their ranks or even temporary assignment to the tasks commonly performed by them "it need not be said, to a superior workman was the most effective mode of insult that could be pursued." (418)

The superordinate position of the skilled workers derived from three distinct sources upon which not all the skilled were functionally able to draw: 1. semi-autonomy as producers based on long experience and craft knowledge of which latter capital's managers had not yet taken full possession; as a result, skilled workers as individuals and often as unified groups exerted residual control over the quality and quantity of production as well as over the choice, organization and maintenance of the means of production; 2. de facto foremanship on the basis of which they exercised control of scheduling and assignment of work tasks, training, recruiting, hiring, firing and promotion of less skilled laborers; and 3. forms of contracting and subcontracting by means of which skilled workers became virtual employers and perceived exploiters of unskilled laborers. (419) Quasi-monopolization of one or more of these sets of controls by trade unions formed a fourth source, located, to be sure, outside the production process. To the extent that the relatively undeveloped stage of the forces of production compelled capital/management to acquiesce in such control systems, a powerful incentive for cooperation between one stratum of the working class and certain industrial fractions of the capitalist class to control and discipline segments of the less skilled and organized industrial proletariat was released. The new and intensified forms of capital accumulation and the accompanying reorganization of work and authority flows undermined the original foundations of this working class bifurcation (420)--but neither immediately nor unilinearly. Thus, for example, the machine-making and munitions industries, which under the shock of the extra-economic imperatives of World War I had undergone a transformation of the skill structure ("dilution"), subsequently experienced a lapse into prewar conditions.

During 1919 the extensive readaptation of the machine-shops, and the great demand for new tools ... facilitated the ab-

sorption, often in new situations, of all the skilled engineers. ... The great bulk of the "dilutees," including
substantially all the women, received their discharge on
the cessation of their jobs of "repetition work" on munitions
of war, the employers preferring, in face of the immediate
demand, to avoid trouble, to revert to the old methods and
to get back their former staffs, rather than engage in the
hazardous enterprise of reorganising their factory methods.
... There has apparently been a continuous increase in the
proportion of machines demanding less than full skill ...
and therefore of "semi-skilled" men in employment, without
(owing to the expansion of the industry as a whole) any
reduction in the number of skilled men. (421)

But even at the height of wartime "dilution," the effect of the
more elaborate division of labor and of the introduction of
female labor "was an upgrading of the men," (422) whose positions of leadership within the manual work force were considerably strengthened by the insertion of locations within the division
of labor staffed by workers without any practical experience
or craft overview and hence wholly reliant and dependent upon
those with such backgrounds and knowledge. (423)
The performance by individual artisans or groups of artisans
of several or all functions simultaneously underscored the
complexity of class relations generated by the multiplicity of
socio-economic roles assumed by the skilled stratum. Semi-
autonomous workers, for example, might be employed in industries with or without attached laborers; yet even where they
exercised no direct control over the unskilled, the latter's
heteronomy revealed their classical proletarian origins and
status whereas the former's limited autonomy derived from pre-
capitalist relations of production. Although many of these
craftsmen may never have been independent small commodity
producers, many had been, others might venture into self-
employment in the future and still more may have speculated
about it. Their divergent career paths provided them with a
different outlook on the finality of dependent employment
status. (424) The contrasts between the work routines of
those with more than a modicum of autonomy and those with
virtually none at all had a powerful impact on the perception
of the degree and extent of degradation within dependent employment as well as on the urgency and kinds of measures that
would have been necessary to eliminate the sources of that
degradation. (425)
The exercise of de facto foremanship, on the other hand,
not only brought the labor aristocracy into direct confrontation
with the less skilled but inserted it, nolens volens, into the

172

authority structure of the factory as an agent of capitalist discipline. Although individual latitude and attitudes as well as the necessity of simultaneously satisfying minimum trade union standards and rules may have rendered enforcement of this discipline more or less benign, their dual role as highly trained producers, who could be replaced only with great difficulty, and of executors of specifically capitalist labor controls permitted ambiguities of class allegiance to arise. Regardless of these ambiguities, however, and of the widespread enmity and contempt that existed between the controllers and the controlled within the labor force, employers never suspended their suspicions of the reliability of their proletarian agents: the advent of Taylorism signaled the progressive absorption of these supervisory positions into explicitly non-proletarian strata. (426)

Subcontracting, finally, in its pure forms of "co-exploitation" of less skilled workers by the more skilled and capitalists together, represented an avenue by which members of the working class might gain temporary or permanent access to the industrial employing class. Two caveats are, however, in order. First, the number of labor aristocrats fitting this category was small compared to that constituting the ranks of the semi-autonomous workers and the de facto foremen; and second, the pure or extreme form of subcontracting, in which co-exploitation was unambiguous, appeared much less frequently than the mixed forms. These restrictions underscore the fact that the typical labor aristocrat was not the classical subcontractor; indeed, it has been suggested that

> subcontract as a general system might well favour the emergence not so much of an aristocracy of labour as of a struggling, and often not particularly prosperous, mass of small masters and sweaters some of whom succeeded in rising clear into the employers' stratum while others relapsed from time to time into wage-labour. (427)

But the extreme type of co-exploiting contractors earning huge weekly wages did flourish--particularly in the iron and steel and iron shipbuilding industries. In the latter, for example, where the relation between platers and their helpers was likened to that between "taskmaster and serf," (428) the general secretary of the union complained of insubordination and lack of subservience among the laborers and helpers. (429) Antagonism between the two groups was made more acute by the fact that the platers successively resisted efforts by their helpers "to secure piecework rates, in order that their remuneration might bear some proportion to the rapidity and intensity of work, the pace being set by the platers." (430) Given the helpers' unchanged day-rates, the platers' earnings were in part a function of the incremental output that resulted from the increased pace of work that the platers, spurred on by the incentive of piece-rates, imposed on the helpers. (431)

In certain branches of the iron and steel industry the system of co-exploitation reached its most developed form: some contractors not only engaged in no manual labor, but, like absentee owners, often left the mills entirely for holidays. (432) The struggle of the unskilled in this industry against what they perceived to be and formulated as a dual structure of authority, dependence and exploitation and as an extreme form of intra-working class income inequality found organizational expression not only in oppositional movements within the Associated Iron and Steel Workers of Great Britain (433) and the British Steel Smelters' Amalgamated Association, (434) but also in the conflict between these two unions concerning the relative weight to be assigned to the interests of the minority of highly skilled tonnage workers, contractors and subcontractors and to the majority of less skilled workers. The ultimate victory of the latter and of the organizational principle of industrial unionism as opposed to craft unionism (and more generally of new unionism over old unionism) (435) proved in no small part to be a function of advancements of capitalist rationalization and the need on the part of the latter's agents to centralize managerial authority over the labor force and the organization of production. (436)

This last point demonstrates--with respect to a crucial industrial case--how little differentiated are analyses that ascribe an invariant "strategy" to employers and to the employing class in general of supporting and fostering labor aristocracies on all levels as agents of bourgeois ideology, commissioned to disorient the putative underprivileged minority of spontaneous radicals. (437) In point of fact, to the extent that such consciously formulated and implemented policies played a societally significant part, employers exhibited sufficient flexibility to maneuver unskilled, lowpaid and unorganized groups into undermining the skilled labor monopolies of labor aristocracies whose customs and prerogatives had become obnoxious to continued profitability. (438)

Less extreme forms of co-exploitation did not presuppose (439) actual subcontracting and tended to be concentrated in industries (such as cotton spinning) in which experience rather than formal apprenticeship separated the skilled from the unskilled. (440) Moreover, in a series of other industries (e.g., mining) co-exploitation was preserved by means of various patently biased systems of wage payment. (441)

In contrast with the vast majority of the English working class, whose position within the class structure was unambiguously determined by its absolute dependence on and subordination to the class owning and controlling the means of production and employment and whose lack of difficult and expensive to acquire skills made it, insofar as individuals were concerned, easily dispensable, the skilled upper stratum of the industrial proletariat occupied several locations within the class structure. As dependent producers--and this was their predominant status--labor aristocrats were subject to the same fundamental system of exploitation in which the less skilled were embedded. As semi-autonomous craftsmen they escaped some of the more severe forms of incapacitation, infantilization and degradation which inhered in the heteronomous work patterns of the unskilled. In the exercise of these "prerogatives," which had been conceded or tolerated by capital, the skilled shared attenuated segments of the freedom characteristic of pre-capitalist producers or of those outside the nexus of capitalist relations of exploitation. The fact that the unskilled enjoyed virtually none of this type of freedom served to underscore, in the consciousness of both strata, the differential life-chances of each. As de facto superintendants of less skilled labor, the artisan group embodied the authority of the common class antagonist while ultimately still subject to it. The emergence of formal functional foremanship eliminated much of the ambiguity in this relationship, in part by transplanting numerous former aristocrats of labor into an intermediary stratum that was generally acknowledged as owing its existence, material privileges and allegiance to employers. And finally, as contractors and subcontractors the skilled appeared publicly as exploiters of the less skilled--a relationship, however, that was complicated by the fact that they in turn were themselves wage laborers and union members.

Because many labor aristocrats functioned in several or all of these roles simultaneously, (442) their self-image as a stratum distinct from--now cooperating, now conflicting with--the two major classes was enhanced. The fact that their unique socio-economic position at the level of the individual establishment derived in large part from their national proliferation, interconnectedness and increasing unification--within the trade union movement--reinforced their objective and subjective cohesiveness as a discrete entity rather than as fortunate isolated individuals.

D. Trade Unions, Politics and the Aristocracy of Labor

> One can understand how an ignorant ordinary labourer may
> fancy there is something clever in determining that only a
> certain number of bricks (below the right number) shall
> be put into a hod, under the impression that another man
> must be engaged, as all the bricks must be carried up;
> forgetting how soon and how simply machinery may supersede
> the whole of this labour; but it is difficult to understand
> how a skilful and intelligent bricklayer can allow himself
> to be dictated to as to the use of his hands. ... (443)

The three decades preceding World War I witnessed formidable
changes in the composition and direction of the British trade
union movement. Nevertheless, certain fundamental features of
the traditional craft organizations proved resistant, in various
degrees, to attacks from within and without. At the outset of
the period under review, several years prior to the emergence
of New Unionism, a non-socialist sympathizer insisted that
trade unionism had failed to make advances.

> In two generations now it has shown itself utterly power-
> less to reach the residuum, or even materially to combine
> the great average mass. ... (U)nionism in its average, and
> certainly in its lower types, tends to sectional and class
> interests; it divides trade from trade, members from non-
> members; and especially it accentuates that sinister gulf
> which separates the skilled and well-paid artisan from the
> unskilled labourer, and from the vast destitute residuum.
> Our industrial competition forces these classes into perma-
> nent antagonism. Unionism too often deepened this antago-
> nism into bitter and unsocial war. (444)

This not uncommon criticism (445) continued to be repeated
long after large numbers of the less skilled had created their
own organizations. (446)
Although it was generally acknowledged that several of the
traditionally more rigidly self-contained unions of the skilled
were prompted by the--competitive threat (447) of the--auto-
nomous organization of the less skilled to relax admission
requirements, (448) many unions persisted in excluding the
unskilled outright (449) while others conferred subordinate
membership status on them. (450) In still other unions, attempts
by the national leadership or a socialist minority to accommodate
the realities of the transformation taking place with regard to
the differential demand for skilled, semi-skilled and unskilled
labor were thwarted by the rank and file. (451) Formal ap-

prenticeship programs were in some instances used to bar the unskilled; (452) in many trade unions the entrance fees and weekly dues were too onerous for the unskilled to afford. (453)

In spite of variations from union to union, (454) overall the organizational fractionation of the working class diminished notably. It remains to be seen, however, what impact this enhanced degree of cohesion had on the older unions and, more specifically and centrally, whether such unions proved more committed to the framework of ownership, authority, control and distribution of wealth posited by capital than did the newer unions of the less skilled. Did, in other words, the skilled and their unions act as a brake on the socialist movement in Britain? (455)

The evolution of New Unionism during the closing decade of the nineteenth century and the opening decade of the new century disillusioned many socialists who had been its enthusiastic supporters and founders. (456) Between the flush of initial attempts at general organization of the unskilled and the move toward industrial unionism during the years of the "workers' rebellion" immediately preceding the war, (457) New Unionism became a "cautious, limited and conservative 'sectional' unionism," (458) which recruited "a great many men who ... commanded that power to make themselves scarce" (459) and whose job monopolies, closed shops and "special interests had to be safeguarded." (460)

It is, to be sure, true that the new unions joined the Labour Representation Committee (the forerunner of the Labour Party) with much greater alacrity than the older unions. (461) But this allegiance derived in large measure from the weakness of the new unions and their corresponding need for state intervention in order to attain various improvements in working and living conditions--which the older unions achieved by means of collective bargaining--rather than from a strategy of supporting socialist legislation. (462) Moreover, the leadership of some unions of the unskilled was as antisocialist as that of many of the old unions. (463)

On the other side of the divide of trade unionism, the leftward movement of craftsmen and their unions (464) was fostered by renewed and intensified opposition to trade unions by employers from the 1890s onward and by the state in connection with the Taff Vale judgment (1901) and Osborne judgment (1909) by the House of Lords which served to discourage unions from striking and engaging in political activity. (465) Working class sectionalism was undermined even more effectively by the impact of mechanization on the skill structure and competitive labor market position of the craft unions. (466)

Struggles over these issues underlay the decision of many of the older unions to affiliate at the outset with the Labour Representation Committee so that by joint political action they could "hold on to what they had achieved by industrial action. ..." (467) Moreover, the skilled were by no means under-represented in the rank and file membership of socialist or left-wing political organizations. (468) Finally, the skilled and the unskilled do not appear to have held perceptibly divergent views concerning such major foreign political involvements as the Boer War (469) and World War I. (470)

On the eve of the war the skilled and their organizations no longer controlled the labor movement as they had three decades earlier. As the material conditions of manual workers became more homogeneous, the latter's political-economic representation became more integrated and unified. With the tendential erosion of the objective basis of the isolation, autonomy and privilege of the labor aristocracy, the framework began to crumble within which the labor aristocracy and the employing, investing and ruling classes could view each other as potential allies. In spite of the fact that in many instances national collective bargaining agreements "represented a joint victory for employers and trade union leaders over the hostility of a rank and file," (471) "the great unrest" (472) of the last prewar years revealed that if a tacit class collaborationist quid pro quo had ever existed, neither side now regarded accommodation as tenable or even desirable. With the decline in the standard of living, both capitalists and workers insured that stable and predictable industrial relations could no longer be buttressed by reinforcing the structural privileges of one stratum. (473) At the same time it was still uncertain whether the stable organizations of the unskilled were as threatening as the elemental spontaneity of the unorganized had once been. (474)

Part II
Continental European Labor Aristocracies

The skilled and steady employments are not cumbered with clowns and idiots. (1)

Chapter 8
Germany

A. The Revolution of 1848

In Germany, as elsewhere, significant wage differentials among various sectors of the manual working class can be traced back to the period prior to the rise of industrial capitalism. (1) But just as it was shown to be conceptually inappropriate to infer the existence of a labor aristocracy from the presence of wage differentials in eighteenth century Britain, so too it is unwarranted to speak of one for the German states in the early nineteenth century. Given the fact that industrialization and proletarianization set in at a later point in time in Germany, (2) a self-reproducing proletariat failed to appear before the last quarter of the nineteenth century. (3) At mid-century, the German working class was as backward as German industrial capitalism. (4) Consisting of a number of disparate groups of numerically unequal strength, manual workers had not yet coalesced into a unified socio-economic, let alone politically conscious class. (5)

In 1846, the number of factory workers (551,244) exceeded the number of wage-dependent craftsmen (384,783) in Prussia, but with the addition of the master craftsmen (457,365), the aggregate artisanate was considerably larger than the industrial proletariat. (6) Although clearly expanding, the Prussian (7) factory working class still accounted for but one of every ten manual workers, whereas agricultural laborers, day laborers and servants constituted more than one-half of the manual working class. (8) In Berlin, the largest German city, only one inhabitant in forty was classified as a worker in 1847. (9)

In spite of the undeveloped state of the German working class, it has been suggested that by 1848 the factory worker, particularly in iron foundries and locomotive works, (10) had become a labor aristocrat, who

> refused to play the role of downtrodden plebeian which socialist theory had chosen for him. He remained faithful to king and fatherland ... and he resented the insistence

of the left that he was a proletarian. For it was humiliating to be identified with an uprooted artisan who had neither work nor hope nor pride. As the aristocrat of the lower classes, the factory employee felt himself far above the destitute handicraftsman, and he held on tenaciously to the sense of social superiority which made his hard life more endurable. (11)

This retrojection of the existence of a labor aristocracy to the Germany of 1848 requires close scrutiny. First, the distinction between factory operatives and artisans is overdrawn (12) in the sense that it evokes the image of two sectors, each internally homogeneous and impervious to recruitment from the other. In point of fact, factory workers in the 1840s were recruited largely from among small peasants and agricultural laborers on the one hand and former artisans who had been deprived of their "independent" economic status by the triumph of machine industry, on the other. (13) In particular, the key industry of machine making, which as a new branch of production could not fall back on a core of skilled workers, preferred formerly skilled carpenters, smiths and millwrights for training purposes. (14) Although the temporary bottleneck in the supply of skilled industrial workers may have induced some firms to patronize such employees, which, in turn, may have tempered the latter's rebelliousness, (15) the familial and social background of these workers probably differed but little from that of non-aristocrats. Moreover, the former's alleged "superiority" did not make the machinists, for example, immune to the mass layoffs of these years. (16)

Second, this stratum of workers was not identical with the whole body of factory operatives. Rather, it overlapped with those employed in relatively new branches--such as machine making and metallurgy--which required larger numbers of skilled workers. In the much larger industries of textiles and clothing the advanced degree of mechanization permitted the employment of unskilled workers, symbolized by the extensive use of women and children. (17)

Third, the artisanate did not undergo a uniform process of ruinization and proletarianization. Although many crafts--such as spinning, weaving, nail making and brewing--did succumb to the competition of machine production, others--such as building, printing and baking--were able to maintain themselves or even to expand. (18) Consequently, it is impermissible to contrast the industrial worker and the artisan since many of the former were unskilled and experienced deteriorating conditions whereas many of the latter still enjoyed relative prosperity.

182

This dichotomous image is, fourth, inadequate because it obscures the fact that numerous artisans became active participants in radical or revolutionary movements not because they had suffered absolute immiseration, but rather because the increasing scale of production limited the number of journeymen who could become self-employed or small masters. This intra-generational consciousness of the ineluctability of wage labor caused them to "experience the oppressive distinction between entrepreneur and worker doubly," since their first-hand knowledge indicated to them that their employers possessed no virtues that they themselves had not acquired. (19)

The ascription, finally, of labor aristocratic status to a body of largely unorganized (20) workers is problematic in light of the socio-historical specificity traditionally associated with the term. (21) For labor aristocracies in nineteenth century capitalist societies differed crucially from the less opaque products of the ruling class tactic in precapitalist societies of patronizing certain sectors of the exploited classes in order to forestall the formation of a solidary political opposition. The salient difference between these two contexts consisted in the fact that pre-capitalist ruling classes endeavored to maintain their position in relation to a fundamentally atomized underclass. (22) Their tactics flowed from policies consciously formulated on a superordinate political level (23) or, alternatively, were implemented directly by local property owners. Common to such politics were the substantial element of initiative on the part of the ruling classes and the virtual passivity on the part of the privileged stratum of the exploited classes.

In modern, capitalist labor aristocracies, on the other hand, bourgeois policy assumed a distinctly subsidiary role, whereas objective economic and derivative political processes became paramount. At the same time, labor aristocrats, though not necessarily having reflected on the societal ramifications of their actions, entered into complicated political-economic negotiations with industrial employers and the state in order to secure a status inaccessible to other proletarian strata. Since such procedures were not restricted to individual plants or firms, (24) but extended to nation-wide industries or to national political institutions, they presupposed a bargaining agent that could act effectively and uniformly on behalf of this stratum. This agent almost invariably proved to be a non-universal trade union organization (since universal membership would have complicated or even precluded the conferral of stratified privileges). Attempts, on the other hand, to by-pass trade unions, that is, to elevate certain groups of unorganized workers to a favored position, differed in political character from the classical mechanisms of erecting privilege. These highly conscious and aggressively anti-unionist efforts commonly stemmed from sectors of the employing class that perceived either their sectional interests or the aggregate societal equilibrium as menaced by an intractable trade union or socialist movement. (25)

For the foregoing reasons, then, the introduction of the notion of a labor aristocracy into the analysis of Germany at the time of the revolution of 1848 confuses historically disparate phenomena.

B. A Comparison of the Craft Basis of Trade Unionism in Germany and Britain

That fundamentally different national political-economic forces shaped the rise and consolidation of trade unionism in Britain and in Germany is indicated, negatively, by the fact that craft unions predominated in both countries; it would, in other terms, be unwarranted to reduce the differences in the sociopolitical orientation of the labor movements in these two countries to that which was common to them--namely, the similar (and in part identical) industrial sectors and occupational groupings from which members were recruited as well as the narrow organizational structure of the unions. (26)

This similarity in the composition of the membership applied to the predominance of artisans not only during the years prior to 1848, (27) but to the entire period before World War I. Thus both the Lassallean trade unions (coordinated by the Allgemeiner Deutscher Arbeiterschaftsverband) and the more Marxist-inspired unions affiliated with the First International (Internationale Gewerkschaftsgenossenschaften), which were founded in the latter part of the 1860s and forced into dissolution by Bismarcks's repressive legislation in the mid-1870s, recruited their members chiefly from the skilled trades; bricklayers, carpenters, tailors, shoemakers, woodworkers, bookbinders, bakers and metal workers were particularly well represented. (28) A similar pattern emerged from the first comprehensive enumeration of trade unionists published in 1878. (29)

Contemporary Social Democrats were acutely aware of the difficulties involved in organizing the unskilled industrial proletariat. The central organ in exile of German Social Democracy during the period of the Anti-Socialist Law (30) adduced two reasons to explain why German factory workers had not been organized: 1. individual plant and firm welfare programs presumably diverted the attention of workers from the underlying cause of their exploitation; and 2. their wages were too "miserable" to enable them to afford to pay union dues. (31)

The two components of this explanation are contradictory; for if wages were in fact very low, it does not seem plausible that "welfare" plans could have been effective enough to forestall all attachment to socialist politics. And indeed, as Der Sozialdemokrat proceeded to point out, although the factory proletariat was not organized, it did support and vote for Social Democracy. (32) Such informal participation indicates that high dues may have rendered mass membership impossible at that time; (33) it also underscores the inflexibility of the Social Democratic movement, which was willing to accept an undemocratic principle of organization that relegated the bulk of the proletariat to passive membership.

Der Sozialdemokrat also maintained that only workers in small and medium-sized firms were organized because the master employing five to twenty journeymen did not possess the means to bind them to his shop; nor, on the other hand, did the journeymen become subject to the same type of dependency that characterized the relationship between factory proletarians and factory owner. The craftsmen's skill insured not only greater autonomy vis a vis the individual employer but also the status and respect inhering in a "person." (34)

Although theoretically plausible and historically reflective of the empirical evolution of trade unionism in various countries, this argument was manifestly at variance with the conceptualization of the genesis of class conflict set forth by the doctrinal leaders of German Social Democracy, Marx and Engels. For they perceived political-economic class struggle as arising from a radical transformation of skilled artisans (as well as of peasants and small tradesmen) into unskilled factory proletarians, dehumanized, alienated from their work and product, an appendage to machine and employer, concentrated in ever larger plants and subject to increasingly homogeneous living conditions. (35) To be sure, it is possible to view the situation in Germany as an early stage in the development of the labor movement corresponding to the comparatively retarded development of German industrial capitalism. (36) Even after the rise of large-scale industry in Britain and Germany, however, the vast majority of industrial proletarians remained outside the organized labor movement whereas skilled tradesmen in smaller firms formed the core of membership. (37)

The fact that craftsmen rather than industrial laborers provided the bulk of trade unionists well into the twentieth century compelled Marxists to seek an explanation of this deviation from the expected course. (38) They emphasized, inter alia, the fact that in certain areas of Germany (such as Rhenish Bavaria), in which peasant in contradistinction to feudal estate farming had been the dominant form of land use, the recruits to urban industry were small peasants and agricultural workers who were not only frugal but also "possessed by the property-devil," that is to say, "ideal workers in the sense of the exploiting bourgeoisie." (39)

Apparently dissatisfied with earlier attempts at explanation, Marxist historians have recently undertaken to prove that the dominance of skilled tradesmen in small and medium-sized firms was "not coincidental, but rather socio-economically founded." (40) In a curious inversion of the traditional Marxist critique of the reactionary role of guild traditions in Germany, the latter have been invested with a progressive spirit of solidarity that has been alleged to have united such journeymen as printers, carpenters, shoemakers and masons at a time when they perceived the transformation their occupations were undergoing. (41) To the extent that industrialization not only undermined craft traditions by means of mechanization and the intensified division of labor, (42) but also impaired or rendered almost hopeless the prospect of achieving economic independence, (43) it is plausible that craftsmen undergoing proletarianization banded together in opposition to embryonic capitalist exploitation. (44) Many artisans, on the other hand, particularly at the time of the revolution of 1848-1849, reacted to the threat of proletarianization by demanding the suspension of industrial freedom (Gewerbefreiheit), the introduction of which had marked a major superstructural victory for the agents of capitalist forms of enterprise. (45)

An extended version of the foregoing explanation has stressed that a significant proportion of skilled trade unionists toward the close of the nineteenth century represented precisely such proletarianized craftsmen. (46) This particular form of dequalification presumably radicalized this stratum, whereas the surplus agrarian population, which formed a large segment of the unskilled factory work force, did not bring with it a tradition of collective resistance or organization. (47) Yet analysis of the supposedly retardant influence of the absence of forms of struggle specific to capitalist exploitation reveals the existence of gaps in the aforementioned thesis; for as the example of the masons, the great majority of whom were recruited from villages and rural areas and whose education more closely resembled that of rural day laborers than that of craftsmen or modern industrial workers, (48) demonstrates, even within the framework of German society agrarian origins did not necessarily preclude the formation of militant anti-capitalist trade unions. (49)

The first result of the preceding discussion confirms the claim that skilled workers, often employed in craft shops, rather than industrial proletarians predominated in the trade union movements of nineteenth century Britain and Germany. If subsequent analysis indicates that a comparable labor aristocracy did not arise in Germany, it may be concluded that monopolization of the trade union movement by the skilled was not a sufficient condition for the generation of a labor aristocracy. Derivatively, the fact that unskilled laborers were not in the forefront of the labor movement in Germany should draw attention to the unfounded prejudice, often espoused in Marxist historiography, that they were imbued with revolutionary consciousness; for as Marx observed, "numbers weigh only in the balance, if united by combination and led by knowledge." (50) Mere subjection to exploitation in developed capitalist forms did not guarantee short-term consciousness of this new social relationship let alone the emergence of collective measures to combat it. (51) Mere concentration and centralization of capital and labor did not automatically sublate the atomization of industrial recruits; the latter's self-consolidation as a coherent social force proved to be a much more complex and tortuous process than nineteenth century theorists had imagined. (52)

C. From the Revolution to the Expiration of the Anti-Socialist Laws

The type of labor aristocracy that impressed observers during the latter half of the nineteenth century differed considerably from that which had supposedly arisen in 1848 and even more radically from that which manifested itself after the rise of the large central unions affiliated with the Social Democratic Party in the 1890s. If the function of the labor aristocracy in the 1840s had been to stand aloof from revolutionary movements, its role was said to be more activist in the period from the 1850s through the 1870s. For at this time the liberal bourgeoisie, consolidated organizationally in the Fortschritts-

partei, sought to gain a foothold in the urban working class,
which was in the process of being molded by capitalist industrialization. The primary vehicle of this effort to influence
certain proletarian strata--Worker Education Societies (Arbei-
terbildungsvereine)--was launched in the 1860s in connection
with attempts by the bourgeoisie to forge alliances that could
exert political pressure on the ruling absolutist-feudal
classes. (53)

> The bourgeoisie needs ... a large staff of intelligent
> workers which the elementary school under the domination
> of the orthodox church no longer furnished. It was there-
> fore concerned, wherever possible, to combine trade and
> continuation schools with the worker education societies,
> which could be and really were of use to the workers. If
> in this way it was able to imbue an elite of workers with
> its spirit, which these sergeants of the bourgeoisie then
> conveyed to the masses of workers, then it profited doubly.
> ... The mayor of Leipzig once enunciated it honestly in an
> official speech: the purpose of worker education societies
> was to cultivate an aristocracy of workers. ... (54)

According to this conception, then, the rising industrial
bourgeoisie also confronted the dual problem of recruiting and
training qualified workers for new production processes and
of insuring both their subordination within the authority
structure of capitalist enterprises and their general loyalty
to profit-making property. The specific function of the labor
aristocracy in this context derived from the peculiar conflicts
generated by class relations during a historically unique
transition to self-reproducing capitalist relations of production.
For until the latter began to enforce their own strict discipline,
extra-economic measures were required to overcome pre-
industrial barriers. (55) Although the governmentally sanctioned
violence and harsh legislation that accompanied the rise of
British capital (56) were not lacking in Germany, they were
more conspicuously accompanied by efforts at cultural co-optation than in Britain where the earlier development of a labor
movement with its own traditions stymied such endeavors. In
particular, atomized rural recruits appeared to offer successful
objects of attention in Germany where an embryonic labor
aristocracy antedated developed capitalist relations but could
not mature into a lasting and stable stratum once the capitalist
bourgeoisie had made its peace with the politically ruling
classes and settled upon a course of confrontation with rather
than integration of the working class.

Yet even during the period in which the bourgeoisie aspired to imbue segments of the proletariat with its views, success was neither profound nor widespread. Mehring maintained that the liberal bourgeoisie had been doomed to failure because it had undertaken to organize members of the workers education societies as a politically energetic auxiliary force in relation to other strata of the working class and simultaneously to render them weak-willed vis a vis the bourgeoisie. (57) The successful infiltration of the membership and capture of the leadership by Social Democrats also contributed to the ultimate failure of these societies. (58) In this regard the Berlin machinists, a bastion of the modern skilled industrial worker, appear to have been exceptional. (59)

Although owners of large industrial enterprises did pursue policies, such as intentional wage differentiation, designed to undermine solidarity within the work force, (60) this strategy did not originate in the 1870s. (61) On the whole, however, this decade, especially after the Gründerkrise, marked as it was by declining profitability (62) and real wages (63) as well as by a rise in labor's share of national income, (64) witnessed the consolidation of capital and labor as antagonistically organized political-economic classes. The rise of "yellow" unions, sponsored by employers, and the opposition of entrepreneurs to the liberlization of combination laws (65) foreshadowed the enactment of the Anti-Socialist Laws a few years later. The fact that politically organized workers still represented an "elite" did not diminish the single-mindedness with which the police harassed and persecuted them. (66)

With the advent of the Anti-Socialist Laws (in force from 1878 to 1890) and the virtual proscription or dissolution of the entire Social Democratic trade union movement, (67) integrationist tendencies were deprived of any basis that might have promoted them. The increasingly severe oppression and penalties of these years, which embittered all Socialists and virtually all trade unionists, insured a manifestly antagonistic relation between the working class on the one hand and the ruling classes and their state on the other. (68)

In the context of this intensified class repression, some Social Democrats began to voice the view that the "ideological" orientation of the German movement--in contradistinction to that of Britain--could be traced back exclusively to the current political persecutions. (69) The adherents of this position seemed to imply that the English or "normal" course of events was preferable. Those, however, who welcomed the explicitly political direction of the German labor movement, argued that

189

England, not Germany, represented the aberration. For although in England, too, trade unionists constituted a "labor aristocracy so to speak," the world market basis for this stratum was no longer available to Germany; consequently, a labor aristocratic imitation of English relations was "virtually out of the question." (70)

Despite the contrasting values attaching to these two views, both shared a common if implicit assumption--namely, that the formation of anti-capitalist consciousness had been (e.g., in Britain and the United States) and would continue to be (e.g., in Germany) impeded by the democratization of the bourgeois state. (71) To be sure, the peculiar class alignments in Germany promoted the perception of economic exploitation as political repression. (72) Yet the alleged attenuation of class conflict by means of its restriction to the economic sphere deviated too obviously from Marx's doctrine to be incorporated into the Social Democratic catechism. (73) Socialists were therefore eager to seize on the association of the rise of British socialism with the decline of Britain's world industrial domination as proof of the exceptional status of a national labor aristocracy. (74) Deprived from the outset of monopoly profits similar to those accruing to British capital, Germany would never, so argued Der Sozialdemokrat, be able to sustain a national labor aristocracy. (75)

Social Democracy remained ostracized even after the lapse of the Anti-Socialist Laws. Thus Rosa Luxemburg, who, like many leftists, viewed the desire on the part of the trade union movement for greater autonomy in relation to the Social Democratic Party with suspicion, conceded in 1902 that "the German police state untiringly takes care, by means of legislative attacks ... of drumming this character of class struggle into the trade union movement." (76) In spite of the willingness of some liberal groupings to enter into electoral coalitions with the Social Democrats, (77) the state and the ruling classes fostered an openly adversary relationship with organized labor. (78) Politically organized efforts on the part of oppositional bourgeois elements, on the other hand, to reconcile the working class with the existing social system proved short-lived and unsuccessful. (79)

D. From 1890 to the First World War

1. Comparative Growth of Trade Union Membership

Trade union membership in Germany remained the privilege of a small minority until after the turn of the century. The transformation of the unions into mass organizations was facilitated by the expiration of the Anti-Socialist Laws and the onset of a period of economic expansion which began in the mid-1890s. (80) The trade unions in existence until this time had been created by socialist parties prior to the advent of developed capitalist relations of production; partly as a result of these precocious origins, German trade unions "remained uninfluential until growing industrial conflict had impressed the need for organization on a large part of the working class." (81)

Although the German population was fifty to sixty per cent greater than that of Britain during the four decades preceding the First World War, (82) it was not until the 1880s that the secondary sector in Germany employed more persons than the corresponding sector in Britain.

Table 29. The British and German Labor Force in Construction, Mining, Manufactures and Industry, Census Years, 1871–1911 (83)

Great Britain

	Total (in millions)	Share of total occupied population (in per cent)
1871	5.3	43.1
1881	5.7	43.5
1891	6.5	43.9
1901	7.7	46.3
1911	8.6	46.4

Germany

	Total (in millions)	Share of total occupied population (in per cent)
1871	5.0	28.9
1875	5.4	29.2
1882	5.9	29.6
1895	8.0	34.0
1907	10.8	38.4

By this time, the rate of increase of industrial employment in Germany began to exceed that in Britain by a considerable margin. Thus, whereas industrial employment rose by 83.1 per cent in Germany during the quarter-century between 1882 and 1907, the three decades between 1881 and 1911 witnessed a rise of only 50.9 per cent in Britain. Nevertheless, as the prewar period drew to a close, the sector of the economy that had historically lent itself most readily to labor organization still accounted for a greater share of aggregate employment in Britain than in Germany. At the same time, the little-organized agricultural sector employed 35.1 per cent of the occupied population in Germany, but only 8.3 per cent of that in Britain. (84)

Not until a decade before the First World War did German trade union membership exceed one million; (85) on the eve of that war, British trade unionists remained considerably more numerous than their counterparts in the German trade union movement affiliated with the Social Democratic Party (i.e., the so-called free trade unions).

The relatively undeveloped state of German trade unionism is also documented by the fact that British strikes were larger and longer. Although there were about twice as many work stoppages in Germany (between 1890 and 1913) as in the United Kingdom (between 1893 and 1913), the number of workers involved per work stoppage was almost seven times larger in the United Kingdom. (87)

A comparison of the aggregate degree of organization in both countries further illustrates the more circumscribed character of German trade unionism. If domestic servants, farmers and their families and members of the armed forces and of the liberal professions are omitted, the proportion of workers organized in the United Kingdom in 1888, 1901 and 1910 was six, fifteen and seventeen per cent respectively. If only adult male manual workers are considered, the corresponding degrees of organization rise to ten, twenty-five and thirty per cent respectively. (88) The explosive growth in membership during the years immediately preceding the First World War increased the density of organization still further.

In Germany, trade unionists accounted for approximately 5.4 per cent of male wage workers, sixteen years and older, employed in industry (including mining and construction), trade and transport in 1895. (89) By 1907 the corresponding degree of organization had risen to 25.6 per cent. (90)

These figures underestimate the real differences between Britain and Germany inasmuch as they exclude the agricultural sector in the latter country. For whereas in England and Wales

Table 30. British and German Free Trade Union Membership, 1891-1913 (in millions) (86)

	United Kingdom[a]	Germany[b]		United Kingdom[a]	Germany[b]
1891	c	0.3	1902	2.0	0.7
1892	1.6	0.2	1903	2.0	0.9
1893	1.6	0.2	1904	2.0	1.1
1894	1.5	0.2	1905	2.0	1.3
1895	1.5	0.3	1906	2.2	1.7
1896	1.6	0.3	1907	2.5	1.9
1897	1.7	0.4	1908	2.5	1.8
1898	1.8	0.5	1909	2.5	1.8
1899	1.9	0.6	1910	2.6	2.0
1900	2.0	0.7	1911	3.1	2.3[d]
1901	2.0	0.7	1912	3.4	2.5
			1913	4.1	2.5

[a] Membership at end of year.

[b] Average annual membership

[c] Before 1892 data collection was not comprehensive.

[d] From 1911 on the data do not include the membership of the Domestics and Agricultural Laborers unions, which were however relatively small.

fewer than 600,000 males above the age of fifteen were employed as non-familial agricultural laborers and servants in 1901 and 1911, (91) the corresponding numbers for Germany were more than twice as great in 1907; with the addition of non-all-year-round workers, the figure becomes four times greater. (92) Inclusion of these workers reduces the proportion of adult males in trade unions to below one-fifth in 1907. (93)

These global averages conceal significant variations among branches and occupations. Thus in 1896, thirty-seven per cent of printers, thirty-three per cent of coppersmiths, thirty-two per cent of glove makers and twenty-two per cent of litho-graphers were organized; in contrast with these relatively skilled workers, fewer than three per cent of textile workers and fewer than one per cent of construction laborers were

organized. (94) Data for the early 1900s indicate a similar
differential. Thus, whereas more than seventy-one per cent
of the printing industry, thirty-nine per cent of the building
trades and thirty-seven per cent of the metal and machine
making industry were organized in 1911, only twenty-one per
cent of general factory workers and sixteen per cent of textile
workers were organized. (95)

These aggregate and sectional limitations of the trade union
movement appeared so self-explanatory to some Social Democratic
leaders that they were at times disposed to view universal
organization of wage workers not only as impossible but also
as unnecessary. As a result, the party tended, particularly
until the early 1890s, to act passively with regard to the
furtherance of specifically trade unionist goals. (96) At the
party convention in 1893 (97) Wilhelm Liebknecht and August
Bebel declared that increasing concentration and centralization
of capital would soon render trade union struggles ineffective
and political struggles essential. The state, moreover, by
assuming control of various insurance systems, would undermine the basis upon which unions recruited members. (98)
The party could readily accept the minimal degree of trade
union organization as long as it remained convinced that the
politically revolutionary situation in Germany rendered universal
organization of workers qua wage earners superfluous. (99)
This almost fatalistic approach was not restricted to the
analysis of German conditions. Examining the far from universal
organization of the British working class, both Kautsky and
Bernstein concluded that trade unions would always be confined
to an aristocracy of the working class. (100)

Distracted by the alleged superfluousness of universal
organization, Social Democrats failed to explain why so few
German workers joined trade unions. (101) It appears, however,
that political resistance by employers as well as the patriarchal
relations to which many workers were subject in rural areas,
small handicraft shops and some large factories induced the
party leadership to believe that legally compulsory membership
was, to be sure, advantageous, but also politically
utopian. (102)

Such short-sighted views (103) paradoxically reinforced precisely what the party was combating--the restriction of the
labor movement to an elite stratum. (104) In contrast with the
party, the policies of which had become a contradictory amalgam
of revolutionary Attentismus (105) and practical reformism, the
trade unions, by concentrating on the improvement of working
conditions within capitalism, did not lose sight of the importance
of broadening their membership. (106) Unlike British trade

unions, German labor organizations did not engage in widespread exclusionary practices (107) such as exacting high dues. (108)

2. The Industrial Skill Basis of German Trade Unionism

The basic reason for this less selective or elitist approach to intra-industry organization lay in the generally more rapid, sudden and comprehensive nature of industrialization in Germany. For as a result of this more condensed process of socio-economic change, the pre-capitalist and early capitalist industrial customs and traditions of entrepreneurial organization (109) and of the workplace that characterized Britain well into the twentieth century never consolidated themselves as relevant conservative forces in German capital-labor relations. Thus, for example, the "co-exploitation" of less skilled workers by more highly skilled co-working subcontractors in iron and steel manufacture, shipbuilding, cotton manufacture and mining, which constituted one of the principal microeconomic and microsocial sources of an intra-plant and intra-union labor aristocracy in Britain, was largely absent in Germany. (110)

Moreover, the fact that the repression of early trade unions had tended to sever the links between superior living conditions on the one hand and generalized societal recognition of an intermediary position with respect to social class, status or prestige on the other, meant that the socio-political gulf between economically better and worse-situated strata of the German working class did not assume the same proportions as in Britain. (111) Finally, the relatively late emergence of unions among the new skilled workers of the metallurgic industries, in which a long tradition of artisan-small master relations was lacking, meant that a major sector of what constituted the British labor aristocracy never arose in Germany. Thus in spite of the heavy concentration of skilled occupations in these industries, the principal labor organization in this field, the Deutscher Metallarbeiter-Verband, embraced all occupations, having become by 1913 a mammoth union with well in excess of 500,000 mambers. (112)

The skilled metallurgical workers have recently been cast in the role of the "motor of Wilhelmine labor reformism." (113) Apart from the failure of the adherents of this thesis to explain how such a category of workers was able to seize control of the labor movement, (114) no documentation has been provided that such control was ever established during the prewar period. Although these "new" skilled workers may have represented the new direction that industrial skills subsequently

195

took in the twentieth century, during the prewar years they accounted for but one sector of the skilled. As was the case in Britain and elsewhere, the artisans of those branches that had not yet been revolutionized by machinery (such as masons, carpenters, tailors, bookbinders and others) still exercised considerable authority within the labor movement. Thus despite the fact that the number of organized metal workers increased at twice the rate of increase of total union membership between 1892 and 1913, (115) unionists in the largely skilled, non-revolutionized trades still represented the largest contingent of trade union members on the eve of the First World War. (116)

Although capital-labor relations indisputably assumed a different quality in an iron and steel mill employing in excess of 1,000 workers (117) from that which obtained in a cabinet-making workshop employing five or fewer persons, (118) no unambiguous correlation existed between plant size on the one hand and the stage of technological development or capital-labor relations on the other. Thus if foundries and smelteries are excluded, in which as early as 1895 97.8 per cent of employees worked in units employing more than fifty persons, (119) the metalworking and machine-making industries--the citadel of the "new" skilled worker--are seen to have more closely resembled branches generally considered technologically backward than the thesis of "the mass worker" suggests was the case. (See Table 31.)

Thus as late as 1907, the average unit in the building trades was larger than that in metalworking, while the average number of persons employed by machine-making plants was only marginally greater than that in the printing trades. Indeed, in that year these two metallurgical branches employed more persons in plants with five or fewer persons (408,703) than the building and printing trades. (121) This unanticipated result is explained by the heterogeneous structure of the metalworking and machine-making branches; for these were characterized by several sub-branches employing large numbers of workers in individual plants and a larger sector of sub-branches producing non-standardized commodities in much smaller plants. While ironworks employed on the average seventy-eight persons and sheet metal and tin plate plants 176 persons, smiths employed but two or three in 1907; similarly, while plants producing steam engines and locomotives employed on the average 265 persons and cannon foundries 503 persons, producers of wagons and various instruments employed fewer than ten. (122)

Given the large number of "new" skilled workers employed by small firms and the fierce resistance to unionization by

**Table 31. Plant Size for selected Branches in Germany,
1895 and 1907** (120)

	Percentage of persons occupied in plants with fewer than five persons	Average number of persons per plant
Metalworking		
1895	44.9	4.0
1907	29.0	6.1
Machine-making		
1895	22.1	6.6
1907	12.2	11.9
Building trades		
1895	27.0	5.3
1907	20.2	7.5
Printing trades		
1895	16.4	9.0
1907	12.8	11.1

large capitalists in heavy industry who were, especially during
the decade prior to the First World War, increasingly organized
in anti-trade union and anti-Social Democratic Party employers'
associations, (123) the claim that this stratum of workers
achieved "the first historically significant status quo between
capital and labor" in Germany (124) is highly questionable. To
the extent that a "status quo" occurred at all, it was the
historically antecedent accomplishment of the traditional artisans
in small establishments the (mostly working) proprietors of
which had not been in a position to exert counter-pressure on
largely organized workers beyond that flowing from market
factors. (125) The absence of developed methods of surplus-
value production further weakened these small employers, who
in almost all capitalist countries became the first sector to
recognize trade unions.

Despite attempts to ascribe to the "new" skilled workers a
positive attitude to their work, which allegedly tended to
transform them into "professionals," vitally interested in the
use-value aspects of production, (126) by the first decade of
the twentieth century they too were subject to the socio-techno-

logical development that Marx had described for the textile industry. (127) More specifically, "an enormous leveling of the masses of workers was going on, in part gradually, in part violently," whereby some unskilled workers (including women) experienced upward mobility within the occupational ranks of the branch. (128)

Among the "new" skilled workers who escaped dequalification, however, the trade unionistic monopolization of special skills that had founded the peculiar position of the traditional skilled artisans in relation to employers and the unskilled reappeared. (129) In most unions, for example, the increasing division of labor was ultimately responsible for the integration of unskilled workers into the unions of the skilled as it was gradually recognized that standards could not be defended let alone raised while potential cheaper competitors remained outside the organizations. (130) Nevertheless, for a period of years many skilled workers rejected organizational mergers with unskilled co-workers as degrading. (131) By the outset of the First World War, however, most of these barriers had been eliminated organizationally if not always attitudinally. (132)

The integrationist moments associated with the particular responsibilities assumed by skilled workers within the sphere of production did not preclude the creation of antagonisms as intense as those which prevailed between the state and employers' organizations on the one hand and the socialist movement on the other. That more strikes and lockouts took place in the building trades than in any other branch during the fifteen years preceding World War I (133) underscored the absence of a "status quo" in the skilled trades. The largest strike/lockout of the prewar period--conducted in 1910 in the building trades--erupted into a class-wide confrontation. A non-Marxist observer of this conflict was so impressed by the centralized management of the lockout by capitalist organizations both within and outside the construction industry that he spoke of an "enormous sharpening of class antagonisms"; employer-initiated class struggle appeared to dominate economic life more and more. (134) Finally, in spite of the general aversion of the trade union leadership to left-wing Social Democratic appeals for a "mass strike," Carl Legien, the chairman of the General Commission of the German free trade unions, was constrained to concede that such concerted action would be practicable particularly in the metallurgical industry and in the entire building industry. (135)

3. German Theories of Skilled Trade Unionists as Labor Aristocrats

This evidence that craft unionists engaged in class-conscious struggles notwithstanding, a tradition comprehending contemporary and subsequent authors, Marxists and non-Marxists, scholars and political activists, exists that explicitly or implicitly casts this stratum in the role of a co-opted labor aristocracy in opposition to a revolutionary or at least revolt-inclined underclass of the unskilled. (136) Thus as early as 1907 a historian of the free trade unions ventured the prediction that the latter, as representatives of the better-situated skilled and unskilled workers, would withdraw from the Social Democratic movement to form a radical reform party, while the mass of the unskilled, the dissatisfied, would continue to support a revolutionary Social Democracy. (137)

In part influenced by the general political conflicts of the Weimar Republic, in the course of which the Communist party propagated the notion of the eventual organizational polarization of the labor aristocracy and of the unskilled/unemployed in the Social Democratic party and the Communist party respectively, (138) a number of authors began to argue that skilled unionists in Germany, as the counterpart of the British "trade union aristocracy," tended toward revisionism; the unskilled were seen as forming the basis of communist, syndicalist and progressive unionist movements. (139) Common to most of these authors was not only the failure to document such claims, (140) but also--and more importantly--the absence of a rigorous analysis of the aggregate socio-economic and political mechanisms that must, according to the logic of such claims, have given rise to and helped perpetuate the existence of a labor aristocracy.

Trotsky, who did proceed along analytic lines, based his view on a conception of revisionism as a constituent historical element of German Social Democracy. Accordingly, the general reformist orientation of the day-to-day politics of the movement resulted from the fact that a revolutionary situation did not objectively exist in Germany. (141) The left-wing of the Social Democractic party, at least prior to the party's advocacy of a policy of national defense during the First World War, maintained a more differentiated, or perhaps merely more optimistic, position that distinguished between the party and the trade unions. The latter, according to Luxemburg, represented "group interests and a stage of development of the labor movement," whereas the party represented "the working class and its emancipatory interests as a whole." (142) The fact that German trade union leaders none the less claimed equality of status for their organizations was based on "an illusion of the quiet, 'normal' period of bourgeois society in which the political struggle of Social Democracy seems to merge with the parliamentary struggle." The latter Luxemburg equated with trade unionistic struggles as reform work within bourgeois society. (143) She perceived the partial autonomization of the trade union movement as a function of the bureaucratization and specialization that accompanied its explosive growth following the fall of the Anti-Socialist Laws. (144) Nevertheless, the German trade unions, which had been founded by Social Democracy whose "doctrine forms the soul of trade union practice," (145) were less likely to follow a reformist path than those of any other country. (146) Ultimately, Luxemburg maintained, the alleged opposition between the party and the unions was nothing more than that "between Social Democracy and the upper stratum of the trade union officials, which however is at the same time an opposition within the trade unions between a part of the trade union leaders and the proletarian mass organized in trade unions." (147) Echoing the sentiments of trade union leaders (148) and prominent Social Democrats, (149) Luxemburg contended that the very fact that a million trade unionists consciously conceived of their unions as Social Democratic organs would insure adherence to revolutionary policies. (150)

Whereas Luxemburg tended to focus on the quality of leadership and thus to retain the hope that an upsurge from below would infuse a practical anti-capitalist spirit into the movement, other leftists regarded the trade union base itself as corrupt. Thus as early as 1906, the Leipziger Volkszeitung, to the editorial board of which Luxemburg belonged, sharply criticized the unions in connection with the then current debate concerning the general strike; proceeding one step further than Luxemburg in rejecting the claim that the unions and the party enjoyed equal status as mutually complementary components of the proletarian class movement, the newspaper charged that "the trade union movement is no class movement at all. It is the movement of the labor aristocracy, not of the working class. It does not have a complementary or antagonistic relationship, but rather no relationship at all to the political class movement." (151) This position, reminiscent of contemporary attacks on the British trade unions by the Social Democratic Federation, (152) formed part of a radical left-wing tradition that insisted that German trade unions had been transformed, during the two decades preceding the First World War, from organs of the revolutionary working class into social-reformist professional associations. (153)

200

Subsequently, the trade unions were portrayed as having sapped the revolutionary energies of the party.

> The unionists, with their anti-revolutionary attitude, may be presumed to have represented more accurately than the Social Democratic Party the mass of German workers. ... By organizing these masses where the party could not, the union leaders were able to transmit the subjective attitudes of the politically passive workers into the Social Democratic Party itself, with the party executive as their agent. In this sense the trade-union conquest made the party more representative of German labor than it had been before 1906. (154)

Such a view is problematic because of its failure to differentiate sufficiently between leaders and the rank and file as well as between the organized and unorganized sectors of the working class. Although the catalog of issues concerning which trade union representatives exerted a conservative influence on party policy (155) expressed real conflicts of interest between the trade union bureaucracy and the radical wing of the party, the fact that the centrist executive of the party acquiesced in various anti-radical demands (156) indicated less divergence of opinion between the two organizations than the aforementioned view suggests. More importantly, however, the latter, based as it is on a formal organizational analysis, which relies chiefly on official sources such as convention proceedings, provides little insight into the attitudes of the rank and file. Specifically, this view confuses "the mass of German workers" with the minority organized in trade unions. It not only conceals the issue of differentiation within the working class, but also inaccurately describes the minority of trade unionists as uniformly passive. It thereby overlooks the fact that the German labor aristocracy constituted a stratum of distinctively active and progressive workers. (157)

Although, as Luxemburg observed, dual membership in a trade union and the party presupposed an extraordinary degree of idealism, intelligence and commitment, which could be expected only in "the most enlightened and intelligent minority of the Social Democratic working class in the metropolises," (158) even non-radical trade union leaders encouraged their members to join the party. (159) And in point of fact, the number of trade unionists willing to undergo the sacrifices associated with dual membership was considerable. (160) An official study, for example, of party membership in Greater Berlin in 1906 (161) ascertained that more than 40,000 of the approximately 250,000 trade unionists in that district were also party members. (162) Disaggregated by trade union, these data do not support the conclusion--implied by the thesis of the trade-unionization of the party--that the more aristocratic trade unions were also those characterized by greater political passivity. For the better-paid and more highly organized trades disclosed an above-average degree of dual members. (163) The Book Printers, Lithographers, Smiths and Upholsterers proved to be the only major exceptions. (164) The Metalworkers accounted for almost one-fourth of the total joint trade union-party membership. (165)

Such evidence supports the argument that the more highly skilled, organized and paid workers did not, in general, pursue purely trade unionistic goals; rather, they represented a more conscious stratum of the German proletariat compared with less skilled workers, whose rates of trade union and party affiliation were considerably lower. (166) A similar study of union-party membership in Frankfurt/Main in1905 not only confirmed that Social Democratic workers were "the elite of the industrial working class," (167) but also introduced a further variable--that of access to self-employment. This claim that a high positive correlation obtained between restricted access to "economic independence" and socialist attitudes ("the intimate nexus between socialism and capitalism") (168) is worth examining more closely.

4. Self-Employment

Table 32 summarizes the relevant data concerning employers and the self-employed in prewar Germany.

From 1895 to 1907, male proprietors as a share of all males occupied in the industrial sector fell from about one-quarter to about one-sixth. (170) This decline was common to all industries except the food industry. The individual values from which the aggregate averages are derived varied significantly--from less than one per cent in mining and foundries to more than one-half in the clothing industry. The other major industries with a below-average share of male owners were (in ascending order for 1907): stone/clay/glass, chemicals, machinery, paper, printing, the building trades, textiles and metallurgy; the other major industries with an above-average share were: wood, leather, food and clothing.

Most of the more highly skilled, paid and organized trades (i.e., machinery, metallurgy, printing and building) belonged to the first group, which, however, also included large-scale industries with many unorganized and unskilled workers (i.e.,

Table 32. Employers and the Self-Employed in German Industry, 1895 and 1907 (169)

	Male owners as a percentage of occupied males		Increase or decrease in the number of male owners from 1895 to 1907	Owners not employing any workers as a percentage of all owners	
	1895	1907		1895	1907
All industry	24.2	17.3	-58,199	60.0	50.0
Mining/foundries	0.5	0.3	369	13.8	5.7
Stone/clay/glass	6.6	5.1	- 280	28.7	19.4
Metallurgy	25.3	16.4	-10,609	37.5	31.1
Machinery	15.0	8.3	3,582	52.4	42.5
Chemicals	10.1	7.1	227	29.9	21.3
Fuels, etc.	10.0	6.3	- 39	22.5	12.0
Textiles	24.4	13.2	-59,522	74.1	62.4
Paper	14.8	10.4	226	39.3	33.9
Leather	30.9	26.0	1,355	46.2	44.1
Wood	35.6	25.6	-19,922	55.4	45.9
Food	27.1	27.6	29,006	25.4	19.4
Clothing	57.5	54.2	-37,003	77.3	71.1
Cleaning	47.6	43.7	19,142	77.7	64.5
Building trades	18.8	13.2	8.547	53.8	36.5
Printing	12.5	11.0	4.515	28.1	24.9
Arts	47.6	40.1	2.207	79.7	71.7

chemicals, paper and textiles). (171) Thus although the better-situated workers had statistically below-average access to economic proprietorship, they not only shared this status with the unskilled (many of whom had considerably less access), but did not suffer an above-average deterioration of such opportunities.

It must be borne in mind, however, that large numbers of the formally self-employed in reality led, as a result of their subordination to larger, capitalist producing and merchandising units (e.g., as subcontractors or cottage industry workers), a "proletaroid" existence. (172) This was particularly true of the proletarianized self-employed artisans who worked alone (Alleinmeister). (173) Their universal tendency to decline as a share of all proprietors underscored their insecure status. (174) Nevertheless, at the turn of the century Alleinmeister still abounded in the clothing, textile, wood, leather, machinery and in sectors of the building industry. (175)

It appears, therefore, that particularly in trades that generated rapidly deteriorating conditions for the self-employed but that also permitted the reintegration of proletarianized Alleinmeister into relatively small producing units that employed workers with a tradition of collective resistance (such as those in the building trades, woodworking and machine-building), conditions for the formation of Social Democratic consciousness were favorable. It was, then, not only or not so much the absolute size of the work unit or the degree of access to self-employment (176) that determined the development of organized solidarity, but rather the confrontation with the consequences of capitalist accumulation and centralization, expressed on the market level as the inability to compete. (177)

The transformation of an Alleinmeister, barely able to eke out a livelihood, into a regularly employed, comparatively well-paid skilled worker in a small firm, generated a peculiar set of capital-labor relations which inevitably left its imprint on the Social Democratic labor movement. Thus many of these former Alleinmeister did not experience proletarianization as immiseration, unlike large groups of their classmates. They not only improved their material status but also came to receive wages in excess of the incomes of many small masters. (178)

Although the similarity of working and living conditions between artisans and small masters created a sector within which conflict was muted or transmuted into patriarchal or quasi-comradely disputes, (179) the very smallness of these units, as expressed in their below-average productivity and degree of mechanization, (180) meant that they were compelled to compensate for their inferior competitive position by trying to exact lower wages and longer hours from their employees. But since it was precisely such small workshops that were most vulnerable in relation to organized artisans, small masters were frequently drawn into anti-trade union alliances which were under the auspices of large capitals. (181) On the other hand, in numerous sectors few mediations connected even the smaller masters and their skilled employees, who had clearly become segregated into a separate socio-economic class. (182)

Advancement by artisans to and within larger units of production was accompanied by a new pattern of income (183) stratification and a tendential intergenerational polarization of affiliation between skilled personnel in supervisory positions and the bulk of the wage-dependent unskilled. (184) Such upward mobility created a conflict of interest between supervisors and their former class "comrades," but it may also have made the gulf between employers and employees seem easier to bridge. (185) Although this conflict may have been mitigated in the case of skilled employees who possessed sufficient control of the work process to ward off what they regarded as pernicious intervention by management, it was exacerbated in large factories in which supervisory personnel and the unskilled were concentrated. (186)

From 1895 to 1907 the number of salaried male administrative, office, technical and supervisory employees in German industry rose from 258,460 to 562,089 or by 117.4 per cent; the share of non-production employees rose during these years from 4.0 to 6.5 per cent. (187) Male technical and supervisory personnel alone rose by 165.2 per cent, thus doubling their share of total male industrial employment. Two industries-- machine-making and construction--, which accounted for 30.0 per cent of male industrial employment, employed 40.9 per cent of all male technical and supervisory personnel in 1907. If in 1907 (1895) there were approximately twenty-three (forty-three) male production workers in all firms with employees for every technical or supervisory employee, then there were twenty-two (seventy-two) in the building trades, fifteen (twenty-four) in machine-making, eight (nineteen) in chemicals and thirty-six (ninety-six) in clothing. (188)

5. National Peculiarities of the German Labor Aristocracy

Contemporary discussions of the possible existence of a labor aristocracy in Germany stressed, even when affirmative, the attenuated version in contrast to the English original. (189) What struck observes as most threatening to the unity of the working class was neither widespread upward inter-class mobility (190) nor some implicit understanding between trade unions and sectors of the capitalist class to the exclusion of the unorganized majority of the proletariat--as was alleged to have been the case in the United States. (191) To be sure, there was no dearth of liberal politicians and academics, centered in the Verein für Socialpolitik, (192) working toward the recreation in Germany of the trade union aristocracy that they admired in England. (193) Little indicates, however, that trade unionists sought such an accommodation or that employers would have accommodated them if approached. (194) Rather, the major impulse to the formation of a cleavage in the working class in the form of the detachment of a privileged upper stratum was perceived, if at all, (195) as having originated more or less spontaneously in the historical fact of the prior organization of the skilled workers. (196)

Although neither the pre-existing objective and subjective heterogeneity of the working class nor the original restriction of trade union membership to the skilled was fortuitous, the subsequent course of proletarian unity was a function, inter alia, of: 1. the effects of capital accumulation on the socio-economic hierarchies within the working class; and 2. the measures which those at the top of the hierarchies took to integrate the less skilled into the general struggle of labor against capital.

1. German Social Democrats, thoroughly in the theoretical tradition molded by Marx, were convinced that the course of industrial development would compress the hierarchy of skills by undermining the basis of the highly skilled. (197) This prediction appeared to them borne out during the prewar years; for census data as well as studies conducted by the Verein für Socialpolitik revealed a reduction in the relative number of skilled workers. (198) The flattening of the skill pyramid as expressed by the absolute and relative expansion of the sector of semi-skilled machine workers at the expense of the skilled and the unskilled motivated Max Weber to remark that this homogenization was accompanied by the constitution of the working class as a social class engaged in class action. (199) Moreover, the fact that wage differentials between skilled and unskilled workers declined, beginning with the latter half of the 1880s, (200) may be taken as an indirect indicator of the narrowing of skill differentials. (201)

Significant gaps in wage levels persisted nevertheless. As late as 1913, hourly rates of skilled building tradesmen exceeded those of their unskilled co-workers by 26.8 per cent; the corresponding differential in annual earnings in cotton spinning amounted to 40.9 per cent. (202) Skilled industrial workers earned, in the years immediately preceding World War I, in the range of 1,500 to 2,400 marks annually while the annual wages of the unskilled fell within the range of 900 to 1,500 marks (averaging 1,100 to 1,200 marks). (203) A study of negotiated (i.e., minimum and not effective) wages, conducted in 1913, of more than 100,000 plants employing more than one million workers, revealed that whereas 42.2 per cent of the skilled males earned fifty-five pfennigs or more per hour, only 20.2 per cent of the unskilled men reached this level; at the other end of the scale, only 3.6 per cent of the skilled, but 12.6 per cent of the unskilled men earned less than thirty-five pfennigs per hour. (204)

These differentials, which were narrower than those obtaining in Britain and the United States, (205) did not enable large numbers of skilled workers to afford bourgeois life-styles. (206) And even if it were true that income differentiation within the working class at the turn of the century had been greater than that between the best-paid workers and the part of the petty bourgeoisie consisting of lower-echelon civil servants, small masters and shopkeepers, (207) this circumstance alone would not suffice to prove that this stratum of workers had coalesced politically and socio-economically with the petty bourgeoisie. Such a conclusion would presuppose the existence of a broader set of material conditions illustrating similar working and living conditions as well as of a conscious policy on the part of the labor aristocracy to distinguish itself from the bulk of the working class. (208)

In this connection average annual incomes of manual workers and, for example, civil servants, did not constitute a commensurable basis for the comparison of lifetime incomes. During the first decade of the twentieth century, for example, approximately fifteen per cent of skilled machinemakers in Berlin earned more than 2,000 marks per annum--about twice the average annual earnings of all industrial workers. (209) Although these wages approached the "bourgeois incomes of civil servants," this "elite" of machinists not only confronted old age without pensions but was forced to withdraw form the skilled labor force--indeed from the ranks of the employable in general--in large numbers before reaching the age of fifty. (210) Thus the insecurity inherent in surplus value-producing labor--as expressed by the disparity between high wage rates and low lifetime earnings--rendered comparisons with other types of income recipients illusory. (211) Analogously, high rates of unemployment meant that high hourly wages did not lead to high annual wages. (212) Skilled building tradesmen, for example, who had once been able to secure their subsistence during the winter months (213) by means of secondary employment in agriculture, were confronted with the fact that the labor-saving mechanization of agriculture rendered this expedient less and less accessible. (214) Unable to survive during the winter on the basis of accumulated savings, "a large number" were compelled to "beg." (215) Moreover, the above-average accident and fatality rates among many skilled workers reduced annual and lifetime incomes even more radically. (216)

2. The evidence pertaining to the attitudes and policies of the unions of the skilled toward the objective forces that shaped intra-working class differentiation is ambiguous. Numerous sources disclose a willingness to accept the existing pattern of material inequalities. This viewpoint applied not only to the refusal on the part of trade unions to press for collective bargaining procedures and institutional arrangements that would have compressed the wage hierarchy, (217) but also to the almost fatalistic toleration by the Social Democratic party of capitalistically generated intra-working class inequalities. In connection, for example, with a debate concerning the salaries of party officials at the party convention in 1892, Wilhelm Liebknecht delivered the following polemic:

> You who are sitting here are after all for the most part aristocrats among the workers as it were--I mean with regard to income. The working population in the Saxon Ore Mountains, the weavers in Silesia would consider what you earn the income of a Croesus. What would you say if the weavers demanded, No one shall have a higher income than they themselves have? Do we who aspire to a more decent human existence want to seek to level down? In bourgeois society equality is just impossible. (218)

Few party members or trade unionists would, presumably, have denied that bourgeois society enforced inequalities that would continue as long as capitalism prevailed; similarly, Liebknecht's audience included few who would have proposed achieving greater equality by reducing the better-paid to the level of the worse-paid. But within the restrictions imposed upon the labor movement by a wage hierarchy that roughly corresponded to a hierarchy of values of labor power as determined by skills levels, it was one of the implicit goals of the party to mold autonomous working class institutions that created embryonic forms of socialist (re-)distribution by inculcating and reinforcing socialist attitudes and behavior. Self-fulfilling prophecies to the effect that "that circle of party comrades is considered the better one which has a better income and a better standard of living" (219) scarcely furthered that goal. And even those who argued that hunger did not constitute the sole motivation of class struggle and that "bourgeois society itself makes certain that the workers were not too well-off" (220) tacitly relegated the low-paid and unorganized workers to a permanently subordinate role within the movement.

The unemployment insurance system represented another area of ambiguity. During the prewar period, that is, prior to the introduction of compulsory state unemployment insurance programs, trade unions performed an important function as insurance agents. In part because the costs were regarded as burdensome, (221) but also because opponents, considering unemployment and hence the alleviation of its consequences as the responsibility of capital, maintained that unemployment insurance funds would lead to a decline of class struggle, (222) many unions resisted the introduction of such systems. If in 1892 only ten unions provided unemployment benefits, (223) two decades later only five failed to offer them; by 1912 more than 2,500,000 members were insured against unemployment. (224) Even if payments replaced but a small fraction of a member's normal wages, (225) they still served to set off recipients from non-recipients.

During this period unions demanded the application in Germany of the Ghent system, which provided for state and communal subsidies to trade unions without interfering with the latter's administrative autonomy. (226) By excluding the unorganized, such a system widened the gulf between them and the organized workers. In cities such as Erlangen in which the Ghent system was practiced, "one could not assign to members of the aristocracy of labor who had become unemployed such lowly jobs as (say) to day laborers or hod carriers." (227) The distribution of money to trade unionists and public works jobs to the unorganized added a new dimension to the existing model of material and psychological inequality. (228)

The rationale underlying trade union support for this system consisted in the latter's tendential enforcement of universal organization. The force of this weapon--which the state perceived and hence refused to enact--was founded upon the belief that whose who had not yet comprehended the necessity of trade union membership did not "deserve" unemployment insurance benefits. (229) To the extent that trade unions succeeded in attracting otherwise excluded strata of the working class--rather than in detaching a privileged stratum from the rest of the class--, they exerted a unifying influence on the proletariat. (230) To be sure, a part of the strong increase in membership during the years following the introduction of the Ghent system in some German cities may be attributed to the desire by new members to participate in the unemployment insurance system. Nevertheless, large numbers of workers (especially women and agricultural laborers) remained unorganized not for lack of interest but because of resistance by employers or insufficient recruitment by the unions. In other words, whereas this system of compelling workers to choose between acting in a collective manner or suffering the consequences of pretending to be able to afford

the life-style of an economically independent bourgeois may have
been appropriate in Denmark, (231) it was inexpedient in
Germany where a majority of those addressed by the unions
did not consist of the free agents presupposed by the system's
underlying principles.

E. Summary

The same economic forces that acted to create a materially
superior stratum of manual workers in Britain were also at
work in Germany--namely, a specific historical stage (232) in
the development of the forces of production as expressed in a
broader range of deskilling than of upward skilling embedded
in the general capitalist laws governing the value of labor
power. A trade union movement also evolved that revealed incipient elitist and isolationist characteristics. (233) Yet these
tendencies were not consolidated in a system of institutionalized
privileges sanctioned by explicit or implicit positive functions
performed for the benefit of the ruling classes. On the contrary,
much more so than in Britain, German employers as a class power
combated the very existence of trade unions until the advent
of the Burgfrieden during World War I. (234) The unions, as
a part of the anti-capitalist Social Democratic movement, which
was treated as an alien body by German capital and the German
state, reciprocated by maintaining an official socialist spirit
quite unknown to the bulk of the established unions of the
skilled in Britain. And even when this anti-capitalism remained
predominantly rhetorical, the fact that the largely non-radical
leadership felt compelled to infuse Marxist terminology into
trade union struggles indicated that the consciousness of the
membership was not purely "trade-unionistic." (235)

Whereas--according to those who have taken the existence
of a labor aristocracy in Germany for granted--the objective
function of a materially privileged stratum of workers in
Germany was to provide the socio-economic basis of reformism
and revisionism, the labor aristocracy in Britain stood outside
of and opposed the socialist movement. What rendered the
notion of a German labor aristocracy particularly unrealistic
was the fact that whereas in Britain a significant opposition to
the labor aristocracy arose as early as the end of the 1880s
among working class socialists, the basic opposition in prewar
Germany was restricted to the left-wing intellectuals of the
party. In Germany no mass-based socialist alternative emerged

210

to the upper stratum of the working class which continued to constitute the core of the socialist movement. (236)

This crucial functional difference between the upper strata of two national working classes underscores the inadequacy of one-sided reliance upon quantitative income criteria in stratification analysis. This stricture applies with special force to authors who include in a labor aristocracy all members of the working class whose incomes exceeded a certain fixed level. (237) For such an approach, associated as it is with the undocumented claim that immiseration leads to heightened class consciousness, (238) creates a logical hiatus which is then filled by ad hoc assertions concerning the non-equivalence of economic or "objective bribery" on the one hand and political or "subjective corruption" on the other. (239)

Apparently aware of the historical absurdity of including the entire corps of skilled German workers--who, numbering almost 5,000,000, accounted for more than half of all industrial workers in 1907 (240)--among the labor aristocracy, the author of the empirically most detailed study of the German labor aristocracy chose to restrict this stratum to the "tip of the skilled workers," in particular to overseers, gangers, foremen, sweaters, paymasters and to a very select group of highly skilled workmen in key positions some of whom functioned as subcontractors. (241) Apart from the issues--already alluded to--associated with the inadequacies inherent in comparisons of the wages of manual workers and the salaries of civil servants and other empirical problems, (242) the aforementioned analysis is fundamentally marred by its failure to mediate firm-level strategies to cultivate a favored group within the work force with the specific macro-social function performed by the German labor aristocracy. (243) Proceeding from an a priori assumption that the creation of the labor aristocracy was a conscious "aspiration" (244) of the capitalist class in general, such an analysis tends to view the formation of this stratum as "artificial"; this implication derives from the notion that "pure" capitalist development would not have brought into being such a counter-revolutionary sector of the working class. Extraordinarily high wages are therefore viewed as having been determined not by the normal workings of capital accumulation but rather by the bourgeois policy of seeking support and causing disruption within the working class. (245)

Although micro-economic wage policies of this type flourished, they were largely geared to shop-level supervisors many of whom also engaged in manual labor. (246) If in fact, however, this circumscribed category of labor aristocrats was perceived by the majority of dependent wage laborers as agents or extensions of capitalist exploitation, (247) then the resentment which class or even trade-unionistically conscious workers presumably bore these supervisors would have prevented the latter from insidiously introducing bourgeois ideology into the labor movement. It is, moreover, unlikely that such management-oriented employees were represented in large numbers in free trade unions or in the Social Democratic party. Indeed, infiltration of the socialist movement was, according to one author, apparently not even the major purpose behind the "creation" of the labor aristocracy. "In order to rally its support within the working class organizationally, the bourgeoisie began to attempt to organize 'yellow' (company) unions." (248) Yet this type of organization, (249) far from undermining the socialist labor movement, actually evoked universal denunciation from the free trade unions as well as from the Christian and Hirsch-Duncker unions. (250) Although the growth of company unions in the years immediately preceding World War I impeded the spread of free trade unions within heavy industry, this entrepreneurial strategy was too obviously part of a general class confrontation to have been interpreted as a sophisticated attempt to "cultivate" a labor aristocracy as a vehicle of bourgeois ideology within the labor movement. (251) Finally, such combative policies stood in sharp contrast to the alleged tactic of simultaneously recognizing the Social Democratic party and trade unions in order to foster the growth of a labor aristocracy qua labor bureaucracy. (252) For although far-sighted liberals such as Max Weber may have understood that outlawing these organizations served merely to radicalize them, the ruling classes were forced to legalize them not as the result of insight into their own long-term self-interest, but rather as a result of Social Democratic resistance to repression.

Thus in spite of important similarities with regard to the socio-economic forces underlying the formation of a materially advantaged stratum of the working class in Britain and Germany, overriding national differences intervened. In contrast to Britain, Germany did not enjoy unparalleled international economic superiority during the formative years of its industrial proletariat; unlike Britain, it did not acquire economically significant colonial possessions. (253) Most importantly, however, no tradition of system-conformist action existed that could have issued in notable economic or political gains for any sector of the working class. (254) In contrast to the contemporary situation in the United States, German radicalism was but little hampered by the (real) prospects of individual economic independence in agriculture or industry or by rapid upward mobility at the expense of immigrant minorities. (255)

Chapter 9
France

The labor aristocracy has, it is generally acknowledged, played a comparatively insignificant part in France. (1) Received opinion will largely be corroborated in this chapter, which is devoted to elucidating the causes of this variant development.

A. The Period prior to the Paris Commune

As in the cases of Britain and Germany, so too with regard to France there is a period prior to which the development of capitalist relations of production and hence of the "modern" class structure was too weak to generate a proletarian stratum whose particular sectional interests could have represented a factor of aggregate societal relevance in stabilizing class rule. Consequently, references, by contemporaries or by subsequent authors, to labor aristocratic strata during such a period reveal themselves, upon closer inspection, to be literary in nature without the precise meaning of the modern concept. (2)
 Determination of an appropriate terminus a quo in France is rendered more complicated by the fact that workers, particularly those in Paris, exerted a decisive influence on revolutionary political life as far back as 1789. (3) But as Marx pointed out with reference to the revolution of 1848:

> The development of the industrial proletariat is in general conditioned by the development of the industrial bourgeoisie. Under its rule alone does it attain the expanded national existence that can raise its revolution to a national one, does it itself create the modern means of production which become so many means of its revolutionary liberation. ... French industry is more refined and the French bourgeoisie has developed in a more revolutionary manner than that of the rest of the continent. But the February revolution, was it not aimed directly at the aristocracy of finance? This fact

proved that the industrial bourgeoisie did not rule France. The industrial burgeoisie can rule only where modern industry shapes all property relations to suit itself, and industry can attain this force only where it has conquered the world market, for the national boundaries do not suffice for its development. But the industry of France asserts itself for the most part in the national market only by a more or less modified prohibitive system. If, therefore, the French proletariat at the moment of a revolution possesses actual power in Paris and an influence that spurs it to a charge beyond its means, in the rest of France it is crowded together at single scattered central points, almost disappearing among the superior numbers of peasants and petty bourgeoisie. The struggle against capital in its developed modern form, in its salient point, the struggle of the industrial wage worker against the industrial bourgeois, is in France a partial fact. ... Nothing more explicable, therefore, than that the Paris proletariat sought to assert its interest alongside the bourgeois interest instead of bringing it to bear as the revolutionary interest of society itself. ... (4)

The subordinate status of industrial capital and of industrial workers vis a vis the agricultural sphere was clearly reflected in the census of 1851.

Table 33. Sectoral Composition of the economically active Population in France, 1851 (in per cent) (5)

Sector	Share
Agriculture	60.8
Large (Manufacturing) Industry	5.7
Small Industry and Commerce	20.0
Liberal Professions[a]	9.6
Domestic Service	3.9
	100.0

[a]Includes those living on property incomes; state pensioners; and state employees.

Whereas more than three-fifths of the working population were engaged in agriculture, only slightly more than one-quarter was employed in the secondary sector; here, in turn, only one-fifth of industrial workers was employed in large-scale industry. But even this sector was characterized by relatively small production units, there having been fewer than ten workers for every master. (6) Three-quarters of the approximately 1.2 million industrial workers (or almost two-thirds of the almost seven hundred thousand male wage workers in manufacturing) were employed in textiles, in which masters were outnumbered by workers by a ratio of somewhat less than fifteen to one. (7) Although some workers were obviously employed in plants or trades in which larger aggregates of wage workers were concentrated, (8) even the bulk of Parisian workers was employed in petty bourgeois enterprises during this period. (9)

Although at mid-century the industrial worker "had not as a rule become a factory hand" and still possessed "a fair chance of becoming a master," he nevertheless "had the interests and point of view of the wage earner." (10) The incipient elements of the working class could look back upon a revolutionary tradition unparalleled in Britain or Germany, (11) yet their overwhelmingly minority status within the class structure meant that the working class had not yet constituted itself objectively as a class. (12)

If the domination of industrial capital was similarly absent in mid-century Germany, (13) the decisive transformation had already occurred in Britain where in 1851 the secondary sector accounted for more than two-fifths of total employment compared to slightly more than one-fifth in the primary sector. (14) France, moreover, continued to lag behind Germany and Britain, so that whereas industrial employment had already exceeded that in agriculture in Germany by 1907, (15) this turning point did not occur in France until after World War II. (16) The relatively slow growth of industrial capitalism in France was further reflected in the declining share of world output and trade accounted for by French manufacturing industry.

The deterioration in France's position was almost as marked as that in the United Kingdom and meant that on the eve of World War I Russia had nearly supplanted France as the fourth largest industrial nation.

Given the comparatively undeveloped capitalist mode of production in France, (17) it is not surprising that most references to labor aristocratic tendencies were motivated by wage differentials that were not necessarily accompanied by differences in socio-political attitudes or behavior. (18) Thus, there is some indication that the share of the best and of the worst-paid wage workers among all Parisian wage earners in-

Table 34. Distribution of World Manufacturing among the four major producing Countries, 1870–1913 (in per cent) (19)

	United States	Germany	United Kingdom	France
1870	23.3	13.2	31.8	10.3
1881–1885	28.6	13.9	26.6	8.6
1896–1900	30.1	16.6	19.5	7.1
1906–1910	35.3	15.9	14.7	6.4
1913	35.8	15.7	14.0	6.4

Table 35. Distribution of World Trade in Manufactures among the four major trading Countries, 1883–1913 (in per cent) (20)

	United States	Germany	United Kingdom	France
1883	3.4	17.2	37.1	14.6
1890	3.9	17.2	35.8	14.5
1899	9.8	19.5	28.4	12.6
1913	11.0	23.0	25.4	10.6

creased during the Second Empire. (21) Yet the list of the
best paid workers (22) or of "privileged" or "aristocratic"
trades (23) reveals, when compared with those trades most
active in socialist movements, (24) that by and large the better
rather than the worse paid were politically active. (25)

This line of reasoning is supported by Marx's description
of the strategy unfolded by the French bourgeoisie after the
February Revolution had driven the army from Paris; in order
to confront the proletariat militarily, the bourgeoisie was left
but one expedient: "to counterpose one part of the proletarians
to the other." Yet the tool of this policy was not the better
paid sector of the working class, but rather the lumpenproletariat, which was recruited into the counterrevolutionary
mobile guard. (26)

This is not to say that references to wage aristocrats during
this period contained no socio-political connotations. (27) Indeed, examples of explicit attempts by employers to divert
workers from political and social action have been documented
for the period of the Second Empire. To this end employers

founded choral societies the members of which were possibly considered labor aristocrats by other workers. (28) Engels, for example, maintained that a conscious subsidiary aim of Baron Haussmann's reconstruction of Paris--the primary purpose of which was to disperse densely populated working class quarters and to render barricade fighting more difficult--was "the training of a specifically Bonapartist construction proletariat, dependent on the government." (29) Bourgeois reformers, moreover, achieved a small measure of success in their attempts to co-opt the producers' cooperative movement which, in order to adapt itself to political conditions during the Second Empire, abandoned its original socialist orientation in favor of accommodating itself to the laws of capital accumulation. If some bourgeois elements "saw it as a way of creating new property owners and thus consolidating the social order," (30) then "the most important association" (31) of this type, namely, the Association fraternelle des ouvriers maçons et tailleurs de pierre, must have appeared as a notable success since more than one-tenth of its members acquired sufficient capital to become entrepreneurs. (32)

Nevertheless, these integrative phenomena remained marginal to the fundamental class alignments of the period which were, in turn, a function of the relatively undeveloped state of French capitalism. The absence, furthermore, of a generally recognized bargaining agent on behalf of significant numbers of workers meant, in conjunction with the widespread hostility of employers and their organizations to existing trade unions, (33) that efforts at co-optation would have resembled pre-capitalist patriarchal patterns of class domination more than the "modern," quasi-spontaneous products of class collaboration. (34)

B. The Third Republic to World War I

Despite general agreement concerning the comparative insignificance of labor aristocratic strata in France, (35) varying explanations have been propounded to account for this divergent development. (36) One major strand of thought on this subject does not emphasize the formation of a labor aristocracy as such but rather the conditions which underlay the distinctive French labor movement. This view adverts to the fact that as a result of the large agrarian population and of the relatively low degree of urbanization, crafts in rural areas and medium-szied towns were in a superior position to maintain themselves. Moreover, the preservation of the independent agrarian population and the constant increase in the number of rentiers provided the basis for a large consumption and luxury goods-producing sector which was characterized by a below-average organic composition of capital, thereby reinforcing the comparatively low degree of capital concentration and centralization in French industry. (37)

The main exponent of this argument considered the absence of the powerful classical sources of replenishment of the reserve army of the unemployed--namely, the proletarianization of peasants and (independent) craft workers, release of labor consequent upon an increasing organic composition of capital and minimal population growth--to have provided the background against which a comparatively strong increase in real wages could take place. (38) According to this reasoning, the combination of favorable market conditions for labor power and a national tradition of political democracy created the basis for the greater strength of manifest reformism/revisionism in France than in Germany. (39) The syndicalist program of direct action and of the general strike was, on the other hand, seen as a function of flagging capital concentration and centralization: in view of the absence of tangible signposts of the evolution of socialism within the womb of capitalism and against the background of a long-term hostile parliamentary majority of the supporters of private ownership of the means of production, class conscious workers felt strongly attracted to radical trade unionism as a form of socialist activity. (40)

Another theoretical approach, though partly complementary to the preceding one, offers a variant interpretation of some of the same forces alluded to by the latter. The proponent of this view posits that narrower wage differentials than those prevailing in Britain

militated against the growth of a labor aristocracy interested only in reforms. French economic growth was neither dynamic enough to raise demanded trades into a labor aristocracy nor catastrophic enough to ruin declining ones, but it was regular enough to maintain steady pressure on the economic position of most trades and to form a more homogeneous skilled proletariat. (41)

Having already gained, according to this view, "some degree" of control over the process of production, such skilled workers resented the "employer as a superfluous parasite" whose removal would have put an end to their exploitation. (42) Given, finally, the probability that skilled workers were, prior to World War I,

undergoing greater real and relative deprivation with respect
to the deterioration of traditional working conditions than factory
workers, the author of this view concludes that, for this period
at least, artisans did not represent a privileged proletarian
minority. (43)

The following evaluation of these sets of arguments will attempt
to arrive at a more adequate analysis by eliminating the inconsistencies inherent in these approaches.

In order to quantify the gradual transformation of the
French class structure, the following indicators are presented
showing the composition of the industrial labor force according
to the categories of employer, self-employed and employee for
France and Germany. In 1882, approximately one-eighth of the
German industrial work force was composed of employers, one-
quarter of self-employed and five-eighths of employees. By
1895, the employers and the self-employed accounted for but
one-tenth and one-sixth respectively, whereas employees accounted for three-quarters of all those employed in industry,
mining and construction. Finally, by 1907, the employers and
the self-employed had each been reduced to one-eleventh,
whereas employees represented nine-elevenths of the total. (44)
In France, on the other hand, the censuses conducted in 1896,
1901 and 1906 revealed scarcely any change at all: employers
constituted approximately one-tenth, the self-employed three-
tenths and the employees three-fifths of all those occupied in
industry. (45) The wage labor-capital relationship became more
widespread at an early stage in Germany and continued to
encompass ever greater segments of industry whereas its scope
remained more or less constant in France.

If the intensity--in contradistinction to the extensity--of
the capital-labor relationship is expressed by the number of
employees per establishment, then the relative backwardness
of French capitalism reveals itself to be less straightforward
than the foregoing data indicated. If the non-employing self-
employed are omitted, (46) then the average number of persons
per establishment in German industry, mining and construction
rose from 5.4 in 1882 to 7.4 in 1895 and, finally, to 9.0 in
1907. (47) In France, on the other hand, the corresponding
figure fluctuated about six for the three census years of 1896,
1901 and 1906. (48) Table 36 shows the composition of French
and German industrial establishments according to size-classes
during the first decade of the twentieth century.

Only about one-sixth of German industrial employees worked
in establishments of one to five employees compared to almost
one-quarter of their French counterparts; this relationship is

Table 36. Share of Wage and Salary Workers employed in Industrial[a] Establishments in Germany (1907) and France (1906) according to Employment Size-Classes (in per cent) (49)

	1-5 workers	6-50 workers	more than 50 workers
Germany	16.2	28.5	55.3
France	24.9	26.3	48.8

[a]Mining, industry and construction

similar to that obtaining for the non-employing self-employed in both countries. As the size-class increased, however, French employees were almost as concentrated as their German counterparts. In fact, a proportionally greater share of French than of German industrial workers was employed in establishments with more than 1,000 employees. In 1906, two-fifths of all French industrial workers were employed in establishments of one hundred or more workers while over one-ninth worked in establishments with more than 1,000 employees. (50) By 1906, the average number of employees per establishment exceeded 500 in the following branches (the average is indicated parenthetically): coal mining (984); tin plate (904); armanents (863); blast-furnace and steel-works (711); wool-combing (694); and plate glass (551). (51)

Thus despite the generally undeveloped state of French capitalism prior to World War I, (52) significant numbers of workers, particularly in mining, metallurgy and textiles, were subject to huge concentrations of capital and experienced their working conditions side by side with large aggregates of wage earners. (53)

Nevertheless, comparatively few French workers--regardless of their position within the division of labor or of their degree of subordination to capital--were trade unionists. (54) In 1881, approximately 60,000 trade unionists were recorded in France (55)--about 10,000 more than in Germany prior to the passage of the Antisocialist Law; by the mid-1890s French trade unionists numbered more than 400,000 but increased rather slowly so that by 1898 German trade unionists already outnumbered them. As World War I approached, French trade unionists exceeded one million but were outnumbered two and one-half to one by their German counterparts. (56) Even this aggregate figure overstates the degree of organization of French industry since about forty per cent of French trade unionists worked in agriculture, trade, commerce and the service sector. (57) Although the members of the unions co-ordinated by the Confederation Générale du Travail, which was formed in 1895, had originally been concentrated in small and medium-sized establishments employing largely skilled workers, (58) by 1914 members from branches of large-scale production, such as mining, textiles and chemicals, began to bulk large within the total membership. Disaggregated by branch, the degree of organization does not appear to correlate significantly with concentration of employment or skill level on the one hand or with militancy or revolutionary policy on the other. Thus in 1914, the building trades, which represented largely skilled workers in small establishments, belonged to the revolutionary wing of trade unionism and were almost one-quarter organized; (59) the metal trades, which were also considered revolutionary, were only one-eighth organized whereas the chemical industry, composed chiefly of workers in large plants, was three-elevenths organized. (60)

This apparently random distribution of characteristics assumes a different meaning when the two basically different types of French labor radicalism are examined. The older unions of the skilled, which had passed through several phases of radicalism during the nineteenth century, constituted the first type. During the Third Republic this radicalism assumed the form of trade socialism, which was based on the "professional privilege" of a stratum of urban (mainly Parisian) workers whose anti-capitalism envisioned no specified place for unskilled industrial workers. Although the latter were not excluded from the movement, little effort was expended to mobilize them, while the issue of immediate corporate seizure of control over individual establishments by local trade unions was scarcely geared to appeal to the unskilled whose immediate economic interests lay elsewhere. (61) This guild-like approach of the unions of the skilled no doubt in part prompted Marx and Engels in the 1880s to liken them to the English trade unions of the period. (62)

This relatively privileged status of the skilled was, however, under attack from progressing industrialization so that the trade unions became involved in attempts to combat the deterioration of working and living conditions associated with dequalification processes. Consequently, the struggles engaged in by the skilled assumed a different character in accordance with the progress of capital in the various branches. (63) But despite the de facto neglect of the immediate interests of the bulk of the unskilled by the trade socialists, the latter's distinctly anti-capitalist orientation (64) renders a comparison with late nineteenth century English trade unionists qua labor aristocrats implausible. Although the thesis according to which this stratum imposed its reformist orientation on the French labor movement as a whole bears some similarity to left-wing Social Democratic analyses in pre-World War I Germany, it remains to be seen whether the charge of aristocratic corruption associated with the latter also applies to the French artisans.

The second type of labor radicalism was to be found in the unions of the unskilled, which originated in connection with the formation of the Parti Ouvrier Français in 1882 by the Marxist Jules Guesde in opposition to the reformist "possibilist" or "opportunist" wing of French socialism. Although the Guesdists shared the Possibilists' appreciation of the importance of uneven economic development as a factor in the creation of politically and socially relevant differentiation within the working class, they drew the conclusion that the skilled urban workers should be rejected as petty bourgeois elements and that organizational efforts should be focused on that sector of the proletariat which represented the future of capitalism--namely, the unskilled industrial workers, who were concentrated in mining, textiles and metallurgy in the northern regions of France. (65) Yet there is little evidence that sharp differences persisted between these two trade union movements especially in light of the latter's relative insignificance and of the ultimate coalescence of both in revolutionary syndicalism. (66)

But despite the relative reformism of the skilled unionists, the implacable enmity shown the non-yellow unionists by the employing class and requited by the former (67) precluded the possibility of the organized artisans' performing any stabilizing function for French capital let alone that of being solicited to act as such agents. Given the considerable wage differentials between skilled and unskilled workers in France, (68) there is little reason to assume that they were responsible for national labor aristocracies elsewhere but not in France. (69)

Although the gradual process of capitalist industrialization and the correspondingly long tenure of petty and non-capitalist sectors of production (70) contributed to the relatively homogeneous structure of the French working class, the comparative unity of proletarian political action can be understood only in the context of the property-owning and class structure, which militated against independent working class politics as they were possible in Britain and practiced in Germany. (71) Under these circumstances it is questionable whether the skilled unionists ever performed a reformist role equivalent to that ascribed to their German counterparts since they--paradoxically--did not "majoritize" the labor movement to the same extent as the latter. The separate existence of Marxist-led organizations of the unskilled in France--which was lacking in Germany--meant that such unions were in a better position to combat reformist tendencies. The almost complete overlap of skilled unionists and Social Democratic trade unionists in Germany, on the other hand, meant that the former, in spite of whatever reformist tendencies they may have exhibited, bore almost the entire burden of working class socialism whereas the organized artisans shared this role in France. (72)

Chapter 10
Labor Aristocracies in other European Countries

The authors who have confirmed the presence of national labor aristocracies in the less industrialized countries of Europe (1) may be classified under two headings: 1. non-Marxist scholars who identify labor aristocrats almost exclusively by their above-average standards of living; and 2. Leninists, who trace the corruption of certain working class strata back to a bourgeois strategy of divide-and-conquer based on colonial or imperialist "super-profits."

The first group is typified by Robert Michels who posited that, "The worker's ultimate goal is to rise into the petty bourgeoisie" or rather "to live like the petty bourgeoisie" while remaining a manual worker. (2) Although this alleged goal may seem innocent enough in itself when identified with the desire for "a better and more carefree existence" of organized workers as a class, (3) it is, according to Michels, a function of the "need for differentiation" among workers which is, on the objective side, encouraged by the production system in modern industrial plants. (4) Drawing on examples from the trade union movement in England, Germany, France, Belgium, Holland, Italy and the United States, (5) Michels asserts categorically that:

> The aristocratic elements of the working class, the best paid, those who approximate most closely to the bourgeoisie, pursue tactics of their own. ... Working-class history abounds in examples showing how certain fractions or categories of the proletariat have, under the influence of interests peculiar to their own sub-class, detached themselves from the great army of labour and made common cause with the bourgeoisie. (6)

Although no societally relevant sections of the organized French or German working classes collaborated with the bourgeoisie prior to World War I--and collaboration during that war encompassed the entire national working class--, and although the English labor aristocracy became increasingly integrated into the aggregate working class once its separate interests and special position began to disintegrate, Michels insists on the emerging bifurcation of the proletariat.

> In the womb of the fourth estate the fifth is already stirring. One of the most crucial dangers for Socialism consists in the ... hypothesis that gradually a series of strata of the working class, by means of the joint action of the general increase of social wealth in union with the most energetic efforts of the workers to elevate their class position, attains a pinnacle on which the workers will, to be sure, not lose the general human feeling of never having enough ..., on which however they will become bourgeoisified and contented to the extent that the ardent longing of the masses, which was born of deprivation, for a fundamentally different social system gradually becomes foreign to them. (7)

To the extent that this analysis has proved to be accurate, it has not been with regard to a privileged minority of the working class but rather to the organized working classes as a whole in their manifest political behavior. Thus even on the level of the seemingly plausible relationship between economic improvement and reformism, Michels' generalization appears unwarranted.

A labor aristocracy may, as already noted, arise under specific historical conditions of internal uneven development in which the manual working class becomes highly differentiated in the process of production and segmented into strata experiencing disparate working and living conditions. A modern labor aristocracy, however, further requires a national organization of bargaining agents on behalf of the owners of skilled labor power within a general political framework that would permit and/or enforce the stratified distribution of democratic rights within the proletariat. Although these conditions restrict the phenomenon of a labor aristocracy to countries undergoing capitalist industrialization and characterized by national trade unions, they admit the possibility of the formation of a labor aristocracy in countries other than the most highly developed capitalist ones. (8)

It is possible, for example, to point to the Scandinavian countries for instances of manifest organizational divisions within the working class. The fact that the skilled in Denmark before World War I exhibited little interest in organizing the unskilled derived in part from and, in turn, reinforced the social barriers between the two groups. (9) In Sweden, too, the unskilled in the building trades were forced to form their own union (in 1891) because the unions of the unskilled refused to admit them. (10) Yet in both countries the unskilled became significant forces within the trade union movement. In Denmark their general union soon became the largest in the country, representing, by 1900, almost three-tenths of all unionists and attaining a membership almost four times as large as the next largest union. (11) The unskilled workers of the Swedish building trades expanded to include the unskilled of other branches, thereby becoming a mjaor organization. (12) The fact, however, that an extraordinarily high percentage of the--relatively small number of--industrial workers in these countries belonged to trade unions (13) virtually precluded the possibility of the rise of a semi-autonomous proletarian political elite. If the trade union movements in Scandinavia, which were even more closely associated with the Social Democratic Party than was the case in Germany, proved to be reformist, then this tendency applied to the movement as a whole and was neither restricted to nor borne exclusively by a minority of better-paid workers. (14)

There are few countries for which systematic studies have uncovered labor aristocracies with a long-term continuity of aggregate societal relevance. In Switzerland, workers in Geneva were divided in the 1860s into two groups typified by: watch-makers, who were skilled, Swiss citizens with political rights and relatively high standards of living; and construction workers on large projects, who were largely low-paid foreigners without political rights. (15) Whereas the former, who considered themselves aristocrats within the working class, (16) were "for the most part satisfied with their lot" and believed they had "nothing to gain by the social revolution," the latter did not see any means of leaving their poverty "than a social revolution involving the complete and collective emancipation of all workers." (17) But in connection with capital-labor conflicts in the Geneva construction industry between 1868 and 1870 (18) the watchmakers became involved in the aggregate workers' movement so that Marx entered into a tactical alliance with them in order to combat Bakunin's influence in Switzerland. (19) Apart from episodic phenomena, the labor aristocracy does not appear to have asserted itself in pre-World War I Switzerland. (20)

In Italy, the existence of large wage differentials (21) and an "internal colony" in the South (22) proved, even in the presence of paternalistic attempts by employers to create localized labor aristocracies, (23) insufficient to transform the organized skilled into a labor aristocracy. (24) The un-reservedly repressive policies of the state and of employers toward working class organizations exerted a unifying influence on the Italian proletariat that partly compensated for the divisive impact of the North-South regional bifurcation on the occupational and skill structure as well as on the working and living conditions of the working class. (25)

In Austria-Hungary the dimension of ethnic fragmentation was superimposed on regional segmentation. (26) Although the German speaking workers of Lower Austria and Bohemia have been characterized as labor aristocrats on the basis of their domination of the skilled occupations and of their higher standards of living, (27) the separatist German nationalist movement in Bohemia and Moravia refrained from making common cause with employers in spite of their diatribes aimed at ethnic Slavs who, in their view, were being employed by (German-speaking) capitalists to lower prevailing wage levels by threatening traditional standards. (28) Despite the fact that Czech nationalist groups also avoided alliances with employers' associations, Austria-Hungary (29) may offer the example of a capitalist class that enjoyed the benefits of a disunited working class without having had to distribute "crumbs" to either of the latter's factions. (30)

The primary weakness of Lenin's explanation of reformism consists in its lack of mediations. (31) For even if his description of the economic mechanism channeling colonial or imperialist "super-profits" to a restricted stratum of or to an entire national working class were accepted as theoretically sound, (32) the links Lenin analytically forged to a corresponding labor aristocratic consciousness were no stronger than those sketched in Hobson's supra-historical view of the use to which economic parasitism had always put colonies--namely, as a type of bread and circuses to "bribe its lower classes into acquiescence." (33) And even if this connection were granted, Lenin provided no reasonable let alone rigorous explanation of how this numerically small upper stratum of the working class was able to majoritize the entire class. (34)

This almost exclusive reliance on factors related to the world market (35) has meant that Leninist writers have found it difficult to account for the appearance of labor aristocratic tendencies in countries that possessed no colonial or imperialist advantages to fall back on as a "bribery fund." In the case of a recent study of the Russian working class, this difficulty is avoided at the price of voluntaristically overthrowing Lenin's entire conceptual structure: in order to explain why metal workers in St. Petersburg, who received high wages from firms realizing monopolistically high profits, were not labor aristocrats but, rather, members of the revolutionary vanguard, a Soviet scholar reverts to the argument that these high wages did not

represent a bribe but, rather, compensated the skill and
intensity of labor associated with the work. (36) Although this
argument may be correct, it offers no general method of mediat-
ing economic and sociopolitical factors. (37)

It is almost axiomatic that a Leninist study of a country as
backward as capitalist Bulgaria concludes that the labor aristocracy was of little significance. (38) Analogously, writers in
the Leninist tradition trace the rise of a Swedish labor aristocracy to the transformation of Sweden's trade and capital
position in connection with World War I, despite the fact that
the Swedish labor movement had been reformist earlier as
well. (39)

In summary, then, few studies have demonstrated the
existence of a long-lived, politically relevant labor aristocracy
outside of the major capitalist nations of Europe prior to World
War I. Although reformist tendencies prevailed in several
countries (such as Denmark and Sweden), the progressive role
assumed by the upper stratum of the working class differed
so sharply from that of the conservative English labor aristocracy that application of the same concept to both phenomena
becomes misleading if not false. In several other instances,
moreover, no proof was forthcoming that laboristic reformism
owed more to the attitudes of the economically privileged strata
than to those of the working class as a whole.

Appendix. South Africa: A Racial Aristocracy of Labor?

The example of an economically, politically and socially privileged
sector of workers in South Africa raises claims to particular
analytic interest in consequence of the extraordinary clarity
that appears to surround the issue of a labor aristocracy in
that country. Thus even those who consider the notion otherwise "politically and intellectually suspect," perceive the unique
possibility of demostrating "scientifically the existence of an
authentic labour aristocracy." (40)

Yet in spite of the obvious advantages accruing to white
workers, the racial dimension brings into focus an important
political and theoretical question that is more difficult to resolve
in other contexts--namely, what are the advantages accruing
to the capitalist class? An examination of this issue will also
contribute to an understanding of the effects of a labor aristocracy on the stability of a national capitalist mode of production
as well as to that of the nature of the subjective mediations

acting on the agents of the ruling class in motivating the latter to adopt a labor aristocratic strategy of industrial relations.

The issue of the conscious structuring of aggregate class relations assumed a different character in South Africa in the late nineteenth and early twentieth century from that which had been familiar from the European capitalist countries. Whereas the spontaneous dynamic of capital accumulation in Europe, based on a prior accumulation that had created a property-less proletariat, had sufficed to reproduce its necessary exploitable human material and to render general labor recruitment superfluous, a decision had to be made in South Africa whether to encourage the immigration of white Europeans, to recruit low-wage Asians or, finally, to devise methods to diminish the native "Africans' high 'leisure preference.'" (41) In contrast, the historical conditions underlying the formation of another white settler colony, Australia, created a radically different class constellation: given the absence of a large aboriginal population and the relatively free access to land, capitalist class formation in the sense "that a larger group of identical people was exploited for a whole lifetime by another group of identical people" (42) was delayed until the twentieth century. The absence of a large aboriginal population, whose destruction or expropriation might have created strong ties between workers and capitalists/landowners, as well as the antagonisms between the largely convict immigrant population and the ruling classes (43) did lead to the emergence of a militant labor movement which, favored by the high costs of immigration and the lack of large-scale industry, was able to thwart attempts by employers to organize mass immigration. (44) A third type of English settler colony, the United States, was marked by a two-fold labor recruitment policy: after the Civil War in principle released black slave labor for industrial capitalist exploitation, mass immigration of Irish and non-English speaking Europeans was systematically encouraged.

This tripartite division of the working class in the United States (i.e., ex-slaves, immigrants and whites of longer residence) reintroduces the question of the factors motivating capitalist labor strategy. (45) Why did the capitalist class--to the extent that an aggregate policy emerged from the needs of individual capitals--opt for one source of labor rather than for another? More specifically: did factors other than the lowest possible wage level and the greatest possible immediate profit enter into the formulation of a labor policy?

Some authors deny that extra-economic factors have played a part in capitalist motivations. One sociologist, for example,

230

in opposing the view that capitalists play off various fractions of the working class against one another, insists that the former prefer laissez faire on the labor market while any politically motivated decisions result from employers' having yielded to a labor aristocracy "under duress." (46) According to this view, the alleged capitalist tactic of divide-and-rule implies that capitalists pay one group more than they must, an approach "which would only be rational if paying more to one group enabled them to pay another substantially less. Capital would have to be 'bribing' white labor to help keep black labor cheap." (47)

Although it may be true, in terms of supply and demand on the labor market, that restriction of blacks (or of any other proletarian grouping) to certain departments of the division of labor may in fact exert downward pressure on the wage level of this grouping, such an empirical objection does not form the principal weakness of the aforementioned view. Rather, it is defective because it assumes that which is to be demonstrated--namely, that immediate economic considerations are the only relevant ones to capitalists. It fails, moreover, to distinguish between two possible and not necessarily mutually exclusive strategies: 1. an otherwise disadvantaged group is favored in order to undermine the power of a labor aristocracy; and 2. a labor aristocracy is encouraged or tolerated in order to forestall the organization of the mass of the working class. (48) Both approaches were adopted in South Africa--simultaneously and as historical alternatives.

Hannah Arendt's vision "of a phenomenon that occurs whenever the mob becomes the dominant factor in the alliance between mob and capital" (49) takes to its logical conclusion the aforementioned denial that capitalist labor policies incorporate extra-economic goals. By assuming the working class to be the subject rather than the object of social change, Arendt can ascribe to it--rather than to the capitalist class--the practical insight

> that profit motives are not holy and can be overruled, that societies can function according to principles other than economic, and that such circumstances may favor these who under conditions of rationalized production and the capitalist system would belong to the underprivileged. South Africa's race society taught the mob the great lesson of which it had always had a confused premonition, that through sheer violence an underprivileged group could create a class lower than itself, that for this purpose it did not even need a revolution but could band together with groups of the ruling classes. ... (50)

231

Yet even Arendt is constrained to introduce a major economic element by conceding that, "Imperialism ... was willing to abandon the so-called laws of capitalist production ... so long as profits from specific investments were safe." (51)

Although there were doubtless numerous instances of wage structures that encroached upon normal profits and that only with violence could be covered by Marx's notion of the "moral" component of the value of labor power; (52) and although the racist ideological aspects of imperialism that Arendt analyzes should not be underestimated, (53) capitalist acquiescence in many of the demands by white labor for discriminatory labor market policies must also be seen as part of a long-term strategy to maintain capitalism in South Africa altogether.

In this connection it is crucial to distinguish between the political-economic situation in South Africa in the late nineteenth and early twentieth century on the one hand and that emerging during the post-World War II period. During the latter period the expansion of capital in South Africa became incompatible with the continued exclusion of the native African population from occupations previously reserved for whites; at the same time the joint effect of the increased urbanization of the black population (which was accompanied by an increase in the cost of living) and of growing political instability rendered a narrowing of wage differentials between blacks and whites inevitable. (54) During the earlier period a different constellation of forces obtained. Although diamond mining required little skill at first, as more scientific methods of exploitation were introduced in the 1880s, skilled miners had to be imported, chiefly from Britain, since there was a general lack of qualified labor in South Africa. (55) At the outset the relationship between the skilled whites and the unskilled blacks bore some resemblance to that between labor aristocrats and the unskilled in England in respect of the underlying economic mechanisms; (56) but as non-whites gradually acquired the experience and skill required for certain occupations, and as increased numbers of Afrikaaners became supernumerary in the agricultural sector and thus began to seek jobs as unskilled laborers in urban areas which had theretofore been performed by native Africans, certain groups of Europeans developed a "sectional interest ... to exclude Native competitors." (57)

Competition with blacks--whether for skilled or unskilled positions--meant not only reduced employment opportunities for whites but also an inevitable reduction in white wage levels. The latter resulted not only from the altered configurations of supply and demand but also from the vast gap in the prevailing standards of living between whites and blacks. If white workers' high wages were in some measure a function of black workers' low wages, then even a radically egalitarian and anti-racist trade union policy on the part of the white proletariat could not have avoided the eventual reduction of the white wage level. Under these circumstances the racist ideological superstructure had "reacted back" onto and become integrated into the material base to such a degree that abandonment by white workers of their exclusionary policies toward non-white workers would have been visionary. In point of fact, white workers tended to perceive moves by employers to introduce non-whites in much the same manner in which militant trade unionists throughout the world viewed entrepreneurial tactics that resulted in a deterioration of working and living conditions. (58)

Although attempts by capitalists to employ larger numbers of native black and imported Asian laborers were in part stymied by "the collective strength of white miners," (59) whom it was consequently necessary to "placate," (60) the ruling class was neither indifferent nor hostile to the formation of a white labor aristocracy. Alfred Milner, the British High Commissioner for South Africa, who was instrumental in importing Asian laborers to the mines at the conclusion of the Boer War, expressed the concerns of that class with great clarity. Although the decision to import laborers was dictated largely by the requirements of profitability, (61) Milner, as a representative of the dominant British capitalist class, was acutely aware of the dangers to his class that would have resulted from the increased cohesiveness of the white working class that the movement toward an all-white labor force would have generated. (62)

> We do not want a white proletariat in this country. The position of the whites among the vastly more numerous black population requires that even their lowest ranks should be able to maintain a standard of living far above that of the poorest section of the population of a purely white country. (63)

Milner therefore planned to shift whites out of mining and into what he considered more permanent employment. (64)

Paradoxically, then, capitalists were willing to implement white workers' demands to separate whites and non-whites by trade or industry, albeit for radically different reasons: whereas white workers feared that non-white competition would eventually depress their wages, employers feared that employing large numbers of non-whites in jobs also performed by whites would inevitably lead to "civilized" wages for non-whites and to either a more unified multiracial proletariat or potentially destabilizing unrest on the part of the white working class. Hence the desire of employers to have mining stamped as low-paid, non-white work, with whites performing almost exclusively supervisory tasks. (65)

General Smuts, the South African Premier during much of the post-World War I period, conceptualized the dilemma confronting South African capital during a parliamentary debate of a minimum wage bill. (66)

> Our wages paid to skilled workers in South Africa are far in excess of what are paid in any other country, except America, and we were able to do it because we paid the black man such a low wage. The native only receiving two shillings a day we could afford to pay 20s. to the white man and more. ... Supposing a black man in future is not paid 2s. but the civilized wage of 5s. ... Can we, after that, continue to pay the skilled man 20s or 25s.? Naturally that man's pay must come down. There will not be enough to go round and keep the industries going. ... (67)

This view would suggest that white workers and white employers, as classes on the aggregate societal level, not only shared in but also vied for the exploitation of non-white workers. That is to say, apart from any gains stemming from firm-level co-exploitation or subcontracting, the entire economic chain regulating prices of production, aggregate redistribution of surplus value qua profit and wages must have been so structured as to insure white workers a share of the surplus labor expended by black workers regardless of whether specific whites worked in branches or firms employing non-whites. (68)

Marxist and non-Marxist scholars alike have argued along these lines. Among the latter, Doxey has promoted this view forcefully by pointing to "an 'inner' privileged society," which has been "subsidized by surpluses created by the low-paid non-whites." (69)

> With a national income per capita only a fraction of that of Canada, the United States and Australia, white workers in South Africa have been able to command incomes almost on a par with those received by workers in those countries. (70)

On the assumption that differences in skill level and/or intensity of labor between white and non-white workers alone cannot account for wage differentials, the foregoing argument appears logically unassailable. The same validity attaches to a recent attempt to demonstrate quantitatively that white workers have been sharing in the surplus value produced by black workers. (71)

It is simplistic, however, to present the complex socio-economic and political-economic causality underlying the formation of the South African labor aristocracy as the economic pay-off to the latter "in return" for its "political support for the State." (72) For historically it was not the capitalist class that initially solicited political allegiance from the white working class in exchange for European-level wages, but rather the white proletariat that insisted on such wages and contributed to the election of a Boer government (i.e., one not controlled by the economically dominant British cpaitalist class) that, over the years, induced and compelled employers to discriminate against blacks and Asians. (73)

Capitalist acquiescence was a function not only of the pressure exerted by the Boers and the white working class, but also of the lack of a feasible alternative. Skilled workers had to be imported during the nineteenth century; even if the inclination had been present, it would not have been possible to train black workers quickly enough. But white workers from Europe could not have been paid less than they had been accustomed to in their countries of origins, for otherwise they would have been unwilling to emigrate. Similarly, once employed, these workers would scarcely have permitted capitalists to reduce their wages to near-African levels. If they had chosen to resist by recourse to arms, the employing class might have had no alternative to arming a black labor aristocracy--a very unlikely strategy. The capitalists had, in other words, to become reconciled to the long-term presence of a white working class whose wages would in part represent a drag on profits extracted from black labor. But given this enormous source of exploitation and the nearly monopolistic control of world diamond and gold output, (74) the joint appropriation of surplus value did not result in rates of profit below those obtained elsewhere in the capitalist world. (75)

The fact that South African capitalists had at their disposal the world market-mediated wherewithal to meet white workers' demands for Lenin-like crumbs and even whole loaves, provided the objective economic basis for the "alliance" between white workers and capitalists. That this cooperation did not come about solely as a result of pressure from the former may also be conjectured on the basis of the need British cpaitalists had for the presence of a white working class as a buffer between it and the mass of the non-white proletariat. White proletarians served, moreover, as a alibi for the bourgeoisie by destroying the perfect overlap between class and race. (76)

Chapter 11
Results

He that puts not constantly the same sign for the same idea, but uses the same words sometimes in one and sometimes in another signification, ought to pass in the schools and conversation for as fair a man, as he does in the market and exchange, who sells several things under the same name. (1)

In a number of crucial areas the present study has arrived at conclusions that diverge sharply from the postulates of the Marxist and non-Marxist political and scholarly literature.

1. The basis upon which the peculiar position, role, privileges and power of national labor aristocracies rested was the possession and control, that is, the access to the acquisition and monopolization, of relatively complex manual industrial skills.

2. Although this skill-base in some instances coincided or overlapped with ethnic (Austria-Hungary), racial (South Africa), religious (Ireland) or regional (Italy) proximate sources of working class divisiveness, the latter functioned authoritatively only insofar as they served to circumscribe the success of those segments of the class which might realistically have aspired to the status of the skilled. Skill was, in other words, the element common and essential to all national labor aristocracies, whereas the other, chiefly ascribed, characteristics were, with reference to the capitalist mode of production, accidental. (2) Being an unskilled Irish Protestant, Northern Italian or German-speaking Austrian was associated with certain superior social and often political and economic conditions by virtue of the power residing in these larger groups to withhold vital skills. (3)

3. The skill structure itself underwent dramatic changes in accordance with the qualitative and quantitative requirements of varying rates, conditions and forms of capital accumulation. The concomitant intersecting processes of skilling and de-skilling involved on-going restratification of the working class, which threatened and ultimately dissolved numerous preserves of proletarian privilege while elevating new groups into new

236

positions of authority. With very few exceptions, no super-ordinate proletarian positions were free of considerable insecurity during the lifetime of their occupants let alone during that of the particular trades to which they were attached.

4. The skill hierarchy was subject to an overriding tendency toward greater compression and compactness. Although certain forms of technological progress thwarted this general trend toward increased homogeneity during some periods, and although the deteriorating conditions and growing insecurity associated with de-skilling often exacerbated intra-working class tensions, the tendential equalization of working and living conditions provided an effective basis for organizational and political unification. (4)

5. The upper stratum of skilled workers itself comprehended disparate sectors: traditional craftsmen and artisans, such as jewelers, watchmakers and saddlers, working in very small units and producing entire commodities; carpenters and masons working at many different sites with many different men, building dissimilar structures, some of which however would have been familiar to distant ancestors; machinists in medium-sized shops performing precision work with relatively new tools and outside longstanding traditions; and skilled iron and steel workers, massed in hundreds and thousands, earning the highest working class wages--in part by coexploiting the un-skilled--under highly unsanitary and dangerous conditions. Thus although their living conditions may have borne a tolerable resemblance to one another's, their work routines and rhythms, their relations to employers and co-workers, their traditions, organizations and futures set them apart from one another. In this important sense they constituted not a unified but an asynchronous stratum--rooted in production processes antedating and destined to be swept away by capitalism as well as in those of the most advanced industrial sectors.

6. The peculiar unity of this stratum derived, in the first instance, not from their common front over against the less skilled, but rather from their resistance in their individual trades and occupations to the new form of industrial heteronomy which was obscured by contractual autonomy: they were the first workers to struggle for and to secure, in a systematic and institutionalized manner, a modicum of substantive protection against the imperative of self-expanding capital. Through their trade unions they initiated a permanent process of undermining "the passive society of workers" (5) which the capitalist organization of labor had created out of formerly self-conscious agents of production. At their inception, then, the organiza-

tions of the skilled performed a progressive, that is, future-oriented, potentially classwide role of which employers and the state took a dim view. Such a stratum was not artificially created by the bourgeoisie for ideological reasons, but arose spontaneously within the framework of developing industrial capitalism.

7. Although the exclusion of the less skilled from these organizations reflected and deepened an already existing dichotomy within the working class, the gap between the corresponding standards of living was not unique in the history of dependant classes. (6) What proved to be new was the differential scope of public and, more particularly, political expression associated with this organizational stratification. But as long as formally undemocratic political procedures discriminated against the entire working class indiscriminately, and as long as trade unions were outlawed, subject to rigorous restrictions and vigorous prosecution, or merely randomly tolerated without formal recognition, socio-economic fissures found little politically relevant room for expansion. In Britain this situation was not fundamentally altered until the passage of the Second Reform Bill and the legalization of trade unions in the 1860s and 1870s. (7) The partial enfranchisement and organization of the working class created the possibility of a politically efficacious autonomization of the interests of one stratum of the working class to the neglect or even at the expense of the whole class in the name of which politics were being conducted.

8. There is some evidence that during the period between this juncture and the rise of unions of the unskilled and a socialist movement in the 1880s and 1890s, British employers and the British state on the one hand and trade union leaders, with at least the tacit approval of many members, on the other hand, engaged in a form of quid pro quo that did not substantiate the unions' self-proclaimed role as the representative of aggregate labor power. That the extent of this active class collaboration remained limited can be explained by the distinction between a labor aristocracy surrounded by an otherwise politically inert working class (such as was the case in Britain from the 1850s through the 1870s) and one confronted with and hostile to a radical movement of the less skilled. (8)

9. Little doubt can, however, attach to the conclusion that the pronounced gap in economic conditions between the labor aristocracy and the remainder of the working class also served to bifurcate this class socially both at the point of production and in major spheres of daily reproduction. The self-image of the labor aristocrats as the respectable segment of the

manual working class, poised midway between the unskilled and the petty bourgeoisie, was confirmed by their interaction with these strata and the latter's attitudes toward them. (9)

10. In contradistinction to the foregoing socio-historically specified conception of the labor aristocracy, that used by Marx and Engels--and more emphatically by many in their school and parties--referred, superficially, to any body of comparatively well-paid workers devoid of radical, socialist or revolutionary leanings. Such usage not only deprived the notion of any meaningful applicability as a research tool, but was, as an abstraction, false; elevated to an inflexible dogma, guiding political practice, it contributed to catastrophic class alignments. (10)

11. Where, as in most of Europe, the aforementioned specific political framework was absent--chiefly because the proletariat as a whole was openly disadvantaged--, no labor aristocracy in control of national working class politics emerged. On the contrary, the better-situated workers in many countries formed the core of the leading left-wing movements; firm-level or localized attempts to cultivate patronal relations of loyalty were not coordinated horizontally or vertically to forge national or class-wide links. (11) In other instances, moreover, entire work forces proved to be the target of such tactics, which were thus deprived of a stratum-specific dimension. (12)

12. The world market did not fulfill an overriding causal role--attributed to it by Engels, Lenin and others--in fostering a British (or any other) national labor aristocracy. Britain's international industrial dominance coincided in part with a prominent phase in the career of the British labor aristocracy. Yet the obvious interconnections must not be allowed to mask the fact that the essential preconditions of the latter were given independently of the former. To be sure, some plausibility attaches to the argument that the accrual of world market-mediated "extra-profits" enabled the British capitalist class to seek an accommodation with a thin upper stratum of workers, whereas the loss of these gains enforced an abandonment of such a strategy. But it is, a priori, also reasonable to conclude that the attainment of high rates of profitability and accumulation, in part without reference to the conditions of exploitation of the domestic working class, dispensed the bourgeoisie from the need to pursue any concerted policy at all towards the British proletariat; analogously, the disappearance of such a favorable international constellation may have necessitated a more cautious and conciliatory class policy designed to avoid the socio-political instability associated with the requirements of intensified forms of compensatory domestic

exploitation. Empirical evidence lends little credence to either of these arguments.

13. Apart from Britain, the only zones in which the existence of societally significant national labor aristocracies was verified were the British-settled colonies of South Africa and North America. There the superimposition of racial and ethnic dimensions gave rise to markedly variant mechanisms of privilege and accommodation that called for the elaboration of alternative explanations. Only one of these national labor aristocracies was examined at length.

14. The indiscriminate journalistic, scholarly and political use of a diluted and ahistorical version of the notion of an aristocracy of labor has proved to be misleading and pernicious. As the present study of the nineteenth century has illustrated, each putative national labor aristocracy must be considered as a highly complex phenomenon sui generis. In light of the vast shifts in class structure, economic relations and national and international forms of political struggle since that time, such a caveat would seem almost gratuitous today.

List of Abbreviations

HMSO   Her/His Majesty's Stationery Office
MEW   Karl Marx and Friedrich Engels, <u>Werke</u> (40 vols.; Berlin (DDR): Dietz, 1958-1968)
P.P.   Parliamentary Papers. The volume number, which is necessary for locating the publication cited, refers to the year preceding it; the page number refers to the individual publication and not to the whole colume.
PSS   V.I. Lenin, <u>Polnoe sobranie sochinenii</u> (5th ed., 55 vols.; Moscow: Gosudarstvennoe izdatel'stvo politicheskoi literatury, 1958-1965)

Notes

Notes to the Preface

1 William A. Dobson, president of the Bricklayers' and Masons' International Union, Proceedings of the Nineteenth General Convention of the United Brotherhood of Carpenters and Joiners of America, held in Fort Worth, Texas, September 16-28, 1916, p. 344.

2 See the relevant reporting in the New York Times of May 9, May 16 and May 21, 1970; Richard Schwartz, "Man in Gray and the Violence", New York Post, May 12, 1970, p. 3, cols. 1-2 and p. 90, cols. 1-4; Pete Hamill, "Hard Hats and Cops", ibid., p. 47, cols. 1-3; Engineering News-Record, May 28, 1970, p. 5; Gilbert Burck, "The Building Trades versus the People," Fortune, LXXXII, 4 (October 1970), 96-97; Fred J. Cook, "Hard-hats: The Rampaging Patriots," Nation, June 15, 1970, pp. 712-17. Cf. John Brooks, The Go-Go Years (New York: Waybright & Talley, 1973), pp. 6-10; Richard F. Hamilton, Class and Politics in the United States (New York: Wiley, 1972), p. 498 n. 103.

3 The appearance of a number of British doctoral dissertations in the 1970s, devoted to intensive studies of local labor aristocracies, represented an empirical breakthrough.

1 Attributed to John Frey, one-time president of the Metal Trades Department of the American Federation of Labor, by Max Nomad, Rebels and Renegades (New York: Macmillan, 1932), p. 361. Cf. Fair Wages Committee, Minutes of Evidence taken before the Fair Wages Committee, P.P. 1908, Vol. XXXIV, Cd. 4423, Q. 4952 at p. 203.

2 Only a sample of the most important works may be alluded to: Peter Townsend, Poverty in the United Kingdom (Berkeley: University of California Press, 1979); W.G. Runciman, Relative Deprivation and Social Justice (Berkeley: University of California Press, 1966); John Westergaard and Henrietta Resler, Class in a Capitalist Society (Harmondsworth: Penguin, 1976 (1975)); James O'Connor, The Fiscal Crisis of the State (New York: St. Martin's, 1973); Horst Kern and Michael Schumann, Industriearbeit und Arbeiterbewußtsein (Frankfurt/Main: Europäische Verlagsanstalt, 1973 (1970)); Samuel Bowles and Herbert Gintis, Schooling in Capitalist America (London: Routledge & Kegan Paul, 1976); P.M. Blackburn and Michael Mann, The Working Class in the Labour Market (London: Macmillan, 1979); Chavdar Kiuranov, Sotsialni klasi i sotsialna stratifikatsia (Sofia: Nauka, 1977); Stanley Aronowitz, False Promises (New York: McGraw Hill, 1974 (1973)); Gavin Mackenzie, The Aristocracy of Labor (London: Cambridge University Press, 1973); A.N. Mel'nikov, Sovremennaia klassovaia struktura SShA (Moscow: Mysl', 1974); Robert Blauner, Alienation and Freedom (Chicago: University of Chicago Press, 1973 (1964)); Duncan Gallie, In Search of the New Working Class (Cambridge: Cambridge University Press, 1978); John H. Goldthorpe et al., The Affluent Worker: Industrial Attitudes and Behaviour (Cambridge: Cambridge University Press, 1970); Serge Mallet, La Nouvelle Classe ouvrière (Paris: Editions du Deuil, 1963); Dean Morse, The Peripheral Worker (New York: Columbia University Press, 1969); Sidney Willhelm, Who Needs the Negro? (Cambridge, Mass., 1970); Martin Osterland et al., Materialien zur Lebens- und Arbeitssituation der Industriearbeiter in der BRD (Frankfurt/Main: Europäische Verlagsanstalt, 1973); Projekt Klassenanalyse, Materialien zur Klassenstruktur der BRD, Part 2: Grundrisse der Klassenverhältnisse (1950-1970) (Westberlin: VSA, 1974); Alain Touraine, La Conscience ouvrière (Paris, Editions du Seuil, 1966).

3 Again a small sample must suffice: William J. Wilson, The Declining Significance of Race (Chicago: University of Chicago Press, 1978); Nathan Glazer and Daniel Patrick Moynihan, Beyond the Melting Pot (Cambridge, Mass.: MIT Press, 1965 (1963)); Allison Davis et al., Deep South (Chicago: University of Chicago Press, 1949 (1941)); John Dollard, Caste and Class in a Southern Town (3rd ed.; Garden City: Doubleday, 1957 (1937)). The immense literature on immigration--within Europe as well as to the United States--should also be consulted. On the organizational level, the institutionalized framework of industrial relations, as embodied in the decisions of the National Labor Relations Board, codifies the dichotomized internal structure of groups of craft and non-craft workers belonging to the same unions and employed in the same plants. See Stephen I. Schlossberg and Frederick E. Sherman, Organizing and the Law (rev. ed.; Washington, D.C.: Bureau of National Affairs, 1971 (1967)), pp. 146-53.

4 See, for example, "Construction Workers: Fallen aristocrats," Economist, August 28, 1976, p. 26; "Winpisinger. Forging a 'new left' coalition," Business Week, February 21, 1977, p. 78.

5 See, for example, C. Wright Mills, The New Men of Power (New York: Harcourt, Brace, 1948), pp. 116-20, 130-31; E.E. LeMasters, Blue-Collar Aristocrats (Madison: University of Wisconsin Press, 1975).

6 See, for example, Jürgen Kuczynski, Die Geschichte der Lage der Arbeiter (Berlin (DDR): Akademie, 1968), pp. 33-57; idem, ibid., Vol. 37: Eine Weltübersicht über die Geschichte der Lage der Arbeiter (Berlin (DDR): Akademie, 1967), pp. 119-23; Philip S. Foner, History of the Labor Movement in the United States, Vol. 2: From the Founding of the American Federation of Labor to the Emergence of American Imperialism (New York: International, 1955), pp. 438-39.

7 Ulf Kadritzke, Angestellte--Die geduldigen Arbeiter (Frankfurt/Main: Europäische Verlagsanstalt, 1975), pp. 99-102.

8 Heiner Minssen and Werner Sauerborn, "Der Massenarbeiter und das Kapital", Gesellschaft. Beiträge zur Marxschen Theorie, No. 10, ed. H.-G. Backhaus et al. (Frankfurt/Main: Suhrkamp, 1977), p. 156.

9 Schriften des Vereins für Socialpolitik, Vol. 138: Verhandlungen (1911) (Leipzig: Duncker & Humblot, 1912), p. 149.

10 Ralf Dahrendorf, "Industrielle Fertigkeiten und soziale Schichtung", Kölner Zeitschrift für Soziologie und Sozialpsychologie, VIII (1960), 560.

11 Minssen and Sauerborn, "Der Massenarbeiter", p. 156.

12 Ibid.

13 Kadritzke, Angestellte, pp. 130, 137.

14 Cf. the critical observations by Christel Neusüss, Imperialismus und Weltmarktbewegung des Kapitals (Erlangen: Politladen, 1972), pp. 78-93.

15 John H. Goldthorpe et al., The Affluent Worker in the Class Structure (Cambirdge: Cambridge University Press, 1969), p. 9.

16 Marc Linder, Der Anti-Samuelson, I (Gaiganz: Politladen, 1974), 131-58.

17 This undifferentiated quantitative approach mars the pioneering work by E.J. Hobsbawm, "The Labour Aristocracy in Nineteenth-Century Britain", idem, Labouring Men (Garden City: Doubleday, 1967 (1964)), pp. 321-70; this essay first appeared in Democracy and the Labour Movement, ed. John Saville (London: Lawrence & Wishart, 1954), pp. 201-39. Cf. John Field, "British Historians and the Concept of Labor Aristocracy", Radical Historians Review, No. 19, Winter 1978-1979, pp. 61-85.

18 Journals of the House of Commons, From November the 29th, 1775 to October the 15th, 1776, Vol. XXXV, pp. 491, 695; Elizabeth W. Gilboy, Wages in Eighteenth Century England (Cambridge, Mass.: Harvard University Press, 1934), pp. 19, 23, 254-57, 274-76; Gustav Steffen, Studier öfver lönsystements historia i England, Part I: Före 1760 (Stockholm: Lorenska Stiftelsen, 1895), Figures I and II; James E. Thorold Rogers, Six Centuries of Work and Wages (new ed., rev.; London: Sonnenschein, 1886 (1866)), p. 327; E.H. Phelps Brown and Sheila V. Hopkins, "Seven Centuries of Building Wages", Economica, N.S., XXII, 87 (August 1955), 195-206.

19 See James W. Thompson, An Economic and Social History of the Middle Ages (300-1300) (New York: Century, 1928), p. 791.

20 The distinction between productive and unproductive labor within the manual working class was empirically of minor significance during the period under review. Moreover, the progressive subsumption of unproductive labor under capitalist forms of management makes it doubtful whether this division is directly relevant to the issue of intra-working class stratification.

21 Karl Marx, Das Kapital, I (2nd ed.; Hamburg: Meissner, 1872 (1867)), 18-21; idem, Das Kapital, III (1894), MEW, XXV, 151-52. Cf. Udo Ludwig, Harry Maier and Jürgen Wahse, Bildung als ökonomische Potenz im Sozialismus (Berlin (DDR): Dietz, 1972), pp. 72-126.

22 Kingsley Davis and Wilbert E. Moore, "Some Principles of Stratification", American Sociological Review, X (1945), 242-43. Cf. the cautious yet incisive critique by Melvin M. Tumin, "Some Principles of Stratification: A Critical Analysis", ibid., XVIII (1953), 387-94. Empirical studies of class structure and stratification have frequently proved less tendentious than their theoretical counterparts. Compare, for example, Theodor Geiger, Die soziale Schichtung des deutschen Volkes (Darmstadt: Wissenschaftliche Buchgesellschaft, 1972 (1932)) and idem, Soziale Umschichtungen in einer dänischen Mittelstadt, Acta Jutlandica, Samfundsvidenskabelig Serie 4, XXIII, 1 (1951) with idem, Die Klassengesellschaft im Schmelztiegel (Cologne: Kiepenheuer, 1949). Cf. Frank Parkin, Marxism and Class Theory: A Bourgeois Critique (New York: Columbia University Press, 1979).

23 Davis and Moore, "Some Principles of Stratification", pp. 242-44, 246-47; cf. Wilbert E. Moore, Industrial Relations and the Social Order (rev. ed.; New York: Macmillan, 1957 (1946)), pp. 568-92; Kurt B. Mayer, Class and Society (Garden City: Doubleday, 1955), pp. 41-42; Richard F. Hamilton, "The Behavior and Values of Skilled Workers", Blue-Collar World, ed. Arthur B. Shostak and William Gomberg (Englewood Cliffs: Prentice-Hall, 1964), pp. 42-57; Robert S. Lynd and Helen Merrell Lynd, Middletown (New York: Harcourt, 1930 (1929)), p. 74.

24 See the very suggestive work by Rudolf Bahro, Die Alternative (Frankfurt/Main: Europäische Verlagsanstalt, 1977).

Notes to Part I

1 "Capital and Labour", recited at a public dinner, also attended by employers, of the Boiler Makers' Society in Hull on September 28, 1872, was cited approvingly by a general secretary and historian of the union, D.C. Cummings, A Historical Survey of the Boiler Makers' and Iron and Steel Ship Builders' Society from August, 1834, to August, 1904 (Newcastle: Robinson, 1905), pp. 86-87.

1 Some of the more useful studies of this period include: J.L. Hammond and Barbara Hammond, The Town Labourer 1760-1832 (London: Longmans, Green, 1919 (1917)), pp. 288-305; Sidney and Beatrice Webb, The History of Trade Unionism (new ed.; London: Longmans, Green, 1902 (1894)), chaps. 2-3; M. Beer, A History of British Socialism, I (London: National Labour Press, 1921 (1919)), 160-347.

2 See Richard K.P. Pankhurst, William Thompson (1775-1833) (London: Watts, 1954), pp. 118-21 and passim; Michael Vester, Die Entstehung des Proletariats als Lernprozeß. Die Entstehung antikapitalistischer Theorie und Praxis in England 1792-1848 (Frankfurt/Main: Europäische Verlagsanstalt, 1972 (1970)), pp. 258-80.

3 William Thompson, Labour Rewarded (New York: Kelley, 1969 (1827)), pp. 75-76.

4 See the discussion of the theories of equalizing differences and non-competing groups in Chap. 5.

5 Thompson, Labour Rewarded, p. 22.

6 Ibid., p. 32.

7 Ibid., p. 27. See Webb, History of Trade Unionism, 1902 ed., pp. 37-39.

8 See W. Cunningham, The Growth of English Industry and Commerce in Modern Times, Vol. II, Pt. II. Laissez Faire (6th ed.; Cambridge: Cambridge University Press, 1925 (1882)), pp. 658-60.

9 Thompson, Labour Rewarded, pp. 27, 81.

10 Ibid., p. 81.

11 Ibid.

12 See J.L. Hammond and Barbara Hammond, The Skilled Labourer 1760-1832 (London: Longmans, Green, 1920 (1919)), passim; E.P. Thompson, The Making of the English Working Class (New York: Vintage, 1963), p. 523.

13 See Maurice Dobb, Political Economy and Capitalism (2nd ed.; London: Routledge & Kegan Paul, 1968 (1937)), pp. 246-47.

14 See "Remarks on Trades' Unions," The Poor Man's Guardian, No. 132, December 14, 1833, pp. 397-99.

15 See Witt Bowden, Industrial Society in England towards the End of the Eighteenth Century (New York: Macmillan, 1925), chap. 4; Christopher Hill, Reformation to Industrial Revolution (Harmondsworth: Penguin, 1975 (1967)), pp. 260-67.

16 Thompson, Making, p. 549; E.J. Hobsbawm, Labouring Men (Garden City: Doubleday, 1967 (1964)), p. 17.

17 See Hammond and Hammond, Town Labourer, pp. 112-42.

18 On the reform movement and the Reform Bill, see The Life of Edward Baines, by his son, Edward Baines (2nd ed.; London: Longman, 1859 (1951)), pp. 129-30; Elie Halévy, A History of the English People in the Nineteenth Century, III: The Triumph of Reform (1830-1841), tr. E.I. Watkin (New York: Barnes & Noble, 1961 (1923)), 3-59; E.L. Woodward, The Age of Reform 1815-1870 (Oxford: Clarendon, 1954 (1938)), pp. 75-83; G.D.H. Cole, A Short History of the British Working-Class Movement 1789-1947 (new ed.; London: Allen & Unwin, 1952 (1925)), pp. 63-69, 94-95. Cf. the literature cited below in chap. 5 sect. G.

19 On Combinations of Trades (London: Ridgway, 1831), p. 68.

20. Ibid., p. 58 Cf. the corroborative remarks by Daniel Guile, corresponding secretary of the Ironfounders' Society, on the role performed by artisans in inhibiting the success of continental-type revolutions or even

of Chartism; Fifth Report of the Commission appointed to inquire into the Organization and Rules of Trades Unions and other Associations (London: HMSO, 1868), P.P. 1867-1868, Vol. XXXIX, Q. 8753 at p. 20.

21 See Zygmunt Bauman, Klasa-Ruch-Elita (Warsaw: PWN, 1960), p. 72

22 On Combinations of Trades, p. 68. Cf. A Short Address to Workmen, on Combinations to Raise Wages (London: Knight, 1831), pp. 9-10.

23 "To the Members of the Unions," The Pioneer, I, 3 (September 21, 1833), 17.

24 See G.D.H. Cole, Attempts at General Union (London: Macmillan, 1953), pp. 104-105.

25 "Remarks on the Late Meeting at the Mechanics' Institute," The Poor Man's Guardian, No. 172, September 20, 1834, p. 257.

26 "The Relative Rights of Labour and Capital Discussed," ibid., No. 171, September 13, 1834, p. 251.

27 "The Small Masters at Their Dirty Work Again," ibid., No. 173, September 27, 1834, pp. 265-66.

28 See Equality, "Hints for the Emancipation of Labourers," ibid., No. 172, September 20, 1834, p. 261; Equality, "Capital and Labour Considered," ibid., No. 192, February 7, 1835, p. 419; cf. however "Great Meeting on Islington Green on Behalf of the Operative Builders," ibid., No. 169, August 30, 1834, pp. 233-35.

29 L. Pumpiansky, "Zur Geschichte der Anfänge des englischen Trade Unionismus. Organisationen und Kämpfe der englischen Arbeiter in der ersten Hälfte des neunzehnten Jahrhunderts," Ergänzungshefte zur Neuen Zeit, No. 13, August 9, 1912, pp. 2, 4, 52. See however the remarks on the polarization of classes in Britain, France and Germany in chaps. 5, 7-9 below.

30 "Political Unions," Carpenter's Monthly Political Magazine, I (December 1831), 127.

31 Alexander Somerville, The Autobiography of A Working Man, by "One Who Has Whistled At The Plough" (London: Gilpin, 1848), p. 145. Cf. Benjamin Disraeli, Sybil or The Two Nations (London: Oxford University Press, 1925 (1845)), pp. 165-66.

32 Second Report from the Select Committee on Combinations of Workmen, Ordered, by The House of Commons to be Printed, 30 July 1838, QQ 4174-4176 at p. 19 Cf. Third Report from Select Committee on Artizans and Machinery, P.P. 1824, Vol. V, p. 190. See below chap. 7 on co-exploitation.

33 Cole, Attempts, passim, provides a running account of anti-trade union struggles during the period through 1834.

34 First Report from the Selct Committee on Combinations of Workmen, P.P. 1837-1838, Vol. VIII, Q. 1954 at p. 108.

35 Ibid., QQ. 2118-2120 at p. 130. See also Alison's anonymous article, "Practical Working of Trades Unions," Blackwood's Edinburgh Magazine, Vol. XLII, No. CCLXIX (March 1838), 281-303. Cf. Webb, History of Trade Unionism, 1902 ed., pp. 153-56; Neil J. Smelser, Social Change in the Industrial Revolution (Chicago: University of Chicago Press, 1959), p. 329; H.A. Turner, Trade Union Growth and Structure (London: Allen & Unwin, 1962), pp. 108-38.

36 William B. Adams, English Pleasure Carriages (Bath: Adams & Dart, 1971 (1837)), p. 188.

37 The Man, I, 24 (December 22, 1833), 190-91.

38 First Report of the Commissioners Appointed to Inquire as to the Best Means of Establishing an Efficient Constabulary Force in the Counties of England and Wales (London: HMSO, 1839), p. 70.

39 Ibid., p. 86. Cf. First Report from the Select Committee on Combinations of Workmen, Q. 2122 at p. 131. Owenites feared that the successes of hostile strikes would cause the Unions, "like aristocracy," to become devoted to bad purposes. See A Mechanic, "Unions and Strikes." The Crisis, and National Co-operative Trades' Union Gazette, IV, 6 (May 17, 1834), 46.

40 See J.H. Clapham, An Economic History of Modern Britain. The Early Railway Age 1820-1850 (Cambridge: Cambridge University Press, 1926), pp. 555-60; T.S. Ashton, "The Standard of Life of the Workers in England, 1790-1830," Capitalism and the Historians, ed. F.A. Hayek (Chicago: University of Chicago Press, 1965 (1954)), p. 155; R.M. Hartwell, "Introduction," J.L. Hammond and Barbara Hammond, The Rise of Modern Industry (9th ed.; London: Methuen, 1966 (1925)), pp. xv-xxxi; Malcolm I. thomis, The Town Labourer and the Industrial Revolution (London: Batsford, 1974), pp. 147-64. For the more traditional or "pessimistic" view, see Hammond and Hammond, Town Labourer, pp. 95-111; Hobsbawm, Labouring Men, pp. 75-121; Thompson, Making, chap. 6; Jürgen Kuczynski, Die Geschichte der Lage der Arbeiter unter dem Kapitalismus, Vol. 23: Darstellung der Lage der Arbeiter in England von 1760 bis 1832 (Berlin (DDR): Akademie, 1964), pp. 114-36.

41 See Elizabeth W. Gilboy, Wages in Eighteenth Century England (Cambridge, Mass.: Harvard University Press, 1934), p. 4; M. Dorothy George, London Life in the XVIIIth Century (3rd ed.; n.p.: London School of Economics, 1951 (1925)), pp. 155-213.

42 Thompson, Making, p. 522.

43 For an analysis of the complicated reasons underlying the import of Irish laborers during this period, see Sidney Pollard, "Labour in Great Britain," The Cambridge Economic History of Europe, Vol. VII: The Industrial Economies: Capital, Labour and Enterprise, Part I: Britain, France, Germany and Scandinavia, ed. Peter Mathias and M.M. Postan (Cambridge: Cambridge University Press, 1978), pp. 108-12. See also Karl Polanyi, The Great Transformation (Boston: Beacon, 1971 (1944)), passim.

44 See Webb, History of Trade Unionism, 1902 ed., pp. 38-39, 74; Thompson, Making, p. 814.

45 Thompson, Making, pp. 239, 262; Webb, History of Trade Unionism, 1902 ed., pp. 76-77.

46 The fact that a stable, intergenerational, "hereditary" stratum of unskilled laborers had not yet been consolidated, contributed to the convergence of political aims. See William Thornton, Over-Population (London: Longman, 1846), p. 56.

47 For an illuminating socio-economic overview of this period, see Adolf Held, Zwei Bücher zur sozialen Geschichte Englands (Leipzig: Duncker & Humblot, 1881).

1 See however the dissenting view by D.J. Rowe, "The London Working Men's Association and the 'People's Charter,'" Past and Present, No. 36, April 1967, pp. 73-86; idem, "Rejoinder," ibid., No. 38, December 1967, pp. 174-76; idem, "The Failure of London Chartism," Historical Journal, XI, 3 (1968), 472-87.

2 "A Letter to the Earl of Durham on Reform in Parliament, by Paying the Elected. London: 1839," Westminster Review, No. LXII, April 1839, p. 264.

3 Edouard Dolléans, Le Chartisme (1830-1848), I (Paris: Floury, 1912), 12.

4 Max Beer, A History of British Socialism, II (London: Bell, 1929 (1919)), 25. cf. ibid., I, 313. See also the speech made by Thomas Attwood before the House of Commons on July 12, 1839 as reported in Hansard's Parliamentary Debates, Third Series, Vol. XLIX, col. 226.

5 Mark Hovell, The Chartist Movement (2nd ed.; Manchester: Manchester University Press, 1925 (1918)), pp. 47-48; cf. ibid., p. 144. See also Reg Groves, But We Shall Rise Again. A Narrative History of Chartism (London: Secker and Warburg, 1938), pp. 20-22. The rather petty bourgeois nature of the political movements in contemporary Birmingham has found many interpreters. See Friedrich Engels, Die Lage der arbeitenden Klasse in England (1845), MEW, II, 418; Trygve R. Tholfsen, "The Artisan and the Culture of Early Victorian Birmingham," University of Birmingham Historical Journal, IV, 2 (1954), 146-66; Albrecht Beck, "Politisches Verhalten und sozioökonomische Fundierung Birmingham 1815-1850" (Inaugural-Dissertation, Albert-Ludwigs University, Freiburg im Breisgau, 1971), passim; J.T. Ward, Chartism (London: Batsford, 1973), p. 79.

6 "The New World, A Democratic Poem, Dedicated to the People of the United Queendom, and of the United States," Notes to the People, I (1851), 2.

7 Iorwerth Prothero, "Chartism in London," Past and Present, No. 44, August 1969, pp. 83-84. See idem, "The London Working Men's Association and the 'People's Charter,'" ibid., No. 38, December 1967, pp. 172-73.

8 Groves, But We Shall Rise Again, p. 20.

9 I.J. Prothero, "London Chartism and the Trades," Economic History Review, Second Series, XXIV, 2 (May 1971), 209-10; James B. Jefferys, The Story of the Engineers 1800-1945 (n.p.: Lawrence and Wishart, n.d. (1945)), p. 18. Cf. Jellinger C. Symons, Arts and Artisans at Home and Abroad (Edinburgh: Tait, 1839), p. 157; Webb, History of Trade Unionism, 1902 ed., p. 152.

10 F.C. Mather, Chartism (London: Historical Association, 1966 (1965)), p. 14.

11 Herman Schlüter, Die Chartisten-Bewegung (New York: Socialist Literature Company, 1916), p. 55.

12 Elie Halévy, Histoire du peuple anglais du XIXe siècle. Vol. III. De la crise du Reform Bill à l'avènement de Sir Robert Peel (1830-1841) (2nd ed.; Paris: Hachette, 1928 (1923)), p. 305.

13 Ibid., p. 306.

14 See Northern Star, March 31, 1838, p. 4 cols. 2-3; ibid., July 7, 1838, p. 3 cols. 5-6; see however ibid., February 24, 1838, p 4 col. 3.

15 Cited by Dolléans, Chartisme, I, 379, without a source.

16 Ibid., I, 388.

17 See Arthur D. Gayer et al., The Growth and Fluctuations of the British Economy 1790-1850, I (Oxford: Oxford University Press, 1953), 354-55; R.C.O. Matthews, A Study in Trade Cycle History: Economic Fluctuations

in Britain 1833-42 (Cambridge: Cambridge University Press, 1954), passim.

18 See Francis Place, Add. Ms. 27819, ff. 5-12, from August 1, 1841, London Radicalism 1830-1843, ed. D.J. Rowe (n.p.: London Record Society, 1970), pp. 148-49; Hansard's Parliamentary Debates, Third Series, Vol. LXVI, col. 640, for February 15, 1843; McDouall's Chartist Journal and Trades' Advocate, No. 18, July 31, 1841, p. 137; Samuel Laing, National Distress (London: Longman, 1844), p. 19.

19 Beer, History, II, 139.

20 Webb, History of Trade Unionism, 1902 ed., pp. 158-59.

21 Ibid., pp. 157-60. Cf. Hovell, Chartist Movement, p. 169.

22 Preston William Slosson, The Decline of the Chartist Movement (New York: Columbia University Press, 1916), pp. 115-68.

23 Halévy, Histoire, III, 306.

24 See Gayer at al., Growth, I, 354-55.

25 Webb, History of Trade Unionism, 1902 ed., pp. 166-67.

26 The Morning Chronicle (London), September 10, 1840, p. 2 col. 6. Cf. J.D. Tuckett, A History of the Past and Present State of the Labouring Population, II (London: Longman, 1846), 547, who reproduced the words of Laing, National Distress, p. 54.

27 See David Jones, Chartism and the Chartists (New York: St. Martin's, 1975), Table 1 at pp. 30-32.

28 Ibid., Table 4 at pp. 134-37.

29 Some of these strikes originated in renewed demands by employers that employees sign "the document," abjuring affiliation with trade unions. See Statement of Facts Connected with the Turn-Out in the Lancashire Building Trades (Manchester, 1846); Friedrich Engels, "Nachträgliches über die Lage der arbeitenden Klassen in England. Ein englischer Turnout," MEW, II, 591-603; Webb, History of Trade Unionism, 1902 ed., p. 175.

30 Webb, History of Trade Unionism, 1902 ed., pp. 168-78.

31 Ibid., p. 174.

32 "The Trades' Conference," Northern Star, X, 447 (June 6, 1846), 4 cols. 5-6; see also p. 6 cols. 3-6, p. 7 cols. 1-3.

33 Northern Star, X, 495 (April 17, 1847), 8 col. 5.

34 Ibid.

35 Carpenters, plumbers, painters and stonemasons were among the most overrepresented occupational groups in the membership of the Manchester Unity of Oddfellows in the years 1846-1848, one of the most important friendly societies of the period. See P.H.J.H. Gosden, The Friendly Societies in England 1815-1875 (Manchester: Manchester University Press, 1961), Tables 11 and 12 at pp. 74-75.

36 "Trades Unions," The Labourer, I (1847), 34. Cf. the letter by an officer of the Boilermakers' Union, Alexander Fletcher, "The Persecuted Shoemakers," Northern Star, XI, 551 (May 13, 1848), 7 cols. 2-3, in which he spoke of "aristocratic notions" and sectionalism.

37 William Peel, "Labour and Trade," The People's Paper, No. 15, August 14, 1852, p. 3 col. 4.

38 See below chap. 4. The trade unionist environment that Jones challenged in the 1850s differed from that which prevailed during the Chartist era. As an example of the changing perception of trade unions, J.S. Mill added to the third edition of his Principles, which appeared in 1852, four years after the first edition, a passage in which he chided unions of the skilled, such as the Amalgamated Society of Engineers, for hindering the "emancipation of the working classes at large" by means of their

exclusionary policies toward "their fellow-labourers." See John Stuart Mill, Principles of Political Economy, ed. W.J. Ashley (London: Longmans, Green, 1926 (1848)), p. 936.

39 Ernest Jones, "The Middle-Class Franchise--Why Will It Injure The Democratic Cause?," Notes to the People, I (1851), 31-32.

40 Hansard's Parliamentary Debates, Third Series, Vol. XCVII, cols. 458-60; Henry Mayhew, London Labour and the London Poor, III (New York: Dover, 1968 (1861)), 233-43.

41 Elie Halevy, A History of the English People in the Nineteenth Century, IV: Victorian Years 1841-1895, tr. E.I. Watkin (New York: Barnes & Noble, 1961 (1946)), 244-45.

42 F.C. Mather, Public Order in the Age of the Chartists (Manchester: Manchester University Press, 1959), p. 82, delimits this role even further: "It is true that working-class special constables were enrolled in large numbers, especially in 1848," but this often took place at the instigation "of their employers, who did not scruple to hold the threat of dismissal over the heads of those who refused to be sworn in." The major motive on the part of employers was to secure the good behavior of their employees, whose jurisdiction as special constables was often restricted to their workplaces. For specific instances of coercion or attempted coercion by employers, see Northern Star, XI, 544 (March 25, 1848), 2 col. 5; ibid., XI, 548 (April 22, 1848), 6 cols. 1-2; ibid., p. 6 cols. 5-6.

43 See Engels, Lage, pp. 451-53.

44 A contemporary observer ranged the higher order of mechanics ("'skilled laborers'") together with shopkeepers as a class situated between professionals, clerics and tradespeople on the one hand and the remaining laborers on the other. Although this author considered the earnings of the skilled sufficient to insure respectability and to maintain comfort in old age, he ranked the skilled among the non-privileged classes, of which they formed the highest order. See William Dodd (An Englishman), The Laboring Classes of England (2nd ed.; Boston: Putnam, 1848 (1847?)), pp. 9-11.

45 See m. Dorothy George, London Life in the XVIIIth Century (3rd ed.; n.p.: London School of Economics, 1951 (1925)), p. 156. Cf. J.H. Clapham, An Economic History of Modern Britain. The Early Railway Age 1820-1850 (Cambridge: Cambridge University Press, 1926), pp. 166-68.

46 See Mayhew, London Labour, III, 221-33.

47 Two distinct cases must be recognized here: 1. technological transformations that substituted unskilled for skilled labor by means of machinery and further division of labor; and 2. the employment of unapprenticed, less skilled workers who performed low-quality "slop" work. Although artisans of this period were threatened mainly by the latter, mechanization also effected some displacement. See Pioneer, No. 4, September 28, 1833, pp. 28-29; The Builder, XII, 570 (May 27, 1854), 281-82; ibid., XVI, 796 (May 8, 1858), 317. See however Hermione Hobhouse, Thomas Cubitt. Master Builder (London: Macmillan, 1971), p. 292.

48 See the discussion of William thompson, chap. 2 above.

49 G. Kitson Clark, The Making of Victorian England (Cambridge, Mass.: Havard University Press, 1962), p. 132, offers no evidence for the claim that in the first half of the nineteenth century the "aristocracy of labour should be grouped with the middle class many of whose prejudices about keeping down the rates and maintaining social order they probably shared..."

50 The immigration of Irish laborers constituted an exception. See Arthur Redford, Labour Migration in England, 1800-1850 (Manchester: Manchester University Press, 1926), pp. 140-42.

51 See Dorothy Marshall, Industrial England 1776-1851 (London: Routledge & Kegan Paul, 1973), p. 104.

52 "The Trades' Union Conference With Mr. Gladstone," Beehive, February 22, 1868, p. 5 col. 3.

Notes to Chapter 4

1 The title of this chapter is taken from the two studies by J.L. Hammond and Barbara Hammond, The Age of the Chartists 1832-1854 (London: Longmans, Green, 1930); and E.J. Hobsbawm, The Age of Capital 1848-1875 (London: Abacus, 1975).

2 See the erroneous contention by W.H. Chaloner, The Skilled Artisans During the Industrial Revolution (London: Historical Association, 1969), p. 4. See also Michael J. Piva, "The Aristocracy of the English Working Class: Help for An Historical Debate in Difficulties," Histoire Sociale-Social History, VII (1974), 270.

3 John Saville, ed., Ernest Jones: Chartist (London: Lawrence and Wishart, 1952), p. 48.

4 "The 'Times' and the Wolverhampton Tinplate-Workers," Notes to the People, I (1851), 421-22.

5 Ibid. Cf. "Address of the Progressive Society of Operative Carpenters and Joiners to the Carpenters and Joiners of London," ibid., II (1852), 723; "The Co-Operative Movement. Reply to Mr. Vansittart Neale," ibid., II, 585.

6 See John L. Tildsley, Die Entstehung und die ökonomischen Grundsätze der Chartistenbewegung (Jena: Fischer, 1898), p. 133.

7 See below.

8 See Marx's comments at the "Sitzung der Zentralbehörde vom 15. September 1850," MEW, VIII, 598.

9 Even in the 1880s, when Engels made the Labor aristocracy a key to his analyses of the British working class, he emphasized that only the fear of trade unions compelled capitalists to pay workers the full market value of their labor power. See the series of unsigned editorials written for The Labour Standard, No. 3, May 21, 1881; No. 4, May 28, 1881; and No. 5, June 4, 1881; cited here according to the German translation in MEW, XIX, 251-60.

10 See Marx's strong views on the importance of strikes for working class independence as expressed in his article on strikes in Britain for the New-York Daily Tribune, July 14, 1853; cited here according to the translation in MEW, IX, 169-75. Cf. Marx, "Bericht des Generalrats der Internationalen Arbeiter-Assoziation an den IV. allgemeinen Kongress in Basel," ibid., XVI, 370. For Jones's contrasting view, see "The National Trades' Union," Notes to the People, II (1852), 762.

11 See Phyllis Deane, The First Industrial Revolution (Cambridge: Cambridge University Press, 1965), p. 148; Thompson, Making, pp. 263-64.

12 "Three to One; or, the strength of the working-classes," Notes to the People, I (1851), 511.

13 See Jones's footnotes to a letter by James Crawford, ibid., II (1852), 522 n. 3. In projecting these trends, Jones appeared as a precursor of one strand of Marx's own thinking. See Marx's letter to the People's Paper, No. 98, March 18, 1854, p. 1, cited below in chapter 5. Cf. however Marx's comments on this letter to Engels in his letter of March 9, 1854, MEW, XXVIII, 328. Nevertheless, even Capital contained passages that resurrected the simplistic approach he once shared with Jones. See Günther Herre, Verelendung und Proletariat bei Karl Marx (Düsseldorf: Droste, 1973), p. 180; Henry Collins and Chimen Abramsky, Karl Marx and the British Labour Movement (London: Macmillan, 1965), pp. 47-48. However simplified Marx's remarks may have been, they did not warrant the attacks launched by W.L. Burn, The Age of Equipoise. A Study of the Mid-Victorian Generation (London: Allen and Unwin, 1964), p. 92.

14 See Jones's prediction of deskilling in the building trades in "The Building Trade," Notes to the People, II (1852), 543; cf. however "The National Trades' Union," ibid., II (1852), 763.

15 See "The Iron Trades," ibid., II (1852), 976.

16 On the capital-using and labor-saving wave of investment which preceded this struggle, see Keith Burgess, "Technological Change and the 1852 lock-out in the British Engineering Industry," International Review of Social History, XIV (1969), 215-36; idem, "Trade Union Policy and the 1852 Lock-out in the British Engineering Industry," ibid., XVII (1972), 645-60.

17 Webb, History of Trade Unionism, 1902 ed., p. 196 and p. 196 n. 1.

18 See Jones, "The Amalgamated Iron Trades," Notes to the People, II (1952), 830.

19 Lujo Brentano, Die Arbeitergilden der Gegenwart. Vol. I: Zur Geschichte der englischen Gewerkvereine (Leipzig: Duncker & Humblot, 1871), p. 191.

20 "The Amalgamated Iron Trades," p. 830.

21 Ibid.; Brentano, Arbeitergilden, I, 191.

22 See Webb, History of Trade Unionism, 1902 ed., pp. 199-200. For an earlier example of exclusionary trade unionism, see the testimony by Archibald Alison, sheriff of Lanarkshire, First Report from the Select Committee on Combinations of Workmen; Together With the Minutes of Evidence and Appendix, Ordered, by The House of Commons, to be Printed, 14 June 1838, Q. 2268 at p. 149 and Q. 2297 at p. 153.

23 James B. Jefferys, The Story of the Engineers 1800-1945 (n.p.: Lawrence and Wishart, n.d. (1945)), p. 42.

24 Cited in ibid. Cf. Brentano, Arbeitergilden, I, 225; A. Journeyman Engineer, Thomas Wright, Some Habits and Customs of the Working Classes (London: Tinsley, 1867), pp. 45-55; J.M. Ludlow, The Master Engineers and Their Workmen (London: Bezer, 1852), passim.

25 Webb, History of Trade Unionism, 1902 ed., p. 200.

26 See Jefferys, Story of the Engineers, passim; Brentano, Arbeitergilden, I, 285 n. 436.

27 On William Newton's decision to become a candidate for the House of Commons in 1852, see A.R. Schoyen, The Chartist Challenge: A Portrait of George Julian Harney (London: Heinemann, 1958), p. 224: "Newton's entry into the arena of politics and his broad social views were in fact a refutation of Jones' attacks on" the selfishness of the labor aristocracy.

28 See Brentano, Arbeitergilden, I, 191.

29 Keith Burgess, The Origins of British Industrial Relations (London: Croom Helm, 1975), p. 65.

30 As late as the 1890s, Platt Brothers of Oldham, employing 10,000 workers and possessing a unique domination of certain product markets internationally, negotiated with no unions. See Paul de Rousiers, The Labour Question in France, tr. F.L.D. Herbertson (London: Macmillan, 1896 (original French ed 1895)), pp. 254-56.

31 See Royden Harrison, Before the Socialists. Studies in Labour and Politics 1861-1881 (London: Routledge & Kegan Paul, 1965), pp. 33-39.

32 Jones's animosity toward the Amalgamated Society of Engineers was partly attributable to the latter's--and, in particular, Newton's--refusal to permit him to address a meeting on December 30, 1851. See "The Operative Engineers and Their Employers," The Times (London), December 31, 1851, p. 5 col. 6; "To the London Executive Committee of the Amalgamated Iron Trades," Notes to the People, II (1852), 724-25.

For Engels' assessment of the strike, see his letter to Marx of March 2, 1852, MEW, XXVIII, 35.

33 "Three to One," p. 511.

34 Ibid.

35 "1852 and the Franchise," Notes to the People, II (1852), 838.

36 "Fresh Falsehood of the Financials. The Middle-Class Franchise and the Census," ibid., I (1851), 187. Several of Engels' references to the labor aristocracy during these years were, in tone and substance, not far removed from Jones's. See below chap. 5. Marx and Engels also claimed that the "petty bourgeois" and the "aristocracy of the workers" within the Chartist movement formed a purely democratic fraction, limiting themselves to the Charter and other petty bourgeois reforms; at the same time they believed that, "The mass of workers living in really proletarian conditions belong to the revolutionary Chartist fraction." See Marx and Engels, "Revue. Mai bis Oktober (1850)," MEW, VII, 445. For a similarly exaggerated judgment, see Engels' letter of April 15, 1848 to Emil Blank, ibid., XXVII, 481.

37 See "Congress of Co-Operative and Trades Union Delegates.-- Benefit Societies," Poor Man's Guardian, II, 124 (October 19, 1833), 333.

38 "The 'Times' and the Wolverhampton Tinplate-Workers," p. 422.

39 Jones's notes to the letter by Crawford, Notes to the People, II (1852), 521 n. (1.).

40 Cf. Engels' similar position as elaborated in "The Ten Hours' Question," The Democratic Review, March 1850; cited here according to the German translation in MEW, VII, 228. See also Gareth Stedman Jones, "Working-Class Culture and Working-Class Politics in London, 1870-1900; Notes on the Remaking of a Working Class," Journal of Social History, VII, 4 (Summer 1974), 499-500.

41 For an early statement of Marx's position on trade unions, see his Misère de la philosophie (1847); cited here according to the German translation in MEW, IV, 175-82.

42 See Engels' letter of March 18, 1852 to Marx, MEW, XXVIII, 40.

43 See Marx's report in the New-York Daily Tribune of October 17, 1853; cited here according to the translation in MEW, IX, 346.

44 See Marx's articles in the New-York Daily Tribune of July 1, 1853 and November 18, 1853; cited according to the translations in MEW, IX, 136 and IX, 460-61, respectively.

45 "The Chartists," New-York Daily Tribune of August 25, 1852; cited according to the translation in MEW, VIII, 344. Engels argued that lowering the borough voting qualification would, by enfranchising the "better paid part of the proletariat," ensure some Chartist representation in the cities. See Engels' unpublished manuscript, "England," written in 1852, MEW, VIII, 216. The voting strength of borough artisans was actually diluted by the Reform Act of 1832. See The Life of Edward Baines, by his Son, Edward Baines (2nd ed.; London: Longman, 1857 (1851)), pp. 130-31; Homersham Cox, A History of the Reform Bills of 1866 and 1867 (London: Longmans, 1867), pp. 7-8; J.R.M. Butler, The Passing of the Great Reform Bill (London: Longmans, 1914), pp. 242-43.

46 See Marx's report for the New-York Daily Tribune of December 16, 1853; cited according to the translation in MEW, IX, 535-36.

47 See Marx's report in the New-York Daily Tribune of July 14, 1853; cited according to the translation in MEW, IX, 170.

48 Webb, History of Trade Unionism, 1902 ed., p. 206.

49 Ibid., p. 208.

50 R.W. Postgate, The Builders' History (London: Labour Publishing, n.d. (1923)), chap. 7.

51 T. Young, "Strike of the Operative Stone Masons of Leicester," People's Paper, No. 54, May 14, 1853, p. 3 col. 3.

52 See Hermann Schlüter, Die Chartisten-Bewegung (New York: Socialist Literature Company, 1916), p. 254.

53 Henry Mayhew, London Labour and the London Poor, III (New York: Dover, 1968 (1861)), 233; cf. ibid., III, 221; IV, 28 n.

54 See Gareth Stedman Jones, Outcast London (Harmondsworth: Penguin, 1976 (1971)), pp. 19-32, 338-41; François Bédarida, "Londres au milieu du XIXe siècle: une analyse de structure sociale," Annales, XXIII, 2 (March-April 1968), 269-95; Francis Sheppard, London 1808-1870 (London: Secker and Warburg, 1971), p. 389.

55 See the editorial note, MEW, XXIX, 688 n. 225; and Marx's letter to Engels of November 24, 1857, ibid., p. 218.

56 Marx's letter to Engels, written about January 16, 1858, ibid., p. 260.

57 Letter from Marx to Engels of September 21, 1858, ibid., p. 356. Marx wrote this sentence in English.

58 Letter from Engels to Marx of October 7, 1858, ibid., p. 358.

59 See Jürgen Kuczynski, Die Geschichte der Lage der Arbeiter unter dem Kapitalismus, Vol. 24: Darstellung der Lage der Arbeiter in England von 1832 bis 1900 (Berlin (DDR): Akademie, 1965), p. 124.

60 See Roberto Michels, La Teoria di C. Marx sulla miseria crescente e le sue origini (Torino: Bocca, 1922), passim.

61 See John H. Goldthorpe et al., The Affluent Worker in the Class Structure (Cambridge: Cambridge University Press, 1969), p. 9; Wolf Wagner, Verelendungstheorie-die hilflose Kapitalismuskritik (Frankfurt/Main: Fischer, 1976). passim.

62 See Rufus S. Tucker, "Real Wages of the Artisans in London, 1729-1935," Journal of the American Statistical Association, XXXI, 193 (March 1936), 79; Hans Rosenberg, Die Weltwirtschaftskrise 1857-1859) (2nd ed.; Göttingen: Vandenhoeck & Ruprecht, 1974 (1936)), pp. 71-78; Kuczynski, England von 1832 bis 1900, p. 119; Thomas Tooke and William Newmarch, A History of Prices, and of the State of Circulation from 1792 to 1856, Vol. IV: During the Nine Years 1848-1856 (London: King, 1927 (1857)), p. 175 n.

63 See below chap. 5.

64 Compare the claim by L.A. Mendel'son Teoriia i istoriia ekonomicheskikh krizisov i tsiklov, I (Moscow: IS-EL, 1959), 577.

65 "The Building Trades," Cabinet Newspaper, August 6, 1859; cited here according to the reprint in Ernest Jones, ed. Saville, pp. 209-10.

66 The former refers to the relation between labor and capital, the latter to that between money wages and the prices of wage goods; see Marx, "Lohnarbeit und Kapital," MEW, VI, 413.

67 Marx, Das Kapital, I (Hamburg: Meissner, 1867; reprint: Tokyo: Aoki-Shoten, 1959), 632. For Marx's earlier, cruder, view of trade unions, see his unpublished manuscript, "Arbeitslohn," MEW, VI, 555, written in 1847.

68 Letter of January 29, 1869, MEW, XXXII, 253.

1 As claimed, for example, by V.E. Kunina, "Karl Marx ob angliiskom rabochem dvizhenii," Marx-istorik, ed. E.A. Zhelubovskaia (Moscow: Nauka, 1968), pp. 509-10.
2 See Chapter 4 above.
3 Cf. Engels' letter of October 7, 1858 to Marx, MEW, XXIX, 358.
4 Letter of February 5, 1851, MEW, XXVII, 180.
5 See Asa Briggs, "Social Background," The System of Industrial Relations in Great Britain, ed. Allan Flanders and H.A. Clegg (Oxford: Blackwell, 1954), p. 14; Hansard's Parliamentary Debates, Third Series, XLIX, 226 (House of Commons for July 12, 1839). Attempts to influence workers ideologically were also undertaken by individual employers. Thomas Cubitt, for example, perhaps the largest employer in the building trades in mid-century London, provided evening technical lectures and a lending library for his employees; see The Builder, X, 472 (February 21, 1852), 126; X, 475 (March 13, 1852), 174; XII, 673 (December 29, 1855), 629-30. Cubitt's biographer notes that such measures were "extremely important to the ambitious workman" since the first free public library in London was not opened until 1854; see Hermione Hobhouse, Thomas Cubitt (London: Macmillan, 1971), pp. 296-97. This particular case assumes a wider significance because it casts doubt on Engels' subsequent claim that factory owners protected trade unions as extremely beneficial institutions after 1848; see Engels, "England 1845 und 1885," Die Neue Zeit, III, 6 (1885); this article first appeared in English in Commonweal and was translated into German by Engels; cited here according to MEW, XXI, 192-93. On Cubitt, see also Report from the Select Committee on Masters and Operatives; together with the Proceedings of the Committee, Minutes of Evidence, Appendix and Index, House of Commons, May 15, 1860, C.-3071, Q. 923 at XXII, 76.
6 Manifest der Kommunistischen Partei, MEW, IV, 470. For Engels' assessment of the severity of the depression, see his article, "(Die Handelskrise in England - Chartistenbewegung - Irland)," MEW, IV, 325; it first appeared in French in La Réforme, October 26, 1847. Cf. Marx and Engels, "Revue. Mai bis Oktober (1850)," MEW, VII, 425-32.
7 Cf. Marx's view of savings banks, which split the working class into savers--and hence those with an interest in the preservation of the social status quo--and non-savers; "Arbeitslohn," MEW, VI, 545. Several years after Marx expressed these views a British watchmaker told a Parliamentary committee that capitalists' immediate interests in effect thwarted the formation of such a division within the working class by providing a worker with a disincentive to save: "the fact of his being able to save money is used as a pretense why his wages should be reduced." Report from the Select Committee on Investments for the Savings of the Middle and Working Classes, July 5, 1850, Parliamentary Papers, 1850, Q. 546 at XIX, 50. See also Karl Marx, Grundrisse der Kritik der politischen Ökonomie (Berlin (DDR): Dietz, 1953), p. 197; Thomas Wright ("The Journeyman Engineer"), Our New Masters (London: Strahan, 1873), pp. 101-102.
8 "Revue. Mai bis Oktober (1850)," p. 440.
9 The controversy surrounding Marx's periodization will not be discussed here; see Werner Sombart, Der moderne Kapitalismus, II:2 (2nd ed.; Munich and Leipzig: Duncker & Humblot, 1917 (1902)), 730-99; Josef Kulischer, Allgemeine Wirtschaftsgeschichte des Mittelalters und der Neuzeit, II (Berlin (DDR): Rütten & Loening, 1954 (1928)), 162-63; Maurice Dobb, Studies in the Development of Capitalism (London: Routledge &

Kegan Paul, 1963 (1946)), pp. 142-51; Leo Kofler, Zur Geschichte der bürgerlichen Gesellschaft (Neuwied: Luchterhand, 1971 (1948)), pp. 297-98.

10 Marx does not explicitly deal with the medieval separation of skilled and unskilled laborers; see E. Lipson, The Economic History of England, I. The Middle Ages (12th ed.; London: Black, 1966 (1915)), 324, 388-89; John Clapham, A Concise Economic History of Britain (Cambridge: Cambridge University Press, 1963 (1949)), pp. 253-60.

11 Das Kapital, I (Hamburg: Meissner, 1867; reprint: Tokyo: Aoki-Shoten, 1959), 333. The expression "Arbeitskraft," the plural of which has been translated as "workers," can mean "labor power" as well as the person who expends it.

12 Ibid.

13 Ibid., p. 334.

14 Ibid., pp. 334, 354.

15 Ibid., pp. 353-54.

16 Ibid., pp. 411-12.

17 Ibid., pp. 345-47.

18 Ibid., 355-496. Wolf Wagner, Verelendungstheorie--die hilflose Kapitalismuskritik (Frankfurt/Main: Fischer, 1976), p. 20, points out that these factors were uppermost in Marx's mind when he spoke of the immiseration of employed workers, whereas income-related aspects were stressed with regard to the reserve army of the unemployed, paupers and others.

19 Zur Kritik der Politischen Ökonomie (1859), MEW, XIII, 18.

20 Ibid.

21 In that year, 10,629 men above the age of twenty were reported as goldsmiths, silversmiths, jewelers; see Census of England and Wales for the Year 1861, Volume III: General Report (London: HMSO, 1863), P.P. 1863, Vol. LIII, Pt. 1, Table XIX at p. liv. W.A. Armstrong, the author of a careful reworking of Charles Booth's census summary manuscripts estimates that half of this number represented manufacturers, half dealers; see W.A. Armstrong, "The use of information about occupation," Nineteenth-century Society, ed. E.A. Wrigley (London: Cambridge University Press, 1972), p. 260 and n. (xiv).

22 Kapital, I, 164 n. 18.

23 See the report of a committee of master spinners cited by Marx in ibid., p. 415 n. 188.

24 See An Inquiry into the Nature and Causes of The Wealth of Nations, ed. Edwin Cannan (New York: Modern Library, 1937 (1776)), Book I, Chap. X, Part I, pp. 101-102 and Part II, p. 123.

25 Kapital, I, 164 n. 18; the expression "'skilled'" and "'unskilled labour'" appears in English in the original.

26 Alfred Marshall, Principles of Economics (8th ed.; London: Macmillan, 1969 (1890)), p. 568, appears to confirm the persistence of such customs in his time although his position is ambiguous.

27 Within the tripartite typology advanced by Gerhard Beier, labor aristocrats in such unions formed a feudal value-elite; see his contribution, "Das Problem der Arbeiteraristokratie im 19. und 20. Jahrhundert," Herkunft und Mandat (Frankfurt/Main: Europäische Verlagsanstalt, 1976), pp. 15-18.

28 Sidney and Beatrice Webb, Industrial Democracy (London: Longmans, Green, 1920 (1897)), pp. 454-81.

29 Rudolf Schlesinger, Central European Democracy and its Background (London: Routledge & Kegan Paul, 1953), p. 81, speaks of "a contradiction in terms."

30 This line of reasoning extends one step further a recent criticism of Marx--namely, that his thesis of the leveling of the skill structure was conditioned by the peculiar historical circumstances characteristic of the wave of industrialization that occurred during his creative years; on this basis critics have stated or implied that Marx was unable to foresee the changes in that structure in the course of the twentieth century. See Udo Ludwig et al., Bildung als ökonomische Potenz im Sozialismus (Berlin (DDR): Dietz, 1972), p. 80; V.-M. Bader et al., Krise und Kapitalismus bei Marx, I (Frankfurt/Main: Europäische Verlagsanstalt, 1975), 244 n. 166. The present argument questions the extent to which Marx judged his own period adequately.

31 R.H. Inglis Palgrave, Dictionary of Political Economy (3 vols.; London: Macmillan, 1894-1899), II, 527; Marshall, Principles, p. 171.

32 Palgrave, Dictionary, II, 527.

33 United States Department of Labor, United States Employment Service, Dictionary of Occupational Titles, Part II, Group Arrangement of Occupational Titles and Codes, June 1939 (Washington, D.C.: Government Printing Office, 1939), p. 59.

34 Interestingly enough, the Department of Labor defines semi-skilled and unskilled occupations chiefly in terms of the absence of the characteristics of the skilled occupations; see ibid., pp. 115, 241.

35 On the distinction between the average level of qualification required of various occupations and the individual levels within occupations, see I.I. Rubin, Ocherki po teorii stoimosti Marksa (3rd ed.; Moscow-Leningrad: Gosudarstvennoe Izdatel'stvo, 1928 (1923)), pp. 178-79.

36 In 1850 Henry Mayhew estimated that fewer than one in ten London carpenters and joiners performed skilled tasks; see his letters LX and LXI in the London Morning Chronicle of July 11, 1850 and July 18, 1850 respectively; cited here according to the reprint in The Unknown Mayhew, ed. E.P. thompson and Eileen Yeo (London: Merlin, 1971), pp. 335-55. Cf. Henry Mayhew, London Labour and the London Poor, II (New York: Dover, 1968 (1861-1862)), 316. The Second Report of the Royal Commission appointed to inquire into the Depression of Trade and Industry, Appendix, Part II, C.-4715-I (London: HMSO, 1886), pp. 8, 12, 19, 42-66, 84, contains returns from local trade unions indicating the skill-composition of their membership.

37 See however the illuminating study by Raphael Samuel, "Workshop of the World: Steam Power and Hand Technology in mid-Victorian Britain," History Workshop, No. 3, Spring 1977, pp. 6-73.

38 Data are presented below. Arthur L. Bowley, Wages in the United Kingdom in the Nineteenth Century (Cambridge: Cambridge University Press, 1900), p. 60 and chart facing p. 94; United States House of Representatives, State of Labor in Europe: 1878, 46th Congress, 1st Session, Executive Document No. 5 (Washington, 1879), pp. 30, 402-407, provide data for Britain and other countries. Evidence from modern "underdeveloped" countries, in which working class exhaustion has reached limits unknown in the advanced capitalist world, indicates that physically taxing construction work is not only compensated at a lower rate than manufacturing occupations, but is also often performed by marginalized elements of the population. See United Nations Industrial Development Organization, UNIDO Monographs on Industrial Development, Industrialization of Developing countries. Problems and Prospects, No. 2: Construction Industry (New York: United Nations, 1969), p. 12; Larissa Adler De Lomnitz, Cómo sobreviven los marginados (Mexico City: Siglo XXI, 1975), pp. 20, 73, 75.

39 Kapital, I, 164 n. 18.

40 See Abstract of the Answers and Returns... Occupation Abstract
M.DCCC.XLI. Part I. England and Wales (London: HMSO, 1844), pp. 283-
96.

41 See, for example, Samuel Laing, National Distress: Its Causes and
Remedies (London: Longman, 1844), pp. 49-50.

42 Ibid., p. 52.

43 Marx left this passage unaltered in the second edition; see Das Kapital
(2nd ed.; Hamburg: Meissner, 1872), pp. 186-87 n. 18.

44 Calculated according to the data in Armstrong, "The use," pp. 264, 268;
in particular the number of weavers, spinners and factory hands fell
from 99,000 in 1841 to 13,400 in 1851; see ibid., p. 264.

45 National Distress, p. 22.

46 Ibid., pp. 25, 19.

47 Ibid., p. 27.

48 Ibid. Interestingly, a committee of delegates studying the destitution of
London's artisans and mechanics in 1848 reported on a tripartite division
of which the highest third was employed at wages "wholly inadequate"
to provide themselves and their families with the necessities of life. See
"Aggregate Meeting of the Trades of London," Northern Star, XI, 549
(April 29, 1848), 1 col. 4. Cf. R.S. Neale, "Class and Class Consciousness
in Early Nineteenth Century England: Three Classes or Five?," Victorian
Studies, XII, 1 (September, 1968), 5-32.

49 National Distress, p. 49.

50 Ibid., n.

51 Ibid.

52 Ibid., p. 51.

53 Remarkably enough, even the most orthodox Marxist-Leninists do not
notice the inconsistency involved in locating the rise of the labor aristocracy in mid-nineteenth century Britain in the context of a development
of the forces of production that required additional levels of skill within
a part of the working class. See Horst Bartel et al, ed. Sachwörterbuch
der Geschichte Deutschlands und der Arbeiterbewegung, I (Berlin (DDR):
Dietz, 1969), 104. Jürgen Kuczynski, Die Geschichte der Lage der Arbeiter unter dem Kapitalismus, Volume 24: Darstellung der Lage der Arbeiter in England von 1832 bis 1900 (Berlin (DDR):, Akademie, 1965),
pp. 115-16, refers to the formation of a broad "'hereditary stratum of
the skilled.'"

54 The Webbs pointed out that economists were surprised by the results of
Charles Booth's survey of London, which confirmed socialists' claims
about the prevalence of poverty; see Sidney and Beatrice Webb, History
of Trade Unionism, 1902 ed., pp. 360-68. For an analogous incident
regarding an investigation of land ownership designed to refute claims by
radicals, see S.G. Checkland, The Rise of Industrial Society in England
1815-1885 (London: Longman, 1971 (1964)), pp. 183-84.

55 See Robert Giffen, "The Progress of the Working Classes in the Last Half
Century," Journal of the Statistical Society, XLVI (December 1883), 593-
622. Cf. the critiques by James C. Hutchinson, "Progress and Wages,"
Nineteenth Century, XVI (October 1884), 630-38; and an anonymous author
of "The Progress of Our Working Classes," Economist, XLI (November 24,
1883), 1363-65.

56 See, for example, J. Shield Nicholson, Principles of Political Economy,
I (London: Macmillan, 1893), 120; Palgrave's Dictionary, cited above,
also relied heavily on Giffen's word. In his testimony before the Royal
Commission on Labour, however, Giffen conceded that definitional problems
had rendered it uncertain whether the skilled had increased in relation

to the unskilled; see Royal Commission on Labour, Fourth Report. Minutes of Evidence Taken before the Royal Commission on Labour (Sitting as a Whole), C. 7063-I (London: HMSO, 1893), Q. 8138. Cf. idem, Fifth and Final Report of the Royal Commission on Labour, Part I. The Report, C. 7421 (London: HMSO, 1894), p. 24.

57 "Further Notes on the Progress of the Working Classes in the Last Half Century," Journal of the Statistical Society, XLIX (March 1886), 56, 67.

58 See William Haber, Industrial Relations in the Building Industry (Cambridge, Mass.: Harvard University Press, 1930), p. 29.

59 See the more cautious judgment by J. Shield Nicholson, The Effects of Machinery on Wages (new and revised ed.; London: Allen, 1912 (1878)), pp. 77-92; Paul Mantoux, The Industrial Revolution in the Eighteenth Century, tr. Marjorie Vernon (New York: Harper and Row, 1961 (first published as La Révolution industrielle au XVIII siècle in 1906)), pp. 410, 424-25. Cf. Edward Baines, Jun., History of the Cotton Manufacture in Great Britain (London, Fisher, n.d. (1835)), pp. 433-502; Andrew Ure, The Philosophy of Manufactures (3rd ed., continued in its details to the Present Time by P.L. Simmonds; London: Bohn, 1861 (1835)), p. 23; (James Dawson Burn), A Glimpse at The Social Condition of the Working Classes (London: Heywood, n.d. (1868)), p. 22.

60 Calculated according to data in Charles Booth, "Occupations of the People of the United Kingdom, 1801-81," Journal of the Statistical Society, XLIX (June 1886), 355-59. Women and children were, to be sure, undercounted in 1841; see Phyllis Deane and W.A. Cole, British Economic Growth 1688-1959 (2nd ed.; Cambridge: Cambridge University Press, 1969 (1962)), p. 139. In addition, the number of general laborers rose strongly during these years although classificatory changes in census enumeration procedures render precise comparisons impossible. Giffen was, in any event, not warranted in drawing his conclusions from the minuscule decline in the number of laborers--deriving almost exclusively from the fall in the number of agricultural laborers--from 1871 to 1881; see Robert Giffen, "Some General Uses of Statistical Knowledge," idem, Essays in Finance, Second Series (3rd ed.; London: Bell, 1890 (1886)), p. 342. See also Booth, "Occupations," p. 363; Armstrong, "The use," p. 274 and n. (xxxiv).

61 See George H. Wood, "Real Wages and the Standard of Comfort since 1850," Journal of the Royal Statistical Society, LXXII, Part I (March 1909), 99.

62 Bader et al., Krise, I, 256-58, point out that this process is accompanied by an elevation of the average educational level necessitated by the increased need for basic technological knowledge; as a result, real wages rise.

63 Joseph A. Schumpeter, Capitalism, Socialism and Democracy (5th ed.; London: Unwin, 1966 (1943)), p. 34, expressed a similar opinion.

64 See, for example, Martin Bronfenbrenner, Income Distribution theory (Chicago: Aldine, 1971), p. 260. This author also fails to differentiate between Marx and Ricardo; on the latter's static view of skill differentials, see David Ricardo, On the Principles of Political Economy and Taxation (1817), P. Sraffa, ed., The Works and Correspondence of David Ricardo, I (Cambridge: Cambridge University Press, 1975 (1951)), 20-22; cf. Louis R. Salkever, Toward a Wage Structure Theory (New York: Humanities Press, 1964), p. 31.

65 For Germany, which in the mid-nineteenth century lagged several decades behind Britain industrially, Kuczynski has argued that by 1850 the price of skilled labor power had already lost its "'Kunstwert'"; that is, it had

already become a commodity that was readily reproducible and exchangeable. See Kuczynski, Geschichte, Vol. 1: Darstellung der Lage der Arbeiter in Deutschland von 1789 bis 1849 (Berlin (DDR): Akademie, 1961), p. 352. In other words, the period was long past in Britain in which it could be maintained that skilled labor had not yet been subjected to the law of value.

66 See, for example, Engels' letter of October 28, 1885 to August Bebel; MEW, XXXVI, 376-77. The view mentioned in the text distinguished Marx not only from Smith, Ricardo and other adherents of the notion of "equalizing differences," but also from those economists espousing the notion of "non-competing groups." See John Stuart Mill, Principles of Political Economy, ed. W.J. Ashley (London: Longsmans, Green, 1926 (1848)), pp. 391-93; J.E. Cairnes, Some Principles of Political Economy Newly Expounded (New York: Harper, n.d. (1874)), pp. 65-68. Cf. Salkever, Wage Structure, pp. 57-69. Whereas Marx emphasized skill, Smith and his followers focused on non-pecuniary (dis-)advantages in explaining wage differentials.

67 In this important substantive sense, then, Marx was concerned with the political consequences of a putative labor aristocracy. The rigid semantic approach of Gunnar Olofsson, "Teorier om arbetararistokrati och reformism hos Engels och Lenin," Arkiv (Stockholm), No. 6 (1974), p. 86, leads to a denial of this interest.

68 Engels did specify the one motivation that a recent critic has termed the only "rational" one--namely, that paying one group more enabled capitalists to pay another group "substantially less." See Edna Bonacich, "Advanced Capitalism and Black/White Relations in the United States: A Split Labor Market Interpretation," American Sociological Review, XLI, 1 (February 1976), 44.

69 It was first published in the Bee-Hive, No. 160, November 5, 1864; here it is cited according to Marx's own translation: "Inauguraladresse der Internationalen Arbeiter-Assoziation," MEW, XVI, 5-13.

70 Ibid., p. 5.

71 Ibid., p. 9.

72 Kapital, I, lst ed., 635-99.

73 See Fritz Sternberg, Der Imperialismus (Berlin: Malik, 1926), pp. 60-61, 434-35; cf. the critical essay by Henryk Grossmann, "Eine neue Theorie über den Imperialismus und die Soziale Revolution," Archiv für die Geschichte des Sozialismus und der Arbeiterbewegung, XII (1928), 141-92.

74 Kapital, I, lst ed., 641.

75 See Gladstone's speech on April 16, 1863 in the House of Commons as cited in ibid., p. 639 n. 103. On the controversy surrounding this quotation, see Karl Marx, "(Antwort auf den ersten Artikel Brentanos)," MEW, XVIII, 89-92; "(Antwort auf den zweiten Artikel Brentanos)," ibid., 109-15; F. Engels, In Sachen Brentano contra Marx wegen angeblicher Zitatsfälschung, MEW, XXII, 93-185. Cf. "How Far Have Our Working Classes Benefited by the Increase of Our Wealth," Economist, XXXII, 1587 (January 24, 1874), 93-95; Henry Fawcett, "The Effect of an Increased Production of Wealth on Wages," Fortnightly Review, N.S., XV, LXXV (January 1, 1874), 75-81. In 1866 one of the largest building employers stated "that it does not appear that, as a class, they (building operatives) are better off now than they were many years ago." See "The Condition of Building Operatives," The Builder, XXIV, 1237 (October 20, 1866), 776.

76 See Thomas Carlyle, "Chartism," Century Edition of The Works of Thomas Carlyle in thirty Columes, Vol. 29: Critical and Miscellaneous Essays,

Vol. 4 (London: Chapman and Hall, 1899; reprint: New York: AMS, 1969), p. 126, who states that well-being is indicated not only by wages and steady employment, but also by relations to the employers. This essay first appeared in 1839. Cf. Marx's detailed questionnaire for workers, first published anonymously in Revue socialiste, April 20, 1880; cited here according to the German translation of the original English MS in MEW, XIX, 230-37.

77 Sternberg, Imperialismus, pp. 60-61.

78 Calculated according to data in Occupation Abstract M.DCCC.XLI, p. 289; Census of Great Britain, 1851, Population Tables, II. Ages, Civil Conditions, and Birth-Place of the People, Vol. I (London: HMSO, 1854), Table XXV at p. ccxxiii; Census of England and Wales, 1871. Population Abstracts, Ages, Civil Condition, Occupations, and Birth-Places of the People, Vol. III (London: HMSO, 1873), Table XVIII at p. xxxix.

79 The data for 1851--which are incomplete--refer to size classes, the largest of which is open-ended, covering concentrations of more than 350 men; the data for 1871 provide accurate numbers for establishments and those employed, but represent incomplete returns. See Census of Great Britain, 1851, Table XXX at pp. cclxxvi-cclxxix; Factories and Workshops, August 9, 1871, P.P. 1871, Vol. LXII, pp. 163-64.

80 A similar pattern prevailed in the United States. See National Industrial Conference Board, A Graphic Analysis of the Census of Manufactures of the United States 1849 to 1919 (New York: NICB, 1923), Chart 48 at p. 96 and Table 48 at p. 97.

81 Calculated according to Deane and Cole, British Economic Growth, Table 31 at p. 143.

82 Calculated according to data in Werner Schlote, British Overseas Trade. From 1700 to the 1930s, tr. W.O. Henderson and W.H. Chaloner (Oxford: Blackwell, 1952 (German ed. 1938)), Table 16 at pp. 152-53; the data are stated in current prices.

83 Calculated according to data in B.R. Mitchell, Abstract of British Historical Statistics (Cambridge: Cambridge University Press, 1962), pp. 315-27.

84 Ibid., pp. 64-65.

85 Great Britain, Board of Trade, Labour Statistics, C.-5104 (London: HMSO, 1887), p. 22.

86 Mitchell, Abstract, pp. 64-65; George H. Wood, "Some Statistics relating to Working Class Progress since 1860," Journal of the Royal Statistical Society, LXII, Pt. IV (December 1899), 640-48.

87 Source: Statistical Abstract for the United Kingdom, In each of the last Fifteen Years, from 1844 to 1858, (London: HMSO, 1859), p. 44; Statistical Abstract for the United Kingdom, In each of the last Fifteen Years, from 1856 to 1870, C. 395 (London: HMSO, 1871), p. 126.

88 Calculated according to data in Census of England and Wales. 1891, Vol. IV. General Report, C.-7222 (London: HMSO, 1893), p. 96 Cf. Wood, "Statistics," Appendix III at p. 666 and chart at p. 661.

89 See the data in G.R. Porter, The Progress of the Nation, revised by F.W. Hirst (London: Methuen, 1912), pp. 5-6; B.R. Mitchell, "Statistical Appendix, 1700-1914," The Fontana Economic History of Europe, ed. Carlo M. Cipolla, Vol. 4, Part 2 (London: Collins, 1973), p. 751.

90 Calculated according to data in United States Bureau of the Census, Historical Statistics of the United States, Colonial Times to 1970, Bicentennial Edition, Part 1 (Washington, D.C.: Government Printing Office, 1975), Series C 91-92 at p. 106.

91 See Sidney and Beatrice Webb, History of Trade Unionism, 1902 ed., pp. 183-84. The Amalgamated Society of Carpenters and Joiners, which abolished this benefit in 1886, had never paid a member a subsidy to emigrate; see Amalgamated Society of Carpenters and Joiners (Francis Chandler), History of the Society--1860-1919 (Manchester: ASCJ, 1910), p. 27. Controversy surrounds the issue of the extent to which mid-nineteenth century trade union leaders accepted orthodox political economy's tenets of supply and demand and the wage fund as applied to emigration. See Charlotte Erickson, "The Encouragement of Emigration by British Trade Unions, 1850-1900," Population Studes, III, 3 (December 1949), 248-73; R.V. Clements, "Trade Unions and Emigration, 1840-80," ibid., IX, 2 (November 1955), 167-80.

92 See Joan Robinson, "Marx and Keynes," Collected Economic Papers (Oxford: Blackwell, 1951), p. 142. A partially compensating factor may have resulted from this deceleration of accumulation insofar as the latter assumed the form of a lower organic composition of capital than would have otherwise been the case. See Keith Burgess, The Origins of British Industrial Relations (London: Croom Helm, 1975), p.v.

93 Calculated according to data in C.H. Feinstein, National Income, Expenditure and Output of the United Kingdom 1855-1965 (Cambridge: Cambridge University Press, 1972), Table 1 at p. T4. During the same period, net property income from abroad rose from 2.1 per cent to 5.1 per cent of gross national product; calculated according to data in ibid., Table 18 at p. T44.

94 Leland H. Jenks, The Migration of British Capital to 1875 (London: Nelson, 1963 (1927)), pp. 335, 411-15. Cf. J.A. Hobson, Imperialism (Ann Arbor: University of Michigan, 1967 (1902)), pp. 61-63.

95 Fawcett, "The Effect," pp. 80-81.

96 See R.A. Church, The Great Victorian Boom 1850-1873 (London: Macmillan, 1975), pp. 71-75; Wood, "Real Wages," pp. 102-103.

97 Rufus S. Tucker, "Real Wages of the Artisans in London, 1729-1935," Journal of the American Statistical Association, XXXI, 193 (March 1936), 79-80, 83.

98 Wood, "Real Wages," Table I at p. 93; Bowley, Wages in the United Kingdom, pp. 130-33.

99 Leone Levi, Wages and Earnings of the Working Classes (London: Murray, 1885), p. 6.

100 Arthur L. Bowley, "Changes in Average Wages (Nominal and Real) in the United Kingdom between 1860 and 1891," Journal of the Royal Statistical Society, LVIII, Pt. II (June 1895), Table VII at 248. Cf. Leone Levi, Work and Pay (London: Strahan, 1877); "The Wages and Earnings of the Working Classes," Economist, XLIII (January 17, 1885), 64-65.

101 Calculated according to data in Feinstein, National Income, Table 18 at p. T44.

102 Kapital, I, 1st ed., 641.

103 "Inauguraladresse," p. 9.

104 Michael Mauke, Die Klassentheorie von Marx und Engels (Frankfurt/Main: Europäische Verlagsanstalt, 1970), p. 135, misinterprets these passages.

105 Kapital, I, 1st ed., 654-57; cf. Marx's comment on the working conditions of printers in "Inauguraladresse," p. 8.

106 In the second edition of Kapital Marx entitled this section, "Effect of the Crises on the Best-Paid Part of the Working Class"; Kapital, I, 2nd ed., 697.

107 Kapital, I, 1st ed., 657. Although relatively well paid, iron shipbuilders did not fall within the category of the highest paid workers. See R.

Dudley Baxter, National Income (London: Macmillan, 1868), p. 50; Leone Levi, Wages and Earnings of the Working Classes (London: Murray, 1867), pp. xxxii, 62-63, 116-17, 120; Labour Statistics, Returns of Wages Published between 1830 and 1886 (London: HMSO, 1887), pp. 211, 218-19.

108 Kapital, I, lst ed., 657-60. Cf. the account presented by Wright, Our New Masters, pp. 44-45; J.E. Mortimer, History of the Boilermakers' Society, Vol. I: 1834-1906 (London: Allen & Unwin, 1973), pp. 65-69. According to A.L. Bowley and George H. Wood, "The Statistics of Wages in the United Kingdom during the last Hundred Years. (Part X.) Engineering and Shipbuilding. A. Trade Union Standard Rates," Journal of the Royal Statistical Society, LXVIII (March 1905), 122, trade union rates were not reduced during the years 1866-1868; see, however, idem, "Statistics of Wages. (Part XIV.) E. Averages, Index Numbers, and General Results," ibid., LXIX (March 1906), 160-61 and Diagrams I and III. On the sharp decline in registered net tonnage from 1864 to 1867, see Akademiia nauki SSSR, Institut mirovogo khoziaistva i mirovoi politiki, Mirovoe ekonomicheskie krizisy 1948-1935, ed. E. Varga, Vol. I: Sravitel'nye materialy po istorii krizisov v vazhneishikh kapitalisticheskikh stranakh (Moscow: OGIZ, 1937), p. 493.

109 Cf. Henry Collins and Chimen Abramsky, Karl Marx and the British Labour Movement. Years of the First International (London: Macmillan, 1965), p. 47.

110 See Engels' letter of January 25, 1882 to E. Bernstein, MEW, XXXV, 268.

111 Letter of November 30, 1881, ibid., pp. 237-38. Cf. Jürgen Kuczynski, Zurück zu Marx (Leipzig: Hirschfeld, 1926), pp. 128-29.

112 Cf. Engels' letter to Bernstein of May 22, 1886, MEW, XXXVI, 487; see also his letter of May 23, 1886 to Laura Lafargue, ibid., p. 489.

113 R.S. Neale, Class and Ideology in the Nineteenth Century (London: Routledge & Kegan Paul, 1972), p. 70, states that building tradesmen resembled an urban free peasantry more than any other group did.

114 "Politische Rundschau," Das Volk, No. 16, August 20, 1859; cited according to MEW, XIII, 487-88.

115 See "The Nine Hours Movement," The Times (London), August 23, 1859, p. 5 col. 4; "The Nine Hours Movement," ibid., September 6, 1859, p. 9 col. 1; "Proceedings In Connection With The Strike," The Builder, XVII, 864 (August 27, 1859), 565. The skilled and unskilled workers received different levels of support.

116 G. Shaw Lefevre and Thomas R. Bennet, "Account of the Strike and Lock-Out in the Building Trades of London, 1959-60," Trades' Societies and Strikes, Report of the Committee on Trades' Societies Appointed by the National Association for the Promotion of Social Science (London: Parker, 1860), p. 54.

117 Frederick Harrison, Autobiographic Memoirs, I (London: Macmillan, 1911), 250-54, recreates the state of hardship during the strike.

118 Twenty-Second Annual Report of the Registrar-General of Births, Deaths, and Marriages in England (London: HMSO, 1861), pp. xxxv-xxxvi. Cf. Shaw and Bennet, "Account," p. 75; a letter from a relieving officer to The Times (London), September 3, 1859, p. 10 col. 6.

119 See R.W. Postgate, The Builders' History (London: Labour Publishing, n.d. (1923)), pp. 236-37.

120 J.H. Clapham, "Work and Wages," G.M. Young, ed., Early Victorian England 1830-1865, I (London: Oxford University Press, 1934), 30-31.

121 See "The Carpenters' Strike at Nottingham," The Builder, XII, 590
(May 27, 1854), 281-82; "The Position and Prosperity of the Building
Operatives," ibid., XVI, 796 (May 8, 1858), 317; "Labour Saving Machines
for Builders," ibid., XXVII, 1384 (August 14, 1869), 640; letter by
George Potter entitled, "The Nine-Hours Movement," ibid., XVII, 852
(June 4, 1859), 380-81; cf. the contrary statements by A Working Man,
ibid., XVII, 85 (June 11, 1859), 397; and Thomas Donaldson, ibid.,
XVII, 856 (July 2, 1859), 447. Cf. also Hobhouse, Cubitt, p. 286.

122 J.R. McCulloch, The Principles of Political Economy (5th ed.; Edinburgh:
Black, 1864 (1825)), p. 347. See the undocumented view presented by
J.H. Clapham, An Economic History of Modern Britain. Free Trade and
Steel 1850-1886 (Cambridge: Cambridge University Press, 1932), p. 446.

123 It must be emphasized that both within Britain and between Britain and
Ireland Marx conceived of the antagonism between British and Irish
proletarians, which he characterized as analogous to that obtaining between the "poor whites" and the "niggers" in the post-bellum South, as
"the secret of the maintenance of power of the capitalist class." See his
letter of April 9, 1870 to August Vogt and Sigfrid Meyer, MEW, XXXII,
668-69. Arthur Redford, Labour Migration in England, 1800-1850 (Manchester: Manchester University Press, 1926), pp. 130-42, describes
some important aspects of English-Irish working class relations.

124 "Inauguraladresse," p. 10.

125 See Marx's "Letter to Labour Parliament," People's Paper, No. 98,
March 18, 1854, p. 1.

126 See, for example, W.W. Rostow, The Stages of Economic Growth (Cambridge: Cambridge University Press, 1960), pp. 150-56.

127 "Instruktionen für die Delegierten des Provisorischen Zentralrats zu den
einzelnen Fragen," MEW, XVI, 197-98.

128 See Collins and Abramsky, Karl Marx, pp. 162, 176, for a more sober
account.

129 See Marx's letters to Engels of April 5, 1869, MEW, XXXII, 293 and of
December 4, 1869, ibid., p. 409; cf. Marx's letter of December 28, 1868
to Hermann Jung, ibid., p. 587. On Applegarth, see the editorial in
The Times (London), October 1, 1869, p. 6 col. 5; A.W. Humphrey,
Robert Applegarth (Manchester: NLP, 1913); Asa Briggs, Victorian
People (Chicago: University of Chicago Press, 1970 (1955)), pp. 168-96.

130 Letter to Marx of December 9, 1869, MEW, XXXII, 411.

131 As early as 1866 Marx spoke of betrayal with regard to two trade union
leaders who were accused of concluding compromises with the bourgeoisie;
see his letter of August 31, 1866 to Johann Phillip Becker, MEW, XXXI,
524. Several weeks later Marx appears to have changed his mind; see
his letter of October 13, 1866 to Ludwig Kugelmann, ibid., p. 534.

132 Lujo Brentano, Die Arbeitergilden der Gegenwart. Vol. II. Zur Kritik
der englischen Gewerkvereine (Leipzig: Duncker & Humblot, 1872),
p. 332, claimed that Marx viewed trade unionists with the greatest
contempt as "'kleine Bourgeois.'" Cf. idem, Eine Geschichte der wirtschaftlichen Entwicklung Englands, III:2 (Jena: Fischer, 1928), 458-59.

133 "(Aufzeichnung der Reden von Karl Marx über die Trade-Unions),"
MEW, XVII, 649; the record of this speech, which was made on September
20, 1871, is taken from the French language minutes.

134 Ibid.

135 See the editorial notes, ibid., p. 750.

136 Mikhail Bakunin, Gosudarstvennost' i anarkhiia (1873), Izbrannye
sochineniia, ed. V. Cherkezova, I (2nd ed.; Petersburg-Moscow: "Golos
Truda," 1922), 49-50. Marx excerpted this passage without comment in

1874-1875; see his "(Konspekt von Bakunins Buch 'Staatlichkeit und Anarchie')," MEW, XVIII, 599. Although Bakunin himself wrote a typology of labor aristocrats, whom he saw as created by the patriarchal relations of the old skilled crafts, he formed a favorable impression of British trade unions. See his Vsesvietnyi revoliutsionnyi soiuz sotsial'noi demokratii (Berlin: Steinitz, 1904 (1870)), pp. 60-67, 70-74.

137 "(Aufzeichnung der Ausführungen von Marx über das Mandat Barrys)," MEW, XVIII, 685. This incident contradicts the interpretation of Marx's attitude presented by Siegfried Bünger, Friedrich Engels und die britische sozialistische Bewegung 1881-1895 (Berlin (DDR): Rütten & Loening, 1962), p. 64 n. 42 cont. on p. 65.

138 Letter to Wilhelm Liebknecht of February 11, 1878, MEW, XXXIV, 320; see also Marx's letter of September 27, 1877 to F.A. Sorge, ibid., p. 295, in which Marx pointed to the new paternalistic attitude that certain large capitalists had adopted toward trade unions.

139 See, for example, Engels' letter of November 8, 1867 to Kugelmann, ibid., XXXI, 568.

140 See, for example, Engels, "Die englischen Wahlen," Der Volksstaat, No. 26, March 4, 1874; cited here according to MEW, XVIII, 494-99. Paradoxically, Engels made the granting of certain democratic reforms, which had been demanded by the Chartists, responsible for working class passivity; he also re-introduced the issue of the effects of England's world market dominance and of the corruption of labor leaders. He and Marx returned to this theme again and again during the 1870s. See the following correspondence: Marx to Paul and Laura Lafargue of July 28, 1870, ibid., XXXIII, 126; Engels to Wilhelm Liebknecht of May 27-28, 1872, ibid., p. 475; Engels to Sorge of September 21, 1872, ibid., p. 524.

141 The Webbs also, however, pointed out that the trade unions aided the organizational efforts of agricultural workers from 1872 onwards; see History of Trade Unionism, 1902 ed., pp. 315-18.

142 Ibid., pp. 276-82.

143 Ibid., pp. 303-307.

144 Ibid., pp. 311-12, 322-23. The Webbs noted that as late as 1883 the Trades Union Congress, by a large majority, rejected amendments supporting manhood suffrage; ibid., p. 354.

145 Ibid., p. 359. Cf. F.M. Leventhal, Respectable Radical. George Howell and Victorian Working Class Politics (Cambridge, Mass.: Harvard University Press, 1971), p. 190. Both the Webbs, History of Trade Unionism, 1902 ed., p. 360, and B.C. Roberts, The Trades Union Congress 1868-1921 (London: Allen & Unwin, 1958), pp. 96-97, contend that the laissez-faire views of the leadership reflected, at least until the 1880s, the opinion of the better situated rank and file.

146 "England 1845 und 1885," MEW, XXI, 194. Engels translated this article into German after having published it in The Commonweal, March 1, 1885; it was subsequently absorbed in its entirety into the appendix of the 1887 American edition of Die Lage der arbeitenden Klasse in England and of later editions.

147 Marx, "Letter to the Labour Parliament," p. 1.

148 E.J. Hobsbawm, "The Labour Aristocracy in Nineteenth Century Britain," idem, Labouring Men (Garden City: Anchor, 1967 (1954)), p. 350; Geoffrey Crossick, "The Emergence of the Lower Middle Class in Britain: A Discussion," idem, ed., The Lower Middle Class in Britain 1870-1914 (London: Croom Helm, 1977), pp. 48-49. Cf. also chaps. 7-9 below.

149 Armstrong, "The use," p. 255.
150 See République Française, Ministère du Commerce, de l'Industrie, des Postes et des Telegraphes, Direction du Travail, Résultats statistiques du récensement des industries et professions. Dénombrement général de la population du mars 1896, Vol. IV: Résultats généraux (Paris: Imprimerie National, 1901), p. xvi.
151 Data on French population taken from République Française, Ministère du Travail, Statistique générale de la France, Annuaire statistique, Vol. 38--1922 (Paris: Imprimerie Nationale, 1923), p. 12*. British population data for 1866 taken from Census of England and Wales, 1891, IV, 96; for the 1890s, population data were interpolated on the basis of the data in Census of England and Wales. 1911. Area, Families or Separate Occupiers, and Population, Vol. I: Administrative Areas, P.P. 1912-13, CXI, Cd. 6258 (London: HMSO, 1912), p. 7.
152 Source: Walther G. Hoffmann, Das Wachstum der deutschen Wirtschaft seit der Mitte des 19. Jahrhunderts ((West) Berlin: Springer, 1965), Table 22 at p. 209.
153 German population data taken from Mitchell, "Statistical Appendix," p. 747.
154 The only sectoral exceptions were the much larger armed forces in Germany and France and the much greater representation of the clergy in the latter country. See Armstrong, "The use," pp. 275-78; Hoffmann, Wachstum, Tables 19-20 at pp. 203-205; Résultats statistiques, IV, xvi.
155 The first complete British census to ascertain these two pieces of information was not conducted until 1891. Although Hoffmann estimated the number of independently employed for the latter half of the century, the only two years for which accurate data are available for Germany are 1882 and 1895. Similarly, the French data prior to 1896 are based on estimates. See Census of England and Wales, 1891. Ages, Conditions as to Marriage, Occupations, Birth-Places and Infirmities, Vol. III (London: HMSO, 1893), pp. xiv-xxv; Résultats statistiques, IV, lxxii, 198-99; Hoffmann, Wachstum, Table 22 at p. 209; Statistik des Deutschen Reiches, ed. Kaiserlichen Statistischen Amt, N.S., Vol. 119 (Berlin, 1899), p. 60. See also Gustav Schmoller, Zur Geschichte der deutschen Kleingewerbe im 19. Jahrhundert (Halle: Verlag der Buchhandlung des Waisenhauses, 1870).
156 Although Engels spoke of a change in the "mutual attitude of both classes," he described all initiatives as having been taken by the bourgeoisie; see "England 1845 und 1885," pp. 192-93.
157 See Kapital, I, 2nd ed., 278-302; "Inauguraladresse," p. 11; "Der Klerus und der Kampf um den Zehnstundentag," MEW, VIII, 537-39; first published in the New York Daily Tribune, March 15, 1853.
158 See Engels, "(Konspekt über) 'Das Kapital' von Karl Marx," MEW, XVI, 266-69.
159 See "Die englische Zehnstundenbill," MEW, VII, 233-43; cf. also ibid., pp. 226-32.
160 "England 1845 und 1885," p. 193.
161 A Short History of the British Working-Class Movement 1789-1945 (new ed.; London: Allen & Unwin, 1952 (1925)), p. 228. Cf. however Postgate, Builders' History, pp. 197-98.
162 See, for example, the editorial in The Times (London), July 8, 1869, p. 8 cols. 5-6.
163 See Webb, History of Trade Unionism, 1902 ed., pp. 232-75, 311-12, 322-23; Frances E. Gillespie, Labor and Politics in England 1850-1867 (Durham: Duke University Press, 1927), p. 188.

164 See The Life of Thomas Cooper, Written by Himself (2nd ed.; London: Hodder and Stoughton, 1872), pp. 392-93.

165 Henry Pelling, Popular Politics and Society in Late Victorian Britain (London: Macmillan, 1968), p. 38.

166 See Gareth Stedman Jones, "Class Struggle and the Industrial Revolution," New Left Review, No. 90, May-June 1975, p. 61.

167 V.E. Kunina, Karl Marks i angliiskoe rabochie dvizhenie (Moscow: Mysl', 1968), p. 275, exaggerates this point.

168 Letter of August 11, 1881, MEW, XXXV, 20.

169 Letter of September 12, 1882, ibid., p. 357. See Kautsky, Die soziale Revolution. I. Sozialreform und soziale Revolution (2nd ed.; Berlin: Vorwärts, 1907), p. 40.

170 Letter of August 30, 1883, MEW, XXXVI, 58.

171 Letter to Bebel of October 11, 1884, ibid., p. 216; January 19, 1885, ibid., pp. 274-75. Cf. however Engels' letter of December 27, 1891 to Kautsky, ibid., XXXVIII, 243.

172 Letter of February 3, 1886 to Florence Kelley-Wischnewetzky, ibid., XXXVI, 443.

173 See, for example, his letter of August 30, 1892 to V. Adler, ibid., XXXVIII, 445. The next year, to be sure, Engels conceded that American workers were still enjoying a kind of prosperity no longer known in Europe; in this context he referred to racial and ethnic cleavages as barriers to socialist development in the United States. See his letter of December 2, 1893 to Sorge, ibid., XXXIX, 173.

174 "Appendix" to The Condition of the Working Class in England in 1844 (New York, 1887); cited according to MEW, XXI, 250-51. It should be noted that the text refers to Engels' depiction of the course of events; in reality, the truck system, for example, continued to be employed for decades; see G.W. Hilton, The Truck System (Cambridge: Heffer, 1960).

175 MEW, XXI, 251.

176 Ibid., pp. 251-52. See however Engels' letter of June 17, 1879 to Bernstein, ibid., XXXIV, 379.

177 "England 1845 und 1885", p. 195.

178 Ibid., pp. 196-97.

179 Ibid., p. 197.

180 Letter of October 28, 1885, MEW, XXXVI, 376-77. Engels used the term "Trades Unions" in English.

181 In addition to the literature already cited, see Postgate, Builders' History, pp. 190-91, 220-21; George Howell, The Conflicts of Capital and Labour (London: Chatto and Windus, 1878), pp. 250-54; testimony of Edwin Coulson, secretary of the Operative Bricklayers Society before the Royal Commission on Trade Unions, First Report of the Commissioners Appointed to Inquire into the Organization and Rules of Trade Unions and Other Associations (London: Eyre & Spottiswoode, 1867), Q. 1496 at p. 59 and QQ. 1568-70 at p. 61; see, however, the question posed by Commissioner Thomas Hughes, Third Report, QQ. 4923-30 at p. 42; "Notes on the History and Condition of the Building Trades. Masons," The Builder, XI, 569 (December 24, 1853), 777; a letter to ibid., XX, 992 (February 8, 1862), 102, does contain a proposal for the training of convicts in order to break the control of the supply of labor by trade unions; Pelling, Popular Politics, pp. 44-51; John Platt, an M.P. and owner of the Oldham cotton machinery works, called for the abolition of apprenticeship on the grounds that it encouraged workers to think in terms of a vested interest in their trades; see Hansard's Parliamentary Debates, Third Series, CXCVII, 1365 for July 7, 1869; H.A. Clegg et

al., A History of British Trade Unions since 1889, Vol. I: 1889-1910 (Oxford: Clarendon, 1964), pp. 140-41, 145-46, 156-59, indicate a greater scope for apprenticeship in engineering, printing and building than conceded by the Webbs; it should be borne in mind, however, that the Webbs did not deny the existence of apprenticeship systems but merely that they restricted employers.

182 Source: Schlote, British Overseas Trade, Table 16 at pp. 152-54.

183 See H.A. Turner, Trade Union Growth, Structure and Policy. A Comparative Study of the Cotton Unions (London: Allen & Unwin, 1962), pp. 110-14; Pelling, Popular Politics, p. 52.

184 On wages in mining, see Palgrave, Dictionary, III, 634-35; Wages.-- General Report. General Report on the Wages of the Manual Working Classes in the United Kingdom, C. 6889 (London: HMSO, 1893), pp. 470-71.

185 Deane and Cole, British Economic Growth, Table 56 at p. 225.

186 See P.L. Payne, "Iron and Steel Manufactures," The Development of British Industry and Foreign Competition 1875-1914 (London: Allen & Unwin, 1968), Tables I and II at p. 72; D.L. Burn, The Economic History of Steelmaking 1867-1939 (Cambridge: Cambridge University Press, 1940), Table XXIV at p. 330.

187 See S.B. Saul, "The Engineering Industry," Development of British Industry 1875-1914, pp. 186-237; Paul Gannay, L'Imperialisme économique et la grande industrie anglaise (Paris: Pinchon, 1905), pp. 164-77.

188 Sidney Pollard, The Development of the British Economy 1914-1967 (2nd ed.; n.p.: Arnold, 1973 (1962)), p. 7. See in general Sidney Chapman, Work and Wages. Part I. Foreign Competition (London: Longmans, 1904).

189 Webb, Industrial Democracy, pp. 456-57.

190 Idem, History of Trade Unionism, 1902 ed., p. 416.

191 James B. Jefferys, The Story of the Engineers 1800-1945 (n.p.: Lawrence and Wishart, n.d. (1945)), p. 98.

192 Webb, History of Trade Unionism, 1902 ed., p. 335; J.C. Carr and W. Tapling, History of the British Steel Industry (Cambridge, Mass.: Harvard University Press, 1962), pp. 70-73, 136.

193 Jefferys, Story, p. 166.

194 Mortimer, Boilermakers' Society, I, 109-11, 188; J. Lynch, "Skilled and Unskilled Labour in the Shipbuilding Trade," Industrial Remuneration Conference, The Report of the Proceedings and Papers (London: Cassell, 1885), pp. 114-18; Webb, History of Trade Unionism, 1902 ed., p. 339.

195 Clegg, History, I, 22 n. 7 cont. on 23; Standish Meacham, A Life Aprt. The English Working Class 1890-1914 (London: Thames and Hudson, 1977), p. 143.

196 Sources: Armstrong, "The use," pp. 255-81; Census of England and Wales, 1891, Preliminary Report, C.-6422 (London: HMSO, 1891), p. xiii; calculations by author.

197 Calculated according to data in: Census of Great Britain, 1851, Table 41 at p.c.; Census of England and Wales for the Year 1861, Vol. III. General Report, P.P. 1863, Vol. LIII, Part 1 (London: HMSO, 1863), Table 84 at p. 132; Census of England and Wales for the Year 1871, General Report, Vol. IV, P.P. 1873, Vol. LXXI, Part II, C.--872.-1 (London: HMSO, 1873), Table 103 at p. 111.

198 Census of England and Wales, 1911, Vol. X: Occupations and Industries, Part I (London: HMSO, 1914), Table 26 at pp. 540-51. The statement in the text does not refer to agricultural laborers.

199 Great Britain, Board of Trade, Labour Statistics, C.-5104 (London: HMSO, 1887), p. 20; Webb, History of Trade Unionism, 1902 ed., pp. 492-93.

200 William Allen, secretary of the Amalgamated Society of Engineers, stated in 1867 that two-thirds to three-quarters of the men in his trade belonged to his union; see Royal Commission on Trade Unions, First Report, Q. 576 at p. 28. Since such figures correspond to a much smaller number of employed than indicated by the censuses of 1861 and 1871, Allen may have been referring to the skilled only.

201 Clegg, History, I, Table 6 at 468.

202 Webb, History of Trade Unionism, 1902 ed., pp. 335, 415-418.

203 See John Burnett, ed., Annals of Labour. Autobiographies of British working-class people 1820-1920 (Bloomington and London: Indiana University Press, 1974), p. 251.

204 Factories and Workshops, pp. 271-72.

205 Ibid. Data calculated by author.

206 Jefferys, Story, pp. 15-16.

207 Ibid., p. 57.

208 Alan S. Milward and S.B. Saul, The Economic Development of Continental Europe 1780-1870 (London: Allen & Unwin, 1973), p. 196; John Foster, Class Struggle and the Industrial Revolution (London: Methuen, 1977 (1974)), pp. 224-27, appears to exaggerate the extent of craft destruction during this period.

209 Jefferys, Story, p. 207, estimates that sixty per cent were still skilled in 1914. For estimates for earlier years, see M. and J.B. Jefferys, "The Wages, Hours and Trade Customs of the Skilled Engineer in 1861," Economic History Review, XVII, 1 (1947), 27-42; Labour Statistics. Returns of Wages Published between 1830 and 1886, pp. 186, 188-89.

210 Jefferys, Story, pp. 124, 170; David S. Landes, The Unbound Prometheus (Cambridge: Cambridge University Press, 1972 (1969)), p. 306; E.H. Phelps Brown, The Growth of British Industrial Relations. A Study from the standpoint of 1906-14 (London: Macmillan, 1959), pp. 90-92; J.W.F. Rowe, Wages in Theory and Practice (New York: Kelley, 1969 (1928)), pp. 89-103, 157-58, 263-70; Burgess, Origins, pp. 1-85; idem, "Technological Change and the 1852 Lock-out in the British Engineering Industry," International Review of Social History, XIV (1969), 215-36; idem, "Trade Union Policy and the 1852 Lock-out in the British Engineering Industry," ibid., XVII (1972), 645-60.

211 Webb, Industrial Democracy, pp. 456-57.

212 Ibid., p. 490.

213 Calculated according to data in Labour Statistics. Returns of Wages Published between 1830 and 1886, pp. 210-12, 218-19.

214 Ibid., pp. 149, 151-52, 176.

215 See, for example, (Samuel Smiles), "Strikes," Quarterly Review, CVI (1859), 509; J.M. Ludlow and LLoyd Jones, Progress of the Working Class 1832-1867 (Clifton: Kelley, 1973 (1867)), p. 237.

216 William T. Thornton, On Labour (2nd ed.; London: Macmillan, 1870 (1869)), p. 344; J.S. Mill, "Thornton on Labour and its Claims," Fortnightly Review, V (N.S.), XXX (June 1, 1869), 695-96.

217 Letter of Lord Shaftesbury to Col. Maude, cited by Edward Beesly, "The Social Future of the Working Class," ibid., V (N.S.), XXVII (March 1, 1869), 354 n. 1.

218 See however J. Ward, Workmen and Wages at Home and Abroad or the Effects of Strikes, Combinations and Trades' Unions (London: Longmans, 1868), p. 9.

219 G.D.H. Cole, "Some Notes on British Trade Unionism in the Third Quarter of the Nineteenth Century," International Review for Social History, II (1937), 1-25; Webb, Industrial Democracy, p. 480.
220 E.g., iron puddlers; see Milward and Saul, Economic Development, pp. 198-99.
221 Robert Torrens, On Wages and Combination (Shannon: Irish University Press, 1971 (1834)), pp. 73-80.
222 Thornton, On Labour, p. 292.
223 Ibid., pp. 292-93.
224 See, for example, Derek Aldcroft and Harry Richardson, The British Economy 1870-1939 (London: Macmillan, 1969).
225 Th. Rothstein, From Chartism to Labourism (New York: International, 1929), p. 263.
226 Source: Kuczynski, England von 1832 bis 1900, pp. 9, 86, 154; idem, Die Geschichte der Lage der Arbeiter unter dem Kapitalismus, Vol. 25: Darstellung der Lage der Arbeiter in England von 1900 bis zur Gegenwart (Berlin (DDR): Akademie, 1965), pp. 6, 52.
227 See League of Nations. Economic, Financial and Transit Department, Industrialization and Foreign Trade (n.p.: League of Nations, 1945), Table 1 at p. 13.
228 Sources for 1880 and 1890: S.B. Saul, "The Export Economy 1870-1914," Yorkshire Bulletin of Economic and Social Research, XVII, 1 (May 1965), Table V at 12; for 1899 and 1913: H. Tyszynski, "World Trade in Manufactured Commodities, 1899-1950," The Manchester School of Economic and Social Studies, XIX, 3 (September 1951), 277-78.
229 See W. Arthur Lewis, "International Competition in Manufactures," American Economic Review, XLVII, 2 (May 1957), 579; Alfred Maizels, Industrial Growth and World Trade (Cambridge: Cambridge University Press, 1963), pp. 189, 220.
230 See Kuczynski, England von 1832 bis 1900, pp. 10-11, 89-90, 155-56; Charles Kindleberger, Economic Growth in France and Britain 1851-1950 (New York: Simon and Schuster, 1969 (1964)), p. 271.
231 Calculated according to data in Schlote, British Overseas Trade, Table 16 at pp. 152-53.
232 Source: Saul, "Export Economy," Table VI at p. 13.
233 Aldcroft and Richardson, British Economy, pp. 72-73; see also Saul, "Engineering Industry," pp. 205-11.
234 Schlote, British Overseas Trade, Table 16 at p. 153.
235 Factories and Workshops, pp. 271, 299, 314.
236 Marx cites an example from cotton spinning, which was also a world market dominated by British firms; in this instance gross profits amounted to about 15.7 per cent of the selling price in 1871; see Kapital, I, 2nd ed., pp. 209-10.
237 V.G. Kiernan, Marxism and Imperialism (London: Arnold, 1974), p. 58.
238 Bowley, Wages in the United Kingdom, pp. 122-23.
239 Wood, "Some Statistics," p. 645.
240 See the data for the latter half of the 1860s in Baxter, National Income, passim; Leone, Wages and Earnings, passim.
241 See Labour Statistics. Returns of Wages Published between 1830 and 1886, pp. 148-49; Bowley, Wages in the United Kingdom, p. 70; Carr and Taplin, British Steel, p. 146.
242 Burn, Steelmaking 1867-1939, does point out, however, that wages at the beginning of the twentieth century were more evenly distributed in German iron and steel works than in those of the United Kingdom.

243 See Marc Linder, Anti-Samuelson, III (Gaiganz: Politladen, 1974), 19-24; cf. Tom Kemp, Theories of Imperialism (London: Dobson, 1967), p. 81.
244 Burgess, Origins, p. 5.
245 Payne, "Iron and Steel Manufactures," Table IV at p. 82.
246 See United States Congress, State of Labor, p. 30; J.A. Banks, Marxist Sociology in Action (London: Faber and Faber, 1970), p. 227.
247 See, e.g., William J. Blake, An American Looks at Karl Marx (New York: Cordon, 1939), p. 73.
248 This view is shared by two authors who would agree on little else: Earl Browder, Marx and America. A Study of the Doctrine of Impoverishment (New York: Duell, 1958), pp. 101-102, 106; Paul Mattick, letter to the author of January 5, 1978.
249 Tony Cliff, "Economic Roots of Reformism. A Critical View of Lenin's Theory of Opportunism," The New International, XXIV, 1 (Winter 1958), 43, contends that imperialism actually narrows wage differentials because cheap food imports aid all workers. Detailed budget and income elasticity studies would be needed to resolve this complicated empirical issue.
250 See Hobsbawm, Labouring Men, pp. 374, 381; Porter, Progress, ed. Hirst, pp. 432-53.
251 The other countries are the United States, France and Germany; see Kuczynski, England von 1832 bis 1900, pp. 197-99; idem, Die Entwicklung der Lage der Arbeiterschaft in Europa und Amerika 1870-1933 (Basel: Philographischer Verlag, 1934), passim; L.A. Mendel'son, Teoriia i istoriia ekonomicheskikh krizisov i tsiklov, II (Moscow: IS-EL, 1959), 526-27.
252 A.K. Cairncross, "Did Foreign Investment Pay?," Review of Economic Studies, III, 1 (October 1935), 77.
253 See E.J. Hobsbawm, Industry and Empire (London: Weidenbaum and Nicholson, 1968), Chart 32.
254 Feinstein, National Income, Table 1 at pp. T4-T5; cf. C.K. Hobson, The Export of Capital (New York: Macmillan, 1914), p. 204.
255 Calculated according to Feinstein, National Income, Table 1 at pp. T4-T5. Non-employment incomes comprehend: income from self-employment; gross trading profits of companies; gross trading surplus of public corporations and of other public enterprises; and rent. Cf. J.B. Askew, "Der britische Imperialismus," Ergänzungshefte zur Neuen Zeit, No. 19, July 24, 1914, pp. 37, 39, 41.
256 Baxter, National Income, p. 50.
257 Feinstein, National Income, Table 1 at p. T4.
258 Baxter, National Income, p. 50.
259 See Levi, Wages and Earnings, p. 9, who estimated weekly family income to be thirty-one shillings in 1865; the annual estimate mentioned in the text applies to the 1870s and 1880s as well.
260 Jürgen Kuczynski, "Ökonomische Basis und Zusammensetzung der Arbeiteraristokratie im Wandel eines Jahrhunderts," Zeitschrift für Geschichtswissenschaft, II (1954), 678.
261 See Herbert Feis, Europe the World's Banker 1870-1914 (New York: Norton, 1965 (1930)), p. 31; Jenks, Migration, pp. 178-85. Germany and the United States, on the other hand, relied much more heavily on such investments. See Rudolf Hilferding, Das Finanzkapital (Frankfurt/ Main: Europäische Verlagsanstalt, 1968 (1910)), p. 442; Feis, Europe, pp. 74-75, 79; W.S. Woytinsky and E.S. Woytinsky, World Commerce and Governments (New York: Twentieth Century Fund, 1955), p. 194.
262 Jenks, Migration, pp. 134-57, 419-20.

263 Large numbers of British workmen were exported along with the capital to construct some foreign railways. See Report from the Select Committee on Railway Labourers, House of Commons, July 28, 1846, P.P. 1846, (530) Vol. XIII, QQ. 327-28 at p. 19.
264 See Terry Coleman, The Railway Navvies (London: Hutchinson, 1967 (1965)), pp. 33-50; J.H. Clapham, An Economic History of Modern Britain. The Early Railway Age 1820-1850 (Cambridge: Cambridge University Press, 1926), pp. 406-12; cf. however Pauline Gregg, Modern Britain. A Social and Economic History Since 1760 (5th ed.; New York: Pegasus, 1967 (1965)), p. 103.
265 See Baxter, National Income, pp. 91-92; Thomas Brassey, On Work and Wages (New York: Putman's, 1883 (1872)), pp. 38, 197-98.
266 Select Committee on Railway Labourers, Q. 1041 at p. 63. Testimony to the effect that navvies' wages were double those of ordinary laborers was unsubstantiated; see ibid., QQ. 331-32 at p. 20. Navvies were compelled in some seasons to work seventy hours weekly; ibid., QQ. 1274-75 at p. 75.
267 See Hansard's Parliamentary Debates, Third Series, CXCVII, 1357-64 for July 7, 1869; Arthur Helps, Life and Labours of Mr Brassey (London, 1969 (1872)), p. 78; Select Committee on Railway Labourers, Q. 1302 at p. 77.
268 Checkland, England 1815-1885, p. 138; Robert K. Middlemas, The Master Builders (London: Hutchinson, 1963), pp. 29-118.
269 Select Committee on Railway Labourers, Q. 2278 at p. 157.
270 These portfolio investments were in large part absorbed by foreign government bonds; see Harvey H. Segal and Matthew Simon, "British Foreign Capital Issues, 1865-1895," Journal of Economic History, XXI, 4 (December 1961), 566-81; Matthew Simon, "The Pattern of New British Portfolio Foreign Investments 1865-1914," Capital Movements and Economic Development, ed. John H. Adler (London: Macmillan, 1967), pp. 33-70.
271 A.R. Hall, The London capital market and Australia 1870-1914 (Canberra: Australian National University, 1963), pp. 38, 43-55; cf. Jenks, Migration, p. 72.
272 Hobson, Export of Capital, pp. 66, 236. Cf. Robert Q. Gray, The Labour Aristocracy in Victorian Edinburgh (Oxford: Clarendon, 1976), p. 52.
273 Calculated according to data in Armstrong, "The use," pp. 255-81.
274 See Maurice Dobb, Political Economy and Capitalism (2nd ed.; London: Routledge & Kegan Paul, 1968 (1937)), p. 231.
275 Hobson, Export of Capital, p. 66. William Ashworth, An Economic History of England 1870-1939 (London: Methuen, 1960), p. 22, justifies "the immense number of domestic servants" by "the immense productive energy and enterprise of so many middle-class men" which it purportedly released. Cf. Marx, Grundrisse, p. 184.
276 See Karl Kautsky, "Der Krieg in Südafrika," Neue Zeit, XVII, I (1899-1900), 196-203. See also chap. 7 below.
277 Collins and Abramsky, Karl Marx, pp. 76-77, 289-90; cf. however, ibid., p. 219.
278 Engels, "England 1845 und 1885," pp. 193, 195. On the course of the cost of living, see Kuczynski, England von 1832 bis 1900, pp. 119-20, 197.
279 England 1845 und 1885," pp. 194, 196.
280 Ibid., p. 194.
281 Ibid., p. 195.
282 Factories and Workshops, pp. 271-72, 298-300, 314-15.

283 Ibid. Wage comparisons have been taken from Baxter, National Income, pp. 88-90.
284 Webb, History of Trade Unionism, 1902 ed., Appendix V at pp. 492-93.
285 See ibid., pp. 311-12, 492-95.
286 See J.M. Ludlow, "Trade Societies and the Social Science Association. Part First," Macmillan's Magazine, III (January 1861), 313.
287 See "The Working Classes," Blackwood's Edinburgh Magazine, CI, DCXVI (February 1867), 220-29.
288 Zygmunt Bauman, Klasa-Ruch-Elita (Warsaw: PWN, 1960), p. 72.
289 Ibid., p. 73.
290 Foster, Class Struggle, p. 229.
291 See C.G. Hanson, "Craft Unions, Welfare Benefits, and the Case for Trade Union Law Reform, 1867-75," Economic History Review, Second Series, XXVIII, 2 (May 1975), pp. 257, 259.
292 Royal Commission on Trade Unions, First Report, Q. 924 at p. 40. Harold Perkin, The Origins of Modern English Society 1780-1880 (London: Routledge & Kegan Paul, 1969), pp. 395-96; and Trygve R. Tholfsen, Working Class Radicalism in Mid-Victorian England (New York: Columbia University Press, 1977), p. 277, follow this line of argument.
293 Wood, "Real Wages," pp. 102-103.
294 Ibid.
295 Source: ibid., Table 2 at p. 97. For operatives of unchanged economic grade the decline was even more marked; see ibid.
296 Royden Harrison, Before the Socialists. Studies in Labour and Politics 1861-1881 (London: Routledge & Kegan Paul, 1965), p. 25, asserts but does not substantiate the claim of "the absolute impoverishment in the standards of the masses." Kuczynski's empirical study is methodologically flawed: the fact that he includes among the labor aristocracy all workers of strata with rising standards of living tautologically reduces the mass of workers to a residuum with declining wages. See Kuczynski, Entwicklung der Lage, pp. 14-15, 21.
297 Baxter, National Income, p. 48, pointed out that many workers, reluctant to accept relief because of the attendant humuliation, preferred to "die of starvation."
298 Source: Statistical Abstract for the United Kingdom, In each of the Last Fifteen Years. From 1867 to 1881, C.-3266 (London: HMSO, 1882), Table No. 91 at p. 166; Statistical Abstract for the United Kingdom, In each of the Last Fifteen Years. From 1876 to 1890, C.-6457 (London: HMSO, 1891), Table No. 112 at p. 221.
299 Census of England and Wales, 1891, Preliminary Report, C.-6422 (London: HMSO, 1891), p. xiii; calculation by author.
300 See Porter, Progress, ed. Hirst, pp. 70, 72.
301 Charles Booth, ed., Labour and Life of the People, Vol. II: London Continued (London: Williams & Norgate, 1891), p. 21. On the economic roots of the specific forms of poverty in London, see Gareth Stedman Jones, Outcast London (Harmondsworth: Penguin, 1976 (1971)), passim.
302 Checkland, England 1815-1885, p. 229.
303 See W. Thorp, Business Annals (New York: National Bureau of Economic Research, 1926), Table 10 at p. 78.
304 Wood, "Real Wages," Table 1 at p. 93 and Appendix at pp. 102-103; Bowley, Wages in the United Kingdom, Appendix I, Table I at pp. 130-31.
305 See Booth, "Occupations," p. 354.
306 See G.T. Jones, Increasing Returns (Cambridge: Cambridge University Press, 1933), pp. 94-95, 97, on the introduction of machinery in construction. Jones refers to worker discontent that led to additional supervisory costs which, in turn, acted as a drag on productivity.

307 Tucker, "Real Wages," p. 80.
308 Calculated according to data in ibid. and in Wood, "Real Wages," pp. 102-103.
309 See George Howell, Labour Legislation, Labour Movements and Labour Leaders (London: Unwin, 1902), pp. 392-93.
310 See Michael von Tugan-Baranowsky, Studien zur Theorie und Geschichte der Handelskrisen in England (Jena: Fischer, 1901), pp. 1, 294-96.
311 A.L. Bowley, "The Statistics of Wages in the United Kingdom during the last Hundred Years. (Part VIII.) Wages in the Building Trades--Concluded. London," Journal of the Royal Statistical Society, LXIV (March 1901), 112; idem, Wages in the United Kingdom, pp. 90-95; Wood, "Some Statistics," p. 664.
312 See Bowley and Wood, "Statistics (Part XIV.) E." pp. 160-61.
313 Bowley, "Changes," Table II at p. 234.
314 Wood, "Some Statistics," pp. 664-65. Cf. Depression of Trade and Industry. Second Report of the Royal Commission appointed to Inquire into the Depression of Trade and Industry, Appendix, Part II, Appendix D, P.P. 1886, Vol. XXII, C.-4715 (London: HMSO, 1886), pp. 3-98.
315 See Kuczynski, England von 1832 bis 1900, pp. 203-205.
316 See Bowley, Wages in the United Kingdom, Table facing p. 94.
317 Benjamin Jones, "Discussion," Journal of the Statistical Society, XLIX (March 1886), 95. On unemployment among trade unionists, see Wood, "Some Statistics," pp. 640-48, 661.
318 W. Hamish Fraser, Trade Unions and Society. The Struggle for Acceptance. 1850-1880 (Totowa: Rowman and Littlefield, 1974), p. 213, argues that as early as the 1850s the middle class "began to see significance in the divisions within the working class." Even on the political plane this division did not become relevant until the late 1860s; see Gillespie, Labor and Politics, pp. 8-9, 37-38, 46, 56. Cf. David Kynaston, King Labour. The British Working Class 1850-1914 (London: Allen & Unwin, 1976), p. 19.
319 Burn, Glimpse, p. 30.
320 (Fleeming Jenkin), "Trade Unions: How Far Legitimate?," The North British Review, XLVII, XCV (March 1868), 33.
321 Leone Levi appears to have been an exception; see his "Discussion," Journal of the Statistical Society, XLIX (March 1886), 94. See also the recantation by James E. Thorold Rogers, Six Centuries of Work and Wages (new edition, revised; London: Sonnenschein, 1886), p. 656.
322 See Mitchell, Abstract, p. 64.
323 See Postgate, Builders' History, p. 300; Webb, Industrial Democracy, pp. 508-27; idem, History of Trade Unionism, 1902 ed., pp. 338-40.
324 Kynaston, King Labour, p. 67.
325 See H.M. Hyndman, The Historical Basis of Socialism in England (London: Kegan Paul and Trench, 1883), p. 287; Sidney Webb, English Progress towards Social Democracy, Fabian Tract No. 15 (London: Fabian Society, 1893), p. 8; J.M. Baernreither, Die englischen Arbeiterverbände und ihr Recht (Tübingen: Laupp'sche, 1886), p. 17.
326 Frederick Harrison, "Remedies for Social Distress," Industrial Remuneration Conference, Report, pp. 430, 437.
327 Edith Simcox, "Loss or Gain of the Working Class during the Nineteenth Century," ibid., p. 85.
328 See the comments by George Hines, ibid., p. 122.
329 Giffen, "Further Notes," p. 56, contended that their share had risen; cf. Baernreither, Die englischen Arbeiterverbände, p. 17; Harrison," "Remedies," p. 437.

330 Hobsbawm, Labouring Men, p. 346.
331 Ibid., p. 343.
332 Males over the age of twenty as a share of those employed in manufacturing rose from 48.6 per cent in 1851 to 49.8 per cent in 1881; calculated according to data in Booth, "Occupations," pp. 355-59.
333 From 1833 to 1867 to 1897 the excess of the former over the latter declined from 100 per cent to eighty per cent to sixty per cent respectively; calculated according to data in Bowley, Wages in the United Kingdom, p. 70. The differential between provincial artisans and town laborers stabilized after 1867; ibid. See also idem, Wages and Income in the United Kingdom since 1860 (Cambridge: Cambridge University Press, 1937), p. 46.
334 See K.G.J.C. Knowles and D.J. Robertson, "Differences Between the Wages of Skilled and Unskilled Workers, 1880-1950," Bulletin of Oxford University Institute of Statistics, XIII, 4 (April 1951), 109-27; S. Pollard, "Trade Unions and the Labour Market, 1870-1914," Yorkshire Bulletin of Economic and Social Research, XVII, 1 (May 1965), 100-104.
335 See Postgate, Builders' History, p. 455; Jones, Increasing Returns, pp. 261-62; Bowley, Wages in the United Kingdom, p. 60, chart facing p. 90.
336 See Labour Statistics. Returns of Wages Published between 1830 and 1886, pp. 208-19; cf. however Hobsbawm, Labouring Men, p. 347.
337 Bowley, Wages in the United Kingdom, Table facing p. 122; Hobsbawm, Labouring Men, p. 347, contradicts this.
338 Bowley, Wages in the United Kingdom, Table facing p. 119.
339 Hobsbawm, Labouring Men, pp. 86-87.
340 Simcox, "Loss or Gain," pp. 86-87.
341 Alfred R. Wallace, "How to Cause Wealth to be More Equally Distributed," Industrial Remuneration Conference, Report, p. 369.
342 Lloyd Jones, "Profits of Industry and the Workers," ibid., p. 34.
343 Simcox, "Loss or Gain," p. 90.
344 Wallace, "How to Cause Wealth," p. 369; cf. however Harrison, "Remedies," p. 433.
345 Cf. J.J. Tobias, Crime and Industrial Society in the 19th Century (New York: Schocken, 1967), p. 185.
346 Simcox, "Loss or Gain," p. 90; Harrison, "Remedies," p. 436.
347 Source: Wages.--General Report, p. xxxii.
348 Ibid., pp. xiv, xxviii; the data for the building trades were constructed by using weights for winter and summer rates as indicated in ibid., p. xxviii.
349 Ibid., p. xiv.
350 Ibid., p. 471.
351 Ibid., p. xiv.
352 Condition of the Working Classes. Tabulation of the Statements made by Men Living in Certain Selected Districts of London in March 1887, C.-5228, P.P. 1886, Vol. LXXI (London: HMSO, 1887), Table B at p. 313.
353 Ibid., Table E at p. 317.
354 Charles Booth, ed., Labour and Life of the People, Vol. I: East London (3rd ed.; London: Williams and Norgate, 1891), pp. 34-35; idem, Life and Labour of the People in London (9 vols.; London: Macmillan, 1892-1897), IX, 8-18, 240-41, 372-78.
355 Royal Commission on Trade Unions, First Report, QQ. 2584-85 at pp. 92-93. Comparative occupational mortality rates for 1861 and 1871 do not, on the other hand, point to any clear-cut patterns. See Supplement

to the Twenty-Fifth Annual Report of the Registrar-General of Births, Deaths, and Marriages in England (London: HMSO, 1864), pp. xxxiii-xxxv; Supplement to the Thirty-Fifth Annual Report of the Registrar-General of Births, Deaths, and Marriages in England, C.--1151-I (London: HMSO, 1875), pp. clxx-clxxiii.

356 Twenty-Second Annual Report of the Registrar-General of Births, Deaths, and Marriages in England (London: HMSO, 1861), pp. xlv-xlvi. An additional 5,896 men left letters of administration assessed at £854 each; ibid.

357 Ibid., pp. 174-80; Supplement to the Twenty-Fifth Annual Report of the Registrar-General, pp. xxxiii-xxxv.

358 Source: Twenty-Second Annual Report of the Registrar-General, pp. 174-77; calculations by author.

359 See G. Philips Bevan, "The Strikes of the Past Ten Years," Journal of the Statistical Society, XLIII (March 1880), 42-43.

360 Ibid., pp. 39-42.

361 Ibid., p. 49; Postgate, Builders' History, pp. 295-98.

362 Webb, History of Trade Unionism, 1902 ed., pp. 299-301.

363 Postgate, Builders' History, pp. 303-306, 456; W.S. Hilton, Foes to Tyranny. A History of the Amalgamated Union of Building Trade Workers (London: AUBTW, 1963), p. 164.

364 See Cole, "Some Notes," passim.

365 "The Trades' Union Congress," Economist, XLI (September 15, 1883), 1076.

366 Webb, History of Trade Unionism, 1902 ed., p. 336. François Bédarida, La Société anglaise 1851-1975 (Paris: Arthaus, 1976), p. 90, argues too glibly on this point.

367 Bauman, Klasa, p. 94.

368 See, for example, John Child, Industrial Relations in the British Printing Industry (London: Allen & Unwin, 1967), pp. 120-21. Cf. the Tenth Annual Report of the Amalgamated Society of Carpenters and Joiners delivered by Robert Applegarth in which he praised attempts of employers and of the Union to "meet on a footing of equality"; see The Penny Beehive, No. 446 (April 30, 1870), p. 164; The Beehive supported this position editorially in the next issue--No. 447 (May 7, 1870).

369 Kuczynski, England von 1832 bis 1900, pp. 218-20, is constrained to concede this point in implicit contradiction of Engels.

370 George Dangerfield, The Strange Death of Liberal England (New York: Capricorn, 1961 (1935)), p. 217.

371 See Edward Baines, The Life of Edward Baines (2nd ed.; London: Longmans, 1859 (1851)), pp. 129-30; "The Lesson of the Strikes," The Times (London), August 29, 1859, p. 5. Col. 4. Cf. J.R.M. Butler, The Passing of the Great Reform Bill (London: Longmans, 1914), passim.

372 Geoffrey Best, Mid-Victorian Britain 1851-1875 (New York: Schocken, 1972), p. 260.

373 Testimony of R.D. Baxter in Report from the Select Committee of the House of Lords appointed to inquire what would be the probable Increase of the Number of Electors in the Counties and Boroughs of England and Wales from a Reduction of the Franchise ..., July 16, 1860, P.P. 1860, Vol. XII (455), Q. 1678 at p. 176 and Q. 1689 at p. 177.

374 Hansard's Parliamentary Debates, Third Series, CLXXXVI (1867), 637.

375 Ibid., CLXXXII (1866), 54-55.

376 Ibid., CLXXXVII (1867), 788. Cf. Briggs, Victorian People, pp. 232-63.

377 In 1865-1866, 128,603 electors on the register in England and Wales were "mechanics, artizans, and other persons supporting themselves by daily

manual labour"; they represented 26.3 per cent of the electors in cities and boroghs and 62.3 per dent of male occupiers paying a gross estimated rental ranging between seven and ten pounds sterling annually. See Electoral Statistics, House Parliamentary Representation Returns, P.P. 1866, Vol. LXII, pp. 1-5.

378 Testimony by Baxter in Report from the Select Committee of the House of Lords, Q. 1693 at p. 178.

379 Ibid., Q. 1684 at p. 177.

380 Ibid., Q. 1694 at p. 178.

381 A Daughter of the People, The Working-Classes (London: Murray, 1869), pp. 8-9.

382 Maurice Cowling, 1867. Disraeli, Gladstone and Revolution. The Passing of the second Reform Bill (Cambridge: Cambridge University Press, 1967), p. 51. Bright believed only "the residuum" to be venal, whereas Lowe extended this judgment to the whole working class.

383 See Homersham Cox, A History of the Reform Bills of 1866 and 1867 (London: Longmans, 1868), p. 205. On the extension of suffrage, see R. Dudley Baxter, The Results of the General Election (London: Bush, 1869), p. 17. More generally, see John Lambert, "Parliamentary Franchise, Past and Present," The Nineteenth Century, XXVII (December 1889), 942-62; Charles Seymour, Electoral Reform in England and Wales. The Development and Operation of the Parliamentary Franchise, 1832-1885 (New Haven: Yale University Press, 1915), passim.

384 See Joseph H. Park, The English Reform Bill of 1867 (New York: Columbia University Press, 1920), pp. 51-86; Asa Briggs, The Making of Modern England 1783-1867 (New York: Harper, 1965 (1959)), pp. 409-10, 504; Henry H. Slesser, The Law Relating to Trade Unions (London: Labour Publishing, 1921), pp. 23-43.

385 In 1866 Gladstone declared that a workman paying rates of seven pounds sterling earned twenty-six shillings per week; when lowered to five pounds sterling, as in 1867, such a limit could be attained by a worker earning about 18.5 shillings weekly. According to Baxter, National Income, pp. 50-51, even a large segment of urban unskilled labor earned more than eighteen shillings weekly.

386 See J.R. Vincent, Pollbooks. How Victorians Voted (Cambridge: Cambridge University Press, 1967), p. 25, on rural class interests.

387 See Briggs, Making, pp. 496-523. Ursula Herrmann, Der Kampf von Karl Marx um eine revolutionäre Gewerkschaftspolitik in der I. Internationale 1864 bis 1868 (Berlin (DDR): Tribüne, 1968), p. 168, misinterprets this course of events.

388 See Gillespie, Labor and Politics, p. 188.

389 Secretary Allan of the Amalgamated Society of Engineers informed the Royal Commission on Trade Unions that his union was cautious about expending funds on strikes whereas "the man who has not got a shilling in his pocket has not much to be afraid of." First Report, Q. 827 at p. 37.

390 See Brentano, Geschichte der wirtschaftlichen Entwicklung Englands, III: 1, 552-53.

391 F.B. Smith, The Making of the Second Reform Bill (Cambridge: Cambridge University Press, 1966), p. 9, maintains that in the 1850s and 1860s the terms "artisan" and "workingman" assumed the meaning of skilled as opposed to unskilled worker; for philological refutation, see Statement of the Master Builders of the Metropolis (London: Moyes, 1834), p. 14.

392 In the building trades, for example, Robert Applegarth assisted in the formation of the short-lived General Amalgamated Labourers' Union in

1872; by the end of the 1880s, however, such support was no longer forthcoming. See Postgate, Builders' History, pp. 298, 345. The organizational aid offered the unskilled in the building trades took the form of segregating the unskilled in separate unions. For a poignant illustration of the ralations between the skilled and the unskilled in building, see A Working Man, Reminiscences of a Stonemason (London: Murray, 1908), p. 76.

393 Lujo Brentano, Arbeitergilden, II, 328. For a subsequent prediction of a similar nature for Germany, see Otto Heilborn, Die "Freien" Gewerkschaften seit 1890 (Jena: Fischer, 1907), p. 187. Cf. Max Weber's letter of April 25, 1905 to Brentano, in which Weber criticized Brentano's advocacy of universal branch organization on the grounds that it would impair the "natural leadership" of the upper stratum of skilled workers; cited by Wolfgang J. Mommsen, Max Weber und die deutsche Politik 1890-1920 (Tübingen: Mohr, 1959), pp. 130-31.

394 It is curious that in the 1860s Wright had characterized the trade unions as progressive; see Thomas Wright, The Great Unwashed (London: Tinsley, 1868), pp. 97-124.

395 Wright, Our New Masters, pp. 5-6. Cf. the similar criticisms in A Working Man, Working Men and Women (London: Tinsley, 1879), pp. 104-14 and passim.

396 See Cowling, Disraeli, p. 45; G.D.H. Cole and Raymond Postgate, The Common People 1746-1946 (4th ed.; London: Methuen, 1971 (1938)), p. 390, simplify this process.

397 As Ure emphasized, "the more skilful the workman, the more self-willed and intractable he is apt to become, and, of course, the less fit a component of a mechanical system." Ure, Philosophy of Manufactures, 3rd ed., p. 20; cf. ibid., p. 23. Cf. A.E. Musson, "Class Struggle and the labour aristocracy, 1830-60," Social History, I, 3 (October 1976), 335-56.

398 Fraser, Trade Unions, p. 217.

399 W.W. Craik, A Short History of the Modern British Working-Class Movement (3rd ed.; London: Plebs League, 1919 (1916)), pp. 49-50.

400 On the anti-union practices of large engineering firms, see Musson, "Class Struggle," p. 352.

401 Hermann Schlüter, The Brewing Industry and the Brewery Workers' Movement in America (Cincinnati: International Union of United Brewery Workmen of America, 1910), p. 95, confused this issue by supposing that industries characterized by a higher organic composition of capital employed fewer workers, who therefore found it difficult to conceive of themselves as a distinct class from their employers.

402 Harrison, Before the Socialists, p. 39.

403 See Engels' notice of the strike in The Labour Elector, II, 35 (August 31, 1889); cited here according to MEW, XXI, 382. Cf. Engels' letter of August 11, 1889 to Bernstein, ibid., XXXVII, 260-61; Engels, "Der 4. Mai in London," ibid., XXII, 60-65.

404 Letter of October 17, 1889 to Laura Lafargue, ibid., XXXVII, 288; retranslated from the German translation of the English original.

405 "Foreword" to the 1892 ed. of The Condition of the Working-Class in England in 1844; cited according to MEW, XXII, 277-78.

406 See Engels' letter to Sorge of December 7, 1889, ibid., XXXVII, 320-21; Engels to Conrad Schmidt of December 9, 1889, ibid., p. 325; Engels to Hermann Schlüter of January 11, 1890, ibid., p. 341. Cf. Harry Quelch, Trade Unionism, Co-Operation, and Social Democracy (London: Twentieth Century, 1892), p. 5.

407 Engels' letter to Laura Lafargue of September 1, 1889, MEW, XXXVII, 268-69; Engels to Kautsky, September 15, 1889, ibid., p. 275.
408 Engels' letter to Sorge of April 19, 1890, ibid., p. 393.
409 Engels to Sorge, December 7, 1889, ibid., p. 321.
410 Engels to Sorge, April 19, 1890, ibid., pp. 393-94; Engels to Sorge, August 9-11, 1891, ibid., XXXVIII, 143.
411 Engels to Sorge, March 4, 1891, ibid., p. 46.
412 Hobsbawm, Labouring Men, p. 225. See also Webb, History of Trade Unionism, 1902 ed., pp. 388-408; Clegg, History, I, 55-96.
413 Engels did concede that racism and immigration policy had created a labor aristocracy among the white American-born workers that was consciously nurtured by the bourgeoisie in order to divide and conquer the working class. See Engels' letter of March 30, 1892 to Schlüter, MEW, XXXVIII, 313-14.

1 Stefano Merli, Proletariato di fabbrica e capitalismo industriale. Il caso italiano: 1880-1900 (Florence: La Nuova Italia, 1972), p. 21, overlooks this point in his critique of "pseudo-concepts" such as that of the labor aristocracy.
2 Paul Mattick's view according to which Engels' and Lenin's conceptions of the labor aristocracy referred to the aggregate working class--in the sense of a counterpart to aggregate capital as a magnitude of social class-is untenable; see Mattick's review of Karl Heinz Roth, Die "andere" Arbeiterbewegung, MS, 1975, passim.
3 V.I. Lenin, "Imperializm i raskol sotsializma," PSS, XXX, 173. See Christel Neusüss, Imperialismus und Weltmarktbewegung des Kapitals (Erlangen: Politladen, 1972), pp. 27-33, 42-47.
4 See Lenin, Imperializm, kak noveishii etap kapitalizma, PSS, XXVII, 423.
5 Lenin, "Tselyi desiatok 'sotsialisticheskikh' ministrov," PSS, XXX, 194-95, derived the super-profits of Danish imperialism from the latter's monopoly of the London milk and meat product market.
6 Lenin characterized this as a secondary issue; see "Imperializm i raskol sotsializma," p. 174. Elsewhere he referred to direct and indirect methods without further analysis; see Imperializm, kak noveishii etap kapitalizma, p. 308.
7 Thus in 1914 Lenin hypothesized that higher pay and liberalism-opportunism were everywhere highly correlated with each other; see "Rabochii klass i rabochaia pechat'," PSS, XXV, 230-31. Four years later he spoke of labor aristocrats as having "sold their right to socialist revolution in order to enter into a union with their capitalists against the huge majority of workers..." See "Zakliuchitel'noe slovo po dokladu o tekyshchem momente 28 iiunia," PSS, XXXVI, 463.
8 See Arghiri Emmanuel, L'Echange inégal (Paris: Maspero, 1969), p. 209. Cf. Lenin, "Krakh II Internatsionala," PSS, XXVI, 228; "O karikature na marksizma i ob 'imperialisticheskom ekonomizme,'" PSS, XXX, 107.
9 See Hans-Christoph Schroeder, Sozialistische Imperialismusdeutungen (Göttingen: Vandenhoeck, 1973), p. 70. For examples of this lack of precision, see G. Sinowjew, Der Krieg und die Krise des Sozialismus (Vienna: Verlag für Literatur und Politik, 1924 (original Russian ed. 1917)), pp. 545-46; N. Bukharin, Imperialismus und Weltwirtschaft (Frankfurt: Neue Kritik, 1969 (original Russian ed. 1915)), p. 186. Geoff Eley, "Social Imperialism in Germany. Reformist Synthesis or Reactionary Sleight of Hand?," Imperialismus im 20. Jahrhundert, ed. Joachim Radkau and Imanuel Geiss (Munich: Beck, 1976), p. 72, exaggerates Lenin's precision. Cf. Thomas Hammond, Lenin on Trade Unions and Revolution 1893-1917 (New York: Columbia University Press, 1957), pp. 78-80, 108-11; Peter Hempe, Die "ökonomische Imperialismus-theorie", (Munich: Beck, 1976), passim.
10 Foster, Class Struggle, pp. 212-13.
11 See Horace B. Davis, "Imperialism and Labor: An Analysis of Marxian Views," Science and Society, XXVI, 1 (Winter 1962), 39.
12 Lenin remarked in his Notebooks on Imperialism that workers in New Zealand had been bought by social reforms granted by the "imperialist bourgeoisie"; see Tetradi po imperializmu, PSS, XXVIII, 512.
13 See Anthony Giddens, The Class Structure of the Advanced Societies (London: Hutchinson, 1974 (1973)), p. 285.
14 See Guenther Roth, The Social Democrats in Imperial Germany (Totowa: Bedminster, 1963), p. 8, who contrasts negative integration and conflict institutionalization. Cf. Dieter Groh, Negative Integration und revolutio-närer Attentismus (Frankfurt/Main: Ullstein, 1973), p. 36.

Notes to Chapter 6

15 See Nicos Poulantzas, "On Social Classes," New Left Review, No. 78, March-April 1973, p. 36; Mattick, review of Roth, Die "andere" Arbeiterbewegung, p. 10.

16 The example mentioned in the text is not meant to imply that so-called paternalistic relations inevitably obscure the consciousness of capitalist relations of production. As Eduard Bernstein, Die Voraussetzungen des Sozialismus und die Aufgaben der Sozialdemokratie (Reinbek: Rowohlt, 1970 (1899)), p. 67 n., pointed out, the journeyman employed by a small master mason will know exactly how much labor, materials and other items cost his employer and how much the latter is charging his customer; in other words, surplus labor lies exposed.

17 See Hugh Seton-Watson, The Pattern of Communist Revolution (London: Methuen, 1953), p. 341.

18 See, for example, Gray, Labour Aristocracy, p. 145. It must be noted, however, that the capitalist class as represented by employers' organizations and the state has been known to support quasi-universal organization of a national working class. See Walter Galenson, The Danish System of Labor Relations (Cambridge, Mass.: Harvard University Press, 1952). Within individual branches employers have often encouragedlabor organizations as a means of subjecting competitors to uniform cost pressures. See Gordon W. Bertram and Sherman J. Maisel, Industrial Relations in the Construction Industry (Berkeley: University of California, 1955), pp. 26-27, 32-33, 40.

19 See Gordon Craig, Germany 1866-1945 (Oxford: Clarendon, 1978), pp. 43-49; Theodore S. Hamerow, The Social Foundations of German Unification 1858-1871. Ideas and Institutions (Princeton: Princeton University Press, 1969), pp. 292-307; idem, The Social Foundations of German Unification 1858-1871. Struggles and Accomplishments (Princeton: Princeton University Press, 1972), pp. 183-91, 243-69, 318-36; Ernst Engelberg, Deutschland 1871-1897 (Berlin (DDR): VEB Deutscher Verlag der Wissenschaften, 1967), pp. 14-16, 71-78.

1 David Lloyd George, War Memoirs, I (London: Nicholson & Watson, 1933), 308-309.
2 Although this turning point roughly coincides with the terminal point of the downswing of the second Kondratieff wave and the beginning of the upswing of the third wave, the downward direction of many of the indicators for the years preceding World War I contradicts Kondratieff's schema. See N.D. Kondratieff, "Die langen Wellen der Konjunktur," Archiv für Sozialwissenschaft und Sozialpolitik, LVI (1926), 573-609; cf. David S. Landes, The Unbound Prometheus (Cambridge: Cambridge University Press, 1972 (1969)), pp. 232-34; Ernest Mandel, Der Spätkapitalismus (Frankfurt/Main: Suhrkamp, 1973), pp. 101-37.
3 Willard L. Thorp, Business Annals (New York, NBER, 1926), pp. 167-76; L.A. Mengel'son, Teoriia i istoriia ekonomicheskikh krizisov i tsiklov, II (Moscow: IS-EL, 1959), 78-92.
4 K.S. Lomax, "Growth and Productivity in the United Kingdom," Economic Growth in Twentieth-Century Britain, ed. Derek H. Aldcroft and Peter Fearon (London: Macmillan, 1969), Table 2 at p. 11.
5 E.H. Phelps Brown and S.J. Handfield-Jones, "The Climacteric of the 1890s: a Study of the Expanding Economy," Oxford Economic Papers, N.S., IV, 3 (October 1952), 266-307; D.J. Coppock, "The Climacteric of the 1890s: A Critical Note," Manchester School, XXIV, 1 (January 1956), 1-31; W. Ashworth, "The Late Victorian Economy," Economica, N.S., XXXIII, 129 (February 1966), 17-33; S.B. Saul, The Myth of the Great Depression 1873-1896 (London: Macmillan, 1972 (1969)), pp. 36-52; Phyllis Deane and W.A. Cole, British Economic Growth 1688-1959 (2nd ed.; Cambridge: Cambridge University Press, 1969 (1962)), Table 77 at p. 297.
6 Lomax, "Growth," Table 2 at p. 11. For an overview and interpretation, see Derek H. Aldcroft and Harry W. Richardson, The British Economy 1870-1939 (London: Macmillan, 1969). Cf. W.W. Rostow, British Economy of the Nineteenth Century (Oxford: Oxford University Press, 1968 (1948)), pp. 8, 25-28.
7 Phyllis Deane, "New Estimates of Gross National Product for the United Kingdom," Review of Income and Wealth, Series 14, No. 2 (June 1968), Table 2 at p. 98.
8 Ernst Helmstädter, Der Kapitalkoeffizient (Stuttgart: Fischer, 1969), pp. 60, 268; Thorp, Business Annals, Chart II at pp. 28-29; E.H. Phelps Brown, A Century of Pay (London: Macmillan, 1968), Figure 22 at p. 140.
9 On the underlying methodology, see Willi Semmler, Zur Theorie der Reproduktion und Akkumulation (Westberlin: Olle & Wolter, 1977), pp. 257-72.
10 C.H. Feinstein, National Income, Expenditure and Output of the United Kingdom 1855-1965 (Cambridge: Cambridge University Press, 1972), Table 20 at pp. T 51-52; R.C.O. Matthews, "Some Aspects of Post-War Growth in the British Economy in Relation to Historical Experience," Economic Growth, ed. Aldcroft and Fearon, Chart 2 at p. 87; Deane and Cole, British Economic Growth, pp. 274-77.
11 Calculated according to data in Feinstein, National Income, Table 20 at pp. T 51-52. Cf. Porter, Progress, ed. Hirst, pp. 698-703.
12 Feinstein, National Income, Table 20 at pp. T 51-52; Phelps Brown, Century of Pay, Figure 17 at p. 123.
13 Feinstein, National Income, Table 18 at pp. T 44-45; "total income" includes net property income from abroad. Cf. Deane and Cole, British Economic Growth, Table 65 at p. 247; Phelps Brown, Century of Pay, Figure 20 at p. 135 and Appendix Table, not paginated (at pp. 444-45).

14 For manufactured goods, see Werner Schlote, British Overseas Trade (Oxford: Blackwell, 1952 (1938)), Table 16 at pp. 152-54; for all exports, see Feinstein, National Income, Table 7 at p. T 21.

15 Feinstein, National Income, Table 7 at p. T 21 and Table 18 at pp. T 44-45; cf. C.K. Hobson, The Export of Capital (New York: Macmillan, 1914), pp. 204, 218-19. Capital exports grew more quickly than ever before, outstripping domestic investment in the decade prior to World War I; see Deane and Cole, British Economic Growth, Table 82 at p. 308.

16 For an exception, see A. Sartorius Freiherr von Waltershausen, Das volkswirtschaftliche System der Kapitalanlage im Auslande (Berlin: Reimer, 1907), pp. 388-89.

17 For an exception, see the undocumented claim by Bernard Semmel, Imperialism and Social Reform (Garden City: Doubleday, 1968 (1960)), p. 13.

18 As late as 1891 Pope Leo XIII described the largest part of the people of "infimae sortis" as "in misera calamitosaque fortuna indigne versentur." "Rerum novarum," par. 2. In England and Wales pauperism and vagrancy were on the rise during the quarter-century preceding the war. See Porter, Progress, ed. Hirst, pp. 67-83; W.H. Beveridge, Unemployment (new ed.; London: Longmans, 1930 (1909)), pp. 42-44, 443.

19 Calculated according to Rufus S. Tucker, "Real Wages of the Artisans in London, 1729-1935," Journal of the American Statistical Association, XXXI, 193 (March 1936), 80; cf. the graph at p. 83. See also A.L. Bowley, Wages and Income in the United Kingdom since 1860 (Cambridge: Cambridge University Press, 1937), Table VII at p. 30.

20 Jürgen Kuczynski, Die Geschichte der Lage der Arbeiter unter dem Kapitalismus, Vol. 24: Darstellung der Lage der Arbeiter in England von 1832 bis 1900 (Berlin (DDR): Akademie, 1965), p. 197; ibid., Vol. 25: Darstellung der Lage der Arbeiter in England von 1900 bis zur Gegenwart (Berlin (DDR): Akademie, 1965), p. 155. Cf. Rostow, British Economy, p. 91; Bowley, Wages and Income, Table VII at p. 30.

21 Source: Kuczynski, England von 1900 bis zur Gegenwart, p. 27.

22 United Kingdom, Department of Employment and Productivity, British Labour Statistics. Historical Abstract 1886-1968 (London: HMSO, 1971), Table 159 at p. 305; cf. Porter, Progress, ed. Hirst, pp. 56-57; Kuczynski, England von 1900 bis zur Gegenwart, pp. 32-33.

23 Deane and Cole, British Economic Growth, Figure 7; Kondratieff, "Die langen Wellen," Fig. 1 at p. 579.

24 Th. Rothstein, From Chartism to Labourism (New York: International, 1929), p. 263.

25 See Peter Mathias, The First Industrial Nation. An Economic History of Britain 1700-1914 (New York: Scribner's, 1969), p. 397. Cf. L.G. Chiozza Money, Things That Matter (London: Methuen, 1912), pp. 1-36.

26 See G.D.H. Cole and Raymond Postgate, The British Common People 1746-1938 (New York: Knopf, 1939), pp. 407-409; Semmel, Imperialism, pp. 74-88.

27 Landes, Prometheus, chap. 5.

28 Schlote, British Overseas Trade, Table 17 at pp. 154-55; John Clapham, An Economic History of Modern Britain. Machines and National Rivalries (1887-1914) with an Epilogue (1914-1929) (Cambridge: Cambridge University Press, 1968 (1938)), p. 3. Characteristically, the share of exports destined for the colonies rose; see Aldcroft and Richardson, British Economy, pp. 67-77.

29 For an overview, see S.B. Saul, "The Export Economy 1870-1914," Yorkshire Bulletin of Economic and Social Research, XVII, 1 (May 1965),

5-18; cf. the overly sanguine contemporary, Sidney Chapman, Work and Wages, Part I: Foreign Competition (London: Longmans, 1904).

30 See Clapham, Machines and National Rivalries, p. 25.

31 See data in chap. 5 sect. D. Cf. John Foster, "British Imperialism and the Labour Aristocracy," The General Strike, ed. Jeffrey Skelley (London: Lawrence & Wishart, 1976), p. 7.

32 One of the ramifications of this pattern of investment was the retardation of monopolization in British industry; see Hermann Levy, Monopole, Kartelle und Trusts (Jena: Fischer, 1909).

33 Cole and Postgate, Common People, p. 424.

34 Ibid., p. 425. This kind of argument is not stratum-specific; to the extent that rates of profit were equalized among branches, it is not even restricted to export industries.

35 Willfried Spohn, Weltmarktkonkurrenz und Industrialisierung Deutschlands 1870-1914 (Westberlin: Olle & Wolter, 1977), pp. 88-175, 218-30.

36 The examples of Germany and the United States show that a rising national industrial bourgeoisie may also pursue anti-union policies.

37 Cf. the poem, "Capital and Labour," cited at the beginning of Part I above.

38 Further modifications in the censuses of 1901 and 1911 permitted the collection of information concerning those who worked at home.

39 "Industry" has been defined to include transport, construction, mining, gas, water and electricity supply and general laborers--that is, sectors, VI and IX-XXII of the censuses of 1901 and 1911. Wherever "dealers" were enumerated separately, they have been eliminated from "industry."

40 Sources: Census of England and Wales, 1891, Vol. IV: General Report, C.-7222 (London: HMSO, 1893), Table 5 at pp. xii-xxv; Census of England and Wales, 1901, Summary Tables, Cd. 1,523 (London: HMSO, 1903), Table XXXV at pp. 188-201; Census of England and Wales, 1911, Vol. X: Occupations and Industries, Part I (London: HMSO, 1914), Table 3 at pp. 14-25. On the deficiencies of the data on masters, see Census, 1891, IV, 35-36.

41 In 1911, 70.2 per cent of female employers and 93.1 per cent of female self-employed were occupied in the clothing industry; calculated according to Census, 1911, Vol. X, Pt. I, Table 3 at p. 23. The bulk of these women were in fact "dependent outworkers"; see Clapham, Machines and National Rivalries, p. 183; Porter, Progress, ed. Hirst, pp. 32-34. Cf. Report of the War Cabinet Committee on Women in Industry, Cmd. 135 (London: HMSO, 1919), pp. 8-28.

42 Calculated according to Census, 1911, Vol. X, Pt. I, Table 27 at p. 552.

43 Calculated according to Census of England and Wales, 1911, Area, Families or Separate Occupiers, and Population, Vol. I: Administrative Areas, P.P. 1912-1913, Vol. CXI, Cd. 6258 (London: HMSO, 1912), Table I at p. 1.

44 See the sources mentioned in n. 40.

45 See Census of Production, Final Report on the First Census of Production of the United Kingdom, P.P. 1912-1913, Vol. CIX, Cd. 6320 (London: HMSO, 1912).

46 On the connection between industrial concentration and the rise of the clerical-administrative sector, see Reinhard Bendix, Work and Authority in Industry (Berkeley: University of California Press, 1974 (1956)), pp. 211-26.

47 Source: Census, 1911, Vol. X, Pt. I, Table 27 at pp. 552-57 and the sources mentioned in n. 40; cf. Census, 1891, IV, 87.

48 This category, which is not differentiated according to employee, employer and self-employed, includes dealers.
49 See Paul de Rousiers, Le Trade-Unionisme en Angleterre (Paris: Colin, 1897), p. 53.
50 See H.R. Taylor, "Bricklayers," Workers on their Industries, ed. Frank W. Galton (London: Sonnenschein, 1896), pp. 175-85; Clapham, Machines and National Rivalries, p. 324.
51 See however William H. White, "The Architect and his Artists," The American Architect and Building News, XXXV, 836 (January 2, 1892), 13. Cf. J.H. Clapham, An Economic History of Modern Britain. Free Trade and Steel 1850-1886 (Cambridge: Cambridge University Press, 1932), pp. 120, 130; L.G. Johnson, The Social Evolution of Industrial Britain (Liverpool: Liverpool University Press, 1959), p. 25.
52 See R.H. Inglis Palgrave, Dictionary of Political Economy, I (London: Macmillan, 1894), 60; cf. S.J. Chapman and F.J. Marquis, "The Recruiting of the Employing Classes from the Ranks of the Wage-Earners in the Cotton Industry," Journal of the Royal Statistical Society, LXXV (February 1912), 293-306.
53 Calculated according to Census, 1911, Vol. X, Pt. I, Table 27 at pp. 552-57. The discussion in the text of employers and self-employed persons is based on the sources referred to in n. 40.
54 See also the discussion in chaps. 5, 8 and 9.
55 See the data in Census, 1911, Vol. X, Pt. I, Table 27 at p. 552; cf. George S. Bain, The Growth of White Collar Unionism (Oxford: Clarendon, 1970), Table 2.3 at p. 14.
56 See Women in Industry, pp. 18-20.
57 See Bowley, Wages and Income, pp. 128-29. The linear interpolation and extrapolation for intercensal years carried out by E.H. Phelps Brown and P.E. Hart, "The Share of Wages in National Income," Economic Journal, LXII (June 1952), Table 1 at 276, is constructed on the basis of an uncritical acceptance of Bowley's categorization.
58 See Guy Routh, Occupation and Pay in Great Britain 1906-1960 (Cambridge: Cambridge University Press, 1960), Table 47 at p. 104; E. Cannan et al., "The Amount and Distribution of Income (other than Wages) Below the Income Tax Exemption in the United Kingdom," Journal of the Royal Statistical Society, LXXIV, Pt. I (December 1910), 63, 66.
59 Geoffrey Crossick, "The Emergence of the Lower Middle Class in Britain: A Discussion," The Lower Middle Class in Britain 1870-1914, ed. Geoffrey Crossick (London: Croom Helm, 1977), pp. 12-13, 34-35, 48-52; idem, An Artisan Elite in Victorian Society. Kentish London 1840-1880 (London: Croom Helm, 1978), pp. 248-50.
60 Hobsbawm, "Labour Aristocracy," p. 351. Cf. the unambiguous view of Richard Jones, Literary Remains, ed. William Whewell (London: Murray, 1859), p. 493.
61 C. Wright Mills, White Collar (London: Oxford University Press, 1967 (1951)).
62 See chap. 5 above; cf. Arthur H. Johnson, The Disappearance of the Small Landowner (Oxford: Clarendon, 1909).
63 Sources: Census, 1911, Vol. X, Pt. I, Table 27 at p. 552; Walther G. Hoffmann, Das Wachstum der deutschen Wirtschaft seit der Mitte des 19. Jahrhunderts (West Berlin: Springer, 1965), Table 20 at p. 205. Members of the military have been excluded.
64 See the sources referred to in n. 63; cf. George J. Stigler, Domestic Servants in the United States 1900-1940 (New York: NBER, 1946), p. 4.

65 David Lockwood, The Blackcoated Worker (London: Allen & Unwin, 1958); H.A. Clegg, Alan Fox and A.F. Thompson, A History of British Trade Unions since 1889, Vol. I: 1889-1910 (Oxford: Clarendon, 1964), pp. 214-29.

66 The position of self-employed artisans was a contradictory one inasmuch as they were formally property owners, independent of employers, yet in their work routines resembled skilled semi-autonomous wage workers; the latter in turn occupied a contradictory position between capitalists and wage laborers in the class structure. Erik Olin Wright, Class, Crisis and the State (London: New Left Books, 1978), pp. 63, 82, 86, fails to analyze these two aspects as a whole.

67 Source: Calculated according to Porter, Progress, ed. Hirst, pp. 26-27; Census, 1911, Vol. X, Pt. I, Table 26 at pp. 540-51; cf. ibid., p. cxli.

68 The vast majority of girls were employed in textiles and clothing or as domestics.

69 At the margin of poverty the additional income from children's wages was, to be sure, critical. Cf. Charles Booth, ed., Labour and Life of the People, Vol. I: East London (2nd ed.; London: Williams and Norgate, 1889), p. 50.

70 British Labour Statistics, Tables 102 and 103 at pp. 195-97.

71 Unless otherwise indicated, the discussion of the labor force is based on data previously cited in the text or derived from the sources mentioned in n. 40. The term "occupied population" excludes housewives.

72 Census, 1911, Vol. X, Pt. I, Table 27 at p. 553.

73 British Labour Statistics, Table 196 at p. 395.

74 Clegg, Fox and Thompson, History, I, 469-70.

75 Calculated according to data in Census, 1911, Vol. X, Pt. I, p. cxxviii.

76 Census, 1901, Table XXXV at p. 187.

77 Ibid.

78 In 1901, 78.8 per cent of all women over the age of twenty-five were married or widowed; ibid.

79 On the reasons that motivated married women to work outside the home, see Women in Industry, p. 24. The labor force participation rate of married women varied widely from region to region and from town to town: it reached two-fifths in some towns with a heavy concentration of textile and clothing manufacturing plants. See Porter, Progress, ed. Hirst, pp. 34-35.

80 The proportion of men aged twenty-five to thirty-five engaged in occupations in 1901 was 98.3 per cent; Census, 1901, Table XI at p. 36.

81 Census, 1911, Vol. X, Pt. I, Table 27 at p. 552. On the returns in 1901, see Porter, Progress, ed. Hirst, p. 29.

82 Census, 1911, Vol. X, Pt. I, Table 3 at pp. 14-25; Porter, Progress, ed. Hirst, p. 33.

83 Porter, Progress, ed. Hirst, p. 32.

84 Ibid., p. 30.

85 As early as 1871 cotton factories in England and Wales employed on the average 175 workers most of whom were women; see Factories and Workshops, P.P. 1871, Vol. LXII, p. 271.

86 See Census, 1901, Table XXXV at pp. 197, 199; Census, 1911, Vol. X, Pt. I, p. xxxvi; Women in Industry, p. 23.

87 Census, 1911, Vol. X, Pt. I, Table 26 at pp. 540-51; ibid., p. cxli; Census, 1891, IV, 58.

88 Porter, Progress, ed. Hirst, Table VI at p. 31; Clapham, Machines and National Rivalries, pp. 471-73. Cf. Census, 1911, Vol. X, Pt. I, p. cxli.

89 Adna F. Weber, The Growth of Cities in the Nineteenth Century (New York: Columbia University Press, 1899), pp. 46-47; Werner Sombart, Der moderne Kapitalismus, III: 1 (Munich: Duncker & Humblot, 1927), 389-90, 410.
90 Weber, Growth, Table XIX at p. 47; Porter, Progress, ed. Hirst, p. 19.
91 See Gareth Stedman Jones, Outcast London (Harmondsworth: Penguin, 1976 (1971)), pp. 19-30.
92 Calculated according to data in Census, 1911, Vol. I, Table N at pp. xx-xxi; B.R. Mitchell and Phyllis Deane, Abstract of British Historical Statistics (Cambridge: Cambridge University Press, 1962), pp. 24-27; Porter, Progress, ed. Hirst, Table I at p. 3.
93 Mitchell and Deane, Abstract, pp. 24-27.
94 Of the two remaining cities, Newcastle formed the center of the northern English industrial region; only Bristol lay outside the main manufacturing areas. See the map, reproduced from the census of 1851, at the end of the volume of Clapham, Free Trade and Steel; cf. T.W. Freeman, The Conurbations of Great Britain (Manchester: Manchester University Press, 1959).
95 Calculated according to Mitchell and Deane, Abstract, pp. 24-27; Census, 1911, Vol. I, Table N at pp. xx-xxi and Table I at p. 1.
96 See Sombart, Der moderne Kapitalismus, III: 1, 390; (France), Ministère du travail, Statistique générale de la France, Annuaire statistique, Vol. 38--1922 (Paris: Imprimerie Nationale, 1923), pp. 180-85.
97 Webb, History of Trade Unionism, 1902 ed., pp. 411-14 and the map following p. 478. The allegedly "provincial and smalltown atmosphere of German prewar labor politics" may be traced in part to the lower degree of urbanization in Germany; in part, however, this claim is misleading since industrial workers and especially trade unionists were more heavily concentrated in the large cities than the population at large. See Barrington Moore, Jr., Injustice (White Plains: Sharpe, 1978), pp. 179-80; Statistik des Deutschen Reiches, Vol. 210, 2 (Berlin: Puttkammer & Mühlbrecht, 1910), passim; Wilhelm Heinz Schröder, Arbeitergeschichte und Arbeiterbewegung (Frankfurt/Main: Campus, 1978), pp. 38-40, 49-54; Georg Neuhaus, Die deutsche Volkswirtschaft und ihre Wandlungen im letzten Vierteljahrhundert, II (M. Gladbach: Volksverein, 1913), 253-61; Dieter Groh, Negative Integration und revolutionärer Attentismus (Frankfurt/Main: Ullstein, 1973), pp. 272-85. On England, see Census, 1911, Vol. I, Table L at p. xvii; Vol. X, Pt. I, Table L at p. cxxxii.
98 Cf. J.E. Cairnes, Some Leading Principles of Political Economy Newly Expounded (New York: Harper, n.d. (1874)), pp. 65-68, on the narrow, step by step upward occupational mobility prevailing in nineteenth-century Britain; cf. Jones, Literary Remains, p. 496.
99 See Karl Marx, Das Kapital, III, MEW, XXV, 399-400.
100 See chap. 8 below.
101 See Margaret F. Byington, Homestead (New York: Charities Publication Committee, 1910), pp. 14-16, Table 6 at p. 40; Commission of Inquiry, Interchurch World Movement, Report on the Steel Strike of 1919 (New York: Harcourt, Brace and Howe, 1920), pp. 22, 99, 128, 179, 246; John N. Ingham, "A Strike in the Progressive Era: McKees Rocks, 1909," The Pennsylvania Magazine of History and Biography, XC, 3 (July 1966), 357-58; Abstracts of Reports of the Immigration Commission, 61st Cong., 3rd Sess., Senate Document No. 747, Vol. I (Washington, D.C., 1911), p. 500; John R. Commons, Races and Immigrants in America (New York: Macmillan, 1916 (1907)), pp. 149-50; Gerd Korman, Industrialization, Immigrants and Americanizers (Madison: The State Historical Society of Wisconsin, 1967), p. 66 n. 13.

102 Report of an Inquiry by the Board of Trade into the Earnings and Hours of Labour of Workpeople of the United Kingdom, conducted in 1906-1907 and published between 1909 and 1913; see n. 250.
103 Routh, Occupation, p. 27.
104 Women accounted for a very small share of such workers; ibid., Table 1 at p. 4.
105 Ibid., Table 11 at p. 28. Routh's data have been adjusted to exclude Scotland.
106 Ibid., Table 2 at p. 7.
107 See however R. Dudley Baxter, National Income (London: Macmillan, 1868), p. 68; Labour Statistics. Returns of Wages published between 1830 and 1886, pp. 219, 356-86; Booth, ed., Labour and Life on the People, I, 34-35.
108 Routh. Occupation, Table 11 at p. 28.
109 Cf. chap. 8 sect. D.4 below.
110 Hobsbawm, "Labour Aristocracy," pp. 351-52.
111 In the United States this point coincided with the appearance of unused capacity during the depression of the 1870s; see Alfred D. Chandler, Jr., The Visible Hand (Cambridge, Mass.: Harvard University Press, 1978 (1977)), p. 272.
112 Ibid., p. 281.
113 Gerhard Brandt, Gewerkschaftliche Interessenvertretung und sozialer Wandel (Frankfurt/Main: Europäische Verlagsanstalt, 1975), p. 71; L. Urwick and E.F.L. Brech, The Making of Scientific Management, Vol. II: Management in British Industry (London: Pitman, 1953).
114 Chandler, Visible Hand, pp. 274-75.
115 Frederick W. Taylor, Shop Managemet (New York: Harper, 1912), p. 98.
116 Ibid., pp. 98-99.
117 Ibid., pp. 92-105; Chandler, Visible Hand, pp. 276-77; Bendix, Work and Authority, pp. 212-15.
118 Booth, ed., Labour and Life of the People, I, 53.
119 Taylor, Shop Management, p. 105.
120 Booth, ed., Labour and Life of the People, I, 53. Cf. David F. Schloss, Methods of Industrial Remuneration (3rd ed.; London: Williams and Norgate, 1898 (1892)), pp. 169-226.
121 Wright, Class, Crisis and State, p. 78.
122 Routh, Occupation, pp. 81-85; Booth, ed., Labour and Life of the People, I, 53, 194-95, 259. Cf. however Sidney and Beatrice Webb, Industrial Democracy (London: Longmans, Green, 1920 (1897)), p. 546 n.2 continued on p. 547; Mills, White Collar, pp. 87-91; Leone Levi, Wages and Earnings of the Working Classes (London: Murray, 1867), p. xxiv.
123 This organizational change both reflected and fostered a higher degree of "real subsumption" of labor under capital; see Karl Marx, Resultate des unmittelbaren Produktionsprozesses (Frankfurt/Main: Neue Kritik, 1970), passim.
124 Calculated according to data in British Labour Statistics, Table 196 at p. 395. The entire increase took place during the years 1895-1900, 1905-1907 and 1910-1913.
125 Ibid. and estimates based on data in Webb, History of Trade Unionism, 1902 ed., p. 415 and p. 415 n. 2.
126 Cf. Webb, History of Trade Unionism, 1902 ed., p. 411; Clegg, Fox and Thompson, History, I, 466-67. The figures mentioned in the text have been adjusted to exclude nonindustrial trade unionists as well as members in Ireland and Scotland.

127 Webb, History of Trade Unionism, 1902 ed., pp. 410-11; Clegg, Fox and Thompson, History, I, 466-70.
128 Clegg, Fox and Thompson, History, Table VI at I, 468.
129 Sidney and Beatrice Webb, The History of Trade Unionism (rev. ed.; New York: Longmans, Green, 1920 (1894)), pp. 497-502; Clapham, Machines and National Rivalries, p. 322; Hobsbawm, Labouring Men, pp. 211-40.
130 Webb, History of Trade Unionism, 1920 ed., pp. 503-509; George S. Bain, The Growth of White-Collar Unionism (Oxford: Clarendon, 1970), Table 7A.1 at pp. 214-15; cf. n. 65 above.
131 Census of England and Wales, 1911, Vol. IX: Birthplaces of Persons Enumerated..., P.P. 1913, Vol. LXXVIII, Cd. 7017 (London: HMSO, 1913), Table II at p. v. In 1861 the corresponding figure was 95.3 per cent. Strictly speaking, these data relate to the relative decline in immigrants and do not preclude the possibility, for example, that previous Irish immigrants reproduced more rapidly than non-immigrants; it is unlikely that such an increase compensated for the very large absolute decline in the number of immigrants.
132 Ibid. and ibid., Table I at p. iv; Porter, Progress, ed. Hirst, Table XIV at p. 16.
133 Census, 1911, Vol. IX, Table XI at p. xvi.
134 Ibid.
135 Ibid., pp. xxi, 206-41 and Table XIV at p. xvii. Cf. Clapham, Machines and National Rivalries, pp. 449-51. English outmigration also reached a record plateau during the decade preceding World War I; see Annuaire statistique, Vol. 38--1922, p. 195.
136 Perry Anderson, "Origin of the present crisis," New Left Review, No. 23, January-February 1964, p. 35, argues that English outmigration to British colonies functioned, by draining off many independent working class elements, as a more important safety valve than colonial super-profits inasmuch as it deflected the working class from confronting capitalism. Although this may have been the case, the mechanism was not peculiar to British colonialism since it applied to German emigration to the United States as well. Moreover, three-quarters of English emigrants were destined for the United States and not for the British Empire; see R.C.K. Ensor, England 1870-1914 (Oxford: Clarendon, 1936), p. 271.
137 Statistical Abstract for the United Kingdom, In each of the last Fifteen Years. From 1889 to 1903, 51st Number, Cd. 2192 (London: HMSO, 1909), pp. 284-85; Statistical Abstract for the United Kingdom... From 1901 to 1915, 63rd Number, Cd. 8448 (London: HMSO, 1917), pp. 406-407.
138 Statistical Abstract for the United Kingdom... From 1867 to 1881, 29th Number, C.-3266 (London: HMSO, 1882), p. 166; Statistical Abstract for the United Kingdom... From 1876 to 1890, 38th Number, C.-6457 (London: HMSO, 1891), p. 221.
139 A sharp decline in the number of those receiving relief followed in the wake of the introduction of old age pensions in 1908: see Statistical Abstract for the United Kingdom... From 1901 to 1915, p. 407 n.
140 Porter, Progress, ed. Hirst, Table V at p. 70.
141 Excluding casuals and the insane.
142 Porter, Progress, ed. Hirst, p. 74, notes that the total yearly pauperism of 1,709,436 in 1906 was almost one-half million greater than the figure for 1844.
143 Royal Commission on the Poor Law and Relief of Distress, Report of the Royal Commission on the Poor Law and Relief of Distress, P.P. 1909, Vol. XXXVII, Cd. 4499 (London: HMSO, 1909), pp. 1131-78.

144 Beveridge, Unemployment, pp. 71-75, 143-49.
145 Porter, Progress, ed. Hirst, Table XV at p. 81.
146 Ibid., Table XI at p. 76.
147 Edward Spencer Beesly, Letters to the Working Classes (London: Truelove, 1870), p. 2; first published in the Birmingham Weekly Post, December 4, 1869.
148 W. Mattieu Williams, "Iron," British Manufacturing Industries, ed. G. Phillips Bevan, I (London: Stanford, 1876), 32, 36.
149 See chap. 5 sect A above.
150 Routh Occupation, pp. 28-38, does not describe the procedures he used to arrive at his analysis of manual workers into skilled, semi-skilled and unskilled for the period under review.
151 Census, 1911, Vol. X, Pt. I, Table 26 at p. 551.
152 Ibid., p. cxxii.
153 See, for example, G.T. Jones, Increasing Return (Cambridge: Cambridge University Press, 1933), pp. 84-85, on building tradesmen.
154 See Erich Sperling, Die neue deutsche Arbeiterbewegung (Bonn: Bonner Verlangsanstalt, 1914), p.6; cf. Hobsbawm, Labouring Men, pp. 190, 348-49, 381-83.
155 These manual industrial occupations have been selected according to descriptive criteria contained in various studies of individual trades alluded to in the notes.
156 Sources: Calculated according to data in: Census, 1891, Vol. IV, Table 5 at pp. xii-xxv; Census, 1911, Vol. X, Pt. I, Table 3 at pp. 15-25.
157 This rubric, which includes many unskilled workers, functions as a substitute for the occupation of ironfounding, for which no separate returns were made in 1891. For 1911 this rubric includes all iron and steel manufacturing workers, ironfounders (excluding foundry laborers), stove grate and bedstead makers and iron workers undefined.
158 Includes metal machinists, patternmakers, workers in textile machinery fittings and others.
159 This category includes palters, riveters, painters and others, a small proportion of whom worked on wooden ships.
160 Includes French polishers.
161 Includes furniture dealers.
162 Includes railway coach/wagon makers.
163 Includes sheet, plate, bottle and other glassmakers.
164 Excludes straw hatmakers.
165 Includes other instruments.
166 Includes dealers.
167 Source: Table 15.
168 See Table 9 above.
169 By 1911, two-thirds of these employees were working on railway coaches.
170 If blacksmiths are transferred from the metal to the traditional trades, the growth of the former rises to 54.2 per cent whereas that of the latter declines to 8.3 per cent.
171 This exclusion refers to carpenters, bricklayers, masons, plasterers, erectors, shipwrights, machinists and iron and steel manufacture workers.
172 Calculated according to data in Labour Statistics. Returns of Wages published between 1830 and 1886, pp. 356, 359, 361, 373-74, 386.
173 J.W. Rowe, Wages in Practice and Theory (New York: Kelley, 1969 (1928)), p. 24.
174 Clapham, Machines and National Rivalries, p. 324.
175 A Working Man, Working Men and Women (London: Tinsley, 1879), p. 108. A decade prior to the period under review this anonymous author--whose

work resembles that of Thomas Wright--concluded that the skilled were able to fix the work "of slogging, fetching, hauling, pulling" as "the very highest verge to which the harder manual work can be carried without giving those doing it a too great insight into the trade...." _Ibid_. The fact that men without formal technical training or "detail mastery" of the "minutiae" of a trade increasingly could enter the lower ends of the various skilled building trades indicated that neither machine-age nor pre-industrial skills were being imparted. See Thorstein Veblen, _The Instinct of Workmanship_ (New York: Norton, 1964 (1914)), pp. 307-308. Cf. Charles Booth, ed. _Life and Labour of the People in London_ (9 vols.; London: Macmillan, 1892-1897), V, 100-105.

176 R.W. Postgate, _The Builders' History_ (London: Labour Publishing, n.d. (1923)), pp. 354-55, 371-72; Taylor, "Bricklayers," p. 182; Cyril Jackson, _Unemployment and Trade Unions_ (London: Longmans, Green, 1910), p. 50. See however (Charity Organisation Society), Special Committee on _Unskilled Labour_, Report and Minutes of Evidence (n.p.: Charity Organisation Society, June 1908), QQ. 1698-1700 at p. 233; Clegg, Fox and Thompson, _History_, I, 352.

177 Booth, ed., _Life and Labour_, V, 79-80.

178 Rowe, _Wages_, pp. 24-25. Cf. Robert Noonan (Tressall), _The Ragged-Trousered Philanthropists_ (New York: Stokes, 1914).

179 Eighteen traditional trades result from the transfer of coachmaking to the metal and engineering trades and the transfer of blacksmiths, cutlers, millwrights and wheelwrights to those practicing traditional trades. According to this classification, the number of traditionally skilled rose by 42,434 from 1891 to 1911.

180 Clapham, _Machines and National Rivalries_, pp. 190-92; Webb, _Industrial Democracy_, pp. 407, 464-66, 498-500.

181 _Census_, _1891_, IV, xiv-xv; _Census_, _1911_, X: I, 20-21.

182 _Census_, _1891_, IV, xiv-xv; _Census_, _1911_, X: I, 20-21.

183 Ensor, _England 1870-1914_, pp. 204, 310-22, 532-40.

184 Clapham, _Machines and National Rivalries_, pp. 183-84; Beatrice Potter, "The Tailoring Trade," _Labour and Life of the People_, ed. Booth, I, 209-40, especially I, 212.

185 _Census_, 1891, IV, xx-xxi; _Census_, 1911, X: I, 22-23.

186 Potter, "Tailoring," pp. 212-17.

187 Specifically, dealers, upholsterers and French polishers were not distinguished from cabinetmakers in 1891.

188 Ernest Aves, "The Furniture Trade," _Labour and Life of the People_, ed. Booth, I, 384.

189 See Victor S. Clark, _History of Manufactures in the United States_, Vol. III, 1893-1928 (New York: McGraw Hill, 1929), pp. 259-60; Sidney Pollard, _The Development of the British Economy 1914-1967_ (2nd ed.; London: Arnold, 1973 (1962)), p. 105.

190 Webb, _Industrial Democracy_, p. 478. Cf. Clegg, Fox and Thompson, _History_, I, 170; Paul de Rousiers, The Labour Question in Britain, tr. F.L.D. Herbertson (London: Macmillan, 1896 (French ed.: 1895)), p. 55.

191 Webb, _Industrial Democracy_, p. 707. Cf. _Life and Labour_, ed. Booth, VI, 80-84.

192 _Census_, 1911, X: I, cxlix and ibid., Table LXIII. Cf. however Money, _Things That Matter_, p. 216.

193 R.H. Tawney, "The Economics of Boy Labour," _Economic Journal_, XIX, 76 (December 1909), 518.

194 R.A. Bray, "The Apprenticeship Question," _Economic Journal_, XIX, 75 (September 1909), 413.

195 Source: Table 15 above.
196 On carriage building, see Life and Labour, ed. Booth, V, 233-50.
197 Ibid., VII, 334-49; Clegg, Fox and Thompson, History, I, 32.
198 Webb, Industrial Democracy, pp. 456-57.
199 Webb, History of Trade Unionism, 1920 ed., pp. 490-91. In the early
    1890s the general secretary of the union claimed that ninety-five per
    cent of the relevant workers were organized; see Royal Commission on
    Labour, Minutes of Evidence, with Appendices, taken before Group "A",
    Vol. III, C.--6894-VII (London: HMSO, 1893), Q. 20,725 at p. 39.
200 See however ibid., Q. 20,531 at p. 27.
201 Ibid., QQ. 20,676-21,154 at pp. 33-62.
202 Unskilled helpers had always formed a large proportion of shipbuilders.
    See Labour Statistics. Returns of Wages published between 1830 and
    1886, pp. 210-19.
203 Brandt, Gewerkschaftliche Interessenvertretung, pp. 52-62.
204 Ibid., pp. 62-63. For a comparison with the situation in the 1870s, see
    Williams, "Iron" and "Steel," pp. 1-76; G. Phillips Bevan, The Industrial
    Classes and Industrial Statistics (London: Stanford, 1876), pp. 40, 45.
205 The discussion of the rise of the semi-skilled is resumed below.
206 On the poor quality of employment data in the iron and steel industry,
    see Brandt, Gewerkschaftliche Interessenvertretung, pp. 48-49, 407 n.
    19. Tin plate workers should be included among the skilled, but defini-
    tional changes between 1891 and 1911 precluded comparability.
207 James B. Jefferys, The Story of the Engineers 1800-1945 (n.p.: Lawrence
    & Wishart, n.d. (1945)), p. 122; Rowe, Wages, pp. 263-70.
208 Jefferys, Story of the Engineers, p. 122; Landes, Prometheus, p. 307;
    Keith Burgess, The Origins of British Industrial Relations (London:
    Croom Helm, 1975), pp. 1-85.
209 E.H. Phelps Brown, The Growth of British Industrial Relations (London:
    Macmillan, 1959), pp. 90-92.
210 James Hinton, The First Shop Stewards' Movement (London: Allen &
    Unwin, 1973), pp. 14, 56-100; Rowe, Wages, pp. 89-103.
211 Jefferys, Story of the Engineers, p. 124.
212 See, for example, Edwin A. Pratt, ed., Trade Unionism and British
    Industry (London: Murray, 1904). Cf. Paul Mantoux and Maurice Alfassa,
    La Crise du trade-unionisme (Paris: Rousseau, 1903); and the modern
    scholarly refutation by A.L. Levine, Industrial Retardation in Britain
    1880-1914 (New York: Basic, 1967), pp. 79-110. See however Charles
    S. Myers, Mind and Work (London: University of London, 1920), pp. 17,
    126.
213 Humbert Wolfe, Labour Supply and Regulation (Oxford: Clarendon,
    1923), p. 154. Cf. Women in Industry, pp. 81-85. It was this kind of
    overriding technological movement that created the basis for the rise
    and fall of skill-based labor aristocracies and not the volition of sub-
    jective agents to create or preserve privileges. Cf. the misleading analysis
    by Francis Hearn, Domination, Legitimation, and Resistance (Westport:
    Greenwood, 1978), p. 165.
214 Jefferys, Story of the Engineers, p. 207, estimates that in 1914 sixty
    per cent of engineers were skilled with the remainder equally divided
    between the semi-skilled and the unskilled.
215 The foregoing aggregate data render improbable the claim that large
    numbers of unskilled workers were upgraded to skilled--in contradistinction
    to semi-skilled--positions. See Royal Commission on Labour, Fifth and
    Final Report of the Royal Commission on Labour, Part I: The Report,
    C. 7421 (London: HMSO, 1894), p. 24.

216 See H.A. Turner, Trade Union Growth, Structure and Policy (London: Allen & Unwin, 1962), pp. 110-14; H.A. Clegg, General Union in a Changing Society (Oxford: Blackwell, 1964), p. 3.
217 Clegg, General Union, pp. 3-4; G.D.H. Cole, "Some Notes on British Trade Unionism in the Third Quarter of the Nineteenth Century," Essays in Economic History, ed. E.M. Carus-Wilson, III (London: Arnold, 1966 (1962)), 206; first published in International Review for Social History, II (1937), 1-25.
218 E. Llewelyn Lewis, The Children of the Unskilled (London: King, 1924), p.xv. This criterion must be distinguished from that which defines skill according to whether it enables its possessor to produce a whole product; see Anna Bezanson, "Skill," Quarterly Journal of Economics, XXXVI (1922), 626-45.
219 Rowe, Wages, p. 157; Clegg, Fox and Thompson, History, I, 429.
220 See, e.g., Max Weber, Wirtschaft und Gesellschaft (Cologne: Kiepenheuer & Witsch, 1964 (1922)), p. 225.
221 See, e.g., Ralf Dahrendorf, Class and Class Conflict in Industrial Society (Stanford: Stanford University Press, 1975 (1959; 1st German ed.; 1957)), p. 49; idem, "Unskilled Labour in British Industry" (Doctoral Thesis, London School of Economics, 1956), passim; Clark Kerr, Labor and Management in Industrial Society (Garden City: Doubleday, 1964), p. 218.
222 Dahrendorf, Class, pp. 48-51.
223 Henry Pelling, Popular Politics and Society in Late Victorian Britain (London: Macmillan, 1968), p. 52. Cf. Bowley, Wages and Income, p. 45.
224 It would, moreover, be necessary to determine whether semi-skilled positions were situated closer to skilled or unskilled ones.
225 E.g., in boot and shoemaking; see David F. Schloss, "Bootmaking," Labour and Life of the People, ed. Booth, I, 241-308.
226 Margo Anderson Conk, "Occupational Classification in the United States Census: 1870-1940," Journal of Interdisciplinary History, IX, 1 (Summer 1978), 111-30, correctly criticizes Alba Edwards for having created a tautological American occupational schema by having introduced social criteria (such as sex, wage-level, age, etc.) into his definition of the skill structure instead of having derived social criteria from that structure. Although Edwards' procedure was clearly inferior to one based on a trade by trade analysis of technological developments, there can be no doubt that traditionally the correlation between wage-level, sex and age on the hand and skill-level on the other was so highly positive that it functioned as an adequate indicator in the absence of hundreds of detailed industrial surveys. Cf. Women in Industry, pp. 21-22.
227 Calculated according to data in Census, 1891, Table 5 at IV, xiv; Census, 1911, Table 3 at X: I, 16.
228 Calculated according to data in Census, 1891, Table 5 at IV, xii, xxiii; Census, 1911, Table 3 at X: I, 14, 24. Cf. Hobsbawm, Labouring Men, pp. 185-271.
229 Booth, ed., Life and Labour, VI, 100-102.
230 Charles Booth, "Sweating," Labour and Life of the People, ed. idem, I, 481-500.
231 Changes in census classifications make precise temporal comparisons impossible.
232 As a result of the growth of occupations requiring physical strength, men may have come to constitute a greater proportion of the unskilled.
233 See, however, Lewis, Children of the Unskilled, passim; S.J. Chapman and W. Abbott, "The Tendency of Children to Enter their Fathers'

Trade," Journal of the Royal Statistical Society, LXXVI (May 1913), 599-604; cf. the scattered autobiographical accounts in Paul Thompson, The Edwardians (Frogmore: Palladin, 1977 (1975)), passim; Standish Meacham, A Life Apart (London: thames and Hudson, 1977), p. 178.

234 The fact that the proportion of skilled workers above the age of fifty-five rose from 1891 to 1911 is consistent with this reasoning, but a similar phenomenon also occurred among the unskilled. See Census, 1891, Table V at IV, x-xxv; Census, 1911, Table 3 at X: I, 14-25.

235 Webb, Industrial Democracy, pp. 477-78.

236 Dahrendorf, Class, pp. 50-51, overlooks this possibility in his critique of Marx.

237 Mrs. Sidney Webb, "Minority Report," Women in Industry, p. 294.

238 The field of most intense conflict between the skilled and the semi-skilled embraced the industries of advanced mechanization which were also largely those of the greatest concentration of capital and labor. Significantly, the most concerted radical labor offensive of the period, the so-called triple Alliance of unions representing miners, railway workers and transportation workers, was based in industries dominated by the semi-skilled and unskilled without any tradition of formal or informal subordination or subservience to a stratum of highly skilled workers.

239 H.F. Moorhouse, "The Marxist Theory of the Labour Aristocracy," Social History, III, 1 (January 1978), 63, levels the charge of "naive economic determinism" at Hobsbawm because the latter relied on wage rates in his study of the labor aristocracy. Yet Hobsbawm did not set himself the task of theorizing about the labor aristocracy but rather, taking as his point of departure a modified Leninist version, of providing an empirical survey of material traits. In this respect he broke ground. See chap. 1 above.

240 See, e.g., Routh, Occupation, p. 96 n. 1. Routh fails to mention that this caveat applies to other tables as well.

241 Earnings and Hours Enquiry. Report of an Enquiry by the Board of Trade into the Earnings and Hours of Labour of Workpeople of the United Kingdom. I.--Textile Trades in 1906, P.P. 1909, Vol. LXXX, Cd. 4545 (London: HMSO, 1909), p. xviii.

242 See the comment by ely Devons, An Introduction to British Economic Statistics (Cambridge: Cambridge University Press, 1956), p. 204.

243 Wages.--General Report. General Report on the Wages of the Manual Labour Classes in the United Kingdom; with Tables of the Average Rates of Wages and Hours of Labour of Persons Employed in Several of the Principal Trades in 1886 and 1891 C. 6889 (London: HMSO, 1893), p. 470.

244 The report of 1906 covered about 3,000,000 altogether, or about five times as many as surveyed in 1886.

245 Bowley, Wages and Income, p. 42.

246 Agricultural laborers were surveyed in 1907, but the report was constructed along different lines so that its results cannot be integrated into the aggregate data; see P.P. 1910, Cd. 5460.

247 Wages.--General Report, pp. xxviii-xxix, 148.

248 Bowley, Wages and Income, pp. 48-49; cf. ibid., p. 41.

249 Twenty shillings, the lower limit in Table 18, constituted the weekly income of the "'poor'"--that is, "those whose means may be sufficient, but are barely sufficient, for decent independent life...." Labour and Life of the People, ed. Booth, I, 33. At the other extreme, forty shillings approximated the average weekly income of clerical workers. See Routh, Occupation, Table 37 at p. 79 and Table 47 at p. 104; Cannan et al., "Amount and Distribution," p. 66.

250 Sources: For 1886: calculated according to data in Wages.--General Report, Table at p. 470; cf. the weighted shares in ibid., p. xxxii; for 1906: calculated according to data in: Enquiry, I.--Textile Trades in 1906, pp. 3-4; II.-- Clothing Trades in 1906, P.P. 1909, Vol. LXXX, Cd. 4844, p. 3; III.-- Building and Woodworking Trades in 1906, P.P. 1910, Vol. LXXXIV, Cd. 5086, p. 3; IV.-- Public Utility Services in 1906, P.P. 1910, Vol. LXXXIV, pp. 4-5; VI.-- Metals, Engineering and Shipbuilding Trades in 1906, P.P. 1911, Vol. LXXXVIII, Cd. 5814, pp. 6-7; VII.-- Railway Service in 1907, P.P. 1912-1913, Vol. CVIII, Cd. 6053, p. 2; VIII.--Paper, Printing, etc., Trades... and Miscellaneous Trades in 1906, P.P. 1912-1913, Vol. CVIII, Cd. 6556, pp. 3, 88, 160, 234.

251 The turning point is thirty shillings.

252 See Bowley, Wages and Income, Table VII at p. 30.

253 Source: ibid., p. 42; the percentages of the median were published in British Labour Statistics, Table 79 at p. 156.

254 Bowley, Wages and Income, pp. 41-42.

255 Ibid., pp. 46-47. Cf. W.D. Mackenzie, "Changes in the Standard of Living in the United Kingdom, 1860-1914," Economica, N.S., I, 3 (October, 1921), 211-30. The shift alluded to in the text is revealed even more dramatically when the absolute diminution in the number of agricultural laborers is taken into consideration.

256 The implied relative decline of the unskilled contradicts the findings, based on occupational data, summarized in sect. B.2 above.

257 The very high shares of low-paid men and very low shares of high-paid men recorded in 1886 in branches characterized by a relatively high wage-level--e.g., shipbuilding, engineering and iron and steel manufacture--suggest that part of the difference between the results of 1886 and 1906 is attributable to non-real factors. See Wages.--General Report, p. xiv; Labour Statistics. Returns of Wages published between 1830 and 1886, pp. 210, 219. That 1886 was a year of depression and 1906 one of prosperity also contributed to the discrepancy. See Thorp, Business Annals, pp. 170, 174; Hobsbawm, Labouring Men, p. 331 n. *.

258 These rubrics include boys and girls, who earned about two-thirds and one-half respectively of the adult female wage level. See Wages.--General Report, pp. xxxii, 476; Routh, Occupation, Table 27 at p. 57; Bowley, Wages and Income, Table X at p. 50.

259 Jürgen Kuczynski, Die Entwicklung der Lage der Arbeiterschaft in Europa und Amerika 1870-1933 (Basel: Philographischer Verlag, 1934), pp. 121-13; idem, England von 1832 bis 1900, pp. 200-201; idem, England von 1900 bis zur Gegenwart, p. 28, presents data purporting to capture the differential movements of real wages of the labor aristocracy and the "great mass of workers." The validity of the data is vitiated by Kuczynski's arbitrary definitional operations which transform the composition of the two sectors over time. He thus renders it impossible to trace the pattern of intra-working class income distribution as experienced by real individuals as opposed to statistical groupings. Cf. the objections raised by A. Fogarasi, "Lenins Lehre von der Arbeiteraristokratie und ihre Anwendung auf Fragen der Gegenwart," Unter dem Banner des Marxismus, IX, 4 (November 1935), 352-53.

260 On a related issue, see E.H. Hunt, Regional Wage Variation in Britain 1850-1914 (Oxford: Clarendon, 1973).

261 Charles Booth, ed., Labour and Life of the People, Vol. II: London Continued (London: Williams & Norgate, 1891), pp. 20-24. The "middle class and above" have been excluded and the institutionalized population

has been reapportioned in accordance with Booth's guidelines; ibid.,
p. 23.

262 Calculated according to ibid., I, Table I (pp. 34-35), 51. Booth's
classes 1-19 have been used as the best approximation of the industrial
proletariat. The data include Hackney.

263 Booth, ed. Life and Labour, IX, 371-72.

264 Calculated according to Bowley, Wages and Income, p. 44.

265 B. Seebohm Rowntree, Poverty (London: Macmillan, 1902 (1901)), p. 117.

266 A.L. Bowley and A.R. Burnett-Hurst, Livelihood and Poverty (London:
Bell, 1915), p. 46; Rowntree, Poverty, p. 111; cf. ibid., pp. 86-87 for
definitions.

267 Cf. W. Lawler Wilson. The Menace of Socialism (Philadelphia: Jacobs,
n.d. (ca. 1910-11)), pp. 428-30.

268 Source: "Memorandum on the Consumption and Cost of Food in Workmen's
Families," British and Foreign Trade and Industry (Second Series).
Second Series of Memoranda, Statistical Tables and Charts, prepared by
the Board of Trade, P.P. 1905, Vol. LXXXIV, Cd. 2337, p. 5 and chart
facing p. 3. The distribution of returns among income groups was not
representative of the working class population at large because the
response rate to the questionnaires was higher among the better paid;
ibid., p. 4. The total sample included 1,944 families.

269 Except for milk which was measured in pints.

270 The inquiry did not collect data on the consumption of alcohol and
tobacco.

271 These data on meat exclude sheep's heads, tripe, heart, liver, pig's
fry, tinned meats and rabbits.

272 The data have been converted to American measures, the British pint
being equivalent to twenty fluid ounces.

273 Thompson, Edwardians, passim. On the considerably higher levels of
consumption among contemporary American workers, see Cost of Living
in American Towns, P.P. 1911, Vol. LXXXVIII, Cd. 5609, pp. lxxv-lxix.

274 Source: Calculated according to data in Routh, Occupation, Table 47
at p. 104. Routh's data for manual employees are extrapolations from
the survey of 1906; ibid., p. 103. The data on clerks' wages stem from
a survey taken in 1910 and are apparently not adjusted for the passage
of time; ibid., p. 78. The annual data for manual workers are merely
the arithmetic product of the weekly average wage and fifty-two weeks;
ibid., p. 96 n. 1, 167-68. Employers and proprietors are not covered
by the data.

275 Women's earnings were roughly half those of men at every level; ibid.,
p. 105.

276 Ibid., p. 167, estimates that the unemployment rate among the unskilled
was almost four times greater than among the skilled.

277 See Condition of the Working Classes. Tabulation of the Statements made
by Men Living in Certain Selected Districts of London in March 1887,
P.P. 1887, Vol. LXXI, C.-5228 (London: HMSO, 1887), Table D at p.
316, which indicates that clerks earning 29s. 7d. weekly could afford
to pay rent of 7s. 5d. whereas carpenters, masons and bricklayers
earning about thirty-one shillings paid less than seven shillings weekly
in rent. Even if clerks' rental expenditures were dictated solely by the
status requirements of residing in certain neighborhoods--and were made
possible by scrimping on other outlays--, the resultant geographic and
status segregation from the working class underscored the gap between
skilled manual workers and the lower non-manual salariat.

278 Other income losses, discussed below, may be assumed to have been greater among the skilled than among clerks.
279 Beveridge, Unemployment, Table XIV at p. 74 and pp. 140-41.
280 Ibid., pp. 71-75.
281 Ibid., pp. 75, 138-39.
282 Cannan et al., "Amount and Distribution," p. 66; Routh, Occupation, Table 37 at p. 79.
283 Enquiry... Building and Woodworking Trades in 1906, pp. 24-27; Enquiry... Textile Trades in 1906, p. 26. Cf. Routh, Occupation, p. 82.
284 Routh, Occupation, Table 47 at p. 104 and Table 48 at p. 107, provides some insight into the subsequent compression of the earnings hierarchy.
285 See however Feinstein, National Income, Table 1 at p. T 6 and Table 18 at pp. T 44-45.
286 Booth, ed., Labour and Life of the People, I, 156-71.
287 Source: Calculated according to ibid., Table I (pp. 34-35). Although Booth's data were based on weekly incomes, Booth incorporated regularity of earnings into his classificatory. scheme. The data refer to Hackney as well.
288 The "well-to-do" encompassed the "Lower Middle Class" and the "Upper Middle Class"; ibid., p. 60.
289 This proportion varied from 2.1 per cent in food preparation to 22.5 per cent among sundry artisans.
290 This overlap was smaller in the more affluent parts of London: See Booth, ed., Labour and Life of the People, II, 18-43.
291 See n. 250 for sources; 309,530 or 16.2 per cent of the total of 1,907,973 men covered earned less than twenty shillings.
292 The report of 1906 covered approximately two-fifths of the workers employed in the branches surveyed; this estimate is based on the census returns of 1901 and 1911 and preliminary reports on the earnings survey published in Board of Trade Labour Gazette, XVII, 4 (April 1909), 111; XVII, 9 (September 1909), 291; XVIII, 4 (April 1910), 117; XIX, 9 (September 1911), 328. If this coverage was representative, the number earning more than forty shillings weekly was about 680,000 for these trades. Half of the remaining gap between the number employed in these trades and that included in the male industrial proletariat is accounted for by miners, who, to be sure, received high wages, but whose working and living conditions assigned them to the sphere of the negatively privileged. See Routh, Occupation, p. 86. A large part of the remaining difference is attributable to laborers, virtually none of whom earned more than two pounds weekly. The total of 900,000 mentioned in the text should, then, be regarded as an exaggerated upper limit.
293 Routh, Occupation, p. 167.
294 Ibid., pp. 167-68; cf. Bowley, Wages and Income, p. 52.
295 Unions of the most highly skilled workers paid ten to fourteen shillings weekly; see Board of Trade (Labour Department), Report by the Chief Labour Correspondent of the Board of Trade on Trade Unions in 1899 with Comparative Statistics for 1892-1898, Cd. 422 (London: HMSO, 1900), pp. 240-51.
296 Based on Routh, Occupation, Table 24 at pp. 52-53.
297 See the sources mentioned in n. 255.
298 Routh, Occupation, Table 32 at p. 68, Table 33 at p. 69 and Table 47 at p. 104.
299 K.G.J.C. Knowles and D.J. Robertson, "Differences between the Wages of Skilled and Unskilled Workers, 1880-1950," Bulletin of Oxford University Institute of Statistics, XIII, 4 (April 1951), 109-27.

300 Jones, Increasing Return, pp. 262-63. A major exception was Belfast, where in the 1890s, for example, bricklayers' wage rates were 2.25 times as great as those of their laborers on account of the latter's extraordinarily low level. The fact that Protestants were overrepresented in the skilled trades while Catholics were overrepresented in unskilled jobs contributed to this most explicit instance of a religion-mediated labor aristocracy in the United Kingdom--albeit outside England. See Geoffrey Bell, The Protestants of Ulster (London: Pluto, 1976), pp. 16-23; Michael Farrell, Northern Ireland: The Orange State (London: Pluto, 1976), p. 16.

301 Rowe, Wages, pp. 42-49.

302 S. Pollard, "Trade Unions and the Labour Market, 1870-1914," Yorkshire Bulletin of Economic and Social Research, XVII, 1 (May 1965), 100-104. Cf. A.L. Bowley, Wages in the United Kingdom in the Nineteenth Century (Cambridge: Cambridge University Press, 1900), passim.

303 The data were not analyzed by occupation within these branches in the published materials.

304 Source: Calculated according to the data in the sources mentioned in n. 250. The branches are ranked according to the percentage of full-time men earning forty shillings or more. The published data on railway employees do not distinguish between full-time and other schedules.

305 Source: Calculated according to data in Enquiry... Textile Trades in 1906, p. xvi; Enquiry... Clothing Trades in 1906, p. 4.

306 Wages.--General Report, p. 475. One-quarter of the approximately 1,400 women who in 1906 were classified as fitters or cutters, "living out" and receiving time wages in workshops earned at least forty shillings weekly while 6.7 per cent earned in excess of sixty shillings; Enquiry... Clothing Trades in 1906, p. 41.

307 Less upward shifting was recorded among children. See Enquiry... Textile Trades in 1906, pp. 6-7; Wages.--General Report, pp. 472-75.

308 See British Labour Statistics, Table 36 at pp. 94-95; Bowley, Wages and Income, Table XI at p. 51.

309 This disparity was compressed somewhat among all men since the large number of short-time workers with low earnings shifted the distribution downward.

310 For full-time men the Spearman rank correlation is -0.72.

311 J.C. Carr and W. Taplin, History of the British Steel Industry (Cambridge, Mass.: Harvard University Press, 1962), p. 146, seem to subscribe to this hypothesis of a premium.

312 Brandt, Gewerkschaftliche Interessenvertretung, pp. 63-72, 121-33, 241-54.

313 See the convenient synopsis in Clegg, Fox and Thompson, History, I, 480-82.

314 Bowley, Wages and Income, Table X at p. 50. Cf. Enquiry... Agriculture in 1907, p. xii; Clapham, Machines and National Rivalries, pp. 97-100. The wage data include the value of room and board.

315 Sources: British Labour Statistics, Table 36 at pp. 94-95; Bowley, Wages and Income, p. 42. The aggregate distributive shares were calculated on the basis of the data in the Earnings Enquiry. The average for Food/drink/tobacco was taken from Clegg, Fox and Thompson, History, I, 482. The men earning sixty shillings and above are included among those earning forty shillings and above.

316 13.2 per cent and 10.6 per cent earned forty shillings or more and less than twenty shillings respectively. Cf. Enquiry... Clothing Trades in 1906, p. 152.

317 The exclusion of women, children and discriminated ethnic and racial minorities is crucial to the validity of this proposition.
318 These data refer to all men--not merely to those working full-time; see Enquiry... Metals ... in 1906, pp. 118-19, 121; Enquiry... Textile Trades in 1906, pp. 60-61, 181.
319 E.g.: various building trades laborers, cotton piecers and certain grades of cotton weavers. See Enquiry... Building and Woodworking Trades in 1906, p. 67; Enquiry... Textile Trades in 1906, p. 62. On the wage hierarchy in London, see Booth, ed., Life and Labour, IX, 372-73; cf. E.J. Hobsbawm, "The Nineteenth Century London Labour Market," London, Aspects of Change, ed. Centre for Urban Studes (London: Macgibbon & Kee, 1964), pp. 3-28.
320 Calculated according to the data in Table 19 above.
321 Enquiry... Textile Trades in 1906, pp. 26-27. See however Enquiry... Metals... in 1906, p. 34.
322 Towns of more than 100,000 inhabitants were defined as "large." See Enquiry... Building and Woodworking Trades in 1906, pp. 19-20; cf. ibid., pp. 47-48, on bricklayers.
323 It may have been a peculiarity of the building trades that the differential between large and small towns was greater for unskilled than for skilled labor; this circumstance may have been due to the fact that unskilled building labor was not far removed in nature from the work agricultural laborers were accustomed to performing. Such labor was in surplus not only in non-harvest periods. See ibid., pp. 24-27; Weber, Cities, p. 41. Cf. Eric Hopkins, "Small Town Aristocrats of Labour and their Standard of Living, 1840-1914," Economic History Review, Second Series, XXVIII, 2 (May 1975), 222-42.
324 Regularity must be distinguished from representativeness.
325 Norman B. Dearle, Problems of Unemployment in the London Building Trades (London: Dent, 1908), p. 136.
326 British Labour Statistics, Table 159 at p. 305 and Table 196 at p. 395.
327 Beveridge, Unemployment, pp. 16-21; idem, Full Employment in a Free Society (New York: Norton, 1945), pp. 40-41; Report by the Chief Labour Correspondent... 1899, pp. 240-99.
328 Beveridge, Unemployment, pp. 19-23; idem, Full Employment, pp. 43-44; Royal Commission on the Poor Law, Report, pp. 1131-78.
329 Mitchell and Deane, Abstract, pp. 64-65.
330 Beveridge, Unemployment, pp. 263-72.
331 Calculated according to British Labour Statistics, Table 159 at p. 305 and Table 160 at p. 306.
332 See however Beveridge, Unemployment, p. 21.
333 Ibid., pp. 162-91, especially Table XXVII at p. 168.
334 Booth, ed., Life and Labour, IX, 374-79.
335 Beveridge, Unemployment, p. 267. The benefit could be received for up to fifteen weeks annually.
336 Report by the Chief Labour Correspondent... 1899, pp. 240-49.
337 Clapham, Machines and National Rivalries, pp. 504-507; A Working Man, Working Men and Women, pp. 36-37; J.M. Baernreither, Die englischen Arbeiterverbände und ihr Recht, I (Tübingen: Verlag der Laupp'schen Buchhandlung, 1886), passim.
338 Acceptance of public assistance, which was designed to keep the recipient below the level of "the lowest class" of laborer, brought disfranchisement with it. See Royal Commission on the Poor Law, Report, passim; Sidney and Beatrice Webb, English Poor Law Policy (London: Longmans, Green, 1910), passim; Beveridge, Unemployment, pp. 150-62.

339 Dearle, Problems of Unemployment, p. 98. Cf. Clegg, Fox and Thompson, History, I, 145.
340 Report by the Chief Labour Correspondent... 1899, pp. 240-99; George Howell, Trade Unionism (3rd ed.; London: Methuen, 1900 (1891)), pp. 97-128. In 1895, only 7,254 members of twenty-seven unions, which included nine-tenths of all union members, received superannuation benefits averaging somewhat over seventeen pounds. See Old Age Pensions Committee, Report of the Committee on Old Age Pensions, C.--8911 (London: HMSO, 1898), QQ. 2153-2156 at p. 104 and Appendix G at pp. 151-53.
341 Elie Halévy, A History of the English People in the Nineteenth Century, V: Imperialism and the Rise of Labour, tr. E.I. Watkin (London: Benn, 1965 (1st French ed.: 1926)), 233-36; idem, ibid., VI: The Rule of Democracy, tr. E.I. Watkin (New York: Barnes & Noble, 1961 (1st French ed.: 1932)), 281-85, 288-89.
342 A private pension amounting to approximately eight shillings weekly qualified a pensioner for the full state pension.
343 Baernreither, Die englischen Arbeiterverbände, I, 385-93.
344 Halévy, History, VI, 352-58.
345 Ibid., pp. 99-102; idem, ibid., V, 232-33, 237. Theretofore only members of unions or friendly societies could be compensated indirectly.
346 This differential also applied to losses owing to strikes. Cf. Kerr, Labor and Management, pp. 105-47.
347 Source: Census, 1911, X: I, Table XLIV at cxxv. Navy and army officers were excluded in both years, clergymen and doctors in 1901. The data on females have been deleted since spurious reporting grossly undercounted the number of retired females; ibid., p. cxxv.
348 The share of unoccupied men over the age of sixty-five had also risen between 1891 and 1901; see Beveridge, Unemployment, p. 121; Census, 1891, Vol. IV, Table 5 at pp. x-xxv.
349 Cf. Beveridge, Unemployment, pp. 121-23.
350 Hobsbawm, Labouring Men, pp. 424-27.
351 Source: Census, 1911, X: I, cxxv and Table XLV at cxxvi. Laborers are included among the fitters, turners and erectors; laborers, platelayers, clerks and officials are not included among the railway servants.
352 Cf. Hobsbawm, Labouring Men, pp. 333-34.
353 Significantly, the more modern trade of plumbing showed one of the lowest rates.
354 Dearle, Problems of Unemployment, passim.
355 This factor may also have contributed to the low rates among miners. See Kerr, Labor and Management, p. 109; John Foster, Class Struggle and the Industrial Revolution (London: Methuen, 1977 (1974)), passim.
356 Census, 1911, X: I, cxxv.
357 As an American worker described the situation in the United States prior to the introduction of old age pensions within the national social security system: "'Back in those days, the word retirement really wasn't part of our vocabulary.'" Wall Street Journal, November 26, 1979, p. 21 col. 2.
358 Calculated according to British Labour Statistics, Table 200 at p. 399. Deaths in shipping led the list in most years. Cf. Kuczynski, England von 1832 bis 1900, p. 209; idem, England von 1900 bis zur Gegenwart, p. 34; Hobsbawm, Labouring Men, p. 180 n. 45.
359 Porter, Progress, ed. Hirst, p. 44; Supplement to the Fifty-Fifth Annual Report of the Registrar-General of Births, Deaths and Marriages in England, Part II, Cd.--8503 (London: HMSO, 1897), pp. lxii-cxli.

360 Booth, ed., Life and Labour, V, 165.
361 Ibid., VI, 210-11.
362 Ibid., Vols. V-VIII, passim; Final Report of the Departmental Committee appointed to inquire into and report upon Certain Miscellaneous Dangerous Trades, P.P. 1899, Vol. XII, C. 5909 (London: HMSO, 1899), passim.
363 Cf. the caveats in W.S. Woytinsky and E.S. Woytinsky, World Population and Production (New York: Twentieth Century Fund, 1963), pp. 177-79.
364 This age-group is used because males born in the latter half of the nineteenth century who reached their twentieth year had, on the average, a life expectancy falling within this range. See Annuaire statistique, Vol. 38-1922, p. 203*.
365 Calculated according to Supplement to the Fifty-Fifth Annual Report of the Registrar-General, Pt. II, pp. cxx-cxxvii.
366 E.g., filemakers and leadmakers; ibid., pp. cxxvi-cxxvii.
367 A similar pattern prevailed in other years; see Supplement to the Twenty-Fifth Annual Report of the Registrar-General of Births, Deaths, and Marriages in England (London: HMSO, 1864), Tables XXII-XXIV at pp. xxxiii-xxxv; Supplement to the Thirty-Fifth Annual Report..., C.--1155- I (London: HMSO, 1875), Table 62 at p. clxxi and Table 63 at pp. clxxii-clxxiii; Supplement to the Sixty-Fifth Annual Report of the Registrar-General of Births, Deaths, and Marriages in England and Wales, Pt. II, Cd. 2619 (London: HMSO, 1908), Charts 1 and 2.
368 Source: Seventy-Fourth Annual Report of the Registrar-General of Births, Deaths, and Marriages in England and Wales, (1911), Cd. 6578 (London: HMSO, 1913), Table 28B at p. 88 and p. xli.
369 Ibid., Table 28A at pp. 78, 80.
370 Ibid., Table 28A at p. 77.
371 Cf. Weber, Cities, pp. 343-67.
372 On the evolution of protective legislation, see Otto W. Weyer, Die englische Fabrikinspektion (Tübingen: Verlag der Laupp'schen Buchhandlung, 1888). For a comprehensive survey of the course of working time, see M.A. Bienefeld, Working Hours in British Industry (London: Weidenfeld & Nicholson, 1972).
373 See, for example, British Labour Statistics, Tables 2 and 3 at pp. 30-33. For a counter-example from mining, see Clegg, Fox and Thompson, History, I, 104-105.
374 Brandt, Gewerkschaftliche Interessenvertretung, pp. 115-18, 232-37, also documents the gradual reduction.
375 Booth, ed., Life and Labour, IX, 298-311.
376 Ibid.; Clapham, Machines and National Rivalries, pp. 477-79.
377 In addition to the sources mentioned in the two-preceding notes, see Hans von Nostitz, Das Aufsteigen des Arbeiterstandes in England (Jena: Fischer, 1900), p. 499; Gustav Steffen, Studier öfver lönsystemets historia i England, Second Part (Stockholm, Lorenska Stiftelsen, 1899), Table XXXVIII at pp. 483-86.
378 Census, 1911, Vol. X, Pt. I, Table 19 at pp. 478-79 and Table 26 at pp. 540-51. Cf. J.J. Tobias, Crime and Industrial Society in the 19th Century (New York: Schocken, 1967), pp. 184-85.
379 Defined as two or more persons living in one room. See Booth, ed., Life and Labour, IX, 3-27. Cf. Octavia Hill, Homes of the London Poor (2nd ed.; London: Macmillan, 1883 (1875)), pp. 14-15.
380 Booth, ed., Life and Labour, Vol. IX, Table I at p. 8, Table II at p. 10 and Table III at p. 16.
381 A.L. Bowley, "Earners and Dependants in English Towns in 1911," Economica, I (1921), 101-12. The data were derived from a special tabulation of unpublished census data.

382 Calculated according to ibid., Table V at p. 107 and Table VI at p. 108. Households without an adult male worker have been excluded.
383 Clara E. Collet, "Women's Work," Labour and Life of People, ed. Booth, I, 451; Hobsbawm, Labouring Men, p. 361 n. 49; Jones, Outcast London, p. 83; Thompson, Edwardians, p. 84.
384 Bowley, "Earners," Table IV at p. 106.
385 Women in Industry, p. 24.
386 Ibid.; Jones, Outcast London, pp. 40, 83-84.
387 The last claim cannot be documented without the kind of analysis of local labor contracts that falls outside the framework of the present work.
388 Hobsbawm, Labouring Men, p. 336, estimates that fifteen per cent of the working class were labor aristocrats. Cf. Th. Rothstein, "Das proletarische Elend in England und Deutschland," Die Neue Zeit, XXVII, I (1908-1909), 326. For a recent restatement of the criteria for excluding certain high-paid workers from a labor aristocarcy, see John H. Goldthorpe et al., The Affluent Worker in the Class Structure (Cambridge: Cambridge University Press, 1969), p. 34.
389 Weber, Wirtschaft und Gesellschaft, pp. 223, 225.
390 Men earning three pounds weekly would have ranked above clerical employees and foremen and alongside lower professionals among the upper three per cent of all earned income recipients. See Routh, Occupation, Table 47 at p. 104 and Table 24 at p. 52. If only 1.7 per cent of males covered by the Earnings Enquiry of 1906 attained this level, a very small proportion earned three pounds week-in week-out. A considerable number of these men were subcontractors in the iron and steel industry, who only with some conceptual violence may be included in the working class. "Superaristocrats" were also employed in printing, engineering, boilermaking, shipbuilding, cotton manufacture and on the railways.
391 Weber, Wirtschaft und Gesellschaft, pp. 223-24.
392 Anthony Giddens, The Class Structure of the Advanced Societies (London: Hutchinson, 1974 (1973)), pp. 107-108.
393 Weber, Wirtschaft und Gesellschaft, pp. 223, 225-26; Giddens, Class Structure, p. 107. Insofar as intergenerational mobility was predicated on superior schooling, the unequal distribution of educational opportunities tended to solidify existing relations. See H.Ll. Smith, "Secondary Education--Boys," Labour and Life of the People, ed. Booth, II, 540-41.
394 Giddens, Class Structure, p. 107.
395 This segregation extended to the residential sphere as well; see Crossick, Artisan Elite, pp. 144-45, 248-50; Booth, ed., Labour and Life of the People, II, passim.
396 William Morris, "Art under Plutocracy," Political Writings of William Morris, ed. A.L. Morton (London: Lawrence & Wishart, 1973), p. 78; first delivered as a lecture at Oxford, November 14, 1883 and published in To-Day, February and March, 1884.
397 Webb, History of Trade Unionism, 1902 ed., p. 374.
398 Nostitz, Aufsteigen des Arbeiterstandes, p. 770.
399 Ibid., pp. 771-72. See the review of this book by Rosa Luxemburg, Gesammelte Werke, I: 1 (Berlin (DDR): Dietz, 1970), 738-47; first published in Leipziger Volkszeitung, May 16, May 18 and May 22, 1900. Luxemburg recurred to Marx and Engels' belief in the eventual leveling influence of the collapse of England's supremacy on the world market. Cf. "Vom Zunftverband der freien Gewerkschaft," The Carpenter (United States), VI, 10 (October 1886), 7.
400 Thomas Wright, Our New Masters (London: Strahan, 1873), p. 101.
401 Ibid., pp. 101-103. Cf. Rousiers, Labour Question, p. 262.

402 Royal Commission on Labour, Minutes of Evidence... before Group "A" Vol. III, Q. 20,804 at p. 44.
403 Ibid., Q. 20,801 at p. 44.
404 Ibid., QQ. 20,808-20,810 at p. 44.
405 Gerald Balfour questioning Andrew Noble, chairman of the Iron Trades Employers' Association for Tyne and Wear and vice-chairman and managing director of Sir William Armstrong and Company, Newcastle; ibid., Q. 25,319 at p. 329.
406 See Austin Lewis, The Militant Proletariat (Chicago: Kerr, 1911), p. 32; idem, "Organization of the Unskilled," The New Review, I, 23 (December 1913), 957; William English Walling, "Class Struggles within the Working Classes," Echoes of Revolution, ed. William L. O'Neill (Chicago: Quadrangle, 1966), pp. 48-50; this article first appeared in The Masses, January 1913; Arno Dorsch, "What the IWW Is," World's Work, XXVI, 4 (August 1914), 417; Proceedings of the First Convention of the Industrial Workers of the World (n.p.: New York Labor News, 1905), pp. 575-76. For an earlier formulation, see Carpenter and Builder, I, 9 (September 1879), 161. Cf. Bruno Ramirez, When Workers Fight (Westport: Greenwood, 1978), p. 201 and passim.
407 William English Walling, Progressivism--And After (New York: Macmillan, 1914), p. xv.
408 Ibid., p. vi. Cf. the more differentiated analysis by Sidney and Beatrice Webb, Problems of Modern Industry (new ed.; London: Longmans, 1906 (1898)), pp. xix-xx.
409 David Kynaston, King Labour. The British Working Class 1850-1914 (London: Allen & Unwin, 1976), p. 67, exaggerates this tendency. Cf. Women in Industry, p. 294.
410 Hobsbawm, Labouring Men, pp. 349-51.
411 Crossick, "Emergence of the Lower Middle Class," pp. 12-13, 48-49.
412 Eric J. Hobsbawm, ed., Labour's Turning Point, 1880-1900 (2nd ed.; Hassocks: Harvester, 1974 (1948)), pp. xvii-xviii.
413 Meacham, Life Apart, pp. 26, 143, superimposes contradictions of thought on real ones by denying on the one hand that threats to skills and wages might have persuaded labor aristocrats to join with other workers and yet admitting on the other hand that the same "threat...compelled them to rethink their situation and their strategies."
414 Foster, "British Imperialism and the Labour Aristocracy," pp. 19-21, tries to conceptualize this transformation within the framework of the Leninist dogma of bribery; cf. idem, "Some Somments on 'Class struggle and the labour aristocracy, 1830-1860,'" Social History, I, 3 (October 1976), 357-66, especially 363. See Halévy, History, VI, 445-48, on the proliferation of labor bureaucrats. Cf. Timo Toivonen, "Aristocracy of Labour: Some Old and New Problems," Acta Sociologica, XXI, 3 (1978), 217-28.
415 A Working Man, Working Men and Women, p. 113.
416 Ibid., p. 105. Cf. Thompson, Edwardians, p. 132.
417 A Working Man, Working Men and Women, pp. 105-106. On increasing uniformity in the area of social appearance, namely dress, see Ensor, England 1870-1914, p. 337; cf. however Speech Delivered by John Burns on "The Liverpool Congress" (London: Green, 1890), p. 6.
418 T.J. Dunning, Trades' Union and Strikes (2nd ed.; London: Consolidated Society of Bookbinders, 1873 (1860)), p. 51. The reference was to an incident involving a mason in 1841.
419 Benson Soffer, "A Theory of Trade Union Development: The Role of the 'Autonomous' Workman," Labor History, I (1960), 141-63, especially 141-44.

420 Robert F. Hoxie, Scientific Management and Labor (New York: Appleton, 1921), pp. 123, 126, 129, 130 n. 1, 131 n. 1.
421 Webb, History of Trade Unionism, 1920 ed., p. 642. Cf. Samuel J. Hurwitz, State Intervention in Great Britain (New York: Columbia University Press, 1949), pp. 89-97, 258-76; (Great Britain, Munitions Ministry), History of the Ministry of Munitions, Vol. V, Pt. I (n.p., 1922), pp. 20-21, 167-93 and passim.
422 Women in Industry, p. 85.
423 On the parallel situation in the United States, see n. 101 above.
424 Cf. Hobsbawm, Labouring Men, pp. 349-50.
425 Wright, Class, Crisis and the State, pp. 79-83, loses sight of the complexity of this contradiction by virtue of excluding semi-autonomous manual workers from his typology of "contradictory locations between the petty bourgeoisie and the proletariat." At the other extreme, the sociohistorical specificity of the relationship between the skilled and unskilled proletarian is effaced by subsuming the medieval journeyman under the rubric of labor aristocrat. See, e.g., Karl A. Wittfogel, Geschichte der bürgerlichen Gesellschaft (Berlin: Malik, n.d. (1924)), p. 97; cf. however Douglas Knoop and G.P. Jones, The Mediaeval Mason (Manchester: Manchester University Press, 1933), pp. 4, 94; idem, "The Rise of the Mason Contractor," Journal of the Royal Institute of British Architects, Third Series, Vol. 43, No. 20 (October 17, 1936), p. 1061; Fritz Paeplow, Bauarbeit, Bauarbeiter und Bauarbeiterorganisationen im Altertum, im Mittelalter und in der Jetztzeit, Part I (n.p.: Deutscher Baugewerksbund, 1929), p. 75.
426 Taylor, Shop Management, pp. 56-57.
427 Hobsbawm, Labouring Men, p. 353. Cf. Soffer, "Theory," p. 147.
428 J. Lynch, "Skilled and Unskilled Labour in the Shipbuilding Trade," Industrial Remuneration Conference, The Report of the Proceedings and Papers (London: Cassell, 1885), p. 114.
429 Royal Commission on Labour, Minutes of Evidence... before Group "A," Vol. III, QQ. 20,801-20,802 at p. 44.
430 Webb, Industrial Democracy, p. 291.
431 J.E. Mortimer, History of the Boilermakers' Society, Vol. I, 1834-1906 (London: Allen & Unwin, 1973), pp. 110-11, 188.
432 Arthur Pugh, Men of Steel (London: Iron and Steel Trades Confederation, 1951), pp. 154-65; cf. Brandt, Gewerkschaftliche Interessenvertretung, pp. 66-72.
433 Brandt, Gewerkschaftliche Interessenvertretung, pp. 121-33.
434 Ibid., pp. 243-54.
435 Symbolized by the results of the dispute and strike at Haward Bridge in 1909-1910; ibid., pp. 347-71.
436 Ibid., pp. 128, 393.
437 Even the most sophisticated Leninist authors, such as Foster, accept some form of this basic dogma; for an egregious example, see H.W. Edwards, Labor Aristocracy: Mass Base of Social Democracy (Stockholm: Aurora, 1978).
438 A.E. Musson, "Class Struggle and the Labour Aristocracy, 1830-60," Social History, I, 3 (October 1976), 335-56, especially 352, makes this telling point in an otherwise unreasonable attack on Foster. Musson's view was prefigured in idem, British Trade Unions, 1800-1875 (London: Macmillan, 1972), pp. 15-21, 50-55; idem, Trade Union and Social History (London: Cass, 1974), p. 19. Cf. Halévy, History, V, 248-49.
439 See Hobsbawm, Labouring Men, p. 353.

440 Turner, Trade Union Growth, pp. 110-11; Webb, Industrial Democracy, p. 323; Neil J. Smelser, Social Change in the Industrial Revolution (Chicago: University of Chicago Press, 1959), p. 329; Burgess, Origins, p. 244; Eduard Bernstein, "Technisch-ökonomischer und sozial-ökonomischer Fortschritt," Die Neue Zeit, XI, I (1893), 861; Gerhart von Schulze-Gaevernitz, Der Großbetrieb (Leipzig: Duncker & Humblot, 1898), p. 278.

441 Schloss, Methods of Industrial Remuneration, pp. 169-226.

442 Most commonly they were semi-autonomous workers and de facto foremen as well as wage workers.

443 A Contractor, "Communications on the Strike," The Builder, XVII, 862 (August 13, 1859), 530.

444 Frederick Harrison, "Remedies for Social Distress," Industrial Remuneration Conference, Report, p. 437.

445 See, for example, H.M. Hyndman, The Historical Basis of Socialism in England (London: Kegan, Paul, Trench, 1883), p. 287; Clementina Black, "The Coercion of Trade Unions," Contemporary Review, LXII (October 1892), 553.

446 See, for example, Report of the Seventeenth Annual Conference of the Social-Democratic Federation (n.p. (London: Twentieth Century Press, n.d. 1897)), p. 21.

447 Clegg, Fox and Thompson, History, I, 132, 457.

448 The Amalgamated Society of Engineers is often adduced in this context; see Rousiers, Le Trade-Unionisme, pp. 258-59; Webb, History of Trade Unionism, 1920 ed., pp. 406-407, 420-21; Halévy, History, V, 219-20.

449 Postgate, Builders' History, p. 345. Cf. G.D.H. Cole and W. Mellor, The Greater Unionism (Manchester and London: National Labour Press, 1913), p. 8.

450 Mortimer, History of the Boilermakers' Society, I, 109. On the more progressive position of the Steel Smelters, see Brandt, Gewerkschaftliche Interessenvertretung, pp. 282-85.

451 Jefferys, Story of the Engineers, p. 166; Webb, History of Trade Unionism, 1920 ed., p. 486; Clegg, Fox and Thompson, History, I, 137, 141-42, 444-45.

452 Royal Commission on Labour, Minutes of Evidence... before Group "A," Vol. III, Q. 20,531 at p. 27, Q. 20,805 at p. 44.

453 In 1899, the Amalgamated Society of Carpenters and Joiners collected more than three pounds in fees and dues from new members compared to less than two pounds collected by the Navvies', Bricklayers' Labourers' and General Labourers' Union; calculated according to data in Report by the Chief Labour Correspondent... 1899, pp. 242, 246. Other unions, such as the Engineers, exacted even higher fees; ibid., pp. 240-99.

454 The Cotton Spinners were particularly protective of their traditions; Clegg, Fox and Thompson, History, I, 112. The Steel Smelters proved to be unusually adaptive; Brandt, Gewerkschaftliche Interessenvertretung, p. 390, explains this development in part by reference to the origins of the labor aristocrats in the steel union: not only were they recruited from the ranks of the unskilled, they were also subject to discrimination on the part of the traditional labor aristocrats in the iron industry.

455 Eric Hobsbawm, in his review of Pelling, Popular Politics, in Society for the Study of Labour History Bulletin, No. 18, Spring 1969, p. 53, denies that between the Chartist period and World War I the labor aristocracy envisaged "anything except the improvement of labour's conditions within and as part of British liberal capitalism." The crux is whether labor aristocrats differed radically from non-aristocrats in this regard.

456 See chap. 5 sect. H above.
457 George Dangerfield, The Strange Death of Liberal England (New York: Capricorn, 1961 (1935)), pp. 214-330, offers a vivid account.
458 Hobsbawm, Labouring Men, p. 225.
459 Ibid., p. 217.
460 Ibid., p. 224.
461 Philip P. Poirier, The Advent of the British Labour Party (New York: Columbia University Press, 1958), pp. 139-40; Henry Pelling, The Origins of the Labour Party 1880-1900 (2nd ed.; Oxford: Clarendon, 1965 (1954)), p. 230; Clegg, Fox and Thompson, History, I, 374-76.
462 Clegg, Fox and Thompson, History, I, 54.
463 See, for example, B.C. Roberts, The Trades Union Congress 1868-1921 (London: Allen & Unwin, 1958), p. 191. On the proclivity of laborers to vote for the Tories, see J.R. Vincent, Pollbooks (Cambridge: Cambridge University Press, 1967), p. 17.
464 Hobsbawm, Labouring Men, p. 381; Clegg, Fox and Thompson, History, I, 291-304; Webb, History of Trade Unionism, 1920 ed., p. 676.
465 Halévy, History, V, 214-15; Webb, History of Trade Unionism, 1920 ed., p. 633. Clegg, Fox and Thompson, History, I, 305-422, especially I, 362-63, argue that employers did not take advantage of the opportunities afforded by the Taff Vale judgment to eliminate unions.
466 Rousiers, Labour Question, pp. 75, 362; Hobsbawm, Labouring Men, p. 230. But it is inaccurate to attribute the leftward swing after 1910 to an improvement--rather than to a deterioration--of the market position of the labor aristocracy. See, for example, David Unger, "Labor Aristocrats and Class Consciousness: Some British Patterns," International Labor and Working Class History, No. 13, May 1978, p. 28.
467 Pelling, Origins of the Labour Party, p. 199. Cf. Poirier, Advent of the British Labour Party, pp. 139-40; Hobsbawm, Labouring Men, p. 341. It is noteworthy that the unions of the semi-skilled, such as the Cotton Spinners and Miners, which had succeeded in obtaining the "ponderable and imponderable perquisites of the 'aristocrat of labour'" by assimilating their "position to that of the 'craftsman,'" were among the last to affiliate. See ibid., p. 216; Poirier, Advent of the British Labour Party, pp. 140-42. See R. Page Arnot, The Miners. A History of the Miners' Federation of Great Britain 1884-1910 (London: Allen & Unwin, 1949), passim. S.J. Chapman, "Some Policies of the Cotton Spinners' Trade Unions," Economic Journal, X (December 1900), 467-73, noted that piecers acquiesced in the spinners' domination because they aspired to the latter's position. Clegg, Fox and Thompson, History, I, 297, characterize socialist movements within some craft unions as quasi-opportunistic campaigns against the unskilled.
468 Clegg, Fox and Thompson, History, I, 294; Deian Hopkin, "The Membership of the Independent Labour Party, 1904-10," International Review of Social History, XX, Pt. 2 (1975), 191.
469 Richard Price, An Imperial War and the British Working Class (London: Routledge & Kegan Paul, 1972); Karl Kautsky, "Der Krieg in Südafrika," Die Neue Zeit, XVII, I (1898-1899), 196-203.
470 Report of Proceedings at the Forty-Seventh Annual Trades Union Congress (London: Cooperative Printing Society, 1915), pp. 317-38.
471 Clegg, Fox and Thompson, History, I, 471.
472 G.D.H. Cole, A Short History of the British Working-Class Movement 1789-1947 (London: Allen & Unwin, 1952 (1925)), pp. 317-27.
473 See Clegg, Fox and Thompson, History, I, 471-73, on the "failure of collective bargaining."

474 Even prior to the advent of New Unionism and the mass organization of the unskilled, some unemployed artisans participated in the demonstrations and riots during the depression of the 1880s; see "The Unemployed in London," (London) Times, February 9, 1886, p. 6; "The Riots in London," ibid., February 11, 1886, p. 6. Booth, ed., Labour and Life of the People, I, 597-98, saw "the springs of Socialism and Revolution" in the conditions confronting the regularly employed semi-skilled and unskilled workers.

Notes to Part II

1 Jack London, War of the Classes (New York: Grosset and Dunlap, 1908 (1905)), p. 73.

1 Wolfram Fischer, Wirtschaft und Gesellschaft im Zeitalter der Industrialisierung (Göttingen: Vandenhoeck & Ruprecht, 1972), pp. 258-84.

2 In 1871 one-half of the occupied population in Germany was found in agricultural pursuits compared to one-seventh in England and Wales. See Hoffmann, Wachstum, Table 20 at pp. 204-205; Booth, "Occupations," pp. 426-27; calculations by author. Cf. Walther Hoffmann, Stadien und Typen der Industrialisierung (Jena: Fischer, 1931), passim.

3 See Hans Mottek, Wirtschaftsgeschichte Deutschlands, II (Berlin (DDR): VEB Deutscher Verlag der Wissenschaften, 1972), 229; A. Sartorius von Waltershausen, Deutsche Wirtschaftsgeschichte 1815-1914 (Jena; Fischer, 1920), p. 145; Walter Becker, "Die Bedeutung der nichtagrarischen Wanderungen für die Herausbildung des industriellen Proletariats in Deutschland, unter besonderer Berücksichtigung Preussens von 1850 bis 1870," Studien zur Geschichte der industriellen Revolution in Deutschland, ed. Hans Mottek (Berlin (DDR): Akademie, 1960), pp. 109-40; J.J. Lee, "Labour in German Industrialization," Cambridge Economic History of Europe, Vol. VII, Pt. i, pp. 442-91, 703-709.

4 Friedrich Engels, "Germany. Revolution and Counter-Revolution," New-York Daily Tribune, October 25, 1851; cited here according to the German translation, Revolution und Konterrevolution in Deutschland, MEW, VIII, 10-11. Although it originally appeared over Marx's name, this series of articles, which was published in book form in 1896, was written by Engels.

5 R. Engelsing, "Zur politischen Bildung der deutschen Unterschichten 1789-1863," Historische Zeitschrift, CCVI, 2 (April 1968), 353-54; Werner Conze, "Vom 'Pöbel' zum Proletariat," Moderne deutsche Sozialgeschichte, ed. Hans-Ulrich Wehler (5th ed.: Cologne: Kiepenheuer & Witsch, 1976), pp. 111-36; this article first appeared in Vierteljahrsschrift für Sozial- und Wirtschaftsgeschichte, XLI (1954), 336-64. Cf. Werner Conze, "Möglichkeiten und Grenzen der liberalen Arbeiterbewegung in Deutschland. Das Beispiel Schulze-Delitzschs," Sitzungsbericht der Heidelberger Akademie der Wissenschaften, Philosophisch-Historische Klasse, 1965, 2. Abhandlung, passim; Wilhelm Treue, Gesellschaft, Wirtschaft und Technik Deutschlands im 19. Jahrhundert (Munich: DTV, 1977 (1970)), p. 89; Rudolf Stadelmann, "Soziale Ursachen der Revolution von 1848," Moderne deutsche Sozialgeschichte, p. 144; this article is excerpted from Rudolf Stadelmann, Soziale und politische Geschichte der Revolution von 1848 (Munich, 1948); Wilhelm Wortmann, Eisenbahnbauarbeiter im Vormärz (Cologne: Böhlau, 1972).

6 (G.W.) v. Viebahn, "Die gegenwärtigen Bewegungen unter den Gewerbetreibenden und gewerblichen Arbeitern und die zur Hebung ihrer Lage gemachten Vorschläge und Veranstaltungen," Mittheilungen des Centralvereins für das Wohl der arbeitende Classe, Vol. I: 1848-1849 (Berlin: Veit, 1849), pp. 155-56. Cf. C.F.W. Dieterici, Handbuch der Statistik des preussischen Staats (Berlin: Mittler, 1861), pp. 400-406; Gustav Schmoller, Zur Geschichte der deutschen Kleingewerbe im 19. Jahrhundert (Halle: Verlag der Buchhandlung des Waisenhauses, 1870), pp. 65, 71, 105, 126-27, 369-72 and passim.

7 For data on other Zollverein states, see Georg Neuhaus, "Die berufliche und soziale Gliederung der Bevölkerung im Zeitalter des Kapitalismus," "Grundriss der Sozialökonomik, IX. Abteilung: Das soziale System des Kapitalismus, Pt. I: Die gesellschaftliche Schichtung im Kapitalismus (Tübingen: Mohr, 1926), pp. 364-67.

8 See Conze, "Vom 'Pöbel' zum Proletariat," p. 122; Jürgen Kuczynski, Die Geschichte der Lage der Arbeiter unter dem Kapitalismus, Vol. I: Darstellung der Lage der Arbeiter in Deutschland von 1789 bis 1849 (Berlin

(DDR): Akademie, 1961), p. 220; Karl Obermann, Die deutschen Arbeiter in der Revolution von 1848 (2nd ed.; Berlin (DDR): Dietz, 1953 (1950)), p. 28; idem, "Zur Klassenstruktur und zur sozialen Lage der Bevölkerung in Preussen 1846 bis 1849," Jahrbuch für Wirtschaftsgeschichte, 1973, Part II, pp. 79-120, especially p. 85; P.H. Noyes, Organization and Revolution. Working-Class Associations in the German Revolutions of 1848-1849 (Princeton: Princeton University Press, 1966), p. 21; Theodore S. Hamerow, The Social Foundations of German Unification 1858-1871. Ideas and Institutions (Princeton: Princeton University Press, 1969), pp. 44-83; Becker, "Die Bedeutung der nichtagrarischen Wanderungen," pp. 212-17. For a different view of the advances that the antagonism between labor and capital had made by 1848, see "Die socialen Bewegungen der Gegenwart," Die Gegenwart. Eine encyclopädische Darstellung der neuesten Zeitgeschichte für alle Stände, I (Leipzig: Brockhaus, 1848), p. 88. The anonymous author of this article may have been Lorenz von Stein to judge by the similar language and concepts used by him in his Geschichte der sozialen Bewegung in Frankreich von 1789 bis auf unsere Tage (3 vols.; Hildesheim: Olms, 1959 (1850)).

9 Stadelmann, "Soziale Ursachen," p. 485 n. 13.

10 The contemporary political figure, Stephan Born, Erinnerungen eines Achtundvierzigers (2nd ed.; Leipzig: Meyer, 1898), p. 122, singled out the machinists and printers of Berlin.

11 Theodore S. Hamerow, Restoration, Revolution, Reaction: Economics and Politics in Germany, 1815-1871 (Princeton: Princeton University Press, 1958), pp. 36, 80, 140. Cf. idem, "The German Artisan Movement 1848-49," Journal of Central European Affairs, XXI, 2 (July 1961), 135-52; idem, Social Foundations. Ideas and Institutions, pp. 222-23.

12 See, however, Carl Friedrich von Rumohr, ed., Schule der Höflichkeit für Alt und Jung (2nd ed.; Munich: Medler, n.d. (lst ed.: 1834-35)), pp. 55-56, 61.

13 Mottek, Wirtschaftsgeschichte Deutschlands, II, 229. Cf. Martin Kitchen, The Political Economy of Germany 1815-1914 (London: Croom Helm, 1978), pp. 71-72; Stadelmann, "Soziale Ursachen," p. 148; Alan S. Milward and S.B. Saul, The Economic Development of Continental Europe 1780-1870 (London: Allen & Unwin, 1973), p. 427.

14 Mottek, Wirtschaftsgeschichte Deutschlands, II, 230.

15 Empirically, the record of political militancy among artisans and industrial workers during the revolution of 1848 is controversial. See Hamerow, Restoration, pp. 79-80; Noyes, Organization, p. 265; Obermann, Die deutschen Arbeiter, pp. 175, 320; idem, Deutschland von 1815 bis 1849 (Berlin (DDR): VEB Deutscher Verlag der Wissenschaften, 1967), pp. 311-12.

16 Mottek, Wirtschaftsgeschichte Deutschlands, II, 235-36. For a comprehensive description of living and working conditions, see Pierre Benaerts, Les Origines de la grande industrie allemande (Paris: Turot, 1933), pp. 575-621; Kuczynski, Deutschland von 1789 bis 1849, pp. 215-372; Obermann, "Zur Klassenstruktur und zur sozialen Lage der Bevölkerung in Preussen 1846 bis 1849. Die Einkommensverhältnisse in Gewerbe und Industrie," Jahrbuch für Wirtschaftsgeschichte, 1973, Part III, pp. 143-76.

17 See v. Viebahn, "Die gegenwärtigen Bewegungen," pp. 155-56; Hoffmann, Wachstum, Table 16 at pp. 196-97; Mottek, Wirtschaftsgeschichte Deutschlands, II, 187-90, 231.

18 Schmoller, Zur Geschichte der deutschen Kleingewerbe, passim; idem, Grundriss der allgemeinen Volkswirtschaftslehre (erster, größere Teil; Berlin: Duncker & Humblot, 1901 (1900)), p. 421.

19 Schmoller, Zur Geschichte der deutschen Kleingewerbe, p. 350. For an exaggerated literary account of the reaction of a small master and his employees to the onslaught of industrial competition, see Max Kretzer, Meister Timpe (Berlin: Fischer, 1888).

20 Elisabeth Todt and Hans Radandt, Zur Frühgeschichte der deutschen Gewerkschaftsbewegung 1800-1849 (Berlin (DDR): Freie Gewerkschaften, 1950), p. 103. The combination laws were not repealed until the industrial code of the North German Confederation went into effect in 1869. See Dieter Fricke, Die deutsche Arbeiterbewegung 1869-1914 (Berlin (DDR): Dietz, 1976), pp. 623-24; Theodore S. Hamerow, The Social Foundations of German Unification 1858-1871. Struggles and Accomplishments (Princeton: Princeton University Press, 1972), pp. 337-83; Karl Korsch, Arbeitsrecht für Betriebsräte (Frankfurt/Main: Europäische Verlagsanstalt, 1969 (1922)), pp. 66-88; Karl Erich Born, "Der soziale und wirtschaftliche Strukturwandel Deutschlands am Ende des 19. Jahrhunderts," Moderne deutsche Sozialgeschichte, pp. 275-76; this article first appeared in Vierteljahrsschrift für Sozial- und Wirtschaftsgeschichte, L (1963), 361-76; Mottek, Wirtschaftsgeschichte Deutschlands, II, 243-53.

21 See however Born, Erinnerungen, pp. 134-35.

22 In the ante-bellum South, American slaveowners suggested to white workers that the latter constituted a labor aristocracy in relation to slaves; at the same time "masters helped to create a social hierarchy" among slaves in which "the domestics, artisans, and foremen constituted the aristocracy. ..." See Kenneth Stampp, The Peculiar Institution (New York: Vintage, n.d. (1st ed.: 1956)), pp. 333, 337; Robert S. Starobin, Industrial Slavery in the Old South (London: Oxford University Press, 1970), pp. 144-45, 209-14; Bernard Mandel, Labor: Free and Slave (New York: Associated Authors, 1955), p. 57; Eugene D. Genovese, The Political Economy of Slavery (New York: Vintage, 1967 (1961)), pp. 180-239; idem, Roll, Jordan, Roll. The World the Slaves Made (New York: Vintage, 1976 (1972)), pp. 393-94.

23 On ancient Rome, see Heinrich Wilhelm Bensen, Die Proletarier (Stuttgart: Franck, 1847), pp. 100-133; Perry Anderson, Passages from Antiquity to Feudalism (London: Verso, 1978 (1974)), pp. 53-82.

24 For an example of a firm-level "'Aristocracy of Trade,'" see (United States) House of Representatives, State of Labor in Europe: 1878, 46th Cong., 1st Sess., Executive Document No. 5 (Washington, 1879), pp. 130-31.

25 See Klaus Saul, Staat, Industrie, Arbeiterbewegung im Kaiserreich (Düsseldorf: Bertelsmann, 1974), p. 187.

26 Lenin often argued in this undifferentiated manner. See, for example, "Mezhdunarodnyi sotsialisticheckii kongress v Shtutgarte," PSS, XVI, 72.

27 Todt and Radandt, Zur Frühgeschichte, passim.

28 See Franz Mehring, Geschichte der deutschen Sozialdemokratie, II (Berlin (DDR): Dietz, 1960 (1897-1898)), 316; Fricke, Die deutsche Arbeiterbewegung, pp. 624-53; Werner Ettelt and Hans-Dieter Krause, Der Kampf um eine marxistische Gewerkschaftspolitik in der deutschen Arbeiterbewegung 1868 bis 1878 (Berlin (DDR): Tribüne, 1975), p. 193. Cf. Walther Frisch, "Die Organisationsbestrebungen der Arbeiter in der deutschen Tabakindustrie" (Inaugural-Dissertation, Friedrich-Wilhelm University, Berlin, 1905), passim; Todt and Radandt, Zur Frühgeschichte, pp. 94-95.

29 The data were compiled by August Geib and first published in Pionier, January 26, 1878; cited here according to the reproduction in Correspondenzblatt der Generalkommission der Gewerkschaften Deutschlands, III, 30 (December 18, 1893), 1-5.

30 Alfred Förster, Die Gewerkschaftspolitik der deutschen Sozialdemokratie während des Sozialistengesetzes (Berlin (DDR): Tribüne, 1971), p. 174, attributes the article, which is discussed below, to Eduard Bernstein; on the latter's editorship, see Pierre Angel, Eduard Bernstein et l'évolution du socialisme allemand (Paris: Didier, 1961), pp. 72-79.

31 Leo, "Auf gefährlichem Wege," Der Sozialdemokrat, No. 41, October 4, 1883, p. 1.

32 Ibid., p. 2.

33 Data from 1896, however, cast some doubt on this claim. Although the Printers collected more than fifty-three marks per member in dues that year, most unions exacted annual dues totaling five to ten marks while the Miners paid less than two marks. See C. Legien, "Die Gewerkschafts-Bewegung in Deutschland im Jahre 1896," Die Neue Zeit, XVI, I (1897-1898), 54. Given an annual average labor income of 758 marks in the industrial and craft sectors in 1896, dues constituted about one per cent of a worker's income. See Hoffmann, Wachstum, Table 108 at pp. 470-71. See also Paul Umbreit, 25 Jahre Deutscher Gewerkschaftsbewegung 1890-1915 (Berlin: Generalkommission der Gewerkschaften Deutschlands, 1915), p. 30.

34 "Auf gefährlichem Wege," p. 2.

35 See Karl Marx and Friedrich Engels, Manifest der Kommunistischen Partei, MEW, IV, 468-72.

36 See Engels, Revolution und Konterrevolution in Deutschland, MEW, VIII, 11.

37 See Theodor Cassau, Die Gewerkschaftsbewegung (Halberstadt: Meyer, 1925), pp. 2, 30.

38 Cf. Edward Shorter and Charles Tilly, Strikes in France 1830-1968 (London: Cambridge University Press, 1974), p. 349.

39 Mehring, Geschichte, II, 469.

40 Ernst Engelberg, Revolutionäre Politik und Rote Feldpost 1878-1890 (Berlin (DDR): Akademie, 1959), p. 138.

41 Ibid., p. 137.

42 Mehring, Geschichte, II, 104, instanced shoemaking. Spinners, weavers, brewers, glaziers and hatters had been adversely affacted earlier in the nineteenth century; by the end of the century potters, wheelwrights, cabinetmakers and locksmiths suffered the same fate at the hands of industrial capitalism. See Paul Voigt, "Das deutsche Handwerk nach den Berufszählungen von 1882 und 1895," Schriften des Vereins für Socialpolitik, Vol. LXX: Untersuchungen über die Lage des Handwerks in Deutschland mit besonderer Rücksicht auf seine Konkurrenzfähigkeit gegenüber der Großindustrie, Vol. 9: Verschiedene Staaten (Leipzig: Duncker & Humblot, 1897), pp. 665-67. Cf. Otto Thissen, Beiträge zur Geschichte des Handwerks in Preußen (Tübingen: Laupp, 1901), passim.

43 This was particularly the case in the building trades. See Dieterici, Handbuch, pp. 381, 405-406; Karl Heinrich Kaufhold, "Das preussische Handwerk in der Zeit der Frühindustrialisierung. Eine Untersuchung nach den Preussischen Gewerbetabellen 1815-1858," Beiträge zu Wirtschaftswachstum und Wirtschaftsstruktur im 16. und 19. Jahrhundert, ed. Wolfram Fischer ((West) Berlin: Duncker & Humblot, 1971), Table 1 at p. 172 and Table 2 at p. 175; Hamerow, Social Foundations. Ideas and Institutions, pp. 44-83, especially pp. 70-72. See also Preussische Statistik, XXX: Die Ergebnisse der Volkszählung und Volksbeschreibung im preussischen Staate vom 1. Dezember 1871 (Berlin: Königliches Statistisches Bureau, 1875), 237.

44 See Mottek, Wirtschaftsgeschichte Deutschlands, II, 45-46; for a later
period, see Theodor Geiger, Die soziale Schichtung des deutschen Volkes
(Darmstadt. Wissenschaftliche Buchgesellschaft, 1972 (1932)), p. 92. See
also J. Wernicke, Kapitalismus und Mittelstandspolitik (2nd ed.; Jena:
Fischer, 1922 (1907)). For a theoretical treatment, see Emil Grünberg,
Der Mittelstand in der kapitalistischen Gesellschaft (Leipzig: Hirschfeld,
1932); Annette Leppert-Fögen, Die deklassierte Klasse (Frankfurt/Main:
Fischer, 1974).

45 Milward and Saul, Economic Development, pp. 415-16; Mehring, Geschichte, I, 421-24; Hamerow, Social Foundations. Struggles and Accomplishments,
pp. 49-97, 192-237, 337-83.

46 Wolfgang Schröder, Klassenkämpfe und Gewerkschaftseinheit (Berlin (DDR):
Tribüne, 1965), p. 63.

47 See Engelberg, Rote Feldpost, p. 138.

48 See Fritz Paeplow, Die Organisation der Maurer Deutschlands von 1869
bis 1899 (Hamburg: Bömelburg, 1900), p. 301; Schröder, Klassenkämpfe,
p. 29; "Karl Marx und die Gewerkschaften," Der Grundstein, XXVI, 16
(April 19, 1913), 186-87.

49 See however Julius Goldstein, Arbeiter und Unterehmer im Baugewerbe
Deutschlands, Zürcher Volkswirtschaftliche Studien, Fasc. 5, ed. H.
Sieviking (Zurich and Leipzig, 1913), p. 86.

50 Marx, "Inauguraladresse," MEW, XVI, 12.

51 Although the leading German industrial enterprises had, by 1900, exceeded
their British competitors in size, the work force in the chemical and electrical industries, which formed the basis of Germany's science-based sector,
was largely unorganized. See Knut Borchard, "The Industrial Revolution
in Germany 1700-1914," The Fontana Economic History of Europe, ed.
Carlo M. Cipolla, Vol. 4: The Emergence of Industrial Societies, Part 1
(Glasgow: Fontana, 1975 (1973)), pp. 133-35. Cf. Schröder, Klassenkämpfe, p. 66.

52 Cf. Erhard Lucas, Zwei Formen von Radikalismus in der deutschen Arbeiterbewegung (Frankfurt/Main: Roter Stern, 1976), p. 285.

53 In the 1840s, guild members represented the bulk of those belonging to
artisans' education societies; some of these were criticized at the time for
nurturing an "aristocracy of mama's boys." See Ernst Dronke, Berlin, II
(Frankfurt/Main: Rütten, 1846), 161.

54 Mehring, Geschichte, II, 15. Cf. Hamerow, Social Foundations. Struggles
and Accomplishments, p. 197.

55 On the specific capitalist costs of industrialization, see Barrington Moore,
Jr., Social Origins of Dictatorship and Democracy (Boston: Beacon, 1967
(1966)).

56 In addition to the literature on Britain cited above in chaps. 2-5, see
Arnold Toynbee, The Industrial Revolution (Boston: Beacon, 1956 (1884));
J.L. Hammond and Barbara Hammond, The Village Labourer (new ed.;
London: Longmans, 1913 (1911)); Karl Polanyi, The Great Transformation
(Boston: Beacon, 1971 (1944)).

57 Mehring, Geschichte, II, 19.

58 Hermann Müller, Geschichte der deutschen Gewerkschaften bis zum Jahre
1878 (Berlin: Vorwärts, 1918), pp. 27-30, 47-55.

59 Mehring, Geschichte, II, 104-106. Alfred Schröter and Walter Becker,
Die deutsche Maschinenbauindustrie in der industriellen Revolution (Berlin (DDR): Akademie, 1962), pp. 75-84, 221-49, do not confirm this picture
of a conservative body of workers.

60 See Ettelt and Krause, Kampf, pp. 253-54. For data on wage differentials
between skilled and unskilled workers after 1870, see Gerhard Bry, Wages

in Germany 1871-1945 (Princeton: Princeton University Press, 1960), Table A-14 at p. 365.
61 Kuczynski, Deutschland von 1789 bis 1849, pp. 352-53; idem, Die Geschichte der Lage der Arbeiter unter dem Kapitalismus, Vol. II; Darstellung der Lage der Arbeiter in Deutschland von 1849 bis 1870 (Berlin (DDR): Akademie, 1962), p. 164, concludes that wage differentials shrank along with skill differentials.
62 Hans Rosenberg, "Wirtschaftskonjunktur, Gesellschaft und Politik in Mitteleuropa, 1873 bis 1896," Moderne deutsche Sozialgeschichte, pp. 237-39.
63 Ashok V. Desai, Real Wages in Germany 1871-1913 (Oxford: Oxford University Press, 1968), Table 4.1 at p. 36.
64 Hoffmann, Wachstum, Table 23 at p. 87.
65 Müller, Geschichte der deutschen Gewerkschaften, pp. 155-61.
66 Mehring, Geschichte, II, 304. The Socialist Labor party, which was the product of the merger of the two major socialist parties in 1875, counted fewer than 25,000 members that year. Fricke, Die deutsche Arbeiterbewegung, pp. 92. In 1878, the British Amalgamated Society of Engineers alone could boast of almost as many members (45,408) as the entire German trade union movement (49,055). See Amalgamated Society of Engineers, Jubilee Souvenir, 1901 (London: Co-Operative, 1901). p. 126; Fricke, Die deutsche Arbeiterbewegung, pp. 650-52.
67 Fricke, Die deutsche Arbeiterbewegung, pp. 653-54; Umbreit, 25 Jahre, pp. 3-4.
68 The Printers appear to have been an exception; Fricke, Die deutsche Arbeiterbewegung, pp. 654-55.
69 See the criticism of Heinrich Oehme in "Auf gefährlichem Wege," p. 1.
70 Ibid., p. 2.
71 For a latter-day restatement of this view, see Ralf Dahrendorf, Class and Class Conflict in Industrial Society (Stanford: Stanford University Press, 1975 (1959)), p. 62.
72 Dieter Groh, Negative Integration und revolutionärer Attentismus (Frankfurt/Main: Ullstein, 1973), p. 35.
73 This transformation occurred during the 1920s. See Fritz Naphtali, Wirtschaftsdemokratie (2nd ed.; Berlin: Allgemeiner Deutscher gewerkschaftsbund, 1928). Cf. the critique by F. David, Der Bankrott des Reformismus (Berlin: Internationaler Arbeiter-Verlag, 1932), pp. 85-108.
74 See Bebel's speech in Bericht über die Verhandlungen des Parteitages der Deutschen Sozialdemokratie. Abgehalten zu Schoenewegen bei St. Gallen vom 2. bis 6. Oktober 1887 (St. Gallen, 1887), p. 55; cf. Alfred Marshall, Industry and Trade (London: Macmillan, 1932 (1919)), pp. 640-41.
75 Cf. Alexander Helphand (Parvus), Gewerkschaften und die Sozialdemokratie (Dresden: Kaden, 1896).
76 Rosa Luxemburg, "Arbeiterbewegung und Sozialdemokratie," Leipziger Volkszeitung, No. 125, June 4, 1902; cited here according to Rosa Luxemburg, Gesammelte Werke, I: 2 (Berlin (DDR): Dietz, 1970), 256.
77 See L. Bergsträsser, Geschichte der politischen Parteien in Deutschland (6th ed.; Mannheim: Bensheimer, 1932 (1920)), pp. 114-39.
78 See Karl Zwing, Geschichte der deutschen freien Gewerkschaften (Jena: Fischer, 1922), p. 93.
79 See Bergsträsser, Geschichte, p. 128. Cf. Max Weber's inaugural lecture at Freiburg in 1895, "Der Nationalstaat und die Volkswirtschaftspolitik," Gesammelte Politische Schriften (2nd ed.; Tübingen: Mohr, 1958 (1921)), pp. 23-24.
80 Born, "Strukturwandel," pp. 274-75; Gerhard A. Ritter and Klaus Tenfelde, "Der Durchbruch der Freien Gewerkschaften Deutschlands zur Mas-

senbewegung im letzten Viertel des 19. Jahrhunderts," Vom Sozialistenge-
setz zur Mitbestimmung, ed. Heinz O. Vetter (Cologne: Bund, 1975),
pp. 61-120; Wolfgang Schröder, Partei und Gewerkschaft. Die Gewerkschaftsbewegung in der Konzeption der revolutionären Sozialdemokratie
1868/69 bis 1893 (Berlin (DDR): Tribüne, 1975); Barbara Klaus, Zur Entwicklung von Organisation und Konzeption der freien Gewerkschaften
1875 bis 1893) (Offenbach: 2000, 1976).
81 Rudolf Schlesinger, Central European Democracy and its Background (London: Routledge & Kegan Paul, 1953), p. 49.
82 Calculated according to the data presented by B.R. Mitchell, "Statistical
Appendix," Fontana Economic History of Europe, Vol. 4, Table I at p. 747.
83 Sources: Deane and Cole, British Economic Growth, Table 30 and at
pp. 142-43; Hoffmann, Wachstum, Table 20 at p. 205. Calculations by
author.
84 Hoffmann, Wachstum, p. 205; Deane and Cole, British Economic Growth,
p. 142. The data in the text refer to 1907 for Germany and to 1911 for
Britain.
85 As late as the 1890s guild membership exceeded that of the trade unions.
See Noyes, Organization, p. 374.
86 Sources: (United Kingdom), Department of Employment and Productivity,
British Labour Statistics. Historical Abstract 1886-1968 (London: HMSO,
1971), Table 196 at p. 395; Umbreit, 25 Jahre, Appendix Table 5 at p. 172.
In 1913 the free trade unions accounted for more than two-thirds of total
German trade union membership. See Emil Lederer and Jakob Marschak,
"Die Klassen auf dem Arbeitsmarkt und ihre Organisationen," Grundriß
der Sozialökonomik. IX. Abteilung: Das soziale System des Kapitalismus,
Pt. II. Die autonome und staatliche Binnenpolitik im Kapitalismus (Tübingen: Mohr, 1927), p. 143.
87 British Labour Statistics, Table 197 at p. 396; Umbreit, 25 Jahre, Appendix Table 6 at p. 173.
88 H.A. Clegg, Alan Fox and A.F. Thompson, A History of British Trade
Unions since 1889, Vol. I: 1889-1910 (Oxford: Clarendon, 1964), pp. 466-
67. Webb, History of Trade Unionism, 1902 ed., p. 411, estimated that
one fifth of adult male manual workers was organized in 1892.
89 The figure mentioned in the text was arrived at in the following way.
The 6,697 female members of central unions were deducted, leaving
252,478 males; see Umbreit, 25 Jahre, Appendix Table 5 at p. 172. According to the census of 1895, 4,710,480 males sixteen years and older
were employed in industry as journeymen and workers; see Kaiserliches
Statistisches Amt, Statistisches Jahrbuch für das Deutsche Reich, Vol. 31,
1910 (Berlin, 1910), p. 68. Then the 35,271 males sixteen years and
older who were related to their employers were deducted; see Georg Neuhaus, Die deutsche Volkswirtschaft und ihre Wandlungen im letzten Vie-
teljahrhundert, Vol. II: Landwirtschaft und Gewerbe (M. Gladbach: Volksvereins-Verlag, 1913), Table 42 at p. 182. There thus remained 4,675,209
adult males. For historical and critical methodological accounts of the German censuses, see Die Statistik in Deutschland nach ihrem heutigen Stand,
ed. Friedrich Zahn II (Munich and Berlin: Schweitzer, 1911), 3-44, 181-
234. Legien, "Die Gewerkschafts-Bewegung," pp. 52-53, estimated that
6.24 per dent of occupied males were organized in 1896.
90 The sources and procedures duplicate those of the preceding note. Cf.
Handwörterbuch der Staatswissenschaften, 3rd ed., s.v. "Die Gewerkvereine in Deutschland," IV, 1175.
91 Census of England and Wales, 1911, Vol. X: Occupations and Industries,
Part I (London: HMSO, 1914), p. 543.

92 Neuhaus, Die deutsche Volkswirtschaft, II, 72, Table 28.
93 Ernst Engelberg, Deutschland von 1871 bis 1897 (Berlin (DDR): VEB Deutscher Verlag der Wissenschaften, 1967), p. 356, loses sight of this fact. Cf. however Fricke, Die deutsche Arbeiterbewegung, pp. 690-93.
94 Legien, "Die Gewerkschafts-Bewegung," p. 53. Cf. R. Calwer and J. Jastrow, "Gewerkschaften. Einzelne Gewerbe," Schriften des Vereins für Sozialpolitik, Vol. CIX: Die Störungen im deutschen Wirtschaftsleben während der Jahre 1900ff., Vol. 5 (Leipzig: Duncker & Humblot, 1903), pp. 134-35, 138.
95 "Die deutschen Gewerkschaftsorganisationen im Jahre 1902," Correspondenzblatt, XIII, 33 (August 15, 1903), 516-17. Alexander Helphand (Parvus), Die große Aussperrung und die Zukunft der Arbeiterkämpfe im Reiche (Dresden: Kaden, n.d. (1910)), p. 58, maintained that industries operating large units with many unskilled workers (such as the chemical industry) were the most difficult to organize, but that trades with a large proportion of craft workers employed in small units (such as baking) were also difficult to organize. The building trades contradicted this latter pattern. See Jürgen Kuczynski, Die Geschichte der Lage der Arbeiter unter dem Kapitalismus, Vol. 3: Darstellung der Lage der Arbeiter in Deutschland von 1871 bis 1900 (Berlin (DDR): Akademie, 1962), pp. 287-88; Lederer and Marschak, "Die Klassen auf dem Arbeitsmarkt," p. 162; Fritz Paeplow, Zur Geschichte der deutschen Bauarbeiterbewegung (Berlin: Deutscher Baugewerkbund, n.d. (1932)), pp. 462-64; Gerhard A. Ritter, Die Arbeiterbewegung im Wilhelminischen Reich (2nd ed.; (West) Berlin: Colloquium, 1963 (1959)), p. 112; Heinrich Schild, Das Lohn- und Arbeitsverhältnis im deutschen Malergewerbe des zwanzigsten Jahrhunderts unter dem Einfluß der Arbeitnehmer- und Arbeitgeberverbände (Hannover: Georgi, n.d. (1922)), p. 89.
96 See Protokoll über die Verhandlungen des Parteitages der Sozialdemokratischen Partei Deutschlands. Abgehalten zu Halle a.S. vom 12. bis 18. Oktober 1890 (Berlin: Vorwärts, 1890), p. 214.
97 See Protokoll über die Verhandlungen des Parteitages der Sozialdemokratischen Partei Deutschlands. Abgehalten zu Köln a.Rh. vom 22. bis 28. Oktober 1893 (Berlin: Vorwärts, 1893), pp. 180-223.
98 Ibid., pp. 198-202. A resolution that would have obligated members to join trade unions was voted down; ibid., pp. 221-22.
99 See Eduard Bernstein, "Die soziale Differenzierung in der modernen Arbeiterschaft," Jahrbuch der Angestelltenbewegung, (Vol. 6) (Berlin: Industrie-Beamten-Verlag, 1912), p. 313; Robert Michels, Zur Soziologie des Parteiwesens in der modernen Demokratie (Leipzig: Klinkhardt, 1911), p. 358 n. 1.
100 See Karl Kautsky, "Die Neutralisirung der Gewerkschaften. I," Die Neue Zeit, XVIII, II (1899-1900), 389-90.
101 Kautsky, "Neutralisirung," p. 389.
102 See Bebel's statement in Protokoll über die Verhandlungen des Parteitages der Sozialdemokratischen Partei Deutschlands. Abgehalten zu Hannover vom 9. bis 14. Oktober 1899 (Berlin: Vorwärts, 1899), p. 117. At Siemens alone 27,000 employees were members of the company union. See Lederer and Marschak, "Die Klassen auf dem Arbeitsmarkt," pp. 185-90.
103 See the references to Denmark in chapter 10 below.
104 See Protokoll über die Verhandlungen des Parteitages der Sozialdemokratischen Partei Deutschlands. Abgehalten zu Lübeck vom 22. bis 28. september 1901 (Berlin: Vorwärts, 1901), p. 293.
105 The party could, according to Kautsky, make a revolution as little as the bourgeoisie could prevent one. See Karl Kautsky, "Ein sozialdemo-

kratischer Katechismus," Die Neue Zeit, XII, I (1893-1894), 368. Cf. Bebel's speech in Protokoll über die Verhandlungen des Parteitages der Sozialdemokratischen Partei Deutschlands. Abgehalten zu Jena vom 17. bis 23. September 1905 (Berlin: Vorwärts, 1905), p. 292.

106 Although Legien told a party convention that no trade union leader had ever claimed that unions were anything but palliatives within bourgeois society, this view did not always guide union policy. See Protokoll, 1893, p. 184; John Anthony Moses, "'Carl Legiens Interpretation des demokratischen Sozialismus.' Ein Beitrag zur sozialistischen Ideengeschichte" (Inaugural-Dissertation, Erlangen University, 1965), pp. 186-89.

107 On the exceptional position of the Printers, see August Quist, "Zur Kritik des Gewerkschaftswesens," Die Neue Zeit, XX, I (1901-1902), 242-46.

108 At the time of the amalgamation of the Construction Workers and the Masons it was pointed out that the largely unskilled and low-paid workers in the former organization had been paying higher dues than the organized masons. See Deutscher Bauarbeiterverband, Protokoll über die Verhandlungen des konstituierenden Verbandtages. Abgehalten vom 10. bis 12. Februar 1910 in Leipzig (Hamburg: Bömelburg, 1910), p. 176.

109 See Sidney Pollard, The Genesis of Modern Management (Cambridge, Mass.: Harvard University Press, 1965).

110 See Bernstein, "Die soziale Differenzierung," pp. 306-307; Brandt, Gewerkschaftliche Interessenvertretung, pp. 63-72; cf. chap. 7 above.

111 Schlesinger, Central European Democracy, pp. 63-64.

112 Fricke, Die deutsche Arbeiterbewegung, p. 698. Cf. Karl Kautsky, "Verelendung und Zusammenbruch," Die Neue Zeit, XXVI, II (1907-1908), 548; Protokoll der Verhandlungen des elften Kongresses der Gewerkschaften Deutschlands (1. Bundestag des Allgemeinen Deutschen Gewerkschaftsbundes. Abgehalten zu Leipzig vom 19. bis 24. Juni 1922 (Berlin: ADGB, 1922), pp. 528-29.

113 Karl Heinz Roth, Die "andere" Arbeiterbewegung (4th ed.; Munich: Trikont, 1977 (1974)), pp. 21-25, 36-38. For a trenchant critique, see Heiner Minssen and Werner Sauerborn, "Der Massenarbeiter und das Kapital," Gesellschaft. Beiträge zur Marxschen Theorie 10 (Frankfurt/Main: Suhrkamp, 1977), pp. 141-86.

114 Roth, Die "andere" Arbeiterbewegung, p. 22.

115 Calculated according to data in Fricke, Die deutsche Arbeiterbewegung, Table 102 at p. 672 and Table 105 at p. 698.

116 Calculated according to ibid., Table 105 at pp. 696-99. According to the census of 1907, 61.2 per cent of male, nonfamilial industrial workers had preparatory training; although this proportion had been still higher in 1895, the absolute number of such workers rose by nearly one million between the two censuses. See Kaiserliches Statistisches Amt, Statistik des Deutschen Reiches, N.S., Vol. 102: Berufs- und Gewerbezählung vom 14. Juni 1895. Berufsstatistik für das Reich im Ganzen, Part I (Berlin: Puttkammer & Mühlbrecht, 1897), pp. 8-111; idem, ibid., N.S., Vol. 202,1: Berufs- und Betriebszählung vom 12. Juni 1907 (Berlin: Puttkammer & Mühlbrecht, 1909), pp. 41*, 8-17. Cf. Bernstein, "Die soziale Differenzierung," pp. 290-300; Wilhelm Heinz Schröder, Arbeitergeschichte und Arbeiterbewegung (Frankfurt/Main: Campus, 1978), pp. 54-77.

117 In 1895, for example, 57,709 persons were employed in twenty-nine such mills; see Statistik des Deutschen Reiches, N.S., Vol. 119 (Berlin: Puttkammer & Mühlbrecht, 1899), p. 50.

118 In 1895, 140,404 persons were employed in 51,950 such shops; see Statistisches Jahrbuch für das Deutsche Reich, Vol. 19, 1898 (Berlin, 1898), p. 33.

Notes to Chapter 8

119 Statistik des Deutschen Reiches, N.S., Vol. 119, p. 47.
120 Sources: Neuhaus, Die deutsche Volkswirtschaft, II, 119-20, Table 13a, 122-23, Table 13b; Statistisches Jahrbuch für das Deutsche Reich, Vol. 30, 1909 (Berlin, 1909), p. 76. Calculations by author.
121 Calculated according to data in Neuhaus, Die deutsche Volkswirtschaft, II, 119-20, Table 13a.
122 Statistisches Jahrbuch für das Deutsche Reich, Vol. 30, pp. 77-79.
123 See Gerhard Kessler, Die deutschen Arbeitgeberverbände (Leipzig: Duncker & Humblot, 1907); Adolf Weber, Der Kampf zwischen Kapital und Arbeit (3rd and 4th ed.; Tübingen: Mohr, 1921 (1910)); Lederer and Marschak, "Die Klassen auf dem Arbeitsmarkt," p. 162; Umbreit, 25 Jahre, pp. 59-68; Roswitha Leckebusch, Entstehung und Wandlungen der Zielsetzungen, der Struktur und der Wirkungen von Arbeitgeberverbänden ((West) Berlin: Duncker & Humblot, 1966); Groh, Negative Integration, pp. 102-104.
124 Roth, Die "andere" Arbeiterbewegung, p. 22.
125 Weber, Kampf, p. 187.
126 See Minssen and Sauerborn, "Der Massenarbeiter," pp. 147-48.
127 Dora Landé, "Arbeits- und Lohnverhältnisse in der Berliner Maschinenindustrie zu Beginn des 20. Jahrhunderts," Schriften des Vereins für Sozialpolitik, Vol. 134: Untersuchungen über Auslese und Anpassung (Berufswahl und Berufsschicksal) der Arbeiter in den verschiedenen Zweigen der Großindustrie, Vol. II: Auslese und Anpassung der Arbeiterschaft in der Elektroindustrie, Buchdruckerei, Feinmechanik und Maschinenindustrie (Leipzig: Duncker & Humblot, 1910), p. 322.
128 Ibid., p. 323.
129 Cf. Christel Neusüss, "Produktivkraftentwicklung, Arbeiterbewegung und Schranken sozialer Emanzipation entwickelt anhand der Rätediskussion und der Rationalisierungsdebatte der 20er Jahre," Probleme des Klassenkampfs, VIII, 2, No. 31 (1978), 84.
130 See Alexander Wende, "Die Konzentrationsbewegung bei den deutschen Gewerkschaften" (Inaugural-Dissertation, Marburg University, 1912), p. 15.
131 Ibid., pp. 43-48. Cf. Otto Heilborn, Die "Freien" Gewerkschaften seit 1890 (Jena: Fischer, 1907), pp. 62 n. 40, 154; Cassau, Gewerkschaftsbewegung, p. 97.
132 The merger of the Masons and the Construction Workers in 1910 was a significant step; see Deutscher Bauarbeiterverband, Protokoll. In former times a journeyman in the building trades would have forbidden a helper to address him as "du"; see Wende, "Konzentrationsbewegung," p. 55. On the shift in attitudes among and toward the Printers, see Karl Kautsky, Das Erfurter Programm in seinem grundsätzlichen Theil (9th ed.; Stuttgart: Dietz, 1908 (1892)), pp. 212-13; idem, "Neutralisirung," pp. 390-91; Hans Hinke, "Auslese und Anpassung der Arbeiter im Buchdruckgewerbe mit besonderer Rücksichtnahme auf die Setzmaschine," Untersuchung über Auslese und Anpassung, II, 98; Thomas von der Vring, "Der Verband der Deutschen Buchdrucker im Ersten Weltkrieg in der Revolution und in der Inflationszeit (1914-1924). Die Geschichte einer Gewerkschaft während zehn Krisenjahre" (Inaugural-Dissertation, Frankfurt University, 1965), pp. 342-44; Gerhard Beier, Schwarze Kunst und Klassenkampf. Geschichte der Industriegewerkschaft Druck und Papier und ihrer Vorläufer seit dem Beginn der modernen Arbeiterbewegung, Vol. I: Vom Geheimbund zum königlich-preußischen Gewerkverein (1830-1890) (Frankfurt/Main: Bücherbilde Gutenberg, n.d. (1966)), pp. 141-48. See also Erika König, Die deutsche Sozialdemokratie und die aufkommenden Wirtschaftsmonopole (Berlin (DDR): Dietz, 1958), p. 240.

133 Fricke, Die deutsche Arbeiterbewegung, pp. 764-65; Goldstein, Arbeiter und Unternehmer, p. 71; Otto Liebich, Organisations- und Arbeitsverhältnisse im Baugewerbe (Berlin: Elsner, 1922), pp. 66-67; Alfred Tischer, Der Kampf im deutschen Baugewerbe 1910, Abhandlungen aus dem volkswirtschaftlichen Seminar der Technischen Hochschule zu Dresden, ed. Robert Wuttke, Fasc. 3 (Leipzig, 1912), p. 8.

134 Emil Lederer, "Sozialpolitische Chronik. Die Unternehmerorganisationen," Archiv für Sozialwissenschaft und Sozialpolitik, XXX (1910), 863-64; idem, "Sozialpolitische Chronik. Die deutschen Baugewerkschaften im Jahre 1910," ibid., XXXII (1911), 609-66. August Winnig, Der grosse Kampf im deutschen Baugewerbe 1910 (Hamburg: Deutscher Bauarbeiterverband, 1911), offers insight into the solidly social democratic orientation of the building trades unions which were guided by a notion of built-in conflict with capital that was lacking in contemporary British craft unions. Cf. Helphand, Die grosse Aussperrung; Eduard Bernstein, "Ein bedeutungsvoller Gewerkschaftssieg," Sozialistische Monatshefte, XIV (1910), 879-85; August Bringmann, "Der Unternehmerkampf zur Aushungerung der deutschen Bauleute," Die Neue Zeit, XXVIII, II (1909-1910), 135-39; idem, "Zum Kampfe im Baugewerbe," ibid., pp. 205-10; idem, "Das Ende des Unternehmerkampfes zur Aushungerung der deutschen Bauleute," ibid., pp. 522-31, 586-90; idem, "Um die Freiheit der Bauleute," ibid., XXVIII, I (1909-1910), 929-34; Wilh. Dittmann, "Kapitalskonzentration und Gewerkschaftskampf," ibid., XXVIII, II (1909-1910), 871-75.

135 Protokoll über die Verhandlungen des Parteitages der Sozialdemokratischen Partei Deutschlands. Abgehalten zu Mannheim vom 23. bis 29. September 1906 (Berlin: Vorwärts, 1906), p. 249.

136 This dichotomy is reminiscent of the description of the medieval guild journeymen and of the rabble by Marx and Engels, Die deutsche Ideologie, MEW, III, 52.

137 Heilborn, Die "Freien" Gewerkschaften, p. 189.

138 See Ernst Becker, "Die ultralinke Politik und der Faschismus," (KPD-O), Gegen den Strom, V, 11 (1932); reprinted in Der Faschismus in Deutschland. Analysen der KPD-Opposition aus den Jahren 1928-1933 (Frankfurt/Main: Europäische Verlagsanstalt, 1973), p. 176. Cf. Ossip K. Flechtheim, Die Kommunistische Partei Deutschlands in der Weimarer Republik (Offenbach: Bollwerk, 1948), pp. 204-13.

139 Goetz Briefs, "Das gewerbliche Proletariat," Grundriß der Sozialökonomik, IX, I, pp. 221-22. Cf. G. Sinowjew, Der Krieg und die Krise des Sozialismus (Vienna: Verlag für Literatur und Politik, 1924 (1st Russian ed.: 1917)), pp. 529-61, especially p. 555.

140 See, for example, Boris Goldenberg, "Beiträge zur Soziologie der deutschen Vorkriegssozialdemokratie" (Inaugural-Dissertation, Heidelberg University, n.d. (ca. 1930)), p. 33.

141 Leo N. Trotsky, Der Krieg und die Internationale (n.p.: Borba, n.d. (1914?)), pp. 41-54. Cf. Karl Korsch, Marxismus und Philosophie (2nd ed.; Berlin, 1930 (1923)), pp. 13-20.

142 Rosa Luxemburg, Massenstreik, Partei und Gewerkschaften, idem, Gesammelte Werke, II, 156.

143 Ibid.

144 Ibid., pp. 163-64.

145 Ibid., p. 158.

146 Ibid., p. 157.

147 Ibid., pp. 162-63.

148 T. Bömelburg, the leader of the Masons, declared at the fourth German Trade Union Congress in Stuttgart in 1902 that, "The German trade

unions and German Social Democracy are one." See Handbuch der deutschen Gewerkschaftskongresse, ed. Paul Barthel (Dresden: Kaden, 1916), p. 378.

149 K. Kautsky, "Partei und Gewerkschaft," Die Neue Zeit, XVII, I (1898-1899), 420-23.

150 Luxemburg, Massenstreik, p. 169.

151 Cited by Umbreit, 25 Jahre, p. 77; no date given.

152 See chapter 7 above.

153 See, for example, N. Auerbach, Marx und die Gewerkschaften (Berlin: Frankes, 1922), p. 122.

154 Carl E. Schorske, German Social Democracy 1905-1917 (New York: Wiley, n.d. (first published in 1955)), p. 110.

155 Ibid., pp. 90-115.

156 Ibid., pp. 109-10. The general strike and obligatory May Day strikes were two chief points of contention.

157 See Georg Fülberth and Jürgen Harrer, Arbeiterbewegung und SPD, Vol. I: Die deutsche Sozialdemokratie 1890-1933 (Darmstadt: Luchterhand, 1974), p. 91; Frank Deppe, Georg Fülberth, Jürgen Harrer, eds., Geschichte der deutschen Gewerkschaftsbewegung (Cologne: Pahl-Rugenstein, 1977), pp. 84-85.

158 Luxemburg, Massenstreik, p. 159.

159 August Bringmann, "Klassenkampf, Partei und Gewerkschaft. Eine Richtigstellung," Sozialistische Monatshefte, X, 9 (September 1906), 780-83.

160 Claims concerning the growing "trade-unionization" of the party based on global data that show that trade union membership grew more rapidly than party members or voters remain ecological fallacies unless it can be documented that trade union members were specifically represented in ever larger numbers among party members or voters. See Schorske, German Social Democracy, pp. 12-13; Groh, Negative Integration, pp. 71-72. Trade union leaders, however, formed an increasing share of Social Democratic members of the Reichstag. See Heinz Josef Varain, Freie Gewerkschaften, Sozialdemokratie und Staat (Düsseldorf: Droste, 1956), p. 45; cf. ibid., p. 30.

161 Cf. Konrad Haenisch, "Statistisches zur Neutralisationsfrage," Die Neue Zeit, XVIII, II (1899-1900), 596-99. This study of the Leipzig area in 1898 failed to record dual membership.

162 Statistische Erhebungen über die Partei-Organisation Groß-Berlins 1906 (Berlin, 1907), pp. 138-39; cited by Fricke, Die deutsche Arbeiterbewegung, Table 114 at pp. 730-32.

163 This statement applies, for example, to masons, carpenters, potters, stuccoworkers and bakers; ibid.

164 Ibid. The average shop employing a smith or an upholsterer employed only two to three persons in 1907; see Statistisches Jahrbuch für das Deutsche Reich, Vol. 30, pp. 78-81.

165 Fricke, Die deutsche Arbeiterbewegung, pp. 731-32; calculations by author.

166 The Textile Workers in Greater Berlin formed the only major exception to this finding; the Construction Laborers showed a marginally above-average degree of party membership. Ibid., pp. 730-32.

167 Robert Michels, "Die deutsche Sozialdemokratie. I. Parteimitgliedschaft und soziale Zusammensetzung," Archiv für Sozialwissenschaft und Sozialpolitik, N.S., XXIII (1906), 513-14. Michels excepted the Book Printers from his generalization that it was more difficult to organize low-paid workers than the "labor 'aristocracy'"; ibid., p. 514 n. 65 and p. 517.

168 Ibid., p. 515.
169 Source: Statistisches Jahrbuch für das Deutsche Reich, Vol. 31, pp. 64-67; calculations by author.
170 In 1882 the census revealed that 34.2 per cent of those in industrial occupations were proprietors; calculated according to data in Statistik des Deutschen Reiches, N.S., Vol. 119, pp. 62-63.
171 The census data which distinguish between workers with and without "preparatory training" must be treated with circumspection; see n. 116 above.
172 Werner Sombart, Die deutsche Volkswirtschaft im 19. Jahrhundert und im Anfang des 20. Jahrhunderts (8th ed.; Darmstadt: Wissenschaftliche Buchgesellschaft, 1954 (1903)), pp. 455-64. Cf. Neuhaus, Die deutsche Volkswirtschaft, II, 145.
173 Voigt, "Das deutsche Handwerk," p. 631.
174 See the last two columns of Table 32. Neuhaus, Die deutsche Volkswirtschaft, II, 113-14, Table 9, provides a comparative summary for 1882, 1895 and 1907.
175 The proletarianization of these Alleinmeister is confirmed by their concentration at the low end of Voigt's prosperity index, which expresses the number of house servants per one thousand proprietors and self-employed. Building tradesmen, tailors, shoemakers and cottage-industrial weavers and spinners registered the lowest ratings. See Voigt, "Das deutsche Handwerk," pp. 659-62. For the raw data, see Vierteljahrshefte zur Statistik des Deutschen Reiches, Vol. V (1896), Ergänzung zum dritten Heft (Berlin: Puttkammer & Mühlbrecht, 1896), pp. 7-109; Statistik des Deutschen Reiches, N.S., Vol. 202, pp. 4-120.
176 If only production units with at least one employee are examined, the high negative correlation between the share of proprietors in the total number of those occupied and the size of units, by branch, becomes clear. See Neuhaus, Die deutsche Volkswirtschaft, Table 29b at II, 158.
177 See the overview in Thissen, Beiträge.
178 See Karl Thiess, "Das Berliner Malergewerbe," Untersuchungen über die Lage des Handwerks in Deutschland, Vol. 7: Königreich Preußen, Part 3 (Leipzig: Duncker & Humblot, 1896), pp. 238-39; idem, "Das Berliner Klempnergewerbe," ibid., p. 314. Voigt, "Das deutsche Handwerk," p. 669, estimated that one-half of employing craft masters enjoyed a standard of living above that of the upper strata of the factory proletariat.
179 See Siegfried Nestriepke, Die Gewerkschaftsbewegung, Vol. I: Die deutschen Gewerkschaften bis zum Ausbruch des Weltkrieges (3rd ed.; Stuttgart: Moritz, 1925 (1919)), p. 93.
180 Neuhaus, Die deutsche Volkswirtschaft, Table 47a at II, 196-97.
181 Helphand, Die große Aussperrung, pp. 10-11, 39.
182 See Theodor Kreuzkam, "Das Baugewerbe mit besonderer Rücksicht auf Leipzig," Untersuchungen über die Lage des Handwerks in Deutschland, Vol. 9, p. 608; Adolf Noll, Sozio-ökonomischer Strukturwandel des Handwerks in der zweiten Phase der Industrialisierung unter besonderer Berücksichtigung der Regierungsbezirke Arnsberg und Münster (Göttingen: Vandenhoeck & Ruprecht, 1975), Table VI at pp. 78-80.
183 See Fritz Flechtner, "Das Baugewerbe in Breslau," Untersuchungen über die Lage des Handwerks in Deutschland, Vol. q, p. 420.
184 Marie Bernays, "Berufswahl und Berufsschicksal des modernen Industriearbeiters," Archiv für Sozialwissenschaft und Sozialpolitik, XXVI (1913), 909-10; Thiess, "Klempnergewerbe," p. 314.

185 Josef Schmöle, Die sozialdemokratischen Gewerkschaften in Deutschland seit dem Erlasse des Sozialistengesetzes, Part 2: Einzelne Organisationen, Division 1: Der Zimmererverband (Jena: Fischer, 1898), p. 7. Cf. Paul Merker, Sozialdemokratie und Gewerkschaften 1890-1920 (Berlin (DDR): Dietz, 1949), p. 64.

186 On the rise in the share of supervisory personnel as a function of increasing firm size, see Neuhaus, Die deutsche Volkswirtschaft, Tables 25-28b at II, 147-54. In 1907, unskilled workers constituted thirty-eight per cent of machinists, eighty-nine per cent of chemical workers and ninety-seven per dent of those employed by general construction contractors, who employed more than half of all construction employees; calculated according to data in Statistik des Deutschen Reiches, N.S., Vol. 202, pp. 10, 106; Statistisches Jahrbuch für das Deutsche Reich, Vol. 30, pp. 76, 83.

187 Calculated according to data in Statistisches Jahrbuch für das Deutsche Reich, Vol. 31, pp. 64-65. In 1882 their share had been 2.4 per cent; calculated according to data in Statistik des Deutschen Reiches, Vol. 119, pp. 62-63. For an international overview, see Reinhard Bendix, Work and Authority in Industry (Berkeley: University of California Press, 1974 (1956)), pp. 211-26.

188 Calculated according to data in Statistisches Jahrbuch für das Deutsche Reich, Vol. 31, pp. 64-67.

189 See Cassau, Gewerkschaftsbewegung, p. 125.

190 See Robert Michels, "Psychologie der antikapitalistischen Massenbewegungen," Grundriß der Sozialökonomik, IX, I, p. 265; cf. idem, "Beitrag zur Lehre von der Klassenbildung," Archiv für Sozialwissenschaft und Sozialpolitik, XLIX (1922), 561-93.

191 See however Karl Kautsky, "Die Civic Federation," Die Neue Zeit, XXVIII, I (1909-1910), 132-37. Cf. the unorthodox position adopted by Hannah Arendt, The Origins of Totalitarianism (2nd ed.; Cleveland: Meridian, 1967 (1951)), p. 152.

192 See, for example, Max Weber's speech on the co-optation of the Social Democratic movement in Schriften des Vereins für Socialpolitik, Vol. 125: Verhandlungen (1907) (Leipzig: Duncker & Humblot, 1908), pp. 294-301.

193 See, for example, Gerhart von Schulze-Gaevernitz, Zum sozialen Frieden (2 vols.; Leipzig: Duncker & Humblot, 1890). Cf. Wilh. Düwell, "Kritisches zur Gewerkschaftsbewegung," Die Neue Zeit, XIX, II (1900-1901), 714; Kautsky, "Neutralisirung," p. 390.

194 Fülberth and Harrer, Arbeiterbewegung und SPD, I, 118, speak of the creation of a "yellow labor aristocracy," separate from and outside of the Social Democratic labor movement. Yet the very fact that employers found it necessary to by-pass the outstanding representative organs of the German working class underscored the fundamentally different political outlook of the proletariat in Germany and in England. Cf. Kautsky, "Neutralisirung," p. 394; idem, "Klassenkampf und Ethik," Die Neue Zeit, XIX, I (1900-1901), 241.

195 Cassau, Gewerkschaftsbewegung, p. 96, contended that the large-scale westward migration of East Prussian laborers rendered the creation of a German labor aristocracy virtually impossible; cf. Arthur Dix, "Das Slaventum in Preußen, seine Bedeutung für die Bevölkerungsbewegung und Volkswirtschaft in den letzten Jahrzehnten," Jahrbücher für Nationalökonomie und Statistik, LXX (1898), 561-602. Cf. Hans-Ulrich Wehler, "Die Polen im Ruhrgebiet bis 1918," Moderne deutsche Sozialgeschichte, pp. 437-55, 550-62; this article first appeared in Vierteljahrsschrift für Sozial- und Wirtschaftsgeschichte, XLVIII (1961), 203-35. In light of the

fact that the much more extensive immigration of Eastern and Southern Europeans to the United States resulted in "the elevation of the English-speaking workmen to the status of an aristocracy of labor," it is unlikely that contemporary migration to and within Germany could have affected the upper stratum of native German workers so adversely as Cassau maintained. See Isaac A. Hourwich, Immigration and Labor (New York: Putnam's Sons, 1912), p. 12; cf. ibid., p. 395. In 1907, foreign-born workers accounted for approximately one-sixth of agricultural laborers, one-tenth of unskilled and one-sixteenth of skilled miners, one-seventh of unskilled and one-twenty-third of skilled construction laborers and one-fourteenth of all unskilled industrial workers. See Georg Neuhaus, Die deutsche Volkswirtschaft und ihre Wandlungen im letzten Vierteljahrhundert, Vol. I: Die berufliche und soziale Gliederung des deutschen Volkes (M. Gladbach: Volksvereins-Verlag, 1911), pp. 205, 208; Schröder, Arbeitergeschichte, p. 69. In the forty-two German cities with more than 100,000 inhabitants in 1907, those born in East Prussia accounted for 5.1 per cent of industrial workers while those born outside Germany accounted for 4.7 per cent; the corresponding figures for Berlin were 5.8 per cent and 3.8 per cent. The data on urban areas refer to males only. Calculated according to the data in Statistik des Deutschen Reiches, Vol. 210, 2: Berufs- und Betriebszählung vom 12. Juni 1907, Berufsstatistik, Abteilung IX: Die Bevölkerung nach Hauptberuf und Gebürtigkeit, Part 2: Großstädte (Berlin: Puttkammer & Mühlbrecht, 1910), pp. 2-3, 54-55. The relevant data for the United States may be consulted in Bureau of the Census, Thirteenth Census of the United States taken in the Year 1910, Vol. IV: Population, 1910, Occupation Statistics (Washington: Government Printing Office, 1914).

196 See Carl Legien, "Ziele und Mittel der deutschen Gewerkschaftsbewegung," Sozialistische Monatshefte, IV, 3 (March 1900), 110.

197 Kautsky, Das Erfurter Programm, pp. 213-14.

198 See note 116 above. In construction the share of the skilled declined as the number of unskilled employed by general contractors rose by more than 200,000 between 1895 and 1907. See Statistik des Deutschen Reiches, N.S., Vol. 102, pp. 103-108; ibid., Vol. 202, pp. 60, 106-11. Cf. P.M. Grempe, "Technische Fortschritte im Bauwesen," Die Neue Zeit, XIX, II (1900-1901), 54-58; Hans Grandke, "Die vom Verein für Sozialpolitik veranstalteten Untersuchungen über die Lage des Handwerks in Deutschland mit besonderer Rücksicht auf die Konkurrenzfähigkeit gegenüber der Großindustrie," Jahrbuch für Gesetzgebung, Verwaltung und Volkswirtschaft im Deutschen Reiche, N.S., XXI (1897), 1071-77.

199 Max Weber, Wirtschaft und Gesellschaft (Cologne: Kiepenheuer & Witsch, 1964 (1922)), pp. 225-26.

200 Bry, Wages in Germany, Table A-14 at p. 363; mining proved to be an exception.

201 Jürgen Kuczynski, Die Entwicklung der Lage der Arbeiterschaft in Europa und Amerika 1870-1933 (Basel: Philographischer Verlag, 1934), pp. 24-28, has calculated that the real wages of non-labor aristocrats rose by approximately eight per cent between 1899 and 1914 while those of labor aristocrats remained unchanged. Cf. the undocumented claim by Harry J. Marks, "The Sources of Reformism in the Social Democratic Party of Germany 1890-1914," Journal of Modern History, XI, 3 (September 1939), 355. For an earlier period, see Hans Rosenberg, Große Depression und Bismarckzeit ((West) Berlin: de Gruyter, 1967), p. 50.

202 Bry, Wages in Germany, Table A-14 at p. 363.

203 Heinrich Herkner, "Probleme der Arbeiterpsychologie unter besonderer Rücksichtnahme auf Methode und Ergebnisse der Vereinserhebungen," Schriften des Vereins für Socialpolitik, Vol. 138: Verhandlungen (1911) (Leipzig: Duncker & Humblot, 1912), pp. 126, 128.

204 Paul Umbreit, Der Krieg und die Arbeitsverhältnisse. Die deutschen Gewerkschaften im Kriege (Stuttgart: DVA, 1928), pp. 33-34.

205 See Henry Phelps Brown, The Inequality of Pay (Oxford: Oxford University Press, 1977), pp. 68-81.

206 See B.N. Mikhaelevskii, "O rabochei aristokratii v Germanii nakaune pervoi mirovoi voiny," Voprosy istorii, 1955, No. 1, pp. 104-108.

207 Düwell, "Kritisches zur Gewerkschaftsbewegung," pp. 714-15, does not document this claim.

208 See Heilborn, Die "Freien" Gewerkschaften, p. 153.

209 The aggregate average is based on data in Hoffmann, Wachstum, Table 108 at pp. 470-71.

210 Landé, "Berliner Maschinenindustrie," p. 386.

211 The effects of such insecurity on unskilled machinists, more than one-third of whom earned from 900 to 1,200 marks annually, were more severe; ibid., p. 394.

212 Unemployment in the building trades had a greater impact on the skilled than on the unskilled because the former, being more specialized, found it more difficult to locate other employment; see Liebich, Organisations- und Arbeitsverhältnisse im Baugewerbe, p. 125.

213 See Jürgen Kuczynski, Die Geschichte der Lage der Arbeiter unter dem Kapitalismus, Vol. 5: Darstellung der Lage der Arbeiter in Deutschland von 1917/18 bis 1932/33 (Berlin (DDR): Akademie, 1966), p. 167.

214 Bernh. Quantz, Zur Lage des Bauarbeiters in Stadt und Land (Göttingen: Vandenhoeck & Ruprecht, 1911), pp. 2-4, 14; August Bringmann, Geschichte der deutschen Zimmerer-Bewegung, I (Stuttgart: Zentralverband der Zimmerleute, 1903), 100-101. Cf. the extensive data on annual incomes and expenditures over time in Unterlagen zur Beurteilung der wirtschaftlichen Lebensbedingungen der deutschen Bauarbeiter, Fasc. 1 (Hamburg: Deutscher Bauarbeiter-Verband, 1912), pp. 40-47.

215 Kreuzkam, "Baugewerbe," pp. 615-16.

216 See, for example, Zentral-Verband der Maurer Deutschlands, Der Kampf um die Arbeitsbedingungen (Hamburg: Zentral-Verband der Maurer Deutschlands, 1909), pp. 22-23.

217 See Siegfried Nestriepke, Die Gewerkschaftsbewegung, II (2nd ed.; Stuttgart: Moritz, 1923), 178-79.

218 Protokoll über die Verhandlungen des Parteitages der Sozialdemokratischen Partei Deutschlands. Abgehalten zu Berlin vom 14. bis 21. November 1892 (Berlin: Vorwärts, 1892), p. 122. It is inclear whether Legien's protest against Bebel's defense of high salaries for editors of party organs--Bebel had pleaded that they would return to bourgeois organs if their idealism were taxed too heavily--was motivated by egalitarianism or by hostility toward the presence of intellectuals in the labor movement; see Protokoll über die Verhandlungen des Parteitages der Sozialdemokratischen Partei Deutschlands. Abgehalten zu Frankfurt a.M. vom 21. bis 27. Oktober 1894 (Berlin: Vorwärts, 1894), pp. 71, 73.

219 Legien in Protokoll, 1893, p. 183.

220 Robert Schmidt in Protokoll über die Verhandlungen des Parteitages der Sozialdemokratischen Partei Deutschlands. Abgehalten zu Jena vom 17. bis 23. September 1905 (Berlin: Vorwärts, 1905), p. 247.

221 Goldstein, Arbeiter und Unternehmer, p. 83; Internationaler Sozialisten-Kongress zu Kopenhagen. 28. August bis 3. September 1910 (Berlin: Vorwärts, 1910), pp. 12-16, 105-113.

222 Zwing, Geschichte, p. 60; "Die Gewerkschaften," Die Neue Zeit, III (1885), 525.
223 Zwing, Geschichte, p. 62.
224 Umbreit, 25 Jahre, p. 113.
225 See Gustav Brüggerhoff, "Statistisches über das Unterstützungswesen der deutschen 'Freien' Gewerkschaften" (Inaugural-Dissertation, Marburg University, 1908), pp. 43-49; cf. Schlesinger, Central European Democracy, pp. 56-57. The Printers paid 1.5 marks per diem for ư to 280 days to members who had been in good standing for 750 weeks; members who had paid dues for seventy-five weeks received a smaller sum for up to seventy days. See Robert Michels and Gisela Michels-Lindner, "Das Problem der Arbeitslosigkeit und ihre Bekämpfung durch die deutschen freien Gewerkschaften," Archiv für Sozialwissenschaft und Sozialpolitik, XXXI (1910), 457. At this time the average annual labor income in the printing industry amounted to about 1,400 marks; see Hoffmann, Wachstum, Table 108 at p. 470.
226 See Umbreit, 25 Jahre, pp. 112-15; Armin Michaelsen, "Die Reichsanstalt für Arbeitsvermittlung und Arbeitslosenversicherung" (Inaugural-Dissertation, Marburg University, 1929), pp. 2-4; Mollie Ray Carroll, Unemployment Insurance in Germany (Washington, D.C.: Brookings, 1929), pp. 6-11.
227 Michels and Michels-Lindner, "Das Problem der Arbeitslosigkeit," p. 480.
228 Ibid. Cf. Lederer and Marschak, "Die Klassen auf dem Arbeitsmarkt," p. 145.
229 Cited by Michels and Michels-Lindner, "Das Problem der Arbeitslosigkeit," p. 481.
230 See the analogous argument adduced by Kautsky in connection with the attempt on the part of some trade unions to "neutralize" themselves politically in order to overcome objections to membership by Catholic workers; Kautsky, "Neutralisirung," pp. 391-94. On the denominational trade unions, see Ludwig Frey, "Die Stellung der christlichen Gewerkschaftlichen Deutschlands zu den politischen Parteien" (Inaugural-Dissertation, Würzburg University, 1931); Max Prager, "Grenzen der Gewerkschaftsbewegung," Archiv für Sozialwissenschaft und Sozialpolitik, XX (1905), 280-86; William H. Dawson, The Evolution of Modern Germany (New York: Scribner's, n.d. (1908)), pp. 112-14.
231 Jens Warming, Danmarks erhvervs- og samfundsliv (Copenhagen: Gads, 1930), pp. 563-69. Cf. Encyclopedia of the Social Sciences, s.v. "Unemployment Insurance."
232 Schröder, Arbeitergeschichte, p. 147, approaches this issue ahistorically and schematically.
233 Beier, Schwarze Kunst, I, 141-48, is not convincing in his attempt to refute the charge of aristocratic behavior.
234 See Umbreit, Der Krieg, passim; Friedrich Thimme and Carl Legien, eds., Die Arbeiterschaft im neuen Deutschland (Leipzig: Hirzel, 1915); Werner Raase, Zur Geschichte der deutschen Gewerkschaftsbewegung 1914-1917 und 1917-1919 (Berlin (DDR): Tribüne, n.d. (1969)), pp. 12-27.
235 See Lenin, Chto delat'?, PSS, VI, 30, 56. For an overview of the historical development of German trade unionism from the standpoint of French reformist socialism, see Albert Thomas, Le Syndicalisme allemand (Paris: Société nouvelle, 1903); cf. Hedwig Wachenheim, Die deutsche Arbeiterbewegung 1844 bis 1914 (Cologne: Westdeutscher Verlag, 1967).
236 Even the extremely orthodox Marxist-Leninist, Mikhaelevskii, "o rabochei aristokratii," pp. 105, 108, concedes this point.

237 Ibid., pp. 104-105, fixes the wage level at twice that of a worker of average skill.
238 See, for example, Jürgen Kuczynski, Zurück zu Marx (Leipzig: Hirschfeld, 1926), pp. 128-29.
239 See Jürgen Kuczynski, Geschichte der Lage der Arbeiter unter dem Kapitalismus, Vol. 4: Darstellung der Lage der Arbeiter in Deutschland von 1900 bis 1917/18 (Berlin (DDR): Akademie, 1967), pp. 303-305.
240 Mikhaelevskii, "O rabochei aristokratii," p. 105.
241 Ibid., pp. 104-107.
242 See, for example, the unproven claim that labor aristocrats received wages in excess of the value of their labor power; ibid., p. 105.
243 Cf. Bernstein, "Die soziale Differenzierung," pp. 308-10.
244 Mikhaelevskii, "O rabochei aristokratii," p. 105; cf. Kuczynski, Deutschland von 1871 bis 1900, pp. 325-27.
245 Mikhaelevskii, "O rabochei aristokratii," pp. 105, 107, 109.
246 Ibid., p. 107.
247 See Ulf Kadritzke, Angestellte--Die geduldigen Arbeiter (Frankfurt/Main: Europäische Verlagsanstalt, 1975), pp. 103-107 and passim.
248 Mikhaelevskii, "O rabochei aristokratii," p. 108.
249 Employers began to organize yellow unions in 1905; their membership rose from about 59,000 in 1907 to about 280,000 in 1913 at which time they accounted for one-fourteenth of total union membership. See Hans-Alexander Apolant, "Die wirtschaftsfriedliche nationale Arbeiterbewegung (Gelbe Gewerkschaften) in Deutschland" (Inaugural-Dissertation, Leipzig University, 1926), pp. 13-15, 41.
250 On the politically "neutral" Hirsch-Duncker unions, the membership of which exceeded 100,000 by the early years of the twentieth century, see "Die Stärke und Tendenz der Hirsch-Duncker'schen Gewerkvereine," Correspondenzblatt, VII, 52 (December 27, 1897), 321-23; Dawson, Evolution, pp. 112, 114; Lederer and Marschak, "Die Klassen auf dem Arbeitsmarkt," p. 142.
251 See Saul, Staat, p. 187; cf. Karl Kautsky, "Was nun?," Die Neue Zeit, XXI, II (1902-1903), 389-90.
252 Mikhaelevskii, "O rabochei aristokratii," p. 110; cf. Karl Kautsky, "Unser neuestes Programm. 4," Die Neue Zeit, XXII, II (1894-1895), 591.
253 See Mikhaelevskii, "O rabochei aristokratii," p. 104; cf. Dawson, Evolution, pp. 386-87; Hans-Ulrich Wehler, Bismarck und der Imperialismus (4th ed.; Munich: DTV, 1976 (1969)).
254 Although universal manhood suffrage accompanied the founding of the German Empire in 1871, the Reichstag was from the outset enfeebled in relation to the Prussian Landtag, which remained a formally undemocratic institution during the prewar period. Léon Duguit, Manuel de droit constitutionnel (3rd ed.; Paris: Boccard, 1918 (1911)), pp. 327-44, provides an overview of suffrage restrictions in Europe. Cf. Hamerow, Social Foundations. Ideas and Institutions, chaps. 4-5, 7; idem, Social Foundations. Struggles and Accomplishments, chaps. 4-7; Schorske, German Social Democracy, pp. 45-49, 171-87; Groh, Negative Integration, pp. 128-60; Ernst Engelberg, Deutschland von 1871-1897 (Berlin (DDR): VEB Deutscher Verlag der Wissenschaften, 1967), pp. 11-23.
255 See however Mikhaelevskii, "O rabochei aristokratii," pp. 103-104.

1 This view has continued to prevail during the post-World War I period. Although radical syndicalists charged, toward the end of the 1920s, that industrial rationalization would result in a bifurcation of the working class into a minority of well-paid labor aristocrats and a majority of unemployed, studies of the Fourth and Fifth Republic have not confirmed the existence of a politically relevant labor aristocracy. See Marjorie Ruth Clark, A History of the French Labor Movement (1910-1928), University of California Publications in Economics, VIII, 1 (April 15, 1930), 148; Richard F. Hamilton, Affluence and the French Workers in the Fourth Republic (Princeton: Princeton University Press, 1967), pp. 130-33; Alain Lipietz, Le Tribut foncier urbain (Paris: Maspero, 1974), p. 64 n. 9.

2 For a similar, Spanish example, see Raymond Carr, Spain 1808-1939 (Oxford: Clarendon, 1966), p. 447.

3 See Friedrich Engels, "Die europäischen Arbeiter im Jahre 1877," MEW, XIX, 129; first published in English in The Labor Standard (New York), III (March 24, 1878).

4 Karl Marx, "Die Klassenkämpfe in Frankreich 1848 bis 1850," Neue Rheinische Zeitung. Politisch-ökonomische Revue, Heft 1, January 1850, pp. 15-16; cited here according to Karl Marx/Friedrich Engels, Gesamtausgabe (MEGA), Erste Abteilung, Vol. 10 (Berlin (DDR): Dietz, 1977), p. 127.

5 Source: Ministère de l'Agriculture, Statistique de la France (Paris: Imprimerie Imperiale, 1855), pp. xx-xxiv; calculations by author.

6 Calculated according to data in ibid., pp. xxi-xxii.

7 Ibid.

8 See Bernard Moss, The Origins of the French Labor Movement 1830-1914. The Socialism of Skilled Workers (Berkeley: University of California Press, 1976), pp. 17-18, 171 n. 46. It is unclear whether this author uses the expression "semiartisanal mode of Parisian production" in a literary or rigorous Marxist conceptual manner.

9 In 1847 there were five workers for every employer. See Pierre Vinçard, "Le Prolétariat français aux XIXe siècle," Colins, L'Economie politique, I (Paris: Librairie Générale, J.G. 1856), 222; cf. Abel Chatelain, "Une grande industrie motrice française attardée: Le Bâtiment," Annales: Economies, Sociétes, Civilisations, XIII, 3 (July-September, 1958), 575.

10 J.H. Clapham, The Economic Development of France and Germany (4th ed.; Cambridge: Cambridge University Press, 1968 (1921)), p. 75.

11 As Moss, Origins, pp. 8-20, notes, the labor movement in France--and here France proved to be no exception--arose among the skilled rather than among unskilled factory workers. Although it is Moss's merit to have analyzed the pecularities of "trade socialism" of the skilled, he throughout confuses the traditional skilled, who were undergoing de-skilling, with the new industrial skilled.

12 See Arthur Louis Dunham, The Industrial Revolution in France 1815-1848 (New York: Exposition, 1955), pp. 178-212.

13 In 1852 about fifty-five per cent of the employed were located in agriculture and twenty-five per cent in mining, industry and crafts; calculated according to data in Hoffmann, Wachstum, Table 20 at p. 204.

14 See Deane and Cole, British Economic Growth, Table 30 at p. 142.

15 Hoffmann, Wachstum, Table 20 at p. 205.

16 See B.R. Mitchell, "Statistical Appendix 1920-1970," The Fontana Economic History of Europe, ed. Carlo M. Cipolla, Vol. 6: Contemporary Economies, Part 2 (Glasgow: Collins and Fontana, 1976), p. 659; Claude Fohlen,

"France 1920-1970," ibid., Part 1, p. 76, presents an instructive graphic representation of twentieth century French labor force evolution.

17 Roger Price, The Economic Modernisation of France (New York: Wiley, 1975), argues that the ancien régime was not overcome until about 1880.

18 This appears to have been the case in any event after the decline of the French guild system. See E. Levasseur, Histoire des classes ouvrières et de l'industrie en France de 1789 à 1870, II (2nd ed.; Paris: Rousseau, 1904 (1867)), 237.

19 Source: League of Nations, Industrialization and Foreign Trade, Table 1 at p. 13.

20 Source: Lewis, "International Competition in Manufactures," p. 579.

21 Calculated according to data in ibid., II, 712-13; Vincard, "Le Prolétariat français," p. 223; Georges Duveau, La Vie ouvrière en France sous le Second Empire (5th ed.; n.p.: Gallimard, 1946), p. 320; Moss, Origins, pp. 15-16.

22 Henri Sée, Französische Wirtschaftsgeschichte, II (Jena: Fischer, 1936), 239, names miners, building tradesmen and iron and glass foundry workers for 1847; on the latter, see Joan W. Scott, The Glassworkers of Carmaux (Cambridge, Mass.: Harvard University Press, 1974).

23 Duveau, La Vie ouvrière, pp. 306, 396-98, mentions watchmakers, printers, some building tradesmen, bakers, puddlers, forgers, some mechanics, spinners and engravers.

24 See Moss, Origins, pp. 8-12.

25 It should be stressed that even relatively well-paid workers led very Spartan lives; see for example the description of the leisure activities of a Paris carpenter and his family in the 1850s by F. Le Play, Les Ouvriers européens. V: Les Ouvriers de l'occident, IIme Série--populations ébranlées envahies par la nouveauté ... (2nd ed.; Tours: Mame, 1878 (1855)), 439-40. Cf. Kuczynski, Geschichte, Vol. 33: Darstellung der Lage der Arbeiter in Frankreich seit 1848 (Berlin (DDR): Akademie, 1967), p. 43.

26 Marx, "Klassenkämpfe," p. 132.

27 For a further example of such neutral designations, see Edmond About, Le Progrès (4th ed.; Paris: Hachette, 1867 (1864)), p. 48, who speaks of printers as an "aristocratic" category of the working class whereas ragpickers and sewermen "bring up the rear." Cf. Georges Renard, Les Travailleurs du livre et du journal, III (Paris: Doin, 1926), 52.

28 Duveau, La Vie ouvrière, pp. 482-83.

29 Friedrich Engels, Zur Wohnungsfrage, MEW, XVIII, 260. On a different segment of the construction proletariat, see Abel Chatelain, "La Main d'oeuvre et la construction des chemins de fer au XIXe siècle," Annales. Economies, Sociétés, Civilisations, VIII, 4 (October-December, 1953), 502-506.

30 Moss, Origins, p. 49.

31 See J.S. Mill's enthusiastic description in his Principles of Political Economy, pp. 779-80 n.

32 See Republique Française, Ministère du commerce, de l'industrie, des postes et des télégraphes, Office du Travail, Les Associations professionelles ouvrières, Vol. IV: Industries du bâtiment.--Transports.--Industries diverses (Paris: Imprimerie Nationale, 1904), p. 223. Although Duveau, La Vie ouvrière, p. 306, characterizes masonry as one "des professions plus humbles," the wage differential between masons and their helpers amounted to approximately sixty per cent during the Second Empire; see Levasseur, Histoire, II, 713. The low prestige associated with bricklaying may have derived from the fact that the mason was "le paysan devenu

ouvrier"; see Fernand Borie, L'Ouvrier maçon (Paris: Doin, 1924), p. 142.

33 See W. Lexis, Gewerkvereine und Unternehmerverbände in Frankreich, Schriften des Vereins für Socialpolitik, Vol. XVII (Leipzig: Duncker & Humblot, 1879), passim.

34 Kuczynski, Geschichte, Vol. 32: Darstellung der Lage der Arbeiter in Frankreich von 1789 bis 1848 (Berlin (DDR): Akademie, 1967), p. 37, neglects this point in his ahistorical comparison of the eighteenth and nineteenth centuries.

35 See however Daniel Ligou, Histoire du socialisme en France (1871-1961) (Paris: Presses Universitaires de France, 1962), p. 16.

36 Kuczynski, Frankreich seit 1848, p. 157, merely confirms this distinction for the period 1871-1918 without any attempt at causal explanation.

37 Sternberg, Imperialismus, p. 517.

38 Ibid., pp. 517, 520-21, 529-32. With 1871 as the base year, real wages of the employed rose more in France by 1900 than in Germany, England or the United States; such comparisons vary according to the years selected. See Mendel'son, Teoriia i istoria, II, 526-27. Cf. the radically different conclusions reached by Eliane Mossé, Marx et le problème de la croissance dans une économie capitaliste (Paris: Colin, 1956), pp. 176-77.

39 Sternberg, Imperialismus, p. 532.

40 Ibid., pp. 533-34. Cf. Clapham, Economic Development, p. 276.

41 Moss, Origins, p. 15.

42 Ibid., p. 19. Moss argues in a self-contradictory fashion here since he previously pointed to joint action by such workers and their employers against larger capitalist manufacturers or contractors; ibid., p. 18. The attitudes of workers toward their immediate employers were obviously shaped in large part by the size of the shop and, derivatively, by the function and income of the employer.

43 Ibid., p. 43.

44 Calculated according to data in Statistik des Deutschen Reiches, N.S., CII, 62-63; Statistisches Jahrbuch für das Deutsche Reich, Vol. 31, 1910, pp. 64-65. Cf. Wl. Woytinsky, Die Welt in Zahlen, II: Die Arbeit (Berlin: Mosse, 1926), 12, 23.

45 Calculated according to data in République Française, Ministère du Commerce, de l'Industrie, des Postes et des Télégraphes, Direction du Travail, Service du Recensement Professionel, Résultats statistiques du recensement des industries et professions, Dénombrement général de la population du 29 mars 1896, IV: Résultats généraux (Paris: Imprimerie Ntionale, 1901), 198-99; idem, Résultats statistiques du recensement générale de la population effectué le 24 mars 1901, IV: Population présente. Résultats généraux (Paris: Imprimerie Nationale, 1906), 500-501; Mme. Cahen, ed., "La concentration des etablissements en France de 1896 à 1936," Études et conjoncture, IX, 9 (September 1954), 857-58, 862. The censuses conducted prior to 1896 did not include the self-employed as a separate category but assigned them to the categories of employer and employed; see République Française, Ministère du Commerce, de l'Industrie, des Postes et des Télégraphes, Office du Travail, Statistique générale de la France, Résultats statistiques du dénombrement de 1891 (Paris: Imprimerie Nationale, 1894), pp. 421, 424-28, 430-31, 436-43. Cf. also E. Levasseur, Questions ouvrières et industrielles en France sous la Troisième Republique (Paris: Rousseau, 1907), pp. 270-75.

46 The purpose of this approach is to isolate the wage labor sector although even establishments employing merely several workers may be only

marginally capital-accumulating. The share of the non-employing self-employed ("isolés") varied sharply--from virtually nil in mining and metallurgy to almost three-fifths of the work force in the clothing industry; see République Française, Ministère du Travail et de la Prévoyance Sociale, Direction du Travail, Statistique générale de la France, Résultats statistiques du recensement générale de la population effectué le 4 mars 1906, Vol. I--Part 2: Population présente totale (Paris: Imprimerie Nationale, 1910), pp. 111-16.

47 Calculated according to data in Neuhaus, Die deutsche Volkswirtschaft, II, 113, 116-17, 124.

48 See Recensement générale 1906, I:2, 119. These data include the transport and state industrial sectors which raise the average slightly. The fact that two sets of data on employees were included detracts from the usefulness of the French data; see ibid., pp. 182-83 and n. 7. The foregoing averages are based on the less inclusive set of data; use of the more inclusive data raises the average somewhat but not to the German level. Similarly, the German averages are inflated by the fact that they include owners whereas the French data refer to employees and workers alone; adjustment of the German data for 1907 reduces the average number of employees and wage earners per establishment to 8.1--still about one-third greater than the corresponding figure for France.

49 Source: Calculated according to data in Neuhaus, Die deutsche Volkswirt-schaft, II, 113, 116-17, 124, 147; Recensement générale 1906, I:2, 182. Cf. Woytinsky, Welt in Zahlen, II, 25.

50 Recensement générale 1906, I:2, 182.

51 Ibid., p. 120. For an interntional comparison, see Peter N. Stearns, Lives of Labor (New York: Holmes and Meier, 1975), Tables I-III at pp. 155-58. Cf. Levasseur, Questions, p. 279.

52 See Sée, Französische Wirtschaftsgeschichte, II, 420-21.

53 In 1906, 680,542 industrial employees, accounting for 18.2 per cent of all such employees, were employed in establishments with more than 500 employees; calculated according to data in Recensement générale 1906, I:2, 182.

54 As, however, David J. Saposs, The Labor Movement in Post-War France (New York: Columbia University Press, 1931), p. 135, notes, many of the unorganized were "'class conscious' in the continental European radical labor sense." A relatively low degree of organization still characterizes French workers; see the international comparison in Frankfurter Allge-meine Zeitung, July 18, 1974, p. 10.

55 See Paul Louis, Histoire du mouvement syndical en France, I: de 1789 à 1918 (Paris: Valois, 1947), 125.

56 For the French data, see Annuaire statistique, 1922, p. 46; Ernest Mahaim, "Die Gewerkvereine in Frankreich," Handwörterbuch der Staats-wissenschaften, ed. J. Conrad et al., IV (3rd ed.; Jena: Fischer, 1909), 1191. For the German data, see Umbreit, 25 Jahre, App. Table 5 at p. 172.

57 Annuaire statistique, Vol. 35--1914 et 1915 (Paris: Imprimerie Nationale, 1917), p. 134.

58 See Val R. Lorwin, The French Labor Movement (Cambridge, Mass.: Harvard University Press, 1954), p. 41.

59 See Recensement générale 1906, I:2, 192; Lorwin, French Labor, p. 44; Annuaire statistique, Vol. 35, p. 134. See, in general, Raymond Joran, L'Organisation syndicale dans l'industrie du bâtiment, Thèse pour le doctorat (Paris: Savaète, 1914), passim. Cf. J. Barberet, Le Travail en

France. Monographes professionelles, III (Paris: Berger-Leurault, 1887), 273-382, on carpenters.

60 Recensement générale 1906, I:2, 188, 190; Annuaire statistique, Vol. 35, p. 134; W. Kulemann, Die Berufsvereine, Erste Abteilung: Geschichtliche Entwicklung der Berufsorganisationen der Arbeitnehmer und Arbeitgeber aller Länder, Vol. 4: England--Frankreich--Belgien--Holland--Luxemburg--Dänemark--Schweden--Norwegen (2nd ed.; Berlin: Simion, 1913 (1900)), p. 270.

61 See Sternberg, Imperialismus, p. 535.

62 See Engels' letter of November 23, 1882 to Marx, MEW, XXXV, 118-19; cf. Marx's reply of November 27, 1882, ibid., p. 120. See also Claude Willard, Le Mouvement socialiste en France (1893-1905). Les Guesdistes (Paris: Éditions Sociales, 1965), p. 318.

63 See Edward Shorter and Charles Tilly, Strikes in France 1830-1968 (London: Cambridge University Press, 1974), pp. 216-17; Stearns, Lives of Labor, passim, appears to overrate the speed of technological change; on the construction industry in particular, see ibid., pp. 157-65. Especially among masons struggles centered not so much on technical change as on the use of piece work; see Martin Nadaud, Memoires de Leonard. Ancien garçon maçon (Paris: Egloff, 1948 (1895)), pp. 200-201. The extent of industrialization may, as a result of the extremely strenuous and dangerous aspects of production processes associated with some stages of industrialization, not be accurately measured by the development of the share of female and child employment in various branches; see the data for the 1860s and 1890s in Annuaire statistique de la France, Vol. 18, 1898 (Paris: Imprimerie Nationale, 1898), Table 264 at p. 230.

64 For monogrpahic insight into this area of consciousness, see P. Du Maroussem, La Question ouvrière, I: Charpentiers de Paris. Compagnons et indépendants (Paris: Rousseau, 1891), 226-29, 242-46 and passim.

65 Moss, Origins, pp. 25-26, 109-10, 113, 120.

66 On the occupational composition of the membership of the Parti Ouvrier Français, see Willard, Le Mouvement socialiste, pp. 46-47, 334-39, 597-98.

67 As Theodore Zeldin, France 1848-1945. I: Ambition, Love and Politics (Oxford: Oxford University Press, 1973), 230, notes, the radical building tradesmen were in retrospect not so menacing as they appeared during the years prior to World War I. None the less, the strike record underscores the seriousness with which workers and employers conducted their struggles; see Louis, Histoire, I, 221-22.

68 See Carl von Tyszka, Löhne und Lebenskosten im 19. Jahrhundert (Frankreich, England, Spanien, Belgien) (Munich-Leipzig: Duncker & Humblot, 1914), Table 1 at pp. 7-8.

69 Especially since France was the destination of a large sub-stratum of low-paid immigrant workers from Italy, Poland, Spain and North Africa; the number of foreigners in France almost tripled between 1851 and 1881, exceeding one million before World War I. See Werner Sombart, Der moderne Kapitalismus, III:1 (Munich-Leipzig: Duncker & Humblot, 1927), 397; Saposs, Labor Movement, pp. 119-21; Sée, Französische Wirtschaftsgeschichte, II, 439-40; Die Wirtschaft des Auslandes 1900-1927, ed. Statistischen Reichsamt, Einzelschriften zur Statistik des Deutschen Reiches, No. 5 (Berlin: Hobbing, 1928), pp. 69-71. It is noteworthy that, since most of the immigrant wage earners occupied unskilled positions, opposition to immigration stemmed not so much from a putative labor aristocracy as from unskilled French laborers. See Peter N. Stearns, Revolutionary

Syndicalism and French Labor (New Brunswick: Rutgers University Press, 1971), p. 58.

70 See W.A. Cole and Phyllis Deane, "The Growth of National Incomes," _The Cambridge Economic History of Europe_, ed. H.J. Habakkuk and M. Postan, Vol. VI: _The Industrial Revolutions and After: Incomes, Population and Technological Change_ (I) (Cambridge: Cambridge University Press, 1965), pp. 11-13; Kindleberger, _Economic Growth in France and Britain_, pp. 171-72.

71 See Karl Marx, _Der achtzehnte Brumaire des Louis Bonaparte_, MEW, VIII, 198-99, on the importance of the peasantry for class politics in France. On the class structure in France, see _Recensement générale 1906_, I:2, 110. Cf. Karl Kautsky, "Klasseninteresse-Sonderinteresse--Gemeininteresse," _Neue Zeit_, XXI, II (1903), 240-45, 261-74.

72 The situation in Paris differed from that in the rest of France: in Paris almost four-fifths of the employed male population were wage and salary workers in 1901 and 1906. But Paris accounted for but one-fourteenth of the French population in 1910-1911 and but one-ninth of all males in manufacturing industry, so that national class politics were determined by the composition of the French "desert" and not in the metropolis. The foregoing figures were calculated on the basis of data in _Recensement générale 1906_, II: _Population présente_ (Paris: Imprimerie Nationale, 1909), 18; ibid., I:2, 182; Mitchell, "Statistical Appendix 1700-1914," pp. 747, 750; Willard, _Le Mouvement socialiste_, p. 250.

1 See Carl Brinkmann, "Die Aristokratie im kapitalistischen Zeitalter," Grundriss der Sozialökonomik, IX. Abteilung: Das soziale System des Kapitalismus, I. Teil: Die gesellschaftliche Schichtung im Kapitalismus (Tübingen: Mohr, 1926), p. 32.
2 Robert Michels, Zur Soziologie des Parteiwesens in der modernen Demokratie (Leipzig: Klinkhardt, 1911), p. 277 and p. 277 n. 1.
3 Ibid., p. 277.
4 Ibid., p. 278.
5 For a rehearsal of historical examples of the lack of solidarity between skilled and unskilled workers, see Otto Rühle, Illustrierte Kultur- und Sittengeschichte des Proletariats, I (Frankfurt/Main: Neue Kritik, 1971 (1930)), pp. 258-68.
6 Robert Michels, Political Parties, tr. Eden and Cedar Paul (New York: Dover, 1959 (1915)), pp. 290-91. Part of this passage was not included in the original German edition.
7 Michels, Zur Soziologie des Parteiwesens, pp. 283-84.
8 The notion of a labor aristocracy has recently been applied to the independent developing nations of Africa with the modification, inter alia, that labor aristocrats are said to be situated in the most advanced sector of the economy rather than in the artisanal trades. This privileged stratum is seen, moreover, as one elite among several competing for consumption advantages rather than as a social stratum involved in a contradictory position within two classes. See Giovanni Arrighi and John S. Saul, "Socialism and Economic Development in Tropical Africa," Journal of Modern African Studies, VI, 2 (August 1968), 141-69, especially 149, 151, 162; cf. the critical articles by Keith Hinchliffe, "Labour Aristocracy--Northern Nigeria Case Study," ibid., XII (1974), 57-67, and P. Waterman, "The 'Labour Aristocracy' in Africa--Introduction to a Debate," Development and Change, VI, 3 (July 1975), 57-73.
9 See Galenson, Danish System, pp. 18, 22.
10 See Sigfrid Hansson, Den sevenska fackföreningsrörelsen (Stockholm: Tidens Förlag, 1923), pp. 28, 30-31.
11 Calculated according to the data in the semi-official trade union publication, Oversigt over fagforenings-bevaegelsen i Danmark i tiden fra 1871 til 1900, ed. J. Jensen and C.M. Olsen (Copenhagen: Bording, 1901), table at pp. 296-97. On the union of the unskilled, see Axel Olsen, Dansk Arbejdsmands Forbund gennem 50 aar 1897-1947 (Copenhagen: Grafisk Institut, 1947).
12 Hansson, Den svenska fackföreningsrörelsen, p. 51.
13 In 1900, 76.6 per cent of adult male industrial and handicraft workers in Denmark were organized; the 21.7 per cent degree of organization among women above the age of eighteen exceeded that among males in many contemporary countries. See Oversigt, ed. Jensen and Olsen, pp. 173-74; two-fifths of the males between the ages of eighteen and twenty-two were excluded as apprentices. The aggregate number of male workers on which these figures were based amounted to 100,000. Building tradesmen in Copenhagen were almost one hundred per cent organized by 1885; by 1901 eighty-five per cent of all male and thirty per cent of all female workers in Copenhagen were unionists. See Georg Nørregaard, Arbejdsforhold indenfor dansk haandvaerk og industri 1857-1899 (Copenhagen, 1943), pp. 357-58. For an earlier period, see Henry Bruun, Den faglige arbejder-bevaegelse i Danmark indtil aar 1900, Part 1: Til ca.

1880 (Copenhagen: Selskabet for Udgivelse af Kilder til Dansk Historie, 1977 (1938)), passim.
14 Galenson, Danish System, pp. 12-14, offers one explanation of "the consistent moderation of Danish labor ideology." For the somewhat different pattern in Norway, see Walter Galenson, Labor in Norway (Cambridge, Mass.: Harvard University Press, 1949), pp. 15, 20-22, 59-63.
15 See the journal of the First International in Switzerland, L'Egalité, I, 9 (March 20, 1869), 1.
16 See Erich Gruner, Der Arbeiter in der Schweiz im 19. Jahrundert (Bern: Francke, 1968), p. 549.
17 Marc de Préadeau. Michel Bakounine. Le Collectivisme dans l'Internationale. Étude sur le mouvement social (1868-1876) (Paris: Rivière, 1912), pp. 142-43; cf. Fritz Brupbacher, Marx und Bakunin (Berlin: Die Aktion, 1922), pp. 67-69; E.H. Carr, Michael Bakunin (New York: Vintage, n.d. (first published in 1937)), pp. 375-80.
18 See Karl Marx, "Die Aussperrung der Bauarbeiter in Genf," MEW, XVI, 431-33.
19 Préadeau, Bakounine, pp. 143-44; Gruner, Arbeiter in der Schweiz, pp. 615-16.
20 For the post-World War II period one author has tried to show that native Swiss bank employees have enjoyed relatively high salaries as a result of bank profits stemming from the large amounts of "capital in flight" deposited in Swiss banks. See Jean Ziegler, Une Suisse au-dessus de tout soupçon (Paris: Seuil, 1976), p. 91. Although this economic mechanism is plausible, Ziegler has not even pretended to have demonstrated that Swiss bank employees have therefore become ardent supporters of Swiss "secondary imperialism."
21 See United States Congress, State of Labor in Europe: 1878, pp. 30, 286-303.
22 See A.M. Rumyantsev, ed., Structure of the Working Class (New Delhi: People's Publishing House, 1963), p. 104.
23 See Merli, Proletariato, pp. 456-57.
24 Ibid., pp. 546, 560. For a different view of the labor aristocratic tendencies created by the North-South division, see Hobsbawm, Labouring Men, p. 357; Gwyn A. Williams, Proletarian Order. Antonio Gramsci, Factory Councils and the Origins of Communism in Italy 1911-1921 (London: Pluto, 1975), pp. 24, 30, 55; G.D.H. Cole, A History of Socialist Thought, Vol. III, Part II: The Second International 1889-1914 (London: Macmillan, 1970 (1956)), pp. 734-36, observes that Italian Socialists refrained from placing a high priority on the struggle for universal suffrage because they feared "being swamped by the mass of illiterate and uninformed voters, especially in the south. ..."
25 See Maurice F. Neufeld, Italy (Ithaca: Cornell University, 1961), pp. 317-20, 328-29, 350-52; Daniel L. Horowitz, The Italian Labor Movement (Cambridge, Mass.: Harvard University Press, 1963), pp. 46, 79; Shepard B. Clough, The Economic History of Modern Italy (New York: Columbia University Press, 1964), pp. 163-69; Sidney G. Tarrow, Peasant Communism in Southern Italy (New Haven: Yale University Press, 1967), pp. 12-39.
26 See the masterful overview by Otto Bauer, Die österreichische Revolution (Vienna: Wiener Volksbuchhandlung, 1923).
27 Hans Hautmann and Rudolf Kropf, Die österreichische Arbeiterbewegung vom Vormärz bis 1945 (Vienna: Europaverlag, 1974), pp. 98-104.
28 See Andrew G. Whiteside, Austrian National Socialism Before 1918 (The Hague: Nijhoff, 1962), passim; cf. also idem, The Socialism of Fools.

Georg Ritter von Schönerer and Austrian Pan-Germanism (Berkeley: University of California Press, 1975). On the evolution of Austrian trade unionism, see Julius Deutsch, Geschichte der österreichischen Gewerkschaftsbewegung (Vienna: Brand, 1908), pp. 318-19 and passim.

29 On the specific conditions of the heterogeneity of the Hungarian working class, see Cole, Second International, pp. 568-70.

30 See Whiteside, Austrian National Socialism, passim. Although the German speaking workers may have viewed ethnic Slav workers as "coolie"-like competitors, the situation in Austria differed radically from that prevailing on the West Coast of the United States in the 1870s and 1880s where the introduction of Chinese labor not only permitted white workers to abandon unskilled positions in favor of skilled ones, but also induced trade unions to form alliances with employers. See Alexander Saxton, The Indispensable Enemy. Labor and the Anti-Chinese Movement in California (Berkeley: University of California Press, 1971).

31 See above chap. 6. Cf. Projekt Klassenanalyse, Leninismus--eine neue Stufe des wissenschaftlichen Sozialismus? (Westberlin: VSA, 1972), pp. 329-36, 404-10.

32 For a general discussion of the economic consequences of imperialism for the working class, see Otto Bauer, Die Nationalitätenfrage und die Sozialdemokratie (2nd ed.; Vienna, 1924 (1907)), pp. 476-91; Joseph Schumpeter, Imperialism (and) Social Classes, tr. Heinz Norden (Cleveland and New York: World, 1965 (first appeared in Archiv für Sozialwissenschaft und Sozialpolitik, XLVI (1919))), pp. 85-87.

33 J.A. Hobson, Imperialism (Ann Arbor: University of Michigan Press, 1967 (1902)), p. 194. Lenin attached great significance to this statement; see his Tetradi po imperializmu, p. 306; Imperializm, p. 400.

34 See, for example, Lenin, "Krakh," pp. 249-50. For critical views of Lenin's position, see Paul Sering, Jenseits des Kapitalismus (Lauf: Nest, 1946), p. 220; Michael Harrington, Socialism (New York: Saturday Review, 1972), p. 148.

35 Lenin also recurred to the argument that labor aristocracies could be cultivated by the "bribing" of a part of an autochthonous working class and the simultaneous "boundless and shameless exploitation" of low-wage immigrants who were deprived of political rights. See Lenin, "K peresmotru partiinoi programmy," PSS, XXIV, 371.

36 E.E. Kruze, Polozhenie rabochego klassa Rossii v 1900-1914 gg. (Leningrad: Nauka, 1976), p. 291.

37 Cf. A.G. Rashin, Formirovanie rabochego klassa Rossii (Moscow, 1958), passim.

38 See Liuben Berov, Polozhenieto na rabotnicheskata klasa v Bulgariia, mimeo (Sofia: VII "Karl Marx," 1965), pp. 19-20, 33, 47.

39 See Rumyantsev, ed., Structure, pp. 112-14. On Sweden's capital position, see Eli F. Heckscher, An Economic History of Sweden, tr. Göran Ohlin (Cambridge, Mass.: Harvard University Press, 1954), pp. 210-11, 278-80. Cf. Tom Kemp, Theories of Imperialism (London: Dobson, 1967), p. 81. A study of the Netherlands, a country with access to huge colonial incomes prior to World War I, concluded that the economic advantages accruing to the Dutch working class were virtually nil. See "V. Die Kolonialfrage. A. Bericht des Genossen Van Kol, namens der Sozialdemokratischen Arbeiterpartei Hollands. Die Kolonialpolitik Hollands," Propositions et projets de résolutions avec rapports explicatifs présentés au Congrès Socialiste International de Stuttgart (18-24 Août 1907) (n.p., n.d.), pp. 317-22.

40 See the editorial "Introduction" to Robert Davies, "The White Working
Class in South Africa," New Left Review, No. 82, November-December
1973, pp. 38-39.
41 W.H. Hutt, The Economics of the Colour Bar (London: Deutsch, 1964),
p. 49.
42 Jürgen Kuczynski, Geschichte, Vol. 27b: Die alten englischen Dominions
(Berlin (DDR): Akademie, 1965), p. 275.
43 See B. Fitzpatrick, British Imperialism and Australia, 1783-1833 (London:
Allen & Unwin, 1939); idem, The British Empire in Australia. An Economic
History 1834-1939 (2nd ed.; Melbourne: Melbourne University Press, 1949
(1941)), p. 126.
44 See Kuczynski, Dominions, pp. 265-300, especially pp. 268, 272, 274-75,
299. On the Australian labor movement, see the encyclopedic work by
T.A. Coghlan, Labour and Industry in Australia (4 vols.: London: Oxford
University Press, 1918). Cf. these interpretative works: B. Fitzpatrick,
A Short History of the Australian Labour Movement (Melbourne: Macmillan,
1968 (1940)); E.W. Campbell, History of the Australian Labour Movement.
A Marxist Interpretation (Sydney: Current Book, 1945); Robin Gollan,
Radical and Working Class Politics: A Study of Eastern Australia, 1850-
1910 (Melbourne: Melbourne University Press, 1960).
45 The factors underlying the expansion of the labor force are objective
economic ones over which capitalists exercised little control. The issue
under discussion concerns the nature of the labor to be recruited as well
as the mode of recruitment.
46 Edna Bonacich, "A Theory of Ethnic Antagonism: The Split Labor Market,"
American Sociological Review, XXXVII, 5 (October 1972), 557. Hutt,
Colour Bar, pp. 179-80 and passim, also elaborates this position.
47 Edna Bonacich, "Advanced Capitalism and Black/White Relations in the
United States: A Split Labor Market Interpretation," American Sociologial
Review, XLI, 1 (February 1976), 44. Cf. Norval Glenn, "Occupational
Benefits to Whites from Subordination of Negroes," ibid., XXVIII, 3
(March 1963), 443-48; idem, "White Gains from Negro Subordination,"
Social Problems, XIV, 2 (Fall 1966), 159-78; Michael Reich, "The Economics
of Racism," Problems in Political Economy, ed. David M. Gordon (Lexing-
ton: Heath, 1971), pp. 107-13; Albert Szymanski, "Racial Discrimination
and White Gain," American Sociological Review, XLI, 3 (June 1976), 403-
14.
48 Bonacich, "Advanced Capitalism," p. 38, shows an implicit acknowledgment
of the possibility of the simultaneous application of two strategies. Cf.
Allison Davis et al., Deep South (Chicago: University of Chicago Press,
1949 (1941)), pp. 460-62, 478-80.
49 Arendt, Origins of Totalitarianism, p. 204.
50 Ibid., p. 206.
51 Ibid., p. 204.
52 For an early reference, see James Steuart, An Inquiry into the Principles
of Political Economy, I (London: Millar and Cadell, 1767), 311-19.
53 Arendt fails to distinguish consistently between the so-called poor whites,
who at the close of the nineteenth century constituted one-fifth of the
Afrikaaners and one-tenth of the white population, and the remainder of
the white working class, which did not uniformly expect or demand
"permanent emancipation from work." See Arendt, Origins of Totalitarianism,
pp. 185-207, especially pp. 194, 198; cf. Sheila T. Van der Horst, "The
Effects of Industrialisation on Race Relations in South Africa," Industrialisation and Race Relations, ed. Guy Hunter (London: Oxford University Press, 1965), p. 116.

54 Analyses of more recent economic developments in South Africa may be consulted in F. Lee, Südafrika vor der Revolution (n.p., n.d. (ca. 1966)); and H. Adam, Südafrika (Frankfurt/Main: Suhrkamp, 1969).

55 See G.V. Doxey, The Industrial Colour Bar in South Africa (Capetown: Oxford University Press, 1961), p. 22; C.W. de Kiewiet, A History of South Africa (Oxford: Clarendon, 1942), p. 95.

56 The wage differentials were, however, much larger; at the turn of the century skilled white immigrant miners received as much per day as unskilled blacks received per week. See Van der Horst, "Effects," p. 114; cf. Kuczynski, Dominions, p. 471.

57 Sheila T. Van der Horst, Native Labour in South Africa (London: Oxford University Press, 1942), p. 157.

58 Even Kuczynski, Dominions, p. 468, interprets the miners' strike of 1907-- which, he fails to mention, was directed against the employment of Asian contract laborers--as against the deterioration of working conditions. For an example of European socialist opposition to immigration, see the discussion contribution by Fritz Paeplow at the Internationaler Sozialisten-Kongress zu Stuttgart. 18. bis 24. August 1907 (Berlin: Vorwärts, 1907), p. 119.

59 Doxey, Industrial Colour Bar, p. 23.

60 Van der Horst, Native Labour, p. 242. The decision, in 1907, to repatriate the 10,000 Chinese laborers, who had been imported in 1904, did not constitute a complete victory for white workers since the Chinese were in part replaced by native Africans. See de Kiewiet, History of South Africa, p. 146; Elie Halévy, A History of the English People in the Nineteenth Century, V: Imperialism and the Rise of Labour, tr. E.I. Watkin (London: Benn, 1965 (first French ed. 1926)), 376-78; idem, ibid., VI: The Rule of Democracy 1905-1914, tr. E.I. Watkin (New York: Barnes and Noble, 1961 (first French ed. 1932)), 27-34.

61 A decade later the State Mining Commission stated that given wage differentials, employment of whites instead of blacks would wipe out profits in half of the mines; see Doxey, Industrial Colour Bar, p. 122. For a similar claim with reference to higher minimum wages for blacks, see the speech by Mr. Marwick in Union of South Africa, Debates of the House of Assembly, Second Session, Fifth Parliament. 13th February to 25th July, 1925. Vol. 3 (13th February to 15th April.) (Cape Town: Cape Times, n.d.), col. 1720.

62 Cf. H.J. Simon and R.E. Simon, Class and Colour in South Africa 1850-1950 (Harmondsworth: Penguin, 1969), pp. 82-83.

63 South Africa. Further Correspondence relating to the Affairs of the Transvaal and Orange River Colony, P.P. 1904, Vol. LXI, Cd. 1895 (London: HMSO, 1904), p. 42.

64 de Kiewiet, History of South Africa, p. 146.

65 White supervisors, in particular gang leaders, shared in the increased earnings resulting from the rising productivity of black gold miners while the real earnings of the latter stagnated for decades. See Francis Wilson, Labour in the South African Gold Mines 1911-1969 (London: Cambridge University Press, 1972), pp. 46-48.

66 Even Kuczynski, perhaps the most dogmatic modern exponent of the Leninist conception of the labor aristocracy as a creature of the bourgeoisie, is compelled to speak of the "complexity of employment problems from the standpoint of the ruling class," which is torn between "status" and profit requirements. See Kuczynski, Dominions, p. 445.

67 Union of South Africa, Debates, March 30, 1925, col. 1602. Cf. ibid., cols. 1586-1603, 1651-1853.

68 In the 1920s it was claimed that virtually all white workers were "in the position more or less of foremen"; ibid., col. 1591.
69 Doxey, Industrial Colour Bar, p. 122.
70 Ibid., p. 120.
71 See Robert Davies, The White Working-Class in South Africa," New Left Review, No. 82, November-December 1973, pp. 40-59. Davies' article is vitiated by the fact that the author concentrates on differential changes in productivity over time as proof of the increasing super-exploitation of blacks without considering differential skill levels between blacks and whites at one point in time or over time. For recent occupational data by race, see F.E. Rädel, Progress or Exploitation? (n.p. (Capetown): Miller, 1978), Table 4 at p. 23. For a more cautious restatement, see Robert Davies, "Mining Capital, The State and Unskilled White Workers in South Africa, 1901-1913," Journal of Southern Africa Studies, III, 1 (October 1976), 41-69.
72 Davies, "White Working-Class," p. 51.
73 This was particularly the case during the 1920s and 1930s in connection with the so-called civilized wage policy, which was enforced by the government by means of wage regulations, tariff manipulation, direct subsidies and government contract discrimination. See Van der Horst, Native Labour, pp. 252-66. On the crucial election of 1902, see Halévy, History, VI, 34.
74 South Africa accounted for seventy-six per cent of the world's diamond production in 1919; in 1913 it accounted for thirty-eight per cent of world gold output--a share which rose in the following years. See Wirtschaft des Auslandes 1900-1927, pp. 808-10.
75 See Union of South Africa, Union Office of Census and Statistics, Official Year Book of the Union, No. 6--1923 (Pretoria: Government Printing and Stationery Office, 1924), p. 688, for data on gross profits and fixed capital for various manufacturing sectors from 1915 to 1921. For more recent data on mining profits, see Linder, Der Anti-Samuelson, IV, 132 n. 165.
76 For a more generalized treatment of the racial aspects of capital-labor relations, see E. Franklin Frazier, Race and Culture Contacts in the Modern World (Boston: Beacon, 1968 (1957)), pp. 127-74.

1 John Locke, An Essay concerning Human Understanding, ed. A.C. Fraser, II (New York: Dover, 1959 (1690)), 143-44.
2 The sexual division of the working class has received little attention in this study as a result of the virtual exclusion of women from the ranks of the skilled. An examination of the capitalist transformation of the sexual division of labor--as it pertains to the issues raised here--constitutes an important desideratum of research.
3 To some degree the situation among unskilled whites in the ante-bellum American South and in South Africa differed: as a result of the necessities of mere political survival in the context of a large enslaved or numerically dominant conquered race, whites of all classes acted on ostensibly non-economic grounds to distribute formal political power more democratically among themselves. Even in these zones, however, economic advantage and exploitation ultimately underlay such considerations. See however the remarks attributed to Lord Milner by Beatrice Webb, Our Partnership, ed. Barbara Drake and Margaret I. Cole (New York: Longmans, Green, 1948), p. 352.
4 Cf. the discussion of the interaction between intra-class inequalities and the distance between adjacent classes by Stanisław Ossowski, Struktura klasowa w społecznej świadomości (Lodz: Zakład narodowy im ossolinskich we wrocławiu, 1957), pp. 85-88. On the rational "class-oriented action" symbolized by some national working class movements, see Mancur Olson, Jr., The Logic of Collective Action (rev. ed.; New York: Schocken, 1971 (1965)), pp. 102-10.
5 Karl Renner, Die Rechtsinstitute des Privatrechts und ihre soziale Funktion (Tübingen: Mohr, 1929 (1904)), p. 47.
6 See, for example, the description in P.A. Brunt, Social Conflicts in the Roman Republic (London: Chatto & Windus, 1971).
7 See the insightful comments by A.V. Dicey, Lectures on the Relation between Law and Public Opinion in England during the Nineteenth Century (2nd ed.; London: Macmillan, 1930 (1905)), pp. 240-75.
8 The labor aristocracy in the United States from the 1880s onward approximated this model more closely than did the British labor aristocracy. See G.D.H. Cole, The World of Labour (2nd ed.; London: Bell, 1915 (1913)), pp. 133, 135; L.I. Zubok, Ocherki istorii rabochego dvizheniia v SShA 1865-1918 (Moscow: IS-EL, 1962), pp. 134, 243, 277; S.M. Askol'dova, Nachalo massovogo rabochego dvizheniia v SShA (Moscow: Nauka, 1966), pp. 79, 218; Louis Vigouroux, La Concentration des forces ouvrières dans l'Amerique du nord (Paris: Colin, 1899), p. 346; Bernard Mandel, Samuel Gompers (Yellow Springs. Antioch Press, 1965 (1963)), pp. 224-25.
9 The rigidity of pre-capitalist class structures precluded the transformation of the superior material conditions of a dependent stratum into the politically sanctioned transcendence of a given class position. On the specific conditions obtaining under feudalism, see Heinrich Bechtel, Wirtschaftsstil des deutschen Spätmittelalters (Munich: Duncker & Humblot, 1930), pp. 44-56, 213-24; Josef Kulischer, Allgemeine Wirtschaftsgeschichte des Mittelalters und der Neuzeit, I (Berlin (DDR): Rütten & Loening, 1954 (1928)), 213-14; Edgar S. Furniss, The Position of the Laborer in a System of Nationalism (Boston: Houghton Mifflin, 1920), pp. 222-29; E. Lipson, The Economic History of England, I: The Middle Ages (12th ed.; London: Black, 1966 (1915)), 388-89; Sombart, Der moderne Kapitalismus, II: 2, 835-36. See, however, W. Cunningham, The Growth of English Industry and Commerce dcuring the Early and Middle Ages (5th ed.; Cambridge: Cambridge University Press, 1927 (1882)), pp. 346-47; Lujo Brentano: On

the History and Development of Gilds, and the Origin of Trade-Unions (London: Trübner, 1870).

10 The most glaring example was the Weimar Republic. See Karl Dietrich Bracher, Die Auflösung der Weimarer Republik (2nd ed.; Stuttgart: Ring, 1957 (1955)); A. Enderle et al., Das rote Gewerkschaftsbuch (Hamburg: Association, 1973 (1932)); Eva Cornelia Schöck, Arbeitslosigkeit und Rationalisierung. Die Lage der Arbeiter und die kommunistische Gewerkschaftspolitik 1920-28 (Frankfurt/Main: Campus, 1977).

11 On the ultimately unsuccessful attempt in Germany in the 1860s, see R. Meyer, Der Emancipationskampf des vierten Stands, I (2nd ed.; Berlin: Bahr, 1882 (1872)), 199.

12 See David I. Kulstein, Napoleon III and the Working Class (n.p. (Sacramento?): The California State Colleges, 1969); cf. however Meyer, Emancipationskampf, I, 30; Friedrich Engels, Die preussische Militärfrage und die deutsche Arbeiterpartei (1865), MEW, XVI, 71-72. These latter two contemporaries stressed the stratum-specific component of the attempt by Napoleon III to create an "artificial" proletariat in the luxury goods-producing industries.